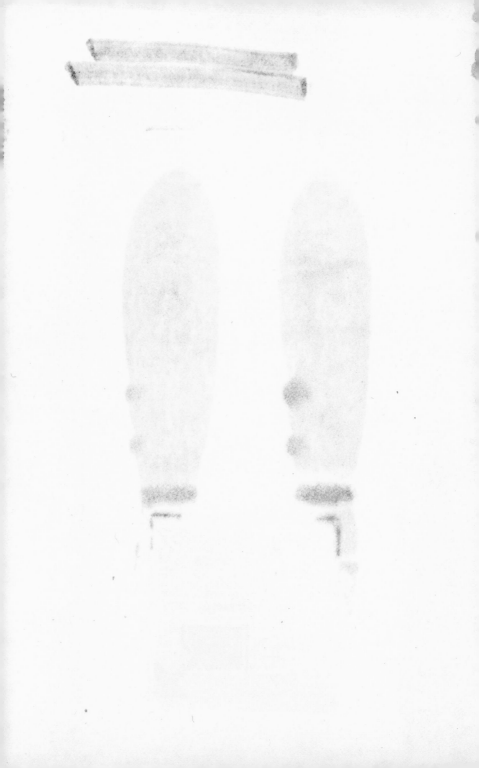

Love, Laughter and Tears

My Hollywood Story

by Adela Rogers St. Johns

LOVE, LAUGHTER AND TEARS
SOME ARE BORN GREAT
THE HONEYCOMB
TELL NO MAN
FINAL VERDICT

Adela Rogers St. Johns

Love,
Laughter
and Tears

My Hollywood Story

DOUBLEDAY & COMPANY, INC., GARDEN CITY, NEW YORK 1978

ISBN: 0-385-12054-0
Library of Congress Catalog Card Number 76–50786
Copyright © 1978 by Adela Rogers St. Johns
All Rights Reserved
Printed in the United States of America
First Edition

Dedication

I offer this book to three women—
Colleen Moore Hargrave, longtime cherished friend
Kristen St. Johns Wolf, beloved granddaughter
Betty A. Prather, newfound friend and modern patron of the arts
—with my affection, admiration and gratitude. Without
their constant support and encouragement the completed
manuscript would not have become a reality.

Acknowledgments

I would like to give heartfelt thanks to those who have helped me in so many ways while I was working on this book:

My daughter, *Elaine St. Johns*, who worked long and hard to assist me in every way in organizing and presenting the material. My son, *Mac St. Johns*, who gave me loyal moral support, collected photographs, checked facts and dates; if any errors occur you may be sure that was the time I *didn't* call him. *Victor Palmieri*, who, despite his own far-flung business obligations, first undertook with kindness, understanding and humor the Care and Feeding of Authors, which includes protection, surcease from financial worries and a strong arm to lean upon—and my grandson, *George St. Johns*, who came on in the second quarter to complete the task with tact, intelligence and good cheer.

My team at Doubleday & Company—publisher *Sam Vaughan*, and my favorite editor, *Ferris Mack*, men of wit, wisdom and patience who know that the greatest thing you can give a writer is *confidence*, and who have never failed me.

Four dear friends, *Ann Moray*, *Ruth Sheldon Knowles*, *Herminia Orena Marsh* and *Dick Boehm*, who extended helping hands and words of cheer at crucial and difficult moments.

My niece, *Tory St. Johns*, and *Kermit Arnds*, manager and proprietor respectively of the lovely Desert Inn at Desert Hot Springs, where they gave me care and kindness while this book was being written.

And finally, with some awe and great respect, *Carole Strasser* and *Nancy Bender,* who can type flawlessly, swiftly and eagerly, and in my case did just that.

Adela Rogers St. Johns
Desert Hot Springs, California

Contents

	Page

Chapter One: MOTHER CONFESSOR OF HOLLYWOOD — 1

Chapter Two: THE KING OF COMEDY AND THE QUEEN OF CLOWNS — 25

Mack Sennett and Mabel Normand
with
Marie Dressler, Bing Crosby, The Bathing Beauties, and *Fatty Arbuckle* — 26

Chapter Three: THE BIG FOUR — 71

Griffith, The Star Maker — 72
The Enigma of Charlie Chaplin — 84
Mary and Doug, the Royal Couple — 95
King and Queen of the World

Chapter Four: THE BEAUTIFUL AND THE DAMNED — 137

Wallace Reid — 138
Barbara La Marr — 147

Chapter Five: ONE OF A KIND   153

    Gloria Swanson   154
    Rudolph Valentino   164
    Bebe Daniels   179
    Lon Chaney   196
    Colleen Moore   208
    Clara Bow   228

Chapter Six: LOVE HOLLYWOOD STYLE   245

    The Garbo-Gilbert Interlude   246
    Gary Cooper's Love Story in Three Acts   252
    Jean Harlow and William Powell   270
    The Drama of Ingrid Bergman   281

Chapter Seven: THE MIRACLE OF TWO COWBOYS   295

    Tom Mix   296
    Hopalong Cassidy   302

Chapter Eight: THE MAGNIFICENT GABLE   311

with
Esther Williams, Joan Crawford, Carole Lombard

Love,
Laughter
and Tears

My Hollywood Story

Chapter One

Mother Confessor of Hollywood

Shooting?

The tall, melancholy, cadaverous young man, wearing a black hat with the soft brim pulled down over his right eye, used that word when he spoke to our city editor, who was indeed a terrible man according to the age-old newspaper tradition about city editors. In fact, J.B.T. Campbell was the most terrible of them all which meant that he was the most dedicated to always having a *shooting* on the front page if possible. Thus when the young man beside his desk used that word, Campbell was instantly all attention.

He was, the young man said, shooting now. *But* unless he got the money to pay off his crew *today* there wouldn't be any shooting tomorrow. This so appalled Campbell that he allowed the young man, who said his name was *Griffith*, to pass the hat in the city room of the Los Angeles *Herald*, the newest, youngest of the nationwide chain of Hearst newspapers. Must have been the day after payday because he raised $286 and departed with it, only a shade less gloomy than when he came in. Campbell watched him go and then beckoned me, the newest, youngest cub reporter on his very new young staff.

"Shooting?" Campbell said to me.

Already I knew that it was against the law so far as Campbell was concerned to go to press without one on the front page. As the deadline approached we were sent helter-skelter to the outlying jails and police stations to find that pièce de résistance from Shakespeare to Dickens to Conan Doyle to Agatha Christie to the Press. Now here one of them had come looking for him. "Hadn't you better go out and see what or who it is he's shooting?" Campbell's glare turned into a grim grin. "He looks more like Hamlet than anybody I've seen in a long time. It might be Ophelia?"

To the Hamlet of the legendary D. W. Griffith, it was. As I close my eyes and see it again, David Wark Griffith, credited by many as the Founding Father of Films as we know them, was what he was, a stage actor who must once himself have played the melancholy Dane, and with him comes the ideal casting for Ophelia. The fair, fragile, mythical heartbreak of Lillian Gish. If we want to transpose a lot of Shakespeare into the daily life of mad stupendous tumultuous young Hollywood, we had a clown called Fatty Arbuckle for Falstaff, to be victim of a mass mistake, *Midsummer Night's Dream* could be enacted with that little man of big talent, one Mickey Rooney, playing Puck, though Mickey had four or five wives and I don't think Puck had any. Mickey's wistful pursuit of a happy marriage was unbroken and to the last syllable of recorded time. I remember when my daughter's brothers asked him to stay away from our home on The Hill because, they said, they did not want to see their sister married to a movie star particularly Mickey Rooney—so plainly Mickey's intentions had, as usual, been entirely honorable.

For all his sex shenanigans, Mickey was a *good* man. Kind and neighborly. The way I was brought up by my father I was never able to confine morality nor immorality entirely to sex. Of the seven deadly sins only one deals with sex and even that one not exclusively. But then, as the excellent man Menninger said as a book title, *Whatever Became of Sin?* Might that be one reason we're having so much trouble around the country?

How I run before the wind as I take off on this voyage into the Golden Days from the incredible beginning of The Movies to their drab and dreadful end! As they disappear not with a bang but a whimper. I must try to settle a point here and now. There is so much to tell it would run into encyclopedic volumes. Such fabulous stories of love laughter and tears. Of world-loved and world-hated people. Of everything raised to its Nth degree. They press upon me, one shows me a glimpse of another, one spectacular personality has to be joined to another—as Cecil B. DeMille is to Gloria Swanson, as Bebe Daniels, my choice for Hollywood's real-life heroine, is to Harold Lloyd, forever master of gag comedy, for

Bebe went to Harold's studio dressed up in her Aunt Alma's clothes when she was only thirteen and got the job as his leading lady. As all the Stars at Metro-Goldwyn-Mayer including the Barrymores and Garbo and Gable and Crawford were to Louis B. Mayer. As the top box office star of years, Colleen Moore, the original Flapper, was to Scott Fitzgerald who wrote, "I was the spark that lit up Flaming Youth, Colleen Moore was the torch. What little things we were to have caused all that trouble!"

Clark Gable, the all-time and forever Star of Stars.

The other day Howard Strickling, who practically invented the Press Agent, heading the MGM publicity department for the many years when MGM was the greatest studio and producing company ever known or to be known, said, "If it hadn't been for you, Adela, there might have been no Clark Gable."

Even to me this sounds fantastic. Yet in a thrilling and amusing way, an oddly *practical* way, it could be true. Once when Clark Gable wanted *out*—out of The Movies, out of studios and cameras and putting on costumes and make-up, out of handling the adulation and pursuit by women he didn't want having lost the only one he did, I was working on some scripts with and for him and managed to persuade him to keep on. Before that—to make *Gone with the Wind* which he resisted passionately, partly because he definitely disliked David O. Selznick, the producer, but mostly because he said he could never live up to what people expected of him as Rhett Butler. *They'll lynch me in Atlanta,* he said. Remembering the opening night *in* Atlanta, this sounds now even more idiotic than it did then. For that turned out to be the night when they really made him the King. A title Spencer Tracy had hung on him in a half-kidding, half-serious fashion. With perhaps just a touch of the well-known Tracy sarcasm thrown in.

Clark was King all right. On top of the world in those days just before World War II. And the truly spectacular personality that must join him is that unique star, Carole Lombard Gable. For Carole was unique. Together these two lived a vibrant, vivid story of love *and* laughter for a few short years. Then, when Carole's plane crashed into a mountain in Nevada, came the tears. Clark's fans, even his close friends, didn't see them. He was still the King to his public until the day of his death nineteen years later. But Clark Gable was never the same man again, as you will see. The light had gone out of his life.

Yes, the King is dead. I do not know who now lives in the rambling ranch house in the San Fernando Valley that Carole created for him.

But the Queen, our Queen Mary, is still very much alive and doing well, thank you, reports and dark rumors to the contrary notwithstanding. And still lives in her castle. I saw her there the other day.

Mary Pickford.

No other woman ever born was known and loved by as many people as the little girl with the golden curls, born Gladys Smith, who became Mary Pickford. This, my children, in the days before World War I, the era of the Model T Ford, when skirts were just above the ankle, Pancho Villa in the flesh was leading his guerrillas, and *Pollyanna* was a best-seller.

So long ago? As close as yesterday.

During that First World War I can still see Mary Pickford, America's Sweetheart, the only one we ever had, as clear as clear; and with her Charlie Chaplin, the beloved Little Tramp, and Douglas Fairbanks, whose swashbuckling *Mark of Zorro* and *Three Musketeers* invented for all time the Captain Midnights, the Supermen and such heroes as now shine on television. I see them as the first adoring *fans* mobbed them when they toured America selling Liberty Bonds in those early days of this our twentieth century which is even now drawing to a close. "A snip of your curls, Mary" "Let us touch you!" "We love you, Mary."

There had never been anything like it before. We shall not see their like again, I fear.

I thought of this, I always do, when I went to see Mary Pickford. For it shows for how short a time in the historical sense the whole amazing unparalleled phenomenon of *Hollywood* existed. To me it seems only a few years ago that Hollywood and all the word stands for existed only as a wide lazy boulevard running through a small foothill village in the sunshine of Southern California. I used to walk back and forth along it to high school, my books under my arm, and stop to pick poppies at the corner of what is now Hollywood and Vine. Today, Hollywood Boulevard is in actuality a garish, rather frightening street, lined with cheap shops and tawdry, flashy cafes and joints. After dark I wouldn't care to walk it without a police escort but I fear this is true today of most American main streets. It continues to be hard for me to believe of my country yet I admit it is true.

And Mary Pickford lives—not too far from it in the same mansion on the same hillside in Beverly Hills which Douglas Fairbanks gave her as a wedding gift. They decided to call it *Pickfair*.

And before I started this memoir of my Hollywood, where The Movies began, I thought I ought to go and see Mary, to stir my memory of the great days and quicken my heartbeat about what it was *really* like.

Love laughter and tears didn't *begin* with Mary Pickford! It didn't begin in the laboratories of Thomas A. Edison in New Jersey, either. It began with Mack Sennett and Mabel Normand and Charlie Chaplin, who gave us the laughter; it began with D. W. Griffith who contributed the *tears* certainly in *Birth of a Nation* and *Broken Blossoms,* and some of the love.

You know where it began?

It began with *Mary Pickford.*

I know. I just said it didn't. But as I think about it I come to the conclusion that in the sense of that *moment*—that heartbeat—that pulsing presence that was the beginning of life itself—The Movies began when the world fell in love with Mary Pickford.

After Mary the heavens above Hollywood were brilliant with stars.

But she was the first.

For the only time, the United States of America which had fought to throw off a monarch and become an alleged republic, had a Queen. The world, still divided into many lands and kingdoms and distances, had an Empress.

The Duchess of Windsor always looked to be sure the chair was *there* before she sat down on it.

Queen Elizabeth never looks. She knows it is there.

Mary Pickford, a Canadian-born child-actress of no education who indeed became Empress of the World, came to a moment when she didn't look. She knew her throne was there.

But her daughter-in-law, wife of young Douglas Fairbanks, a girl whose screen name was Joan Crawford, put on an extra pair of step-ins when she at last made it to Pickfair, the *only* social control and dictatorship Hollywood ever had, for fear that when she saw Mary Pickford Fairbanks in the drawing room at the foot of the majestic curving stairs she might find her knees wouldn't support her and go tail over teacup.

And Mary was still there, atop her little hill, with the world spread before her. It came to me with the force of a command that I had better go and *see* her.

My People, Mary Pickford once said to me, and meant the whole wide wonderful world and everybody in it. And she was *right*. They had been *her* people. I must go to Pickfair and talk to *Mary*.

"What does she talk about?" a London newspaper correspondent asked me, when I mentioned that I had seen her the day before. He was *polite*, but I knew that he had been refused an interview with Mary Pickford, that his paper in England had carried the headline NO ONE CAN INTERVIEW MARY PICKFORD and others that said the same thing—many others—from Greenland's icy mountains to India's coral strand. They had often come around the world on the chance of seeing Mary Pickford, of speaking a few words to her.

All had been refused.

By her husband, Buddy Rogers. By her wonderful secretary, Esther Helms. By her prime minister, Matty Kemp, who was even then readying a Mary Pickford Festival to take place in London under the patronage of Queen Elizabeth. And a great mystery has been made to surround her.

But I don't go to *interview* her. We gab, as we used to do when we had what we called hen parties in those early days when the girls got together and the men went off to the fights. After all, besides her beloved childhood *chum*, Lillian Gish, who else is there? Who else is there with whom she can talk over old times, the golden glorious nonpareil days, the years of her reign, as it were.

"What does she talk *about?*" the noted English correspondent
wanted to know.

"Oh," I said airily, "of shoes . . . and ships . . . and sealing
wax . . . and cabbages and kings."

I should do his work for him!

I thought about it, just the same. Quite a lot. What does this
Queen of The Movies and Empress of the world, left behind by
the times, yet with her past when she *was* Queen and Empress
still around her in an aura as Napoleon's was at St. Helena and
Elba, what *does* she talk about?

What do *we* talk about, two old friends—oh, how fortunate I
have been, how fortunate I *am,* to have seen her *live* that life
which no other woman has ever equaled, to have kept a friendship
that once was as valuable an asset as a newspaperwoman could
have and now it is still an honor to know a woman who has become a legend in our own time.

I have to pause here to remember what we talked about the
first time I met her. As a working member of the national press I
had been summoned to the presence to answer what Queen Mary
rightly judged was for her a matter of life and death. That day in
late 1919 our Mary was more a myth than a mortal—and the
mortal, madly in love for the first time, was on the verge of de-
stroying the myth. Surrounded by family, protected by producers
and studios, Mary lived her private life in an impenetrable ivory
tower as shrouded in the golden fog of fantasy as Cinderella or
Snow White.

I think the difference in that time and the time today is that we
wanted to *keep* her that way. We wanted someone to idolize,
someone to love. Nobody was intent on stripping her of her ermine and crown or putting out her shining light. For years and
years nobody even asked whether the most famous curls of all
time were real or not. Nobody wanted to find out that Ma Pickford—that most extraordinary of the many founding mothers—
put them up in rags and kid curlers every night. Nor was it
remembered or brought into mind that this tiny creature whom
all the world loved in her virginal little-girl roles on the screen
was, in reality, a woman in her twenties who had at a moment in
time past secretly married a handsome Irish actor.

Sitting in a little white rocking chair that day, dressed in a little white dress, wearing a blue bow on her curls, Mary Pickford asked me, "Will my people ever forgive me if I divorce Owen Moore to marry Douglas Fairbanks?"

America's Sweetheart a *wife*? Whether to Owen Moore or Douglas Fairbanks?

Mary Pickford, our little Mary, *divorced*?

Hard to believe these days when neither seems to have any value that *marriage* not to mention *divorce* could destroy a public idol, yet you must believe it, you must understand it, to know what Hollywood was really like in those days.

For a scandal involving a *marriage* and a *divorce* had ruined Francis X. Bushman at the very height of his up-to-then unequaled drawing power. Not to be forgotten, the moans and groans of desire and frustration or satisfaction one way or another that filled the Paramount Theater when Frank Sinatra opened there many years later were identifiable with those that shook the nickelodeons in the reign of Francis X. *the first* Bushman.

After having tried thirty-seven professions, including wrestling, bike racing and circus strong man, in 1911 Francis X. Bushman was the favorite leading man of those grand old stock companies around Philadelphia, and thus Essanay Studio in Chicago offered him a contract so big that, much as he looked down on the "flickers," he couldn't refuse. In 1918, when he was indeed Grandma's Pinup Boy, he accepted a Metro deal and came to Hollywood in a style never duplicated.

THE EXALTED SUPERB SOULFUL STUPENDOUS SCREEN STAR, as Metro actually billed him, arrived on a private train with one baggage car to carry his private zoo and aviary and another to transport his fleet of cars, among them a specially-built, gold-plated purple number that cost him $15,000 and knocked all Hollywood *and* Los Angeles for a loop.

As he stood before cheering throngs, beautiful as a Greek statue many of which he resembled, and was acknowledged *the* feminine heartthrob by popular acclaim, it must have seemed impossible to Francis X. Bushman and everybody else that anything could dethrone him. Certainly not his utter devotion to his co-star, Beverly Bayne. Our first cosmic empyrean romantic team, they were, dazzling us with love-light; audiences in every theater swooned at their stately love scenes, especially when in one fell swoop Francis X. discarded the stately and succumbed to purple passion. Today's audiences might not find Francis X. their Ideal Male but I do assure you the audiences of that day would have hissed like cobras at the rugged manner and mean countenance of Charles Bronson or the low-key finesse of Paul Newman.

Surely those audiences would be glad to know that this love they witnessed on the screen had come true?

But they were not. The vision of purple passion was eclipsed by the thought of Mr. and Mrs. Bushman sitting down to a communal platter of ham and eggs.

Furthermore, the divorce suit revealed to the public for the *first time* what Mr. Bushman's contracts had always kept him from mentioning and acknowledging—that he had been married since 1902 and had five children; a secret as well kept as Mary Pickford's curls and for the same reason. Nothing like a wife and five children to destroy the Prince Charming illusion.

Eight secretaries were handling the Bushman fan mail and three porters had to carry the autographed photographs to the postbox. (Records held until the Valentino idolatry was upon us.) When his marriage and large family, his divorce and remarriage to his co-star made the front pages only one secretary was needed to cope with the acid denunciations sent forth against the reigning favorite. Bushman was finished on the screen, not to return till some years later in *Ben Hur*—when it was hoped the public had forgotten both him and it—the scandal. This was to be a whole new personality and stardom—but it never was really. His career and his so-romantic second marriage dissolved but Francis X. Bushman was a man of varied interests and resources. He lived for many years with his third wife in a pretty home near Hollywood where he tended chickens, raised fruit, and his own vegetables and made a living in radio. Happy, healthy and handsome at sixty, the last time I saw him he still loved to reminisce about his great days and the $4,000,000 he spent, lost or gave away.

But *Mary Pickford* tumbled from her throne quietly fading away to tend chickens and raise fruit and vegetables? No no. Mary's career *was* her life, the only one she had known since she was five years old. For her it *was* a matter of life and death when she asked, "Will my people ever forgive me?"

I had an answer for that one—and I proved right. Thus began our friendship. But when I saw her the other day she asked me another question which I'm sure she takes equally seriously—a matter of life-after-death, as it were. There she was, fragile, yes, older, certainly—we are both in our wonderful eighties—but still regal, still Mary Pickford. She had been married to Buddy Rogers, a man of considerable charm, for almost forty years. Yet she asked, "Adela, will Douglas ever forgive me?"

I didn't find any answer this time. When Mary divorced Douglas they were still on top of the world, yet neither of them made another picture. He lived less than four years. Perhaps the answer will come as I retell the whole story. A story that could only have happened in Hollywood. In Hollywood as we *lived* it, Mary and I and those others who are imprinted in our hearts, where we worked, loved, gossiped, survived or didn't survive. A Hollywood that is now *history*.

Someday probably my great-grandchildren are going to ask me if I knew Cleopatra or Joan of Arc and I shall answer simply, "No, but I knew Mary Pickford."

And Jessica will say, "And what did she talk about, Grammy?"

And I will say, She talked about Ireland—about some wonderful people we knew—and her mother, Charlotte, who was one of your grammy's greatest friends and to whom Grammy often went for help and reassurance when Grammy was Mother Confessor to Hollywood.

MOTHER CONFESSOR OF HOLLYWOOD

Sometimes I dream I go to Hollywood again.

I find there the young woman who *was* mother confessor of and to Hollywood—and sometimes I find Hollywood, and it is only in memory that I can go back to it for it doesn't exist any more.

It was Jimmy Quirk who gave me this star billing when he started the first fan magazine and I began writing for it. When I wailed that I was having trouble enough being Mother Goose to a

year-old son and a two-year-old daughter—"You're young," said
Jimmy Quirk in New York, "but so is everyone else out there that
has anything to do with the movies. Hollywood is a very young
town. Not just new—*young*. Why, C. B. DeMille is still in his
thirties, and he thinks he's the grand old man who knows it all."

Thus it seemed all right back there in the Roaring Twenties for
Adela Rogers St. Johns to become Mother Confessor of Hollywood though she was only in *her* twenties and thirties. Often and
often after she went to live and work spang-bang in the middle of
it, she felt herself too young and inexperienced for so momentous
and dangerous a position. For soon with all this beauty and genius
and sex and love-of-life boiling in one little pot things began to
happen that even Shakespeare had hardly thought of.

But there she was *when* the elevator went up and there she
stayed.

Which brings me back to that point I must settle before I set
down in print my real memories of what it was like from its very
beginning on the day I went to see D. W. Griffith *shooting* and
wound up on the Mack Sennett lot to the downfall of The
Movies soon after the advent of The Television.

How can I make anybody *see* Hollywood? As I saw it? I saw so
much. It moved so fast. How can I make you believe it?

One evening at San Simeon, when I had been summoned to
what is now a national monument known as the Hearst Castle
but was then to us who went there often the Hearst Ranch, I sat
next to W.R. at dinner. I suppose we called it the Hearst Ranch,
which Winston Churchill once said was absurd, because it *was*
the Hearst Ranch, all those thousands and thousands of acres of
it, and always had been, since the early days of W.R.'s father,
Senator George Hearst, and his wife, Phoebe Apperson Hearst.
The last time I was there I had lunch with William Randolph
Hearst, Jr., in the old white clapboard house at the foot of Pico
Creek, where his grandmother had lived before her famous son
built the magnificent Renaissance palaces atop the Enchanted
Hill. I had been up there when it consisted of two "cottages"
which could easily swallow a mansion or so, and then three cottages and the gardens, then the Big House, the swimming pool,
the zoo and I had a true and deep affection for it—I still have—

which is why I have never been up the Hill since Mr. Hearst died, though I have been asked each year to give a few descriptive lectures to the guides who escort the public through. To tell them exactly what happened, who slept where, how meals were arranged and what time everybody—but everybody—was to go to the theater and see the movie Mr. Hearst had imported from Hollywood.

Never was a greater movie fan than William Randolph Hearst and of course his mistress and the mistress of the Castle was a movie star named Marion Davies. I will go on the record again and again that she would have been a much bigger star if she hadn't had to cope with Mr. Hearst as her producer. I mean all those ruffles and curls, the elaborate sets and bejeweled costumes —Mr. Hearst smothered Marion with lavishness. She was a great comedienne—I've heard Sir Charles Chaplin on this subject; he regarded her as the best actress of comedy next to Mabel Normand, and not just because at one time Charlie was rumored to be madly in love with Marion. So many men were. "It was hard not to be," Robert Montgomery once said to me. "If you were her leading man you had to keep looking often at Mr. Hearst, and realize that he definitely wouldn't like it! This cooled you off at once."

On this particular evening at dinner at the Ranch, as I sat on Mr. Hearst's left with Gloria Swanson on his right and Marion across the narrow table, with Sam Goldwyn on *her* right and Mr. Richard E. Berlin of the Hearst Service on her left, for some reason I mentioned the tapestry that covered the wall of the dining hall which I was facing. The table would seat roughly as I recall at least fifty to a hundred people comfortably and this tapestry stretched almost the full length. It came to me suddenly that I had never heard Mr. Hearst put forth about the *paintings* in the Big House—but he dearly loved to talk about the tapestries.

This one, the Lord of San Simeon told me, had been made in Italy especially for Catherine de' Medici to take with her when she went to marry the King of France. He didn't tell me but Joe Willicomb, his supersecretary, did later, that he had paid over two million dollars for it. And as W.R. began to tell me about it, he explained why he loved tapestry better than painting. "A tapestry" he said, "can contain many scenes, many people, many combinations. It can have a garden, a forest, a river, and several different casts of people. The King, for instance, coming from his palace—a troop of courtiers—a minstrel serenading a lady on a balcony—they are all separate; you are aware that each has a separate story and a separate case of characters and probably a different time-slot. But they all exist together, *simultaneously*, and that," said Mr. Hearst, "is the joy of the tapestry. It has no time limitations!"

He smiled at me. He said, "You say you have difficulty about dates, the year, day and hour when a thing happened, the decade or century in which certain things took place. I think that is quite all right and quite understandable. Many people think that way. You see events *not* as a narrow reel unwinding in a straight line with scenes presenting themselves one after the other, but as a vast tapestry where everything is registered forever in its over-all relationship to everything else. Certain figures stand out, again in relation to each other. They weave the entire tale together, covering everything. They have the Einstein $E=mc^2$ relativity to each other, but they also exist as one grand picture. We may stop and look with joy or amazement at one scene, one drama, one or two figures at a time, but we may also see it all at once as we see a tapestry . . ."

He was to remind me of this years later when he sent for me not too long before his death. To be close to his doctors he was living in Marion's beautiful house off Coldwater Canyon, behind the Beverly Hills Hotel. I found him in a big chair, quieter than usual, but as usual looking all ways at once. One measure of a great editor is to know how to give an assignment, and Mr. Hearst, the greatest, did it better than anyone else.

"The coming of the motion picture," he said, "was as important as that of the printing press. It has occurred to me that you might do a series putting together the Legends of Hollywood, stories about the movie stars and all they have meant to the world. Much of this may be lost. As you read history and biography you discover how much has been lost about which you long to know."

I protested. "History?" I said. "Me? Dates, sequences, times . . . ?"

"No, no," he said. "Human interest stories convey the truth to more people better than any other method. One grand picture woven as we stop to look with joy or pain or amazement at a drama or comedy here, a tragedy there, a sharp scene with one or two figures at a time. This will make us see it all at once as we see a tapestry . . ."

Called *Hollywood*.
Love   laughter   and tears.
And so it was. Oh, it *was*.

And on my tapestry there are truly the figures of:

Gloria Swanson—my ideal as a Movie Star (Fem.), from that first day I saw her as a Sennett Bathing Beauty to the last time a few Sundays ago when she gave the morning talk on spiritual healing to a packed church not far from Hollywood Boulevard.

Humphrey Bogart—in a few unbelievable days which we spent proving our family tree—and that my Grandma Bogart and his grandfather Dr. Belmot Bogart were brother and sister and both of us had as ancestors a Mohawk squaw and a lady who wore her nightgown to church under a sable cape and once, having cut her throat in despair, sewed it up again with her own darning needle. We felt that this latter ancestress explained some of his star parts and some of my newspaper career.

Clara Bow—whom I knew so well during her short spectacular career—fades out into darkness with a bright tear. She was as fine an actress as ever was on the screen. I know! Clara Bow was the IT Girl, the Sex Symbol of her day—and *not* an actress, but she *was* an actress and the unfortunate concurrence of the two led to the overshadowing of her art by her sex appeal, which was as raw, as primitive, as uncontrolled off the screen as on. Clara, with her exquisite talent, which neither she nor her studio knew how to handle, was actually warped by life ere ever she came to Hollywood. A tragedy it was, as I shall tell. I will always remember sitting on a set one day watching her do a scene from a story of mine called *Children of Divorce*, with Gary Cooper. And Clara Bow so moved the not-easily-moved Coop that he gave the first *performance* of his career.

Here on my tapestry is a single scene where Whitey, the chief of police of the Metro-Goldwyn-Mayer Studios, at last had to force his way into the dressing suite of the great ascending star,

Mario Lanza, because he insisted on keeping it *locked*, with all curtains drawn tightly, and both Howard Strickling, as head of Publicity, and Mr. Mayer, as head of the studio, had begun to worry about a possible scandal such as had once befallen us with Wallace Beery and a too-young girl—and when the door was forced it wasn't a beautiful young girl we found, it was just *food*. Hidden trays of fried chicken and pounds of chocolate cake. And Mario Lanza weeping bitterly as he said, "I'm always hungry! I've been hungry for years. I never get enough to eat—this keeping *thin*. All tenors like Caruso have been men with some fat on them!" As a matter of fact it was all that diet and diet pills that killed Mario Lanza long before his time, as those same diet pills were to be so large a part of the disasters that befell Judy Garland. As great an entertainer as the world has ever known, Fred Astaire said to me once. And Noel Coward agreed.

Over here I see the confrontation between the Noblest Hollywoodian of them all—Katharine Hepburn—and the Sweet Prince of the Barrymores, that Royal Family, wiped out by his foe alcohol.

"Mr. Barrymore," said Kate Hepburn, in this her first movie for which she'd left the New York stage, "you are drunk."

"I may be," said Mr. Barrymore, "but drunk or sober I can still act a young amateur right off the set."

And the girl who was soon to change the world's concept of beauty from curls and curves and cuteness back to the glorification of Donatello or Michelangelo and who was to be the heroine of that Hollywood love classic Tracy and Hepburn, won an admiration from me and George Cukor, the director, and the rest of the people on the set. "Yes," said Kate Hepburn, furiously, "that's why it's so dreadful! Think of what we could do if you were sober enough to help me give a performance such as I ought to give opposite you."

"Miss Hepburn," said Mr. Barrymore, "you have unfortunately jolted me back to comparative sobriety. Let us try what we can do."

Their picture A *Bill of Divorcement* was a classic and Kate's first step to stardom.

I was working at RKO for David O. Selznick writing A *Star Is Born* when she arrived in Hollywood and I have to see, too, the day David took his first look at Katharine Hepburn after Lillie Messinger, powerful head of the Eastern story department, sent her out from New York. Selznick ordered someone, anyone, to send Miss Hepburn right back on the next train. This in the early days of talking pictures when a new type of star, a new type of glamour, was born as Helen Hayes, Bette Davis, Humphrey Bogart, Jimmy Cagney and a wave of comics and song-and-dance artists flooded in from the stage.

I see what Hollywood still calls "Came the Talkies" as a montage; individual scenes against a madly whirling background.

Buddy Rogers saying for three days one simple line, "I must have a talk with you," before stage director George Cukor was satisfied. Joan Crawford hearing her voice, which was warmly wonderful, for the first time in a playback and wailing, "That can't be me!" Then going into hysterics. Unable to remember lines she'd known perfectly two seconds before, Gloria Swanson reading them off her leading man's shirt front. Clara Bow, perfect in rehearsal, fainting when she saw the mike over her head. Strong, silent cowboy Gary Cooper being put behind a davenport to play a scene by Director Frank Lloyd so the camera wouldn't show how his long legs shook every time he opened his mouth. Marion Davies, with a small grin after several gallant tries saying, "Who, me? I s-s-stutter," and moving out of her gorgeous dressing bungalow to make way for Norma Shearer.

And now a new Sex Symbol coming over the horizon, Jean Harlow—her platinum hair shining. There have been, a number of times, physical properties so arresting that they were identification and attributes of stellar magnitude. Valentino's black eyes. Mary's curls and Colleen Moore's bobbed hair. Tom Mix's resemblance to some of his Indian forebears. Douglas Fairbanks' leaps and bounds. Charlie Chaplin's feet. Harold Lloyd's eyeglasses. Gable's own-the-earth walk. Gary Cooper's slow grin. Gloria Swanson's unique ability to wear *clothes*, a dream of every woman's heart even in these poor decadent days of patched Levis and sequined sweat shirts.

Yes, and Jean Harlow's naturally platinum blonde hair. True, true, Harlow had for the camera the perfect body as Pickford had the perfect face. But when on my tapestry I see Jean, who was the Baby to all of us who knew and loved her, it is with that shining aura of silvery hair framing a tear-streaked face as she sat in my room at the Hearst Ranch in the middle of the night with Bill Powell, white and strained, beside her.

It's necessary to weave in some of these dangerous, humorous, loving laughing and weeping tales to really know the stars of Hollywood, for as in all other arts and sciences and politics and even industries, the love life of the stars therein has caused all things both great and small, all triumphs and disasters. The stories I must tell run up and down the spectrum from a lifelong devotion, the real *love* of *Miss* Marion Davies and William Randolph Hearst, to high comedy with Greta Garbo and John Gilbert, to the high tragedy of Ingrid Bergman on the island of Stromboli. Sometimes, as with Gary Cooper, the ingredients are all mixed into one life: the Cowboy and the It Girl, Cooper and Clara Bow, was a comedy skit, a vaudeville blackout, the Cowboy and the fiery Lupe Velez was tragicomedy, for not too long after their tempestuous affair the Mexican firebrand killed herself because, literally, she did not understand the English language. Before the Cowboy finally met *the* girl, Veronica Balfe, who was to become his wife and the real love of his life, there was also the drama of the Cowboy and the Countess, an internationally known beauty and hostess who carried the dazed Coop off first to her castle in Italy and then on safari in deepest Africa.

But for real tears I think the saddest love story in Hollywood has to be that of the lovely, silvery Jean Harlow, the Baby, and the suave, sophisticated William Powell. That night at the Ranch I was Mother Confessor at a scene between those two that I didn't want to watch. It broke my heart. It broke Jean's too. As I must show you so you can know the Baby as we did. For we all loved her. Bill Powell did, too.

Yes, sometimes I dream I go to Hollywood again.

Hollywood. A place, a symbol, a people, a state of mind and heart, an Art, an Industry, a legend second only to Camelot itself. A kingdom like Oz, a glory that was Greece and a grandeur that was Rome, a gilded slum with tinsel covering the drama and heartbreak, a center of the beautiful and damned.

As always, Mr. Hearst was right.

I must record my own memories of the legends I see so clearly on my tapestry.

Not too long before he died Walt Disney, one of our lasting geniuses, persuaded Pola Negri to come out of her retirement in Texas to play a part in *The Moonspinners* filmed in London. It was over forty years since Pola, our first foreign import, had burst upon us as the much ballyhooed "temperamental empress of passion" but she still had the touch. When la Negri descended on a press conference at the Dorchester swathed in black satin with a live cheetah in tow she once more made headlines. A valiant band of youngsters who had never seen her pictures waited each morning in the clammy fog to see her leave for the studio. Why? "We didn't want to miss the chance," they said. "You don't often get a chance to see a living legend."

Today I am The Old Woman of the Sea, Mother Confessor turned custodian of the Legends of Hollywood from first to last. If you live longer than practically anybody you find you have a debt to the past, and I must set them down because, you see, some of those current aren't true. Some aren't living. Some are in danger of being overlooked. Some of the great stars live on—even death couldn't kill Humphrey Bogart. Some live on TV, on the Late Late Show, in the pizza parlors. Some have been too soon forgotten.

Lest we forget.

Wallace Reid—the handsomest man I ever saw. Barbara La Marr—the Too Beautiful Girl. The two most talented young people who ever were in Hollywood. Both dead before they were thirty. Bebe Daniels—*Rio Rita*, a star beloved *in* Hollywood *by* Hollywood who left Hollywood for London where she became an idol and where she died full of honors long after World War II. I want to make sure they live.

Hollywood, as Mr. Hearst predicted, and being a prophet is another measure of a great editor, has indeed become the subject of innumerable histories and biographies by people who weren't *there*. But as the scholars begin to agree that the coming of the films was on a par with the coming of the printing press their painstaking research is all too often like a *dig* in ancient Egypt. Compilation of facts, dates, names, lists of movies made, chronology and critical evaluation just about miss living Hollywood entirely.

On the other hand when I read what is written by those who look only for sensationalism, for ugliness and degradation, my very heartstrings protest. There emerges a false picture and utterly unreal and phony personalities. Can anyone truly believe that the movies and all they have given us came from a gaggle of drunks and degenerates?

I realize that today a lot of readers are more interested in the manure than the rose. They never become aware of the fragrance and color and grace of the rose, or they would be bound to prefer it.

I warn one and all that I am going to try to show the rose, so if your preference is for the manure pick up the smelly inaccuracies of one of those dull lives of Jean Harlow. How it is possible to write books and never be right *once* I cannot figure. Because the real stories are so much better, so much more dangerous and big time and important.

Yes, I have heavies—villains—and stories of terrible deeds and words, good-for-nothings, workers of iniquity. I consider Cecil B. DeMille on a par with Benedict Arnold and Judas, and Paul Bern to be listed with Jerry Sneak whom Samuel Foote, in *The Mayor of Garratt*, called a lily-livered knave. But I have stories, too, of courage and loyalty and faith and hope. And romance and danger.

Many of us stand tiptoe looking back with nostalgia, for life *now* can seem pretty drab and fearsome, and it is almost totally without idols of any kind anywhere in any field. Another reason perhaps for the swelling interest in that merry, madcap and miraculous land of a bygone day. It is as though, it seems to me, I could step back to the lost continent of Atlantis, or the Knights of the Round Table where the triangle of King Arthur and Queen Guinevere and Lancelot can hardly be more world shaking than that of Clark Gable and Joan Crawford, at a time when Clark had a wife named Rhea and Joan had a husband named Douglas Fairbanks, Jr., and yet they were so madly in love with each other, Clark and Joan, that we once trembled for the entire picture business for one more *scandal* might allow the churches and the clubwomen to close the movie houses as they threatened to do after the Fatty Arbuckle insanity.

Hollywood. A reality and a fantasy. Oh, yes. For we made a lot of it up as we went along. Let me show you what I mean. A young lady from Cincinnati named Theodosia Goodman *invented* the Vamp—crystal ball, tiger skin rug, peacock feathers and all.

Nothing like Theda Bara could happen today. She was part of the motion picture's very real amazement. To people who had never seen moving pictures before, Theda Bara *was* what they saw on the screen.

Once when a mother saw her child walking along a quiet New York street talking to a dark, white-faced lady, on recognizing Theda Bara the mother began to shriek wildly, "Save him—save him—The Vampire has my child," and actually called the police.

In your dictionary is a memorial to Miss Bara: A Vamp; a woman who preys upon men. To vamp; To prey upon men, to entice, inveigle, captivate. Such definitions and their usage were put into our language by Theda Bara.

Audiences were torn between fear of The Vampire and a wild desire to have some of her strange power rub off on them. The head of a New York department store pleaded with her, "Please don't come in, Miss Bara. We'll send the gowns to your hotel, but we can't stand any more of these riots." Mobs of women had broken plate glass windows to grab a hat Theda Bara had touched, in the hope that they, too, might be able to make men grovel.

Actually Theda was a gracious, cultured woman who, in 1921, while she was still a big star, quietly married her director, a distinguished Englishman of excellent family named Charles Brabin, and retired from the screen. Theda Bara Brabin became a real Grande Dame in Southern California society and they lived happily ever after.

If you were invited to her home, as I was frequently, you would find a hostess who talked wittily, wisely, of music at the Hollywood Bowl, new pictures acquired by the Museum, of European capitals and artistic celebrities in every field of art who were her close friends.

You would also discover that cuisine for which Theda was famous. Indeed once King Vidor, one of our greatest directors, listening to a stage play in which the leading lady was ordering a gourmet's dream of caviar, snails, squabs and crêpes Suzette, leaned over to his companion, Ethel Barrymore, and said, "Ah, potluck at Theda's."

This is the woman who played *The Serpent of the Nile, The Vampire, The Tiger Woman, Carmen* and forty other pictures in three years to bring in the fortune on which William Fox built his company. How often Fox must have congratulated himself on the sharp eyes of a director named Frank Powell who spotted her among the extras as The Vampire they'd been searching for to star in Kipling's line "A fool there was."

Theda was the first movie star around whom a real publicity campaign was built. She did it herself. "You don't need a press agent," Fox said to her. That was the day he asked her where she was born. "It wouldn't be exciting to say Cincinnati, would it?" said Theodosia Goodman. "Suppose we say the Sahara Desert?"

She also created the name Theda Bara. Columns of print pointed out that the letters of her first name were an anagram of death, those of her second Arab. Further she invented a background. Theda Bara, the public was told, was the daughter of a French painter and an Arabian princess, who had eloped to an oasis in the Sahara.

I remember the first time I interviewed Theda Bara, remember the black velvet, the white face and black hypnotic eyes, the crystal ball, the peacock feathers, the tiger skin rugs. Had I believed it? I think so. It was a terrific show she put on.

"To understand those grand days," Theda Bara said to me the last time I saw her, "with the world of movies so new and all, we have to remember that people believed what they saw on the screen. Nobody had then destroyed the grand illusion. They thought the stars of the screen were the way they saw them. Nobody had knocked down any of their idols. Now—they know it's all just make-believe."

So for years they thought Theda Bara was the wickedest woman in the world. Yet as far as I know there was never one word of gossip about Theda Bara of any kind, anytime, anywhere.

If I am raising words to the Nth degree, if superlatives such as handsomest, wickedest, incredible, even fabulous, stupendous, colossal, pepper these pages, stop to think. So many of those who molded this new Art and Industry had a touch, or more than a touch, of genius. The stars of those times were so brilliant we had to commandeer the name *star* to speak of them. They had to be spectacular, the most beautiful, the sexiest, and at certain sharp moments on my tapestry, one after another, the *greatest*, or they would never have made it to the top in my Hollywood.

They were to come in time to the insipidity of stars of the Seventies—where the leading feminine star is the personification of the age's uglification and the male version is as virile as a rained-on bee.

And for me an attempt to bring back those stars of an era of *greatness* when our idols were the extreme exaggeration of all the charms and virtues and irresistible personalities.

Usually, I don't permit myself IFs, but I have to wonder *if* my life would have been different *if* there had been anybody home in that fly-by-night, castles-in-Spain fighting-off-disaster Griffith Studio to invite me in. *If* my first contact with the fabulous picture business had been David Wark Griffith, with his touch of the melancholy Dane instead of Mack Sennett with his commitment to all the clowns from the Roman Circus down through Shakespeare to his own stage in Edendale.

"Go and see what all the *shooting* is about," my city editor had said.

Of course his (hopeful) misinterpretation of that word shows how little we knew about The Movies. Our ignorance at that early date was almost total. However, when I did find the Griffith Studio on Sunset Boulevard there *wasn't* anybody home. Only a pleasant-looking kid—he said his name was Bobby—and nobody was shooting because Mr. Griffith wasn't there and if I wanted to find somebody who was, why didn't I go out to the Sennett Studios in Edendale? They, said Bobby Harron, were always shooting something out there like Cops. Or Comics.

When I turned back from the gate of D. W. Griffith's studio that day, I drove east by north (I think but since I heard on TV the other day that Reno, Nevada, is farther *west* than Los Angeles I'm not going to be positive about it), anyway I drove out a ways and then on a dirt road over a small foothill and arrived at Edendale and the Sennett Studios and no one at all said me Nay—nor Aye for that matter.

I didn't see any shooting as I went round and round that day. I did see a lot of people, *very* busy in all directions, throwing pies, chasing each other, falling out of or into something. I was irresistibly swept into a Magic World of Make-Believe and Laughter.

No, *my* Hollywood didn't begin with D. W. Griffith.

Nor for *me* did it begin with Mary Pickford.

It began with Mack Sennett, The King of Comedy, on that one ramshackle, first of its kind motion picture *lot* where on my tapestry I see

Mabel Normand
Charlie Chaplin
Marie Dressler
Gloria Swanson
Bebe Daniels
and
The Keystone Cops
and
The Bathing Beauties

Chapter Two

The King of Comedy and the Queen of Clowns

MACK SENNETT AND MABEL NORMAND
with
MARIE DRESSLER   BING CROSBY   THE BATHING BEAUTIES
and FATTY ARBUCKLE

The Magic World of Make-Believe. From time to time, how we all need to flee into it. The far places, the people we need to love and admire, the conqueror of time by which we can go into any past we choose and forward into any dream, this is what The Movies brought to pass. Nowadays this magic world seems composed chiefly of Inferno, Earthquake, Tidal Wave, Nausea and the Jaws of an unfriendly shark. I stay home myself and read. I need a wider choice than The Movies of today give me. Beside the manure, there is still the rose. I have the mirth of Thurber, the original Benchley, the wit and wisdom of Dorothy Parker, and Mr. Pickwick. Sometimes the old supreme Movies.

. . . tragedy, comedy, history, pastoral, pastoral-comical, historical-pastoral, tragical-historical, tragical-comical-historical-pastoral, scenes individable or poem unlimited . . . For the law of writ and the liberty, these are the only men.*

They had it all, those men who actually made the movies, who were responsible for creating this entertainment, this travel and truth, this laughter, by putting together the Arts. The men who said Let There Be Light—and light there was on the silver screen, the first movies, bless 'em all. These presented us with this pack-

* Hamlet: Act II, Scene 2.

age of personality and passion, love and laughter and tears. Theodore Huff, Professor of American Film History at New York University, calls *Intolerance*, D. W. Griffith's second epic, a masterpiece—and I quote—"which ranks with such works of art as Beethoven's Ninth Symphony, Rembrandt's 'Descent from the Cross,' Da Vinci's 'Mona Lisa,' the sculptures of the Parthenon, or with works of literature such as Tolstoy's 'War and Peace,' the poetry of Walt Whitman or Shakespeare's 'Hamlet.'"

Griffith himself was the first to say, "We have found a universal language."

While I agree with this I still cannot accept the now generally held historical platform that the movies were a concept of the fertile brain of David Wark Griffith. Partly due, of course, to the wisdom and indefatigable determination of the morning star Miss Lillian Gish, who has made the idealization and appreciation of David Wark Griffith her life's work. About all anyone would need anytime are the efforts of Lillian Gish, who was there when the first flicker of silver came upon the screen and is still as brilliant, powerful and active as ever.

My admiration for Lillian, that great lady who has never known what the word quit meant, is profound and has been for over sixty years. Just the same I'm glad it was Mabel Normand, our madcap mischief maker, who was the first movie star I knew.

For while the historical-tragical indeed even pastoral epics of Mr. Griffith made critical history, it was the *comical* that controlled the motion picture in the beginning. And it is that laughter, that real spirit-lifting laughter which can mitigate tragedy and wipe away tears that I miss most today.

So that my first choice for immortality upon the Mount Rushmore of Hollywood, should we ever, in memoriam, decide to have so splendid a monument, would have to be the big, rough ex-boilermaker Mack Sennett, the King of Comedy, who wanted above all things to be a grand opera singer. The best he could do was let his uproarious *bellow* ring through that space now called a movie lot to command a chase by his Keystone Cops, or a dunking for his Beauties, or a zany pantomime by his stars, who taken all together were the greatest collection of comics of all time.

And, of course, his star-of-stars, Mabel Normand, forever and ever the Queen of Clowns.

Who was born, Charlie Chaplin once said to me, with the gift of laughter, knowing more about comedy and comedy routine than any of the rest of us ever learn.

That brings me to a moment's pause if I may—once upon a time a comedy writer named Harry Ruskin, who had written blackouts for the Ziegfeld Follies and had a fifty-two-week-a-year contract with MGM to compose the *Andy Hardy* series for Mickey Rooney and routines for Judy Garland and Gene Kelly, and I contemplated a sort of textbook for dramatic schools and cinema classes. It was to include all the basic formula for getting laughs. We were of course bound, then, by what was known as good taste, and it is perhaps to be remembered that none of the box office record breakers of the early movies ever hit a blue note in their laugh-getters. Personally, of course, they knew about *sex*. Professionally, it was a no-no—a taboo, as unprofessional and shabbily vulgar as belching or passing wind. Or as low-down as laughing at your own jokes which of course no real comedian ever did. In fact the great stars like Buster Keaton and Charlie Chaplin and W. C. Fields were melancholy fellows and Harold Lloyd wore those horn-rimmed glasses to give him an air of solemnity.

Mack Sennett knew this always. It is possible to run every single reel of film he ever shot without finding any of the silly innuendos and toilet humor resorted to nowadays to get the jaded and weary laughs of a bankrupt nation.

Somewhere, either in his early years in the ironworks in his home town in Connecticut, or when he haunted the Metropolitan Opera House while carrying his spear in lesser musicals on the fringes of Broadway, or in burlesque, or during his days with Griffith at Biograph Studios, Mack Sennett was touched by the comic Muse Thalia. When he moved from Biograph in New York into more sunlight to do his own *shooting* in that small dusty foothill town of Hollywood, he knew that, if you could bring it real *laughter*, the whole world would indeed laugh with you.

So he took with him that small, dark pixie of a girl named Mabel Normand, whom he loved all his life—Mabel and Mabel only and always—and yet he was to destroy her as mortals always do the pixies and elfs and fairy folk. The Little People. Yes yes yes—Mabel Normand was one of the Little People. And she fell in love with a mortal and that brought her under the sway of Melpomene, who wove the web of tragedy.

The mad night when we pulled her out of the ocean after she jumped off the Nat Goodwin pier, she said to me, "It would have been better if you'd let me go. I don't belong in this world . . ." Nor did she.

Truth to tell, the only place I ever saw Mabel where she *belonged* was at Edendale where Mack Sennett had created the World of Make-Believe around her.

Without any difficulty that first day I got into the Mack Sennett Studios and saw Mack Sennett. Nobody, then and from then on, was as accessible as Mack Sennett. True, his name was already over the main gate in huge letters, on the roof of the principal stage, and beyond question he was The Boss of all he surveyed. But he kept every door and window wide open hoping something exciting would come *in* and also if necessary he could throw anybody he didn't need *out*.

When I proceeded under negligible escort to his two-story tower office I have to say that, impressive as the boss man was, and he was very impressive indeed, he was not the first thing I noticed. Nor yet the second.

First I had to see that his attendant was not the expected secretary but one Abdul the Turk, whom I had encountered not too long before when my father took me to the training camp of the great Stanley Ketchel. For a fleeting moment I was not Miss Rogers of the *Herald* but a teen-age girl on a moonlit strip of beach near San Francisco trembling as she received her first kiss from the handsome Ketchel and trembling later in a suite at the St. Francis when the celebrated trial lawyer, Earl Rogers, gave his only daughter her last spanking for kissing a *prizefighter*. Abdul had somehow strayed out of one dream into another so I pulled myself together and grinned at him. Then I had to see that this office contained not only Abdul the Turk, a small desk and a few chairs, but a gargantuan *bathtub* which dominated us all. Make-a-note-make-a-note, said my mind to me—eight feet long at *least*, six feet wide, five feet deep, why you could drown in that tub and no one would even know you were missing—it might not be a *shooting* but it had to be a story.

"There's nothing quite as stimulating as a bath," said an aggressive voice. And I saw Mack Sennett.

An aggressive man. A large, burly Irishman. A man with heavy eyebrows wearing an expensive Panama hat from which the top of the crown had been removed to reveal a luxuriant growth of dark hair. Make-a-note-make-a-note . . .

"Ventilation," said the great man. "If you want to keep your hair, your scalp has to have ventilation."

Since I had but recently skewered my long, long, thick, thick braids on top of my head with torturous steel pins in the manner of beauty then in vogue I had given little thought to baldness. If I had a secret yearning it was to have less rather than more hair. Still, looking from the tub to the hat to the face beneath it, I was ready to believe in ventilation. There was something very believable, despite his obvious eccentricities, something brooding and earthy about this King of Comedy. Thus I was also ready to believe when I was told later that he employed Abdul full time to keep him in fighting trim though he was a peaceable fellow who rarely raised a fist; that there was a gymnasium on the tower roof, a rubbing table and steam room below; that he held his daily conferences submerged to his chin in his bathtub; that despite the hand-to-mouth existence in those early days the large diamond he wore was real, the coins he clinked constantly in his pocket were genuine $20 gold pieces, his favorite supper was champagne with corned beef and raw onions; that he was not chewing gum but tobacco and that his tobacco shots into flat boxes of sawdust placed at convenient intervals around his domain were unerringly accurate.

In short I was ready to believe not only Sennett, but the topsy-turvy world the other side of the looking glass over which he ruled.

From the tower we could see all twenty-eight random, confused acres of it, the original barn, storehouse office, shacks still casually adrift amidst the new stages. A stucco projection room I later found to contain three pew-like rows of benches for minions and a rocking chair close by a box of sawdust for the master. A sloping hill where even now could be seen a cameraman, a director photographing a maiden in a floral bonnet and velvet cape fleeing a top-hatted gentleman with a mustache so villainous as to be visible to the naked eye from our aerie. Over near Alessandro Street was a large concrete bathing pool close by the actors' dressing rooms from the porches of which it was possible for overheated performers to drop or be thrown into the plunge below. On a large level dirt patch I could see four ordinary-looking men, all of whom seemed to be great and furious tumblers, having an impromptu contest to see who could endure the most fantastic falls, flying figures who left the earth with the ease and grace of the immortal Nijinksy and returned to it as abruptly as any earthbound mortal.

"My cops," said Mack Sennett. "Practicing. Always practicing." And indicated that I was free to roam.

To come upon the Hollywood of those days is like taking off for the moon, landing there and finding it inhabited by all the people we always thought and hoped people would be. Including ourselves. The shining stage star David Warfield, who toured our country from big city to small town for years as the Music Master, when I once interviewed him as The Movies became a solid fact of our existence, said he would never make a movie but not from any of that sense of superiority which so many footlight big-timers showed. Exactly the reverse. He said that The Movies would demand more than he or most other stage bigwigs could offer. "The screen," he said "has only one dimension. To be LIFE-SIZE therefore, the personality must be way over life-size, all motion picture stars will be *exaggerations*—expanded to meet the demands of that *flat* silver sheet. You will see."

Shirley Temple   the exaggerated Little Girl

Clark Gable   the Man

Barbra Streisand   exaggeration of the dying twentieth century's exaggeration and symbol of its bankrupt despair.

Mabel Normand   an exaggeration of that Do You Believe in Fairies? which Peter Pan needed to keep his heart young and happy.

Marie Dressler   the old lady everybody needs in their life.

It is very strange.

I miss Marie more than anybody except Clark. I didn't really have her that much *in* my life, even when Talkies came and she rented my house in Beverly Hills and I moved permanently to live in the Malibu Colony. We used to gather there—Frances Marion, the scenarist, and Hedda Hopper, sometimes Margaret Mayer (Mrs. Louis B.) and Agnes Underwood who down the line succeeded J.B.T. Campbell on the *Herald*. Occasionally Mary Pickford made a queenly appearance. And Joan Crawford, who somewhere along in there was Mary's daughter-in-law. And Jean Harlow. And, when Marie was alone, even Miss Greta Garbo.

For once, since my emotions are sometimes mysterious even to me, I can tell you utterly and completely why and I and everybody who knew her missed Marie Dressler more than anybody.

"What is it you do that makes your pitchers pitch better than other managers' pitchers?" I said once to Red Schoendienst, when he was pilot of the St. Louis Cardinals.

"Only one thing any manager can do for any pitcher," Red said, very seriously. "Give him confidence. That's it. Give him confidence."

I *know*.

So do most other people. *Confidence*. Full trust. Belief in the trustworthiness, reliability and ability of a person or thing or *yourself*. Confidence that you can do what you have to or ought to do. When the hills ahead of you seem too steep to climb, without handhold or foothold, that you can climb them from somewhere. *The difficult we do immediately. The impossible takes a little longer.* Marie, whether or no it was actually her conscious slogan, made you believe it could and should be yours. *Get on with it.* It's worth doing—she injected that into you. And when she prayed you felt that she spoke with a Higher Power face to face.

"Oh, please stay with me," Jean Harlow said to Marie on that first day when Jean had to go back to work after the death of her husband, Paul Bern. A top producer, Bern had shot himself in their luxurious home in Bel Air.

Even a little or professional disappointment was something you took to Marie. A minor hurt in your work—I remember so well that I went to her wailing with chagrin and malediction when I found that Irving Thalberg, then head of Metro-Goldwyn-Mayer, had yielded to his wife Norma Shearer and given her the leading role in my picture *A Free Soul* when I'd been promised Joan Crawford.

MARIE DRESSLER

The Greatest Lady of Hollywood.

The Ugly Duckling who became a commanding Broadway favorite at twenty—and a great movie star at sixty.

In between her first success in the Gay Nineties when an ebullient young clown shared the stage with the glittering Lillian Russell, and the immortal Weber and Fields and the day when an old lady with a punishing jaw made her comeback as Marthy, the waterfront drunk in Garbo's first talkie, *Anna Christie*, Marie Dressler sailed more stormy seas, went higher *up* and plunged further *down*, and did it more often, than any other star who ever came to Hollywood.

Once, when Joan Crawford and I were doing a tea-talk television show, our hostess, I think it was Virginia Graham, was stressing our enduring success in our chosen fields and Joan leaned over and put her hand on my arm and said, "You know what's remarkable about Adela and me? We *survived*." We did indeed. But Marie Dressler did more than survive. She wallowed through each trough of the waves so gallantly, came rumbling to the crest again with such zest, that she *inspired*. She made everyone who knew her feel they could go and do likewise. Thus while I see those two gracious and lovely stars, Lillian Gish and Irene Dunne, in the court of our greatest lady, their passage has always seemed so relatively serene that I have to award top billing to Marie—who overcame, and overcame, and *overcame*.

On the stage at thirteen to help support a frail mother she adored, a large awkward girl without beauty, recognized talent, or influential friends, handicapped then and always by unbelievable stage fright and a memory that balked at learning lines, Marie Dressler was at forty, so Joe Weber told me, "the greatest comedienne the stage ever saw." True grit? Has to be, especially when we know that at the halfway mark, when she was thirty, she was blackballed through total misrepresentation by a powerful manager and spent some time in Coney Island selling peanuts. "I've never turned down an honest job in my life," I once heard Marie say to a faltering female star about to refuse a part because it did

not measure up to her own carefully nurtured sense of self-impor-
tance. "If you can't get what you want, take what you can get,"
she said. "Keep working always, it brings luck."

When Marie's luck turned she came back from Coney Island
bigger, funnier, heartier than ever and for two decades, right
through the dark days of our First World War, let this tired old
world borrow its mirth from her great heart. She toured the
United States. She captured audiences in the musical halls and
theaters of England. Somewhere along in here she invaded enemy
territory when she broke through the barrier which decreed that
actresses were not and could not be *ladies,* hence were socially unacceptable. Marie Dressler, born Leila Koerber in Coburg, On-
tario, Canada, daughter of an unsuccessful German music teacher
who had not spared the rod trying to convince his daughter she
lacked talent, who had failed as a salesgirl and bareback rider in a
circus, had no formal education, had worn *tights* on the stage and
all her life insisted on trying to make her own clothes, was seen
riding in the park with *the* Mrs. Stuyvesant Fish. Having invited
Marie to appear before titled guests Mrs. Fish, wise and witty ar-
biter of New York's Four Hundred, decided Marie was what *Mrs.
Fish* thought a lady should be. Later Mrs. W. K. Vanderbilt, Ida
M. Tarbell, Anne Morgan, sister of the financial colossus J.P.,
agreed. They found in Marie Dressler not only a friend, but an
invaluable and indefatigable volunteer for their philanthropies.
Whether it was selling Liberty Bonds, entertaining in hospitals,
giving benefits, or organizing the American Woman's Association
to help women meet the changed conditions following their eco-
nomic independence, Marie was the dynamo, the supercharger;
she made the magic. The same magic worked in Europe where, although she didn't appear professionally, she was toasted by am-
bassadors, strolled through Italian gardens with cardinals. Dressler
could and did walk with kings but she didn't lose the common
touch. To this I can testify. For it was during these halcyon years
that I met her.

Following her riotous stage success in *Tillie's Nightmare,* in
which Marie sang "Heaven Will Protect the Working Girl,"
Mack Sennett brought her to Hollywood to make her first movie.
Mack entitled his screen version *Tillie's Punctured Romance* and

Marie was on his lot as Tillie that day when he set me free to roam. Thus it was on one of his stages, as topless as Mack's Panama hat, not for ventilation but to let in any available *sunlight*, that I first saw Marie Dressler, her two hundred pounds enveloped in a voluminous dress, her forty-three-year-old face decorated with what we then inelegantly called spit curls. And Marie, with that enormous perception of hers, saw at once a *cub* reporter and let her chuckling warmth settle over me. "Let's talk," she said, "but we'll have to make it snappy. The circus is waiting for its elephant."

So we talked. We talked of Anna Held, the great French beauty much admired by my father and also rather excessively by Florenz Ziegfeld who married her for a while. Rumor had it that Anna Held had resigned from a show rather than try to star in a cast which included the homely face and fantastic proportions of Marie Dressler. Thus had Marie earned the title "star obscurer"— a quaint phrase which meant she stole the show.

"I always feel sorry for beautiful women," Marie said. "Beauty can be a curse. You depend on it and when it goes you have nothing to fall back on. Personality, that's the thing. I'm not conceited but I can always take a roomful of people away from any beauty. Why? Because I work to amuse 'em, to make 'em happy. When they've had a real good look at the beauty they come over to Dressler for laughs. Every woman can develop personality; not all can be beautiful."

I felt my bosoms which, to my great distress, I did not then seem to have a fashionable quantity *of*, swelling. I see now that Marie was more *in* my life from that moment than I had realized. For I heard what she said. I heard it inside—not in my head where thoughts can escape right out through the other ear or the mouth—but in my *stomach*. Where the Chinese believe the soul resides. When you hear with your stomach it stays, becomes a part of you. What Marie said that day became a part of me, and none too soon. For shortly before the Ketchel-first-kiss my father had informed me most kindly that my only claims to beauty were my *eyes* which he said were Killarney blue and put in with a sooty finger. Thus Papa forbade the frills and flounces recommended by my mother whom I didn't like very much but who was a *beauty*,

and converted me to the tailored type so someone might notice
my eyes. And, said Papa, my *ankles*. Which were to be contained
in sensible high shoes so's I'd have ankles instead of ham hocks.
But—without *bosoms*, with only *eyes* and *ankles*, a girl could be
forlorn. And here was this great stage star telling me about *personality*. Something, she said, that would last where my mother's
beauty wouldn't. That'd give a girl confidence.

When Marie spoke of Lillian Russell, the American Beauty
Rose, who was her first intimate friend, she said Lillian was the
toast of two continents because she had a nature like sunshine. "I
learned from her what graciousness, kindness, courtesy meant,"
she said, "and to keep my corns and toothaches and troubles to
myself." She thought Lillian was the exception because she had
beauty and also knew how to make people happy.

It is said that anyone can count themselves fortunate if they
have two real friends. Marie Dressler had dozens. And dozens.
From that day forward I thought of myself as one of them. True,
despite the enormous success of her first picture, Marie returned
to the New York stage and I stayed on in Hollywood but when
we parted on the Sennett lot that day Marie wrapped me in a
bear hug and said, "Be seeing you!" Somehow I knew it was a
promise.

I realize suddenly that I had not intended to write about Marie
Dressler at this point in this book. I figured to give her a passing
mention, save her real story for later, now I must laugh at myself.
It is impossible, always was, to give Marie a passing mention.
Some folks you can fragment, write separately of their love life,
their talent, politics, philosophy, isolate a moment of tragedy, of
passion, of triumph. When Marie Dressler comes *in*—whether
into your life, or your consciousness, or your book—she comes
total and whole. There's no way to leave any of her *out*. So here
she is.

Perhaps it is just as well for when we come, as come we must,
to the scandals, the tragedies, the heartbreaks that beset some of
Mack Sennett's stars, the image of Marie will stand before us, a
beacon of faith and fortitude on that shifting tapestry we called
Hollywood.

I must try for winged fingers to set down a portrait of Marie Dressler as we knew her, as we loved her. And we did.

A formidable foe, indeed a lusty fighter in the cause of righteousness. Dressler once chased Jake Shubert from his theater with a large stage brace for violating, in spirit at least, a contract agreement with *all* the artists appearing at the Winter Garden. During the famous Actor's Equity strike for decent contracts and pay while rehearsing for *all* the artists, Marie led the chorus girls in a parade up Fifth Avenue then kept at bay Abe Erlanger, the American theater czar, simply with the threat of her presence. He wouldn't appear before joint committees of actors and managers if Dressler was there. "No," Erlanger said, "she'll say, 'Vell, Abe?' and then—no no. I couldn't do the managers any good if Marie's there."

A great talent who knew the healing value of both laughter and tears. Of laughter she said to me, "Troubles never seem so big, life can never seem so dark, once you have laughed." Of tears, "The right kind of tears wipe away bitterness and rebellion and hatred. They ease the heart. When I sing sad songs it's just Dressler singing, people weep unashamed."

A gifted clown with such innate dignity she could be the rowdy or the lady with equal ease, often on the same evening. Once, while in Venice with her great friend, Lady Alice Colebrooke, Marie was asked by an American heiress married to an Italian prince to appear at a charity ball. To everyone's surprise Marie, always a soft touch, refused. "I don't like the woman," she said. "She's unkind. She hurts people and thinks her charity ball will make up for it." When they chanced to meet the Princess had heard Marie's remark. "I'm sorry you heard it," said Marie, "but I did say it and I think it's true. You may think me a sentimental old woman but kindness is, to me, one of the great things in life."

"And for dislike of me you refuse your talent to help the poor?" the Princess said.

"I will take a table and come to your ball," Marie said. "But I will not perform—unless it's a flop. Then, well, I'll be there, Your Highness."

Gilda Gray doing the shimmy, a dance which she made famous in the Ziegfeld Follies, was to highlight the evening's entertain-

ment. Titles galore, royalty of three countries, society en masse
looked upon Gilda's shimmy—and were not amused. I remember
Valentino, who really knew all there was to know about dancing,
once saying to me, "If you must do the shimmy, do not shake the
shoulders. Shake only the hips, but just gracefully, lightly, otherwise the shimmy is suggestive and vulgar." Maybe Gilda shook
the shoulders that night, at any rate the guests began to leave
with most of the champagne, proceeds from which were to go to
charity, still waiting in the wings. Without fanfare Marie Dressler
rose and made her way to the orchestra. "Play that shimmy music
again, boys," Dressler said, "and this time put a little pep into it.
There's more of me than there is of Gilda." I can see it now:
Marie, in full evening dress, doing her version of the shimmy
which was quite simply hilarious. Europe was certainly at her feet
that night as they laughed and drank champagne and kept her
there until she was ready to drop.

"You've been very kind," said the Princess.

"It's a nice thing to find in other folks, isn't it?" said Miss
Dressler. "I bid you good night."

A soft touch? Oh, she was. A heart of gold that went right to
the bottom of her pocketbook, wherever that bottom was. In the
lean days at Coney Island she once spent her last dollar on a colorful potted geranium, then gave it to the kid in the shooting gal-
lery for his sick mother. Later, when she passed out Christmas
baskets personally in New York's tenement districts, she became
so concerned with one family, an ineffectual husband, a bevy of
skinny kids, a sick mother, that she returned again and again.
Came the day when she arrived to find the children weeping, the
still body on the bed covered with a sheet and the husband dis-
traught over his inability to bury it properly. Marie parted with
four-hundred-odd dollars, all she had in her purse, and withdrew
tactfully before their united grief. Returning to retrieve her umbrella she found the corpse sitting up counting the cash. It was
typical of Dressler that within a month she bought out a bankrupt shoe company, moved the stock into her flat and invited all
God's children to help themselves. They helped themselves to
shoes, to lamps, to everything in the apartment that was portable
and half the linoleum from her kitchen floor. Thus it was that, despite the enormous sums she earned, when Marie found herself at

fifty displaced by the Flapper and the postwar craze for youth her financial situation was less than security deep.⟩

Now came the lowest of lows as she waited "at liberty" in outer offices while managers slipped out the back door. Broke, she lived at the Ritz and acted as hostess for the Ritz Supper Club. She sold real estate in Florida. She tried movies again, a series of cheap comedy-travelogues made in Europe and financed by that press agent de luxe Harry Reichenbach. Made without director or story the idea was to show beautiful scenery with Marie coming on occasionally with a gag to keep the folks awake. The first one, she told me, showed Marie at the Palace of Versailles where she fell into the lake. They were, she said, pretty terrible. So terrible that for all I know they may still repose in some customs warehouse for no one would pay the duty on them. In those years she did anything and everything except admit she was through although, she admitted to me once with a chuckle, "I knew I was a majority of one." We had been listening together to an evening of Brahms on her radio in the house she rented from me in Beverly Hills and then she said, "Of course I always had the three things essential to life—music, laughter, God. Let us give thanks they're free."

And she always had her wealth of friends. Friends, not lovers, played the star parts in Marie Dressler's life. She was really popular with men. She had married once, briefly, early in her career the handsome young assistant treasurer of a company in which she starred. Her one true love—and in Marie's case that is the appropriate phrase—was a man she couldn't marry. His wife consistently refused him a divorce. So Marie waited. And waited. It was Marie who nursed him through his last painful illness, was at his bedside when he died, paid for his burial. Then she put that away with her corns and toothaches, she never talked about him, she never fell in love again. Instead she said, putting everything she had into it, "Friendship is the crown of life."

At point zero, when it seemed ridiculous to keep herself available for the comeback that wasn't coming, it was two of her friends who kept Marie from sailing for Paris there to sell dresses on the Rue Cambon or open a *pension* at Neuilly for Americans.

In New York—Nella Webb. Herself something of a personality. Nella had been a chorus girl behind Marie in the Gay Nine-

ties. Then she traveled the world giving monologues the while
studying under various masters to become the most popular and
successful astrologer of her day, billed, indeed, as the Astrologer to
the Stars. Often and often from her apartment at the Waldorf,
Nella Webb scanned the heavens to predict their influences on
her famous clients. Marie was her oldest friend, in the stars Nella
read for her a future greater than ever, she must not now turn her
back on her country and her profession. "Wait," said Nella.
"Wait a little longer." And she gave her a specific date.

In Holywood—Frances Marion. Frances was another *cub* reporter Marie had befriended in the long ago, this one when the
stage tour of *Tillie's Nightmare* reached San Francisco. Frances
had become one of the first and most brilliant of the major
screenwriters and eventually a power inside the vast organization
of MGM, where Irving Thalberg listened to her before almost
anyone. Behind a madonna-like face and a shy-and-lady-like manner Frances Marion had the rugged determination of a boa constrictor where a *friend* was concerned and when the rumors about
Dressler's plight reached her Frances was determined that Marie's
light should not go out.

I promised you stories of loyalty. No Hollywood legend would
be complete without the story of Frances Marion's loyalty, bless
her stout little heart. And if I have a debt to the past it is to tell
you at least a little part of it, for Frances was my friend, too, from
the very early days until the day I saw her less than a year ago just
before she departed with, so she told me, great anticipation for
that Tavern at the End of the Road where my old friend Damon
Runyon, the Star Reporter, used to say we shall all meet again
someday.

On a day foretold by the stars Frances Marion, upon whom
Marie Dressler had showered so much love over so many years, decided single-handed to stage a comeback for her old friend. Be assured that Frances was resourceful as well as brilliant. Her first
move was to convert a mediocre novel by Kathleen Norris which
she found in a bottom drawer in the MGM story department into
a magnificent cockeyed comedy, *The Callahans and the Murphys*.
Next she began a careful campaign to convince Irving Thalberg

that he wanted to make it into a picture starring Marie Dressler and Polly Moran. On the date Nella Webb had predicted Frances Marion called Marie Dressler to come to Hollywood. That the finished picture had to be withdrawn, despite plaudits from such unerring experts as Charlie Chaplin, Harold Lloyd and a preview audience that mobbed the two stars, had to do exclusively with the fact that the Irish, in one of their less endearing and totally inexplicable moments, took umbrage. Marie swallowed her disappointment and waited. To Frances the setback was trying, but temporary. She next turned her eye on the part of Marthy in *Anna Christie* and simply wrote Marie into it. Dressler did not "obscure" Garbo, but she certainly let everyone know she was there. Then Frances Marion wrote an original story, *Min and Bill*, for Marie Dressler and Wallace Beery. It won Marie an Academy Award, but she won more than that. For with Min the whole world fell in love with an old lady—the old lady everybody needs in their life.

Let's face it. We *all* do. The old lady who bears her age, not as something to cover with powder and paint, not to have "lifted" from her face with a scalpel, but to be carried with pride. At sixty Marie Dressler was living poetry, perhaps by Browning. "Grow old along with me!" she seemed to encourage. "The best is yet to be/The last of life, for which the first was made." Wherever she went now it was like a royal progress, adoring fans pressed near to look into the ugly-beautiful, tough-tender, old-forever-young face of a great and famous lady, the face of age as age should be—not faltering, fretful, regretful, but dynamic, fearless, laughing and triumphant. Oh, she gave them confidence, she did she did. And to those of us who came knocking on her door she gave as much as we would take—and always a little more.

The secret of Marie Dressler? Of her personality? Her power? Her friendships? She told it to me once in two words. *Prayer. Love.* I had gone to interview her for a four-part Private Life for a national magazine, she told me she had one favorite prayer. She said, "If you can pray this and mean it, it's all you'll ever need." Then very softly she quoted from a verse written many years ago: "Teach me to love not those who first love me,/But all the world . . . Teach me to love."

Marie knew how to love. She knew how to live. So of course she knew how to die. When she knew she was very ill, that there was no hope of recovery, she withdrew to Santa Barbara to spare us what she could. The last time I went up we both knew there was little time left. She was very weak, but she gave me a big smile. "Be seeing you!" she said. Once again I knew it was a promise. Just the same, I miss her.

It is very odd. I do not see the famous Little Tramp here on my tapestry. Yet Marie Dressler was working on the Mack Sennett lot with Charlie Chaplin. A genius, an enigma, a despoiler of young girls, an endowed and gifted talent and more, doing what is impossible for talent is genius, so someone once said. Called many things by press and public, by residents of Hollywood great and small, he was exiled at one point practically for his too left-wing politics. In a day when we weren't too slack to give a damn one way or another, his always seemed to me natural enough for a man who had been starved as a child by what he thought of as the aristocrats of England. When he came back to the movie capital after that long banishment he was cheered in mad welcomes home.

But Charlie got his start on the Sennett lot. While he left after only a year for Essanay and a salary we couldn't *believe*, it was on the stages at Edendale that his beloved little character, the exaggeration of shabby gentility, with his baggy pants, too small derby, walking stick, little mustache and funny walk came into being. And when Chaplin left he took with him all that he had learned. One of the maxims his beautiful statuesque blonde leading lady Edna Purviance told me he repeated often and often was, "It must begin with a laugh and end with a tear, *or* it must begin with a tear and end with a laugh," this to my positive knowledge is a sentiment and an expression and method which he took whole from Mack Sennett. Yet on my tapestry I see Charlie much later, in one poignant scene on a moonlit balcony after a ball given by Miss Marion Davies for William Randolph Hearst. And he is dressed as Napoleon.

Nor do I see Bing Crosby, although some sixteen years later Mack was the first man to tab Crosby's future glory. I see Bing as a blond cheerful-looking youngster sitting with a couple of other youngsters in a corner of my living room and emerging to favor me and my guests with a song from time to time.

BING CROSBY

The whole world, maybe two or three worlds, came in time to know, see, and above all hear Bing Crosby. "White Christmas" is a lot more the song of the American people than that third rate tune, "The Star-Spangled Banner." At least it is when Bing Crosby sings it. I will always remember the first time I heard him sing. Do you know at the very thought a voice like no other I have ever heard before or since begins in my mind, my memory, my soul—all or any of them.

I was giving a small dinner party, I think it was for Clara Bow who had never had a dinner given for her before and it is possible she never had another. At this dinner I had asked one of the studios, Universal I think it was, to send me a little music to enliven the evening. So they came, a trio, and I paid each of them twenty-five dollars, including the one who said his name was Bing Crosby. How was I supposed to know that in time you could put any number of zeros after that and somebody would still pay it.

Bing started by being a good-looking kid, glad and entirely co-operative, singing anywhere he could get somebody to listen to him. When Dixie Lee, a very pretty girl on her way to stardom, married him a good many people tried to talk her out of marrying beneath her. It might in somewise interfere with her career. Nobody had any idea that Crosby had one. Talkies were so new in 1929–30 we really hadn't become conscious of A Voice as a bid for stardom in the motion picture.

Arriving at my dinner party the trio, whom I later identified as the Paul Whiteman Rhythm Boys, placed themselves in front of my Chickering grand piano and began to make background music. Our ears were so accustomed to the onslaught of jazz that at first nobody paid much attention. I can't remember when they began to but suddenly I realized we were in complete silence except for a young man's voice now singing solo one of the simple

Irish ballads. All right, all right, I'm not going to try to tell you what it was like to hear the voice of Bing Crosby singing in the Crosby way which was soon to sweep the world. Remember, we had never heard it before. No one had ever heard it before. This was the beginning of a new world of music, a new era which closed a little while ago somewhere in Spain. We didn't know exactly what had happened to us but we knew for sure it was something. We were enchanted, hypnotized, because it was a brand new experience when Bing Crosby sang to us for the first time. After it ceased people began to come up to me and say, "Whothehellwasthat?"

A couple of months later when the Rhythm Boys had joined Gus Arnheim's band and Bing was doing more solos Mack Sennett spotted him at the Cocoanut Grove and signed him for eight two-reelers to be distributed by Paramount.

"What struck me about the guy," Mack said later, "was that all the stuffed shirts at the Grove stopped dancing and gathered around the bandstand to watch him croon. They came to hear him night after night. He held 'em." And how, demanded his studio colleagues, did the great Sennett plan to fit a *crooner* into slapstick comedy? "I don't care if the guy croons, turns cartwheels, or does card tricks," Mack said, "just so long as he entertains. And Crosby can do just that."

That he could. Oh, *couldn't* he!

I do not here claim that Mack Sennett "discovered" Bing Crosby—every time anyone heard Bing sing he was "discovered" anew—but Mack Sennett it was who put him on the way to all those Roads he was to travel to stardom and into the hearts of the world.

By that time, of course, Mack had left the mad mad world of Edendale behind him.

Here at Edendale I see Marie Dressler—and Mabel. A host of comics and stars as the years slide by: Joe Jackson, Harry Langdon, Harold Lloyd, Slim Summerville, Polly Moran, Louise Fazenda, Chester Conklin, Edgar Kennedy, Charlie Chase, Buster Keaton, W. C. Fields. And very clearly I see, stepping to a fanfare of trumpets and the wheeze of a giant calliope, a long line of Bathing Beauties passing in review.

THE BATHING BEAUTIES

Perhaps there is something in a name, for as the fabulous members of Sennett's troupe flashed up to stardom, fame and fortune or down to disaster and tragedy it wasn't as easy to tack Mack Sennett Bathing Beauty and ex-Mack Sennett Bathing girl onto their names as it was Follies or ex-Follies girl onto Mr. Ziegfeld's lovelies.

Also, whereas with Flo Ziegfeld the girls and glorifying the girls always came first, with Mr. Sennett they came second to the clowns and the comedians.

Nevertheless, the Sennett girls were possessed of a secret which made them outstanding.

More than any of the others, bathing beauties or movie stars, Mabel Normand had the Secret. The Mack Sennett Secret, which he demanded in all girls and knew how to use. This is—was—a secret which has belonged to all the important Sirens of history. It lifted them high above women who possessed merely beauty. Or only Sex, as we overemphasize it today. The secret is being used now to give place and power to distinguished ugliness and add the element of Witchery thereto. Cleopatra had it for sure, Caesar fell for it and entered into it. Queen Elizabeth the First brought it into play strongly when in her middle age she totally captivated young Essex. It helped an American woman named Simpson take a King-and-Emperor off his throne. *Charm* was Mack Sennett's word for it. He was always looking for it and all his girls had it and it wasn't just because they wore the first one-piece bathing suits on the best one-piece figures ever seen. When I asked Mack Sennett about it, many years after he had retired and the old Sennett days were gone forever, he couldn't really explain his secret which probaby was something Eve knew in the Garden of Eden.

Nothing about any of it was premeditated, the way there happened to *be* Sennett girls at all seemed by chance, though Voltaire insists nothing can ever exist without a cause. However—one day while he was reading his morning paper, Sennett decided that all was not well, he felt a sense of dark depression, known as the blues by lesser mortals, take him over. All right, he had the best comics in the business, including that little fellow Chaplin, and that big fellow Fatty Arbuckle, and Ben Turpin and Ford Sterling; his Keystone Cops with the chases Sennett thought up were the biggest box office attraction in a very infant industry. Still, it seemed to him that he ought to have something more, something new and fresh and lovely-to-look-at that would drag the public in to *see* this new medium of entertainment, he wanted to make it grow.

As he bent his attention on the paper he noted that the front page was almost entirely given to the picture of a pretty girl. But the picture of Woodrow Wilson, then President of the United States, was on page five.

"Ah," said the King of Comedy to himself. "Girls, pretty girls. That's what I need." And he clapped his hands and opened up a Pandora's box, out of which tumbled glories and heartaches, scandals, murder, suicide and truly noble worth, the lottery of the beautiful and the damned.

Such illustrious names as Mrs. Darryl F. Zanuck and Mrs. Robert E. Sherwood; such famous beauties as Phyllis Haver and Cecile Evans whose legs were insured for a million dollars; and such bitter tragedy as overtook Marie Prevost and Juanita Hansen.

Two things enter my memory cassette here.

'Tis said that he that pryeth into every cloud is likely to get struck by a thunderbolt, but I'd rather take that risk than the one of missing something.

1.
Teeth.

It seems to me that today as I watch what movies there are, meet a few of the stars and near stars here and there, the thing I see and have to note most is *teeth*.

I do not mean those that are breaking records in *Jaws*. And yet —face it—jaws mean TEETH, don't they? So we have wound up in an era of teeth. Perhaps this is because the dentists and the dental care give most of us better ones—or that replacements can be made that look every bit as good. Nevertheless, and whatever the cause, teeth are *in*—people look at each other tenderly yet show their teeth so that the slightest shift might make it seem they intended to bite rather than kiss. Myself I have never found teeth expressive of much—I mean, there they *are*—teeth. They can neither sigh nor weep, they can neither speak nor sing—and too much and too many of them often block the vision.

I cannot remember any teeth when I think of the Mack Sennett girls. They do not come first—not even fifth—in my reconstructed pictures of Mabel Normand, nor Carole Lombard, nor Phyllis Haver nor even Marie Dressler. That huge porcelain grin that sometimes seems quite able to replace JAWS doesn't appear in any of my mental or actual photographs of the Sennett beauties. I am looking, as of now, at a picture labeled Mack Sennett Comedies. Eight Bathing Beauties are perched on a rock, four of them have their mouths closed, not *shut* like a trap or anything, just gently closed. Three have their lips parted and you can see the edges of their uppers, one has her mouth open in a faint smile. They all look *happy* and you note many charms and beauties about them which I daresay you might not if they were showing all their *teeth*.

The other day I asked a man who had been at the front in France when Bebe Daniels, my choice for our real life heroine remember, was the first woman civilian to visit wounded American soldiers as they were waiting to be evacuated from the front lines after D-Day *if* Bebe was smiling as she walked that dangerous strip of territory between two armies locked in the grip of death. He said Yes—she was—and I could see her! But I *knew*, I knew I knew I knew she wasn't showing those wounded suffering young American G.I.s a lot of cold white *teeth*.

2.

Bathing Suits.

It is true that, although Annette Kellermann first wore a one-piece bathing suit, the evolution of that garment in the historical sense took place on the fair forms of the Mack Sennett Bathing Beauties. An aquatic star in the years before World War I, Miss Kellermann was playing vaudeville when the able sports promoter Jack Curley dreamed up her suit as part of an *act*; ladies no more thought of appearing in such garb on the beach than of wearing tights to a restaurant. Luxury beach suits then were knee-length satin or taffeta with built-in wire frames over bloomers to be worn with slippers, stockings ornamented with garters and rosettes, all topped by hats, and I do mean hats. In which, of course, we did not get wet. For those of us who were a little more athletic we went to the water fully clothed in a three-piece costume plus stockings, slippers and a satin bandeau in which we could dunk in the waves but most definitely not *swim*. Now this is what irked Mack Sennett. Little by little, an inch or two at a time, starting at the neck and shoulders, Mack Sennett changed all that, freeing his Sennett girls—and you and me—for action. That was what motivated Sennett. Nudity as such he resisted, not so much because he was a prude, he was that too, but because he was a showman. To be considered. Especially today. Too much bare *skin* can be as chilling as too much bare *teeth?* At any rate that was not what Mack wanted. He wanted his girls to have freedom of movement.

I do think this is one of the reasons generally overlooked why so *many* of the Mack Sennett Bathing Beauties became movie stars of planet magnitude. If anybody thinks Mack Sennett, the ex-boilermaker, allowed them simply to parade up and down like Miss America aspirants at Atlantic City that anybody is much mistaken. Every Bathing Beauty—clad most often in enticing but decorous bathing suits, which left something for a man to dream of *taking it off*—every Bathing Beauty *worked* and most often at being the other end of a *gag*, or the object of a pursuit by the Keystone Cops or the Sennett comedy teams. They were just as apt to get one of those *pies*, if it would be funnier, or be thrown off a cliff or a balcony or a tower, that's what they were for.

And as a matter of fact the first time I ever saw Gloria Swanson she was being tossed off the top of a cliff by a pursuing gent who had caught her. His name was Wallace Beery and I always felt Gloria must have made him her first husband *because* he caught her, we were inclined in those days to think that if a guy *caught* you, you were supposed to marry him. Wally was another type altogether from Gloria's later husbands, who were all suave, polished men of the world, and if there were things Wallace Beery wasn't, those are them.

Upon occasion I was to hear an ex-Sennett girl say, "Of course I was never one of the bathing girls." Well, they were all so close as to make no never mind and if any of them got by without being photographed in a bathing suit I can't remember who it was. The big and the little. The little and the big.

Gloria Swanson—a little girl from Chicago who became the greatest of all Cecil B. DeMille's many stars, who hit Hollywood without a dime or a friend. She lived to wear jewels, and set fashions for a whole decade of the lusty Twenties, made sensational marriages, and was the most elegant and fabulous of them all—on and off. But she started on the Sennett lot and she wore a bathing suit.

Carole Lombard—the last of the Sennett Beauties to hit the top, the smooth sophisticated star of drawing-room comedies, who became the great love in the life of Clark Gable. Carole came to the Sennett lot as Jane Peters. Mack changed her name and handed her a bathing suit. The rest is Hollywood history.

Mabel Normand—queen of the Sennett lot who, Cecile Evans once told me, "was the guiding genius of every girl who ever worked there." Mabel was a champion swimmer and diver.

How did Mack pick so many winners? Did he have an ideal type?

Vera Reynolds, chosen later by Cecil DeMille as the Perfect Flapper partially because as a Sennett girl she had learned to surfboard, was a little bit of a thing, impish as a chipmunk, and Carmelita Geraghty was a true California-Irish-Spanish señorita with black hair and eyes.

Cecile Evans of the million-dollar legs had red hair and green eyes as did Mary Thurman, who was the college boys' favorite of that day and who died much too young.

Sally Eilers, the last of the bathing girls, was all autumn-leaf brown and about medium in figure while Dorothy Seastrom was a tall girl of the Garbo type and poor little Juanita Hansen, who ruined a blossoming career with drink and drugs, was a thin, delicate petite ash blonde.

Exquisite brown-eyed little Marie Prevost had a round kitten quality both in face and figure while THE Mack Sennett Bathing Beauty, she who finally appeared in and was soon to set the fashion for the one-piece bathing suit, Phyllis Haver, was a pretty-

pretty blue eyed blonde with a figure that always seemed to me broad—or *sturdy*. In 1924 Mack Sennett himself made the public statement that the dark, smoldering, brainy beauty Madeline Hurlock, whose back was probably photographed more often than any other in history, was the most perfectly proportioned girl who ever worked in Sennett comedies.

One of the last times I saw Mack Sennett he was living in state and style at the Garden Court apartments smack in the middle of Hollywood. He had mellowed some, mornings he worked on a book about comedy, afternoons he played golf. I think he still carried his great sorrow about Mabel, we didn't talk about her, instead he talked about his Beauties.

"Of course," Sennett said thoughtfully, "they had to photograph well in bathing suits. They had to have beauty. But you see they worked with clowns and so in a way they had to be clowns."

And he had just told me the Secret.

All of them were clowns.

They had sex plus humor. That's hard to do. It's the greatest combination in the world. They had beauty and they were *funny*. Even the desperately tragic ones like Marie Prevost, who worshiped a man who was always in love with another woman, were all clowns—there are many tragic clowns.

They were picked because they made Mack Sennett chuckle. They were brought up and trained on comedy. They lived and breathed it.

That's their Secret. That's what made them different from all other girls.

Everybody on the old Keystone lot was dedicated twenty-four hours a day to thinking up gags, trying to get fresh ideas for funny business, or a story line upon which to hang those jewels of laughter. There was no dialogue then, no funny lines, and so it had to be all pantomime, the true essence of comedy.

Shooting in the sense that would have satisfied the terrible J.B.T. Campbell on the city desk of the *Herald* there was not, still you took your life in your hands in Mr. Sennett's wonderful world of Make-Believe. A man could lose an eye or a leg or something, while they were trying out a gag. Nothing was sacred. More comedy routines, more practical jokes were invented there in those days than anywhere else in the world. By experts! That's all they did all day and all night. The girls led a tough life, they were always getting thrown out of boats, they hung from cliffs, they went into cages with wild animals, they jumped out of windows.

If things got dull or they ran out of ideas in the middle of a picture, or something that had promised to be a howl went flat, then everybody quit and they went out on the back lot and played baseball, the girls played, too. Wally Beery was the star hitter—and then somebody would think up a gag. Maybe one of the girls. Or Harold Lloyd would think up a new twist on an old one, and they'd all go hustling back to work.

Nobody had any respect for anybody else if there was a laugh to be got. Mack Sennett himself wasn't any safer from a bucket of water balanced over his door or an explosive cigar hidden in his box—Marie Prevost was a great one for explosives—than anybody else and it was a rule that if it was funny nobody could squawk. If it wasn't, you could do anything you wanted to them if you could catch 'em.

Mabel Normand was back of half the gags on the Sennett lot. It was Mabel who rigged Ben Turpin, the irresistible cross-eyed comic, and the bear.

Sennett had animals of all kinds at all times, bears and lions and alligators.

There were any number of wonderful routines possible with a pretty girl, a good comic and a roaring lion or an indignant bear.

There were no doubles on the Sennett lot ever, so when the script called for Turpin to get into bed with a bear, it was Turpin who got into bed with the bear. But this time he balked. He said he would go back to being a janitor the way he was when Sennett found him. Everybody explained to him that the bear was old, toothless, without claws, and filled with a true love for humanity, especially cross-eyed comedians. But Ben was adamant.

Finally, they compromised on a stuffed bear. Knowing well the studio motto—anything for a laugh—Turpin went to Louise Fazenda and borrowed one of the long hatpins which she used to keep her comedy hats in place, and he stuck it right through the bear to be sure. When nothing happened Turpin got in bed, the camera turned.

A split second later came a yell that was probably heard in Kansas City. Turpin came out of bed running, he kept running and they didn't find him for two days. Mabel had crawled in behind the bear and flung both the bear's furry arms around Turpin's neck and the camera got one of the funniest impromptu scenes ever filmed. Under the Sennett code, Turpin couldn't even protest because it got a laugh from spectators and film audiences for months to come.

"Our lives outside the studio were unexciting and circumspect." This, a statement by Miss Lillian Gish, refers to the minions of David Wark Griffith. It could never have been said of Sennett and his merry men. Or his girls. They improvised comedy off the lot as well as on it.

Never will I forget what might well be entitled A Night in the Grand Central Station when Miss Gloria Swanson swiped a pair of skis from the back of an unknown youth waiting for the train to Dartmouth. From there on it was all strictly Mack Sennett. The police got into the chase and behaved exactly like Keystone Cops, the whole place was in an uproar, whereupon Miss Swanson led them gaily back, returned the skis to another dumfounded young man, made a Chaplinesque bow to the roaring, cheering mob, and vanished into her imported car, with chauffeur and footman.

The wonderful romance of Clark Gable and Carole Lombard, started with a moose. Around the Metro-Goldwyn-Mayer lot the great Gable was known variously as the King and the Big Moose. For his birthday just after they met, Carole sent him a large stuffed moose, wired for sound.

Other women, from time to time, had showered Mr. Gable with platinum cigarette cases, silk lounging robes, and paper-thin watches, all to his excessive irritation. It took this ex-Sennett beauty to appeal to Clark's own primitive sense of humor, his well-known love of a silly gag, his eagerness for a laugh.

Cecile Evans, and the fabulous Wilson Mizner, who had made fortunes in gold in the Klondike and in real estate in Florida, and who then became a successful playwright and was cherished in Hollywood as a wit and raconteur—Cecile and Mizner thought up and executed one of the most elaborate gags in the annals of our town.

Mizner thought Cecile was wonderful not only because of her

legs but because she was funny. One night she was dining with him in the Hollywood Brown Derby, which Mizner helped to found so he would have somewhere to entertain his friends, and everybody was talking about the super-super-colossal de luxe opening which was to take place that night at Grauman's new Chinese Theatre. Cecile said, "Let's go," and Mizner said no he never went to such futile affairs, but then Cecile showed him a Mizner way to do it.

First they went to a used car lot and bought the most disreputable secondhand car they could find. Then they went home and got all dressed up, Mizner in white-tie-and-tails, Cecile in all her glory. They got in the old car—Mizner weighed better than two hundred fifty pounds so it tipped a bit—drove it through some mud puddles, and joined the line of new cars opening-bound.

Of course the crowd along the way, peering and cheering, gazing into luxurious interiors filled with ermine diamonds and orchids, where they might discover Douglas Fairbanks and Mary Pickford, Gloria Swanson, Charlie Chaplin, Tom Mix or Theda Bara, broke into roars of laughter as the jalopy and its gorgeously dressed occupants hove in sight, and Mizner and the beautiful Cecile responded with royal bows.

The topper was when they arrived at the red-carpeted entrance with its roped-off mobs of fans. Of course they had no chauffeur. Mizner descended majestically, handed Cecile out and when the doorman—solid in gold braid—protested they couldn't leave the jalopy blocking all the approaching bigwigs, Mizner bowed low and gave it to him for a tip.

Even Marie Prevost never lost the technique for laugh-making that took her to heights as a movie star. When she was my good neighbor at Malibu, she was the darling of that then artistic and exclusive film colony.

On the eve of a comeback—she'd fought a winning battle against putting on weight, she got rounder and rounder, and the fashion had changed to skinnier and skinnier—on the eve of her comeback starring picture, she died suddenly, mysteriously and alone. I remember the papers said "Mystery Shrouds the Sudden Death of Movie Star and Sennett Beauty Marie Prevost." The mystery was never solved. Maybe even our most advanced scientific laboratory tests can't locate a broken heart, the man Marie loved didn't love back; he loved Norma Talmadge.

But she had spiritual courage right to the end. She never let anyone else know, never shadowed a summer holiday for anybody else with her own sorrows, she was always laughing.

Mostly the Sennett girls proved their Secret superior in the matrimonial sweepstakes. The gorgeous intellectual Madeline Hurlock married first Marc Connelly, author of the American classic *The Green Pastures*, and then the Pulitzer Prize-winning dramatist Robert E. Sherwood. Little Marjorie King, one of the loves of Jack Gilbert's hectic career, in the end married millionaire Phil Plant, former husband of Constance Bennett. After spectacular successes in two all-time great pictures, *The Way of All Flesh* and *What Price Glory?*, Phyllis Haver retired to marry New York Mayor Jimmy Walker's closest friend, Billy Seeman, a more-than-wealthy importer whom the Follies girls and debutantes had been chasing for years. And at twenty-two Ruth Taylor, one of the prettiest girls to graduate from Sennett's Custard Pie College, who had soared to stardom as Lorelei in *Gentlemen Prefer Blondes*, decided she preferred Paul S. Zuckerman of the New York Stock Exchange and settled down in a Park Avenue penthouse as neighbor to Phyllis Haver Seeman with complete aplomb. But the marriage that affected Hollywood most was that of the Dresden china doll Virgina Fox, to a skinny, unknown writer without a dime named *Zanuck*. Darryl F. Zanuck became in time the all-powerful, controversial head of Twentieth Century-Fox studios thus making Virginia Fox Zanuck for years and years one of *the* First Ladies of Hollywood. As of this date the Zanucks have been married for over fifty years and I will tell you now, as perhaps a Mother Confessor should not, that in my opinion it would be impossible to be married to Darryl F. for so much as five minutes without the Sennett secret.

"Another Sennett girl makes good." We said it so often it became a Hollywood cliché. As Billy Beck substituted a fan for her bathing suit to become the star fan dancer Sally Rand. As Peggy Pierce became an executive in the transportation department at Warner Brothers. As Carmelita Geraghty, who married writer-producer Carey Wilson, had an exhibition of her paintings in

Paris. Perhaps the biggest international triumph was that of *Irene*, MGM's world famous fashion designer, once Irene Lentz of the Sennett comedies. Or maybe, come to think of it, it was the girl whose name I cannot remember but who became a pirate on a riverboat in China. She would come closest to Mack's own ideal. Except, of course, for Mabel.

MACK AND MABEL

With reluctance, with *reluctance*, with love laughter and tears, we come to the Mack Sennett star-of-stars, Mabel Normand.

Not of this world.

Somewhere, sometime, somehow, most people have come to the moment of truth when quite literally they meet someone they *know* is not of this world. I don't mean out of this world—that can happen here and there to very ordinary people moved by some impulse or vision. Mabel Normand was something else again.

She was a pixie, an elf, one of the little people. She had fey moments when I actually thought I could see—not the wings, perhaps, but the faintest glimmer of them, silver-white and transparent. *I know*—but I did think so, and so did many other people. Charlie Chaplin, for one—Marie Dressler for another. And of course Mack Sennett.

Now—now that she is gone—now that I am looking back across the years I can feel a little sorry for Mack Sennett, too. It can't have been much easier for a mortal to be in love with an elf than for an elf to be in love with a mortal.

Perhaps that explains it all and the disaster that befell.

Hard to believe that the greatest tragedy—stark, fatal, utter destruction-of-*genius* tragedy—of Hollywood's entire history took place on the Sennett comedy lot.

And that it was the simplest, oldest of all triangle plots!

"If she hadn't been my friend," Mabel Normand said to me over and over, "*my friend*. If I'd found him with some other girl—"

"It wouldn't have made any real difference," I said.

After a moment Mabel said, "No, no, I don't suppose it would."

So that was why Mack Sennett and Mabel Normand never married, though this was one of the True Romances—and it's a reason no one would have expected to find in *Hollywood* even in those pioneer days.

And that was why Mabel Normand never got over it. The Laughmaker, the littlest of all Clowns—she kept 'em laughing and she left 'em laughing when she said good-bye as George M. Cohan sang.

But *she* wasn't laughing. I know, because I was holding her hot little hand and almost the last thing she said to me was, "Well, anyhow, *you* know I didn't murder Bill Taylor, but I never blamed *her*."

For of course she knew as well as I did and as well as the district attorney did, who *had* taken the oldest of early Western revenges on Mr. Taylor. But as the D.A., Mr. Woolwine, said to me —I couldn't ever convict her, could I?

And *I* said You can't convict anybody for blowing the head off a rattlesnake that's about to bite your little girl, can you?

The last time I saw Mary Miles Minter on the street in Santa Monica I couldn't *believe* she'd ever been anybody's *little* girl. Not even my blessed Clara Bow put on quite so much excess poundage as that.

Time came when the beloved Little Clown was paid $175,000 a picture (which believe me in that day was fantastic), when Mabel Normand had as much of wealth and fame and luxury and idolatry as any other star in pictures has ever been given, when millions fought to get to see her on the screen, when Samuel Goldwyn, our most artistic impresario and even then a great power in the movies, wanted to marry her.

But from first to last Mabel never loved anybody but Mack Sennett, not even for a minute, just as he never loved anybody but Mabel. That may be one reason that the end of this little genius was such sheer tragedy as it broke all our hearts to see.

"Mabel," I said, over and over, "surely you can *forgive* him. I mean we're taught to forgive until seventy times seven—and this is just once—I think you ought to forgive him."

"You don't understand," Mabel said frantically, and the golden-brown eyes that were always so full of love and laughter were full now of tears that spilled over and ran down the little pointed face. "Of course I forgive him—he knows that—of course I forgive him—but—"

That "but" changed the course of motion picture history.

Mack's mother came from the East to see if she could cure whatever the trouble was, for she loved Mabel deeply. Surely, surely, she said to me, she can forgive him that one foolish moment.

And again and again Mabel said, "I have forgiven him—but—"

I don't know why through the early years of their success together Mack Sennett and Mabel Normand never married. Nobody did. It sounds silly to say they were too busy but I honestly think that was part of it. Those were still pioneer days, remember, filled with great experiments; everything was a gamble. Sennett peddled his own pictures to exhibitors to get money enough to make the next one. Sometimes when the sheriff was on the doorstep he and Mabel worked eighteen hours a day. They were absorbed in this new magic.

When Chaplin deserted him, Sennett put the redoubled burden on Mabel Normand who never faltered, worked until she dropped and somehow during this time as he realized all and everything that Mabel meant to him, his inspiration, he remembered that they were going to get married sometime and asked Mabel to set the day.

They decided upon June—a few months away.

And we must remind ourselves that this would be a very big day and night for Mabel. Casual copulation outside of wedlock was frowned upon. Mabel was a virgin, most of us were, Mae Busch the exception.

What happened I now tell as Mabel herself told it to me. We had been friends since we met the first day at Edendale when Mabel was seventeen. Before I married Ike St. Johns, handsome copy editor on the *Herald*, I used to stay at her apartment on the corner of Seventh and Figueroa when I worked too late to get back to Papa's home in Santa Monica. So—she told me and years later the other girl, who is dead now too, told me it happened this way.

Mae Busch *was* her friend, so that it was in every sense a double betrayal—and worse. For when Mae, whom Mabel had known when they were younger than young and both advertising and illustrator models in New York and Brooklyn, was stranded in Los Angeles by the failure of a road company musical, Mabel took her in, fed and clothed her and finally got her a job with *Sennett*.

Few words and simple tell the poor, common little story.

Not long before the wedding day when Mabel, not yet out of her teens, was like a starry-eyed schoolgirl, buying her trousseau and fitting her wedding veil, she began to hear rumors about "Mike," as she always called Sennett, and her friend Mae. So Mabel did the thing typical for Mabel. One evening when Sennett had worked late, Mabel went over to Mae Busch's apartment, a little ashamed of her own suspicions, and asked Mae, and Mae said it was just a friendship. When Mabel got home she found she had left her purse (she was always forgetting something), and went back to Mae's to get it. The front door of the apartment was locked. As she had often done before, Mabel went around to the back which was not. At first she heard nothing. Then she heard voices, the voice of her friend, the voice of the man she loved. She opened the door.

From that moment until the police came to question her concerning the murder of her friend, William Desmond Taylor, Normand was very busy earning herself the title of Madcap Mabel.

Madcap Mabel

That's what Hollywood—and the world—called Mabel Normand in the years after her break with Mack Sennett, and into her madcap career she put the same genius that she had given her movie career which ended with the murder of Bill Taylor. Hollywood, as you know, has had other madcaps but they were pikers compared to Normand.

When she left Mae Busch's apartment that night Mabel went to the home of Fatty Arbuckle, big, fat Arbuckle whom all the Sennett girls loved like a brother and whose own tragedy was still ahead of him. Minta Durfee, his wife, another former Sennett beauty, was Mabel's dearest friend.

"She was like someone bereft of all her senses," Minta told me later, "snow white, she could hardly walk, all she did was keep saying 'No—oh no no no no.' Like a broken record."

For days, she was in and out of a shock-coma. She was under a doctor's care. When she was herself again—though I think she was never her real self—she would never see Mack nor hear his explanations nor his pleas for forgiveness, nor accept his showers of gifts.

Other women, less broad-minded, less charitable than Mabel have forgiven men. None of her friends agreed with the violent extravagance of her stand against Sennett. All of us tried to persuade her to listen to him. "Of course I forgive him," she said. "He's just somebody else, that's all." In the end we all had to admit that whatever it was that drove Mabel she couldn't help it, there was nothing we could do about it.

When tragedy hits clowns, they are bewildered by it, I think. Like fairies who die when they encounter the cruelty of mortals.

"That one always had the heart of a child," Marie Dressler used to say, "and like a child her heart was broken when anyone was unkind to her. Often clowns have hearts like that, and reality defeats them."

At last, a treaty was arranged. Sennett was never again to speak to her of love, their romance was over forever, but she would finish her contract and then go. So they made *Mickey*—in which she gave a performance of incredible beauty and comedy—and the queen of the Sennett lot abdicated. She went to a Goldwyn contract, the like of which Hollywood had never seen, to a new status as a star of a major noncomedy studio into a new world of the motion picture art and industry which was growing faster and faster on every side, like a beanstalk.

Before she had played her pranks on the Sennett lot, on a small stage, with a friendly audience and with a strong man's protection.

Now they were stuff for the front pages, now the world watched. Mabel, always so dependable, such a hard worker, became temperamental. One day she walked off a super-Goldwyn set because she was bored, and the next time her frantic producer,

Mr. Goldwyn, caught up with her - she was in Paris, buying a cloth-of-gold dress which weighed forty pounds and cost $10,000.

Another time she took twenty friends on a trip to Europe, she gave champagne suppers, she bought gems, threw money to servants, she gave high-diving exhibitions from the highest platform at an exclusive country club, a titled Englishman wanted to marry her and she led him a chase all right.

Then one day, after she returned to New York, Mack Sennett somehow managed to get her on long-distance telephone.

He said, "Get off that merry-go-round and come home. I've got the greatest story you ever had—*Molly O*, it's called. Come back."

Mabel said, "I won't. Besides, I've nine months to go with Goldwyn."

"I'll fix that somehow," Sennett said, "if it was like the old days, I'd make you come home."

After a long pause, Mabel said, "If it was like the old days, Mack, I'd never have left."

It seemed then that she was on top of the world. No real princess could command such sheer idolatry. The admiration, the gifts, the Prince Charmings, the applause that Mabel Normand received. Her beautiful, impish face was known and loved everywhere.

Yet once in those days she said to me, "My pillow's always wet when I wake up in the morning. I guess I cry in my sleep."

Somehow, Sam Goldwyn was persuaded to lend her to Sennett for *Molly O*. I wish I had some of the old reviews. The critics said it was the greatest comedy performance of all time, predicted that it would break all records for a comedy film.

Then one day in 1922 a well-known Hollywood director named William Desmond Taylor was murdered.

I was in Chicago when I heard Mabel's voice saying over the phone, "Please come home. I have to tell you . . . you have to tell me what to do . . ." I turned cold with panic, for by that time the police knew that Mabel Normand, whose *Molly O* was playing everywhere to waiting lines, had been the last person to see Taylor alone. Except the murderer.

Scandal.
Stand by to crash.

The trial of Roscoe "Fatty" Arbuckle for the unsavory death of Virginia Rappe.

The unsolved murder of William Desmond Taylor.

They were unrelated. They were related. And for Mabel Normand the sequence was crucial. *If* Bill Taylor had been shot *before* Fatty took that fateful trip to San Francisco—well, there's no use shuffling that deck.

Nobody, but *nobody* in Hollywood ever connected Mabel with the actual shooting of Taylor in his bungalow at the Alvarado Court near Westlake Park in Los Angeles any more than we could connect Fatty with the death of that screen-extra-cum-amateur-call-girl at a party in the St. Francis Hotel. Both were innocent—both were *cleared*—both were pilloried—both were ruined.

Let us see how such things come to pass.

The Arbuckle case crashed upon us like a sudden Wagnerian overture.

Hollywood was stunned, panic-stricken and incredulous under the charge against Fatty Arbuckle and the storm of vilification that followed.

News of the Arbuckle indictment came to me early because my father, Earl Rogers, was still the Coast's leading criminal lawyer and Joseph Schenck, for whom Fatty went to work when he finally left Sennett, wanted Papa to undertake his defense.

Papa prepared me for what was to come. "Arbuckle's weight will damn him," Papa said. "He is charged with an attack on this girl which resulted in her death. He will no longer be the roly-poly, good-natured, funny three-hundred-fifty-pound fat man everybody loves. He will become a monster. If he were an ordinary man his own spotless reputation, his clean pictures would save him. They'll never convict him, but this will ruin him and maybe motion pictures for some time. Tell Joe I can't take the case; the doctors won't let me, but to prepare Hollywood for tornadoes."

The public fury *was* like a tornado and made us realize the truth in a headline which said, "The Movies Are at the Crossroads."

For the many decent, hard-working people making pictures it came as a blasting shock that they could be suspected of all kinds of evil, suffer irreparable loss of fame and fortune, personal shame and humiliation because of something with which they'd had nothing to do.

It was—oh, it was—so difficult to believe when it happened.

One thing that always seems to me to be overlooked. In a gold rush—in the Klondike—when people struck it rich they were looking for gold. We weren't. We hadn't the vaguest idea there was gold in them there Hollywood Hills. Now that the great golden days of The Movies have come and gone, it is easier to look way back and remember how utterly dumfounded and amazed we all were when in a space of—hours?—days?—actually such a short space of time The Movies of the nickelodeons, the poor little orphan of the stage world, the newest of the arts, the smallest of the industries going around with a tin cup asking for dimes—in that *breath* it had swept the globe to its remotest corners, to become Big Business, the newest major industry in the United States, and the focus for the eyes of the world. Thus the Arbuckle case caught Hollywood unprepared for criticism so threatening, so unrelenting, so prejudging.

Fatty Arbuckle, a boy from Smith Center, Kansas, who had worked his way up as a singing waiter, in stock and burlesque, went to San Francisco over the Labor Day weekend in 1921, accompanied by Freddy Fishback, a director in good standing, and the well-known stage and screen actor Lowell Sherman.

There were then no airplanes flying between New York and Hollywood, it took five days in the train, when we wanted a vacation and some elegant restaurants of which there were few in Hollywood (and Los Angeles for that matter) we went to San Francisco. It had once been known as the wickedest city in the Western Hemisphere and it had the best restaurants on the North American Continent. The Cliff House was famous around the world. Thus Fatty Arbuckle betook himself up there \hoping for a few days of fun probably partly on the Barbary Coast, a well-known section where night clubs and honky-tonks and cafes clustered together and produced the first floor shows, the first new dances such as the Bunny Hug and the Turkey Trot, and much of the best music of our times. During this vacation an extra girl named Virginia Rappe got some alcohol in her system, stripped off her clothes, and plunged Fatty and Hollywood into our first major scandal.

The original newspaper account merely said that Virginia Rappe, film actress, had died in a San Francisco sanitarium, after being taken ill at a party given by screen comedian Arbuckle in his hotel suite. This was quickly followed by charges of attack against Fatty, and by his own statement:

We got to San Francisco late Saturday afternoon and tired with the long drive went straight to a hotel, had an early dinner and to bed. Sunday we did some sightseeing and called on friends across the Bay. On Monday a friend of Fishback's dropped in, told of seeing Miss Rappe at the Palace, and I said I knew her well enough to introduce him. We called her and she readily consented to join us at the hotel. It wasn't a party. A number of people had dropped in, that's all.

After meeting the man, Miss Rappe had one or two drinks with us. She then went into the other room of the suite, began tearing the clothes from her body and screaming.

Mrs. Maude Delmont and another woman rushed into the room. They put Miss Rappe into a tub of cold water, thinking she had hysterics. She said she had gas pains around her heart and couldn't breathe right.

I therefore called the hotel manager, explained what had happened and got a room there for Miss Rappe, as she said she didn't feel she could get back to the Palace. That was the last we heard of her. I left the next morning for Los Angeles to get back to work and heard nothing more until news of her death reached me. I am leaving for San Francisco tonight of my own accord.

Here I would like to give some testimony of my own.

At that time, Miss Rappe had been living only a few blocks from me in Hollywood. The day after Fatty had been indicted on the testimony of several girls and Virginia Rappe's own deathbed statements, the man who did my cleaning came and told me: "I did Virginia Rappe's cleaning. I see where one side says she was a sweet young girl and Mr. Arbuckle dragged her into the bedroom, the other witnesses say she began screaming and tearing off her clothes. Once I went in her house to hang up some cleaning, and the first thing I knew she'd torn off her dress and was running outdoors, yelling, 'Save me, a man attacked me.' There I was standing in the kitchen with my hands still full of hangers with her clothes on them and she was running out hollering I'd tried to attack her. The neighbors told me whenever she got a few drinks she did that. I hated to lose a good customer, but I thought it was too dangerous so I never went back."

I asked those neighbors and they confirmed the story. But you couldn't put that kind of evidence into court! The girl was dead. To blacken her character would only increase public indignation against Fatty, for trying to save himself at her expense.

A man named "Pathe" Lehrman, claiming to be the dead girl's sweetheart, told reporters: "If I meet this beast Arbuckle, I will kill him. I directed him for a year, I had to tell him if he didn't keep out of the girls' dressing rooms I'd have him thrown out of the studio."

Mack Sennett, for whom they both worked, said: "In all the years Fatty worked for me he didn't do a thing anyone could point a finger at. Fatty wouldn't hurt a fly. I never knew him to be mixed up in any brawls or to do an ungentlemanly thing toward any girl. He was a kind, good-natured fat man and a good comic."

Minta Durfee Arbuckle, who had been visiting in the East, rejoined her husband immediately and stuck with him to the bitter end. "I've been his wife all these years," she said. "He could not do such a thing. I know. The only thing he's guilty of is being too good-natured to throw out a lot of those no-goods who come hanging around a movie star and cadge free drinks."

As yet Arbuckle had not been tried. Hollywood's frantic plea that he be given the right of every American citizen to the presumption of innocence until proven guilty did nothing to check the fire and brimstone that fell. Within days, Hollywood became synonymous with Sodom and Gomorrah, motion picture houses all over the United States were bombarded by righteous citizens, burned down in several states, and the Motion Picture condemned as the sinful and deadly agency of all corruption, evil and wickedness.

The jury which, after hearing expert medical testimony, acquitted him in less than a minute the following year issued this collective statement: "Acquittal is not enough for Roscoe Arbuckle. We feel a great injustice has been done him. We feel it our plain duty to give this exoneration on the evidence, for there was not the slightest proof adduced to connect him in any way with the commission of a crime. We wish him success and hope the American people will take the judgment of the fourteen men and women of the jury that Roscoe Arbuckle is entirely innocent and free of blame."

This verdict had no effect upon the people, however. For now five months after the death of Virginia Rappe and before the trial and acquittal of Arbuckle we had the unsolved William Desmond Taylor murder involving Mabel Normand and Mary Miles Minter. Within a short time we had seen the peril, we knew we were on the brink of disaster that might, we believed, forever end the Motion Picture and all its works.

William A. Johnston, a brilliant and honest editor, said: "The publicity thus far has put an unbearable burden of infamy upon the motion picture. Every individual within the industry will in some degree feel the stigma of it. If you in the motion pictures don't protect yourselves, the fair name of the industry, the huge fortunes at stake, the reputation of your own decent, hard-working element, then—and mark this well—the same forces that made you great will rise up to put you out of business overnight, destroy you in the very same magic way in which you were created —by popular favor."

That shows you how serious this crisis in our history was. It was then that we reached out and found the former Postmaster General of the United States, a man above reproach, a man of purity so shining that if he'd been six inches taller we would probably have called him Sir Galahad. As he was about five feet four we called him Will Hays the Czar of Hollywood for we had voluntarily accepted strict censorship by the Hays office.

But it was too late for Fatty Arbuckle and Mary Miles Minter who never worked in films again.

It was too late for Mabel Normand.

Everybody who knew them understood that Mabel and Bill Taylor were only friends. Perhaps I understood it best because she had the same kind of friendship with my father. When Mabel came to see me, she and Papa would sit up all night talking about books, history, great people and philosophies.

William Desmond Taylor was a lot of things to a lot of people. Obviously well educated, well traveled, he was very popular with men. Handsome at forty-five, very man-of-the-world, the ladies thought him most sophisticated, he drew them like a honey pot. Including young Mary Miles Minter who had been entrusted to him by Paramount in hopes that he could make of her another Mary Pickford. But to Mabel Normand, Bill Taylor was her old friend, her teacher. Mabel had as many men friends as any woman I've ever known—and Bill was very close to her. So—she stopped by his bungalow late that February afternoon to pick up the book he'd ordered from France for her.

The next morning they found William Desmond Taylor shot to death. As far as Mabel Normand's life and work were concerned the bullet that killed him might as well have gone through her heart.

When she telephoned me in Chicago she said, "When I got there, Bill was talking on the phone, so I had a bag of peanuts and I sat around eating them and reading the *Police Gazette* I'd brought. That was a gag I had with Bill, I insisted the *Police Gazette* was America, the way *Punch* was England. Well, he hung up and came out and brought me the new book of philosophy he wanted me to read, and Peavy, his colored boy, wanted to go home and Bill said he could, and he left.

"Bill and I talked a while, but I was tired, so I went home too. He put me in my car, the way he always did, and I waved to him and he waved back—and we pulled away, my chauffeur was driving, and—that's the last time I saw him."

I caught the train home the next morning and by the time I arrived the witch hunt had already begun.

Within twenty minutes it was proved to the police and the press beyond any possible shadow of a doubt that Mabel could neither have committed nor witnessed the crime. Except for the murderer, she was obviously the last person to see her old friend alive, but plenty of witnesses saw her leave, saw him stand watching her drive away, knew where she was the rest of the crucial time.

Yet her former worshipers, who had placed her on the highest pedestal, dragged her down like a pack of hyenas. Every unconventional thing the madcap had ever done and at which they had laughed and cheered, every petty piece of spiteful, envious gossip, every little scandal of the kind that always pursues those in the limelight from the gold dress to the narcotic a doctor had prescribed for a badly infected sinus, every merry party she had attended as its life and laughter, her attempt at suicide when she jumped off the pier at Santa Monica after her break with Sennett —all these they turned into stones with which they pelted her—to death.

Drug addict, drunkard, wanton—they shrieked at her. Poor, sick, heartbroken, bewildered little clown, she wasn't any of those things ever.

If you have *really* tried suicide, can you ever be the same? For better or for worse. Maybe such an attempt can free you of the desire, maybe there could be a rush of gratitude that you didn't succeed and the sun is so bright you could shout for joy and the flowers are so beautiful you want to dance around them because you are seeing them once again. *Or*—did you go down into a blackness that you carry with you forever, knowing that someday you will have to walk that dark way?

Mabel had had tuberculosis—we called it consumption—as a child. After we saved her that night under the Nat Goodwin pier —we had all been having dinner at the cafe on the ocean front, and at first when I missed Mabel I wasn't concerned, but when she didn't come back we went out to look. We were just in time to see her jump—after that the illness was active once more. She seemed frail, and I could see her going down into the blackness under this groundless, vicious attack. Which is why I went to see the district attorney, Thomas Lee Woolwine, a lifelong friend of my father's.

Mary Miles Minter

M.M.M. Embroidered on the little chiffon nightgown found hanging in Bill Taylor's closet. Passionate love letters signed by the nineteen-year-old star in the toe of his boot. Mary arriving at the scene, as we say, clawing her way through police lines, sobbing and screaming out of her love for her middle-aged director. And in the background her mother, *the* most possessive and obsessive

Hollywood has ever known. I could hear what somebody said one night at one of our hen parties, "If Bill Taylor doesn't look out that girl's mother is going to shoot him one of these days, she ought to." Faith MacLean, wife of prominent actor Douglas MacLean, who also lived at the Alvarado Court, testified at a preliminary hearing that she heard what sounded like a shot at eight o'clock on the fateful evening; looking out the window she saw a figure come out of Taylor's house—it looked like a woman dressed as a man.

Indeed there was much mystery surrounding William Desmond Taylor. We found he was in truth one William Cunningham Deane-Tanner of County Cork, possibly still married to the girl he left behind when he vanished into the gold fields of the Klondike to be shanghaied on a sailing vessel that rounded Cape Horn and eventually reborn as a top flight director named Taylor in Hollywood. There was his missing valet—never found. The missing gun—likewise. His request a year and a half before his murder for help from the U. S. Attorney to break a drug ring. But there was no mystery to any of us in Hollywood including Tom Woolwine about who shot Bill Taylor, or about the motive.

But the D.A. said to me, "I couldn't convict her, could I?"

And I had to say, "You can't convict anybody for blowing the head off a rattlesnake that's about to bite your little girl, can you? Still you could try. As long as this case remains *unsolved* they're going to persecute Mabel Normand."

Which they did. Mack Sennett stood by her loyally, as did Sam Goldwyn. But within a week of the Taylor murder, Sennett had been compelled to withdraw *Molly O*.

The final stab came because of adoration, loyalty she had awakened. The doctors had told her she must go into the hospital on New Year's Day, almost a year after the Taylor murder, for an appendectomy. So on New Year's Eve she went to a small party at the home of Edna Purviance.

She was driven there and escorted upstairs to the front door by her young chauffeur, an excitable boy who worshiped her, as all her servants did, and who had bought a gun because he believed she needed protection.

A silly young millionaire from the Middle West whom Mabel didn't even know, a suitor of Edna's, was there and as Mabel entered he made some stupid but rather insulting wisecrack about Miss Normand. The boy lost his head and shouting, "You take that back, she's an angel," drew the gun and shot him. The victim recovered, no charges were pressed, *but—*

This last nasty little scandal meant the end of everything for her. To look at her you knew she was, quite literally, dying. Oh she went along breathing for a few years or so. She even got married, to one of the nicest guys I ever knew. Lew Cody was called the Butterfly Man—and he was maybe next to Valentino the most attractive man then on the screen to women. He loved Mabel and cared for her with an extraordinary devotion and with tenderness.

To the end, I never heard Mabel Normand condemn anyone for the injustice that ruined her. All she ever said was: "Why?"

I couldn't answer her then any more than I can now. Perhaps they knew that she wasn't a mortal at all, that she was an elf, who could steal their hearts with laughter.

Times have changed. I know I know.

As far as I can tell, Babe Ruth or Stan the Man Musial could have hit Sandy Koufax, the best pitcher ever, or young Catfish Hunter, now pride of the Yankees. In whatever epoch of the picture business Mabel Normand had entered, she would have been the biggest star in it—I wish we had her now just for a couple of pictures! With Mack Sennett, it might bring The Movies back to their erstwhile grandeur.

Chapter Three

The Big Four

All right. So I admit my memory for dates is unethical and lousy. But sometimes I can *see* them. Right here on my tapestry I can *see* the year 1919. Marie Dressler in a voluminous long skirt and *hat* is parading on Fifth Avenue in support of the Actor's Equity Strike. Jack Dempsey, to become a favorite beau in Hollywood, is crowned Heavyweight Champion of the World. The first daily air mail planes, looking like something my great-grandson Bogart is wont to create with tissue paper and toothpicks, are *flying* between New York and Chicago.

Peace, the peace we have marched for, and prayed for, and paid for, is breaking out all over.

It appears to me, looking all the way back, as a pivotal point where the teeter-totter of history is on balance. The guns of World War I, which forever ended one way of life, are silent. The Twenties which will plunge us into another—give us Prohibition, bathtub gin, gangsters and speakeasies, woman suffrage, the jazz age and the flapper—have not begun.

In Paris the Big Four, Prime Minister Lloyd George of Great Britain, Clemenceau of France, Orlando of Italy, and our own President Woodrow Wilson, dreaming of a League of Nations, are hammering out a peace treaty meant to redesign the world.

And in Hollywood our Big Four of the Movies, Mary Pickford, Douglas Fairbanks, Charles Chaplin and D. W. Griffith are making film history. They form a company called United Artists in which they themselves will supervise the productions, distribute them, and divide the enormous profits. No longer will their films be dominated by bankers, producers, exhibitors, but by a girl from Canada with long golden curls, a Jewish theater actor from Denver, a music hall comedian from London, and a gentleman of the South whose family was impoverished by the Civil War but who, and mark this well for it is part of our story, was descended from kings, the Apt-Griffith Kings of Wales.

In this greatest powerhouse of box office talent yet assembled the executive ability, lack of which defeats so many artists, was Mary Pickford's, as was the money know-how. The vitality and audacity were Fairbanks'. The Art in United Artists was Chaplin, the little starving Cockney from the London gutters, who had to make an X when he signed his first contract, who was hailed as a genius of geniuses and waded through one scandal after another until Joan Barry stripped him of his last remnant of dignity.

And what was to be the contribution of David Wark Griffith, ham actor, egomaniac, hypnotist, witch doctor *and* torchbearer, trailblazer, seer, Star Maker? For he was all those things. Oh yes, he was!

D. W. Griffith, the Star Director of Star Pictures until the last frame of recorded film. Griffith whose name on a theater marquee had stellar drawing power unequaled by anyone on the dark side of the camera until Walt Disney came along. He was to contribute the great important pictures to United Artists—hadn't President Wilson said his *Birth of a Nation* was "like writing history in lightning"?—as well as the stature and stability. Or so we thought at the time. How wrong we were. Even Mary Pickford, who had a prophet's eye when it was on the dollar, could not foresee in 1919 that very shortly David Wark Griffith would be as dead at the box office as a dodo bird.

And all because of a girl.

Many years later I ran into the great D.W. in a popular grill on Hollywood Boulevard called Musso Franks. It was late, we'd been to a picture up the way at the Egyptian Theater. We were all a little embarrassed to see that the lonely, gaunt figure at the table near the back was indeed Mr. Griffith. How are the mighty fallen is always a sad refrain and to any of us in the picture business D.W. would always be the Mighty. He had very obviously had more than one too many for the road, he didn't seem to notice us but I—I remembered him so vividly the opening night of *Birth of a Nation* at Clune's (now the Philharmonic) Auditorium, I remembered the wildly cheering throngs, the elite and powerful of The Industry shoving each other every which way to be allowed to shake his hand, to touch his shoulder. I remember so well that I had to rush to get a story done about it, but first I managed to get near enough to pour out a word of congratulation—of *excitement*—oh, it was such excitement.

Hard to understand now—no, no, any opening night is a big event and any successful opening night is a glorious triumph. But an opening night the first of its kind in the world, the spectacular exultation and celebration of a *first* first night! And the epic it unfolded before our eyes was the most significant, tense, beyond-imagination film we'd ever seen. *Gone with the Wind* which tells exactly the same story and has Clark Gable in his finest role, also the benefit of color, likewise *sound* of battle and bugle, is nonetheless not a better picture. It somehow lacks a reality that was Griffith's trademark.

No, since that first opening back sometime around 1915 when stars and lights and crowds jammed what is today Pershing Square in Los Angeles, I have seen nothing that I can call a greater motion picture. Nor one that swept us and moved almost hysterical audiences to such love and tears. Only a few times has it happened that I am so taken over by comedy or drama that I find it almost impossible to return to the here and now and my seat in the theater. All the others except *That's Entertainment* were within the limitations of the stage. Katharine Cornell in *The Barretts of Wimpole Street*, Helen Hayes in *Victoria Regina*, and Olivier in *Richard III*—I flew across the Atlantic to see that one and it was worth it.

We lived in and with *Birth of a Nation* to an extent that was startling as we came out of it. There too we saw for the first time the power of Lillian Gish to enthrall and transport as I do not believe any other star had or has today.

And at the center of it all was D. W. Griffith who had just made the First Great Movie.

Now here in Musso Franks was that same man, he needed a shave, he needed a clean shirt—it hurt me, it hurt terribly for all of us as though we had let this happen. But I knew, I *knew*, how hard we had tried, I knew the number of chances he'd been given and the—yes, the money that had been invested in trying to give him a comeback.

So—as I went over and sat down opposite him at that back table in that restaurant on Hollywood Boulevard, when I realized most of the bright young things coming in had no idea who this old man was, I wanted to cry.

I didn't have to ask the question. Perhaps he saw it in my eyes, on my face, or read my mind—the actors who used to work under his superlative direction always told me that he could read your mind. He was a mind reader, they said, and a sorcerer. He used white magic and Aladdin's lamp, he used black demonology and voodoo—in his heyday that was, maybe he could still do it.

Oddly enough I remember the *voice* better than I do the face and its expressions. It must have been the voice, I thought, that swayed and moved them, lifted them up to greater performances than have ever been given since—Mae Marsh in *Intolerance*, Lillian Gish in *Way Down East*, Richard Barthelmess in *Broken Blossoms*, Dorothy Gish in *Orphans of the Storm*—I saw audiences lifted out of their seats and he didn't depend on catastrophe and violence. No no—a mother whose child is taken from her, a pair of young lovers on an ice floe, a frail little girl and a gentle Chinaman, a blind girl searching for her sister—we were torn by human emotions we all shared.

Magic.

Remember it seemed magic to us—that silent silver screen, with its moving figures and its moving faces. We had the full impact that can never be repeated except to each child who sees his first movie!

And there sat the man who had given it to us, who had soared to find it, alone and unrecognized. He was still too great an artist of human beings and human behavior to banter small talk or meaningless greeting.

He said, "I never had a day's luck after Lillian left me."

I swear the restaurant rocked—like another California earthquake. It didn't seem possible that he could say that sentence. Oh I wanted to be kind, I wanted to be gentle, I didn't want to kick a

man when he was down down down—but—my father had told
me as the very essence of all decision that must be made there is
Truth, maybe you can't get the whole truth but at least nothing
but the truth as far as you can.

So I said, "But . . . D.W. . . . Lillian didn't leave you! You
. . . you chucked her out for that mediocre girl . . ."

He stared at me and suddenly—suddenly—as though one of his
own dissolve close-ups was taking place before my eyes I saw not
D. W. Griffith, but Mary Pickford, Mary who *did* leave Griffith,
they never got along at all, those two dominant rulers. They
stared each other down one day in the old Biograph Studios on
Fourteenth Street in New York, and when Miss Mary Pickford
walked out to do a play for David Belasco she never came back,
nor did Mr. Griffith ask her. There just wasn't room for those two
on one stage, Dorothy Gish said to me once. And of course the
Pickfords, Mary and Lottie and Jack, and the Gishes, Lillian and
Dorothy, had grown up together in the dangerous, difficult years
of theatrical childhood. Mary it was, as a teen-age pioneer in the
movies, who brought the Gish girls to Biograph and Mr. Griffith
in the first place. And it was Mary who said to me after the break,
"Only a truly great artist who is willing to sacrifice all *ego* can get
along with D. W. Griffith. Lillian could. I couldn't." I wonder—I
suppose being Irish I have to always keep on wondering—what
they might have done *together*. I mean if they could have gone on
being a team.

The day David Wark Griffith met Lillian Gish, who was going
on sixteen at the time, his real career as the pathfinder of The
Movies began. The day he let her go, gripped by an egotistical infatuation for another woman, he signed his own death warrant. I
think she was his soul. He didn't have one of his own. Lillian let
him use hers.

Always, it was whispered, this is Svengali hypnotizing Trilby
again. As far as I am concerned she made herself the Stradivarius
on which he played his great works. For all his greatness, he never
made a great picture without her.

With her, he made motion pictures to which nothing but me-
chanics have been added since. In the years since *Birth of a Na-*

tion, Hollywood has produced not one idea in the art of developing a story, getting it on the screen with full impact for the audience, lifting stars to dramatic heights which D.W. had not already used.

He invented the long shot, the flashback, the close-up, backlighting, you name it. Before his innovations movie scenes were photographed in toto as one would view a stage production. After them the motion picture had a technique of its own.

When Griffith died there was talk of a statue of him as the Pioneer of all motion picture directing, and Samuel Goldwyn, of all Hollywood producers the one who consistently did most for the movies as art, said, "He contributed more than any other person to the establishment of motion pictures as the most important medium of entertainment in existence."

Yet for years before he died, Griffith had no job, made no pictures, and Hollywood was attacked for its ingratitude in allowing genius to languish. The forlorn figure of Hollywood's founding father, penniless, neglected, a martyr to crass commercialism and jealousy—that was the way he was envisioned in his last role.

The truth was different.

To begin with he did not die broke. That the heart of Hollywood could not have permitted. No no, at the time of his death he had in one safe deposit box $7,000 in cash, in another $50,000 in bonds.

Two things were responsible for what Griffith called bitterly his being thrown into the discard.

The first—and here we must remember that the father he adored, a Southern colonel of Civil War vintage, had enjoined upon him his duty to remember those Apt-Griffith Kings—the first was that unless King David could be boss, and by boss he meant to an extent equaled in history only by Napoleon, he wouldn't play.

In this I do not say he was wrong. He had proved himself, he had behind him such success as no one could dispute. He might have gotten away with it, except that his active career ended in a series of bad pictures, without Lillian Gish, which ruined him and set his backers in the red many millions.

The man of whom and to whom in the pioneer days everyone

spoke with bated breath, the man who could be questioned by
nobody alive, including Mary Pickford, turned out to be another
man who gave up his throne and relinquished his empire for a
woman.

Well do I remember the first time many many years later when
I went to Nassau to write the life story of Wallis Warfield Simpson, who by then was the Duchess of Windsor, married to the
man who had given up the Crown of England to become her husband. I'd seen her across a room a few times in London but this
was my first real meeting with her—and I couldn't believe it and I
knew *why* the English women had been so angry with him! He
had abandoned his people, left them without their beloved King
—for *her?* They thought her *un*beautiful, *un*attractive, with big
hands and ugly feet and they never forgave their Prince Charming. So it was with D. W. Griffith when he abandoned the fair
Lillian—the Unattainable Dream Girl Lillian Gish—for a girl
who seemed so *without* everything.

Mary Pickford could say to me, "Will my people ever forgive
me if I divorce Owen Moore to marry Douglas Fairbanks?" And I
could, as Mother Confessor of Hollywood, say *yes yes*—to marry
Douglas Fairbanks. Any woman might have done that—divorce
an ordinary young man to marry *Robin Hood, D'Artagnan, Super-
man!*

They might even have forgiven Clark Gable and Joan Crawford
if they had divorced their respective spouses to marry *each other.*

Nobody ever forgave D. W. Griffith for leaving their adored
Lily Maid of Astolat, the forever romantic and exquisite Lillian,
for *Carol Dempster.*

Carol Dempster. It is a name not often mentioned in life stories of D. W. Griffith. None of the pictures he made with her was
successful, on the record she doesn't look very important to his career. Yet she was all-important.

As I remember her, she was sort of pretty. But as an actress
Carol Dempster was hopeless and everybody knew it except the
Master himself. Or did he?

Was he motivated by passion, vanity or pique?

Much of it I think was sheer vanity.

In his egotism Griffith had come to resent the fact that the audiences as well as the critics now thought Lillian Gish was essential to him.

For weeks he rehearsed Carol Dempster as The Child in *Broken Blossoms*. When this became the stellar picture of 1919, the first United Artists release, New York papers declared it "so exquisite, so fragile, so beautifully and fragrantly poetic" that, said they, Griffith had "far exceeded the power of the written word." It made of Richard Barthelmess a big star and yet, said the critics, "so far as the players are concerned, *Broken Blossoms* is Lillian's film first of all."

Lillian, first of all.

This refrain had been a-building. Was it in Griffith's ears as he rehearsed Carol Dempster for the part of The Child? The excuse was to spare Lillian, who had been ill. But what Harry Carr, a great newspaperman who became Griffith's press agent and only close man friend, told me can be told now. Griffith hoped to train her for that tragic, exciting part. If he could, he intended to throw Lillian to the winds without a qualm.

None of this was Carol Dempster's fault, nor her doing. When she was a pupil, Ruth St. Denis had called her a great potential ballet dancer; Carol meant to go on with that career. Then she danced for Griffith in *Intolerance* and he was determined to make her the greatest Griffith star of all time. Why not?

"Actors can never be important," he said once to Mack Sennett. "Only directors will or should have place and power." To him, his actors and actresses were puppets, he pulled the strings.

There were no stars—but Griffith.

In the beginning, of course, this was true. His was a repertory company for films, his performers played leads, bits, dual roles interchangeably as the story and the director demanded. But as the moviegoing public began to recognize faces and make their own demands, as exhibitors found they could fill their theaters by promising personalities—*Mary Pickford, Charlie Chaplin*—the star system was born, which Mr. Griffith ignored insofar as he was able. Upon occasion he said to Lillian Gish, when time and circumstance had forced him not only to give her screen credit, but to feature her on billboards, "That should be my picture, not yours. It's my film."

He was the Great Teacher—except for serial queens like Pearl

White and Theda Bara and Norma Talmadge, a rare beauty who had so captivated one Joseph Schenck, owner of Palisades Park in New Jersey and millionaire exhibitor, that he married her and set up her own company—except for them I cannot think of one woman star of those early days who was not in some degree, by some road direct or indirect, a Griffith product. Yet as soon as his players reached star stature, could command star pay, he sent them on their way. He said good-bye to Mary Pickford, Blanche Sweet, Mae Marsh, Norma Talmadge's immensely talented little sister Constance, extended his royal good wishes, utterly confident that he had only to wave his hand to mold bigger and better stars.

Lillian Gish, despite other offers, stayed on. Because he was, after all, the Master? Yes, I think so, and because she was, well, because she was Lillian, that truly great artist sans ego. And so came about what were to be called by Griffith historians "the Gish years," and they were the most dazzling of all. After *Broken Blossoms* Griffith made *Way Down East* again with Gish and Barthelmess. It was a smash success; he had converted a mediocre melodrama into a masterpiece, with, as the critics pointed out, the help of his stars.

So he let Barthelmess go—to make the incredibly successful *Tol'able David* under the direction of Henry King.

And now only Lillian remained. Lillian—and Carol Dempster.

Let us set the stage carefully for the crucial act. It is 1921, two years only have passed since the founding of United Artists.

David Wark Griffith makes *Dream Street* starring Carol Dempster. The audience turns thumbs down, but silently Griffith refuses to accept their verdict. He makes *Orphans of the Storm* starring Lillian Gish. It is hailed as "a work of art," shown to President Warren G. Harding at the White House with Griffith and the Gish sisters in attendance. Of Lillian the critics write, "She has a way of reaching right in and straining at your heart strings."

It is now that Griffith suggests they go their separate ways.

Carol Dempster is waiting in the wings. Will Griffith risk all the money he can get, his own included, his prestige, his name, on his furious conviction that he can force her on an unwilling, what-the-hell-is-this public? He does. He makes *One Exciting Night* starring Carol Dempster, the public passes again.

D. W. Griffith never makes another box office success.

There was more to it than that, of course. Times had changed. D. W. Griffith no longer bestrode a narrow world of infant movies. William Fox had Tom Mix, and Westerns were booming. The alert, artistic Goldwyn brought such famed literary names as Rupert Hughes, Kathleen Norris, Mary Roberts Rinehart, into the field. Gloria Swanson, a type of woman D. W. Griffith could never understand, had become a DeMille star.

A handsome young man named George Loane Tucker was crowned with laurels for *The Miracle Man*, Eric von Stroheim starred in a cynical, sophisticated drama, *Foolish Wives*, which he also directed and which brought a foreign note. A young stockbroker, Sam Wood, was hailed for his direction of Wallace Reid in the automobile race classics, the same Sam Wood who later made *Goodbye Mr. Chips*. Critics raved over Fred Niblo's work as director of Douglas Fairbanks in *The Three Musketeers* and above all there was Rex Ingram, who had made a picture called *The Four Horsemen of the Apocalypse*, introducing an Italian dancer to play Julio, young Rudolph Valentino.

Griffith need have feared none of this competition. Griffith was better than any of them, if he had been willing to keep ahead of the parade. But his ego wouldn't let him. He had come to Hollywood ahead of the others. When they followed he returned to the East to build himself a studio at Mamaroneck on Long Island in New York, isolated from changing conditions in the industry.

He might have surmounted this and Carol Dempster's failure. But his break with Lillian Gish was fatal.

Why was this so?

The reason lay in Griffith's heritage from a long line of Southern gentlemen. D.W. may have looked like Sherlock Holmes, as indeed he did, and performed as a Welsh king, but his view of womankind was pure Ashley Wilkes. His manners were so courtly as to be almost stiff, to him his female players were "Miss Mary," "Miss Mae," "Miss Blanche." It was twenty-six years before "Miss Lillian" and "Mr. Griffith" were on a first-name basis—for a course Lillian remained his friend, as much as he would let her, until the day of his death and beyond. As bedroom farces and the flapper swept into the theaters Griffith's basic concept remained; he was shocked when he heard that Marguerite Clark had taken her stockings off on camera. His heroines continued fragile, virginal, noble. This he could not change. But they were successful only because of Lillian Gish. No other actress in the world then or now, not even Maude Adams, could have made believable women of this diaphanous substance.

What was she really like, this girl who was Griffith's supreme masterpiece?

She is not richly proportioned. In height, 5 feet 4, her weight 105 pounds. Her slender feet are small, her limbs shapely, her shoulders narrow. Her face . . . It has often been likened to music. I have found it in the heart cry of Mascagni's *Intermezzo*, in Keats' *The Eve of St. Agnes*, in the *Londonderry Air*.

To say it is spiritual beauty only partly tells the story. It is that of course. But something more. Elfland. Lonely moors. Scores of men have written of Lillian's face, have felt its strangeness. Underneath you feel the magic working on them.

Those are the words of the famous American biographer Albert Bigelow Paine.

This was the girl who, when Griffith put up a huge sum of money to make *Way Down East*, went into severe training, cold baths, long walks on the frozen river in snowstorms, so she could let her long hair and her hand drag in the icy river as she floated toward the falls on a cake of ice, over and over until Griffith was satisfied.

Did she love him? She never loved any other man. I know for a fact that no woman in Hollywood, no sex queen, no glamour girl, ever had over the years as many proposals of marriage from distinguished, wealthy, prominent men as did our Lily Maid. Yet she never married. Certainly she worshiped Griffith as an artist.

The cameras of *Way Down East* were right on top of her, her little face grew blue, her lashes were icicles. When she was half-conscious from the wind and the snow, they would carry her back to the studio.

"There was danger, too," Richard Barthelmess, her co-star, once told me. "They had dynamited the ice and I carried her back, stepping from cake to cake. I was scared silly. But Lillian was superhuman. She lived in the spirit. There was never any other woman like her."

After the picture was released, John Barrymore, then at the height of his fame as the theater's most loved and applauded actor, and never at any time backward with the ladies, wrote a revealing note to D. W. Griffith:

I have not the honor of knowing Miss Gish personally, and I am afraid that any expression of feeling addressed to her she might consider impertinent. I merely wish to tell you that her performance seems to me the most superlatively exquisite and poignantly enchanting thing I have ever seen in my life. I remember seeing Duse when she was at the height of her powers, and Sarah Bernhardt, and for sheer brilliancy and great emotional projection, done with an almost uncanny simplicity and sincerity of method, it is great fun and a great stimulation to see an American actress equal them if not surpass them. I wonder if you would be good enough to thank Miss Gish from all of us who are trying to do our best in the theater.

No critic to this day was more difficult to please than George Jean Nathan. He was one of the legion who wished to marry her, of no one did he ever write such unstinted praise as he bestowed on Lillian Gish. "The smiles of the Gish girl are the tears Strauss wrote into the rosemary of his waltzes. The secret of this young woman's unparalleled acting rests in her carefully devised and skillfully negotiated technique of playing always behind a veil of silver chiffon."

A leading novelist of that time was the magnificent Joseph Hergesheimer who wrote his best-selling *Cytherea* around Lillian, Cytherea being another name for Aphrodite, Venus, the goddess of love and beauty.

Would you not think that even King David might have said to this goddess, "Together we reached these heights, greater lie ahead. Share with me both the credit and the profit of all we shall do, you are as much a part of our work as I am"? He didn't.

Instead he said, not mentioning Carol Dempster, of course, "You should go out on your own, your name is of as much value as mine with the public. I think in your own interest you should capitalize on it while you can."

I still think her own explanation of why he did what he did that day is one of the most heartbreaking things I have ever heard.

"I think he just got tired of seeing me around," Lillian Gish said.

As it turned out, Lillian went on to make *The White Sister*, *The Scarlet Letter* and *Romola* in which she brought to the screen a young English actor named Ronald Colman and a stage actor named William Powell.

Griffith, as we know, never made another picture that mattered.

Slowly, as we sat in the back of Musso Franks cafe on Hollywood Boulevard when D.W. was an old man and had been cut off from Lillian Gish for years, slowly, quietly, with a depth I had never heard in his voice before even when he was directing her as she rocked the cradle in *Intolerance*, he said, "She was my luck, she was my light—I never had any of either after I lost her. Oh God—man can be his own worst enemy, can he not? Can he not?"

THE ENIGMA OF CHARLIE CHAPLIN

I find it extraordinary, here and now, to realize how much and how well I knew Charlie Chaplin, knew the key facts and meanings of him for so little time as I spent with him.

I know that Charlie Chaplin was one of the loneliest souls that ever walked this earth. Famous, truly beloved by many into whose dark or unhappy lives he had brought laughter, he himself was a bastard child who had seen his mother go slowly mad in a poorhouse. A misplaced person always in country, city, associates, women, jobs, friends. Between the genius he truly had and the marks left by his starved, cold, lonely childhood in the great city of London, he was always torn. I have thought often of late that in many ways the boy Charlie and his brother Syd, as they sheltered in an attic and stole morsels of bread, were characters out of

Dickens. The real-life Artful Dodgers, Oliver Twists, Poor Joes who were always *moving on*.

In the new, belittled, rudimentary art medium which the motion picture was, young Charles Chaplin—he was still in his early twenties—young Charlie, with the beloved character of the "Little Fellow" as he called him, became Everyman. As Chaplin developed him, wrote more of his own stories, we had Everyman revealing a gallant soul, a simple courage against odds in face of a hostile, bewildering world, laughter in the midst of loneliness, a shy but never quite hopeful search for love—love of a child, such as he presented in *The Kid*, love of a dog, a flower, a blind girl—in his movies that became increasingly successful. For Everyman, as audiences grew and grew, became more and more pleased to see how close to *tears*, love and laughter could come.

I must pause here to reflect on the dread absence of story line or of confusion that now passes for the *story* of a motion picture.

I won't name the star, it wouldn't be fair, but I went the other day with a top movie star to see a picture he had recently made. Being a writer myself I am perhaps more conscious of story and story line than the average picturegoer, and about halfway through I asked this young star about a slight haziness I felt concerning the story. He said he didn't know either and in fact had never had a glimmer of what the story was supposed to be about. No more, I am sure, did the writer, director or producer. May I say, with gentle melancholy, that this seems to me as much the reason for our sad crop of lousy pictures as the absence of stars that really shine.

I am sure, I dare to say with conviction, that there was more work, more dramatic tragic and comedy technique applied to one Chaplin short than is now to be seen in a whole movie? As long as I stayed awake at an alleged motion picture called *The Exorcist* I could not find any strong buildup for what the ads had told us we were soon to see. I kept feeling that for me to really care enough about exorcism to reach the vaunted vomiting point there should be a fine definite tugging story—such as was in a remarkable play which scored a real success on Broadway not too long ago. It was called *The Tenth Man*, and writer Paddy Chayefsky took pains to build the suspense that made the exorcism matter.

No one—no one has ever taken more exquisite pains to build up the laughter than Charlie Chaplin—since it must always be very close to tears, there must always, at all times and in all ways, be a sound reason, a *story* behind it. I do not remember ever laughing and crying at once as hard as I did at the opening night of that picture in which Charlie gave the birthday party to which nobody came. A simple story carefully built to that single scene with its common denominator—who among us has not played some variation of it in our imaginings on the eve of the ball?—we were laughing and crying at *ourselves*. Thus Everyman had his own enormous following, from San Francisco to Singapore, from Boston to Bangkok. Around the world in eighty seconds, with his sloppy shoes and his derby hat and his cane! With a lifted eyebrow Chaplin could make millions and billions of people laugh in every language, with one look he could bring tears and suspense, nobody can do that any more, can they? But then as far as I know there isn't a single *genius* in the movies today.

As early as *Shoulder Arms* he reached a peak of greatness that put him forever in the ranks of immortal artists, with such tormented geniuses as Mozart, Gauguin, Balzac, Keats, Nijinsky and Edgar Allan Poe. Yes—he belongs there and in any honest appraisal of Hollywood this should be claimed for him. I am a little tired of the constant downgrading of the movies just because they came to a rather sticky end.

"Chaplin is not merely a great comedian," Mr. Hearst, that connoisseur of the films, once said to me after the screening of one of Charlie's films in the private theater at the Ranch. "He is a poet, the poet of the screen."

On the other hand . . .

When it was rumored that the beauteous and astringent star Estelle Taylor was engaged to Chaplin she said to me, "No, I couldn't take that kind of punishment. I will pick my own persimmons. Charlie isn't one of them," and so married Jack Dempsey, the Champ. When Jack got angry he simply threw her out the window, which apparently she found natural and reasonable. Charlie, so Lita Grey, the mother of his first two sons, told me after their sensational divorce, was more subtle, he slashed and poisoned with *words*.

Take your pick. Poet or persimmon. Or a little of each. A many-sided man.

While the gold rolled in he was penny-pinching and poor-mouthed. When he was getting $150 a week from Mack Sennett, exactly a hundred a week more than he had ever before earned in his life, and living in one room at the Los Angeles Athletic Club on downtown Seventh Street, he hid his checks under the bed because he thought they were money. When he went to Essanay at $1,250 a week—he had insisted on the extra $250 for living expenses—he put $1,000 a week away for when the bubble should burst. He had a terror of poverty that came from that dark half of his mind where lived always the thwarted, half-starved, bitter urchin he had been.

"It's not so much cold and hunger," Chaplin once said to a friend, "it's the shame of poverty that gets you."

If that shame gave heartbreak to Charlie's comedy it also distorted his life. When he went back to England to be hailed by the populace and decorated by his king, the cup held bitter dregs. "The joy of earning," he once said to me, "was spoiled by the fear it couldn't last." Even when, three years after he left Sennett, he signed a contract with First National for a million dollars, even the following year when he found himself part owner of that multimillion-dollar combine, United Artists, he lived with that fear, carried it all through his years as a great star. This is understandable.

But what of the women in his life—legal and illegal and *Lolita* if you recall that hideous child of darkness?

Yes, yes, the women in his life were legion, he was rich, famous, and forever entertaining. Pola Negri, that first of Hollywood's foreign invasions, had fascinated Charlie who like all early movie stars was a real movie fan. For a time it was tempestuous little Lupe Velez, a star heartbreaker from South of the Border. Glamorous Paulette Goddard, a much-sought-after leading lady on and off the screen, was the heroine of a mystery that we the Press kept alive for a long time. It was called Are Charlie Chaplin and Paulette Goddard *married?* We never got an answer to this question until 1942 when it was announced that they had gotten themselves a divorce. I never believed that one. But he did marry Mildred Harris when she was just sixteen. Later, Lita Grey's marriage license said nineteen but her birth certificate said sixteen, too. Finally, Oona O'Neill, lovely daughter of that Nobel Prize-winning playwright Eugene O'Neill, and she was eighteen to his getting on for sixty. Little Joan Barry—they never married, Charlie and Joan, but she won a front page paternity suit against him the year after Oona became Mrs. Chaplin. One of the most beautiful blondes men preferred around Hollywood then had what she told me—over and over—was a most exciting and wonderful love affair with the Clown Prince and Claire should have known whereof she spoke. As he could mix love and tears, so, according to Claire Windsor, he could mix sex and laughter and that, as everyone knows, is a triumph.

Already, when he became one of the Big Four of United Artists, the turmoil, the distress, the court fights and humiliations, marriages and love affairs and ugly whispers in Hollywood, never to cease over the years, had begun for Chaplin.

The year before he secretly married starlet Mildred Harris. By the time the press located them, their brief honeymoon at Catalina Island was over, Mildred seemed close to a nervous collapse. Their child, born after what Hollywood considered a short count, lived only a few days. Everyone was furious with Charlie. Mildred Harris, a lovely child with a face as innocent as an angel, was only fifteen when he met her.

When Mildred Harris Chaplin died some twenty years or more after their divorce, on her casket was a great spray of orchids from Charlie. Knowing her, I'm sure Mildred would have said with gentle irony, "Better late than never." There were few enough orchids in the cruel months of her marriage to the Genius. Two dresses, one coat a year, he told her, were enough for any woman. A secondhand rattletrap was "the limousine." Those things were secondary. Imagine an inexperienced child trying to cope with his dark moods, his mercurial changes, his terrible isolation, his temperamental explosions, his unpredictable eccentricities. One day he had adored her. The moment they were married his love changed to a bitter and furious resentment.

Later when Lita Grey, a lush, dark, beautiful Spanish-California girl, found herself in the same spot, she said, "Charlie doesn't really care about anything but his work. He hates anyone who inter-

feres. And he likes scenes." His art was his real life. Yet he was a
fool over women. When he found his emotions had betrayed him
into giving up his freedom, he hated the woman.

In Pola Negri, he met his match. One day they cooed like
doves, the next Charlie said for publication, "I am too poor to
marry. This is a working world. We've all got to stay busy and
keep away from these emotional climaxes."

Having anything to do with the dark-browed gorgeous Polish
star who left audiences limp with her *Madame Dubarry* was no
way to avoid emotional climaxes. Thus the following day a headline read, "Pola and Charlie Mend Broken Love, 'Twas but a
Lovers' Quarrel." Then Pola said, "He is a genius, it was an experience divine. A woman learns from experience, no? I walk the
floor, I cannot sleep, I weep, I cannot marry him. I must live only
for my work. Love is over." Shortly afterward, they were golfing
together at Del Monte. They would be married, but "when
depends on our temperaments," said Pola, and in the end both
decided to live for Art alone.

His numerous affairs included sophisticated, mature, worldly
women . . . but when he went to the altar, when he sired his children, he selected teen-age partners.

All this, part of the news and gossip columns which became so
much part of the world's daily fare.

Yet—

"I never loved but one woman in my life," Charlie Chaplin
once told me.

We were sitting on the balcony of the Ambassador Hotel in
that city of Los Angeles of which Hollywood is a suburb. From
the ballroom behind us came the strains of a dance orchestra
led by Paul Whiteman, playing romantic music in his romantic fashion. A moon gave us a romantic glow, from nearby came
the fragrance of night-blooming jasmine. In this setting to this
music and perfume, I would doubtless have been susceptible to
any tale of which drama can be made. To be told a tender, young,
heartbreaking love story by such a master of minstrelsy as the
world's favorite clown shook my heart from its moorings.

It was during a party Marion Davies had given at the Cocoanut
Grove. This was, I think, before Mr. Hearst had finished the pala-

tial house at the beach which he gave to Marion, and her Beverly Hills mansion wasn't quite big enough for this kind of an affair. It was a masquerade, then the favorite social festivity, as though spending most of their lives dressing up for the camera, they got a rare pleasure out of dressing up just for fun. And it was *fun*, beautiful and picturesque with the top movie stars and the top brass of Hollywood who knew pretty well how to do such things, enjoying themselves in what, I am forced to tell you, was a merry but reasonably innocent way.

To explain just how innocent, it is necessary to interject here that at the best of times William Randolph Hearst had a strong prejudice against alcohol. It was almost as though he foresaw what we know today—that alcohol was to be the curse of our country, the way our enemies hope to conquer us from within. And also because Marion had no prejudice against it at all—to the contrary—and W.R. tried at all times to protect her from this, her personal enemy. I hear them now, Marion saying, "But I never get cross with you when you drink," and W.R. saying, "No, you only get cross with me when *you* drink." So at the Ranch—fine ale and the best beer to drink with luncheon, highballs in the afternoon after tennis or a long horseback ride in the hills, one or at most two cocktails before dinner—Albert, the head butler, and the footmen never offered anybody more than two cocktails, never, and Mr. Hearst went about with little plates of china, anything from Crown Derby to Meissen to Sèvres, offering hors d'oeuvres to one and all. He had a fondness for caviar, and I always felt happy and touched when he brought me a plate with a hefty helping of the little black eggs and chopped onions and small squares of toast. "Eat it right away," he would say, "it's very good for you." After the second round of drinks was passed you had to ask for one and if you asked for one too many you would find your bags packed and Joe Willicomb, that supersecretary and major-domo, bidding you a chilly farewell as he put you in the limousine that was to remove you to pastures new. This was referred to in Marion's charmed inner circle as being "sent down The Hill," and even Marion, whose influence thereon was not inconsiderable, couldn't get you asked back up The Hill again.

On this memorable night of the masquerade Marion had

caused a platform with banquet tables to be build at one end of the Cocoanut Grove, at the other were several small balconies off the big bright ballroom filled with its spectacular guests. I was trying not to drink—something I spent a lot of time and energy on until I was healed of my alcoholism for good by God's answer to my prayer which is the only way alcoholism ever gets healed as far as I know. With Mr. Hearst's aversion to any overindulgence, I had always been very careful at the Ranch—which wasn't too difficult. This night in the Ambassador ballroom where perhaps drink was more plentiful than at most Marion Davies' parties, I was ducking it and I got pretty tired and worn with a ballroom full of normal drinkers so I went out on a balcony to get some fresh air. To my surprise, Charlie Chaplin followed me. We had always known each other as I covered Hollywood and Charlie Chaplin was always news and made a lot of it for us, but we weren't friends as I was friends with Clark Gable and Spencer Tracy and Judy Garland and Joan Crawford later. Not that Charlie was ever up-tight about the Press. I just found him sort of hard to be—at ease?—with. And between us I think he was always afraid of us. He was self-conscious about his social ignorances —or at least at that time I thought so. He didn't eat with his knife, I don't mean that. But—he had to *think* before he did things and that he would one day be knighted by his king and be addressed in his native country as Sir Charles was so far beyond his expectations that if you'd made such a suggestion it would have met with ridicule on his part.

On the Ambassador balcony that night, a long time ago now, this slender, curly-haired, nervous, shy little man sat astride a weather-worn chair wearing the uniform of Napoleon as the Little Corporal, he seemed to be in what I daresay one can simply call a Mood. I had watched him dancing with Marion, who was Josephine as Empress with all the jewels, and they were a fantastic pair, two of the world's leading movie stars at play, and as I watched I wondered about the rumor that Charlie was currently in love with *her*. I knew and had always known that Marion was in love with William Randolph Hearst. Perhaps I knew this because I knew Mr. Hearst so well, working for him those many years I knew all the depth and power of his mind, the dazzle and color of his imagination, I knew it would be easy for a girl or woman to fall in love with him. Most people thought of his strength, wealth, power—many from the White House down were afraid of him. His lighter side wasn't so well known and I always was sure that no one could ever really know him if they'd never been at the Ranch, where he was at home, where he belonged, where to see him on a horse was to get forever the fact that most people missed. William Randolph Hearst was a *Westerner*.

Born in San Francisco, had his first newspaper in San Francisco when his mother bought him the San Francisco *Examiner*, he always and always returned to the Ranch as soon as he could. A small item but—his wife Millicent loathed the West, disliked the Ranch and its way of life, and always preferred the house on Long Island or the one on Riverside Drive in New York City. Marion truly loved the Ranch and its ways and was never so happy as when she was there. Sometimes with guests—from the President and Mrs. Coolidge and Winston Churchill to a group of young actors from her latest picture. Or when she was alone with W.R. and a few friends.

I remember particularly one visit when the only other guests were Colleen Moore and her then husband, John McCormick, and Lord Duveen, of the famed art galleries. Lord Duveen had brought some paintings to show Mr. Hearst and we sat in the big room of the Castle, Mr. Hearst and Marion and Joe Willicomb and John and Colleen and I. And Charlie Chaplin. On each painting, Marion had a comment, specific and sure.

"It's quite amazing," Lord Duveen said suddenly in a surprised voice that made us all turn to look at him. "I don't quite understand it. I know Miss Davies as a motion picture star and a—if you will pardon me—a most fine comedian and the—the lady of this castle. But that—how is it if I may ask Miss Davies that you are likewise a—an authority on art as it were."

While Marion stuttered to find words behind her laughter, Charlie Chaplin said in his most *elegant* very British voice, "But my dear fellow—*he taught her!*" And waved a hand that seemed to hold a monocle at His Lordship, the King of the Castle, and I'm not too sure Lord Duveen didn't go away thinking Charlie Chaplin was His Grace the Duke of San Simeon.

After His Lordship's departure Charlie, whose imitations were in another dimension—his leaps and *entrechats* when he did Nijinsky defied gravity just as had that tragic dancer himself, yet Charlie never had a ballet lesson in his life, his Manolete had all the grace of the great bullfighter, all the pathos of the bull melded into something entirely *else* by the refracting lens of great comedy—that night at the Ranch, Charlie was moved to imitate Lord Duveen. Going from painting to painting to *objet d'art,* gesturing, commenting, he even looked like Duveen. Here we *saw* magic. *Duveen* as Duveen wasn't funny—*Chaplin* as Duveen was.

I saw that scene most clearly sitting on that balcony at the Ambassador beside Charlie. I saw it as an example of his power to fascinate. I knew it wouldn't work on Marion, still I had to wonder if he meant it to. "Go and ask," Mr. Hearst always said to his reporters. "If you want to find out something, *ask!"*

Charlie said, "No, I am not in love with Marion." Then he said, "I never loved but one woman in my life. I love her still. Forever."

Way down deep, I suppose we all feel like that. I know I do. In the soft light, before my very eyes, Charlie seemed to change. There was a—a sweetness. I wouldn't have believed it possible, all the love that had ever been there when he looked down at Jackie Coogan, as The Kid. All the longing that had been in his eyes at his lonely birthday celebration. He talked now while Marion Davies' party went on in the ballroom only a few feet away, so that from time to time we had an accompaniment of soft music. Why, I've never quite known, but in a low vibrant voice he began at once to tell me about the One Girl, the only girl he had ever loved, would always love throughout eternity.

They were all unknowns in third-rate music halls in London and the Provinces. She was half of a pretty bad sister act. She had no future. But as he described her, I heard somewhere the music of "Jeanie with the Light Brown Hair" and I knew he had seen in her not a third-rate music hall act but sheer poetry, music, gardens at dawn, all the loveliness which he had missed.

She loved him, too. They had so little—poor young things. Whispered words in the wings, a stolen walk in Hyde Park, shy glances, a snatched kiss or two. Because her sister disapproved. Her sister was the strong one, ambitious and determined, masterful, and she told Charlie's Dream Princess, "He's a cheap clown, he'll never amount to anything. With your *looks*, you can do a lot better than that."

Only—Charlie's sweetheart didn't care, all she wanted was a home, a child, and the man she loved. At last, she got up the courage to defy her big sister, to tell her she was going to marry the little clown. Anyhow—in spite of—etc., etc. It was a mistake to tell her domineering sister what she intended to do. That night the sisters weren't in their place on the bill. The manager said their booking had been changed. He didn't know where they had gone. Charlie had no money. London was so big and the Provinces, all that is England that lay outside of London, were bigger. He couldn't stand it without her, so he accepted a not very good offer to come to America for vaudeville, hence to Hollywood. One morning he awoke to find himself famous.

"I used to dream she'd go to a cinema in London," he said, with a smile at himself, "and recognize me. Her heart would leap and she would write 'Dear Charlie, now that you are so famous, do you remember me.' I'd rush to her—For years, *for years*, I opened all my own fan mail. [I found this was true: ARSJA.] They thought it was vanity—no. I kept looking for her letter that no one would recognize but me. It never came."

Through the music halls, the booking agents, he tried to locate her when he made his triumphal return to England. Not a trace. Careful as Charlie was with money, it is true that he spent a lot of it on this search.

Then one day, he saw her.

There was a park bench along the Central Park wall on the Fifth Avenue side. Sometimes he sat there for hours, staring at the crowds that passed. She wasn't in England, she and her sister must have come to America. Someone had told him that in America you would always see everybody sooner or later on Fifth Avenue. So there sat the great star still looking for his lost love.

One day, a woman came out of a house across the avenue. She lifted her eyes and seemed to look at him and he sprang up and went to the curb. A man followed her, and a little boy. They got into the big waiting car and drove away. "She was just the same," Charlie told me. "And—I loved her just the same."

I could see it so plainly as he told it. Not the great movie star, but the pathetic funny little man he played on the screen, standing there on the curb with his hat on his arm, watching her drive away up the avenue—Fifth Avenue—part of the parade of cars. Then I could see him give that famous shrug, giving up in despair, put on his hat and, twirling his cane in attempted defiance, walk away alone down the long, empty road—the little figure with the funny feet breaking our hearts once more as he grew smaller and smaller.

"Like that," said Charlie Chaplin, "you only love once."

Perhaps he was always looking for her in other young girls. For my own part, after that strange, spontaneous confession, I have to believe it.

Who knows for what the human heart is searching?

MARY AND DOUG
THE ROYAL COUPLE

Once after Mary Pickford and Douglas Fairbanks had married each other in one of the great world romances, I recall a scene at Pickfair when Douglas—an adventurer *off* as well as *on* the screen, wanted to go off to the Gobi Desert to hunt whatever a man hunts in the Gobi Desert. And Mary, all curls and great shining eyes, didn't want him to go. She wanted him to stay in *Hollywood* and make another movie like *Robin Hood* which had such a spectacular career.

"Mary," Doug said, and that proved how serious he was for usually he called her Tupper or Tuppence or a variety of nicknames as they came to him, "the only thing in the world you really care about is making motion pictures."

And his wife, Miss Mary Pickford to you, said without a smile, "Yes, that is true. And it is the only thing in the world you should care about either. You can take people with you wherever you want to, all the people all the time, back and forth around the world and back and forth into other times. Oh, it's so much more exciting and wonderful than—than real life, isn't it?"

I think it is because Mary Pickford believed that and still does that her enchantment never failed.

And it was because Douglas Fairbanks did not that the most

important marriage in Hollywood came to an end. There was that other woman, of course. But if his Queen Mary could have set aside her crown long enough to don desert boots or go on safari, there never would have been. Of that I am certain.

When I last saw Mary at the famed Pickfair home where she has reigned ever since Douglas Fairbanks gave it to her on their marriage—it had been his hunting lodge—when I saw her so tiny and frail in the magnificent throne bed in the grand bedroom, when I sat beside her and we both looked up with love and reverence at a painting of her mother and my beloved friend, Charlotte Pickford, my heart was joyful and yet it was not. Joyful to find our Mary so bright, so eager, so still Irish witty. Yet one hears tales. The world wags its tongue and since the world is sadly filled with a desire to see evil come to its great ones—no no, I will not admit that! Yes, in madness it somehow killed our great hope, Bobby Kennedy, but I will not believe they wish any ill to the girl who was for so many years America's Sweetheart. The tales are simply the silly gossip of petty meddlers, who gather around the great and want to sound *in* when actually they are as far *out* as it's possible to get.

I want to stop here to *shout* that in spite of all the headlines, as I say, that nobody can get to talk to Mary Pickford, I can and do. And that as an expert ex-alcoholic of some thirty years' standing— the *ex* part I mean—I can promise you that any vicious tales of Mary's "secret drinking," any tales that she spends her life in seclusion *because* of this dark secret, are not only vicious but untrue. Lies. Mean, petty, criminally careless lies.

It is true that Mary spends much of her life in bed—and all of it at Pickfair. In the first place, Pickfair as it exists today is about as near heaven as a gal can get until she passes through the Pearly Gates. In the second place it has been the center of Mary's life for a very long time and holds all her dearest memories of her marriage to Doug Fairbanks, all her years with her family—the happy later years anyhow—Charlotte and Jack and Lottie. She and Buddy Rogers have made it their home since their marriage— where else should Mary Pickford Moore Fairbanks Rogers live?

Also in the past several years, Mary has had two eye operations of nerve-racking proportions.

It is a stately—a *queenly*—bedroom where these days I go to see Mary. It may be St. Helena—or Elba—a small spot of exile in a world she once ruled, it is still called Pickfair. Around it are exquisite and stately gardens, and I as a native Californian am well aware what it takes to keep a *garden* in the semidesert horrors of Southern California. The lawns are not as green as England's, of course, but they are kept as green as possible and roll gently from the spreading white mansion to the swimming pool and on all sides to the white plaster walls. In the old days of Pickfair's palatial glory, Miss Pickford—Mrs. Fairbanks—and occasionally later Mrs. Rogers—for she has been called by all those names—used to come and sit in her own canvas chair under the little pergola and watch her guests at play. I never saw her in the pool, I never saw her in a bathing suit, there nor at Fairford, the big clapboard white house Douglas built on the edge of the Pacific at Santa Monica.

"My People!"

Has any other American woman who ever said that had the *right* to say it?

Mary Pickford had that right and what is more she *meant* it—from the very depths of her heart, as much as ever did Queen Victoria of her Empire.

Today she is still at every moment of her life the Dowager Queen, she is in retirement, but the Royalty is undimmed, the Majesty is still there. In my days as a reporter I have bowed to kings and kissed the hand of a queen or two—no one ever had as much Royalty as did the girl born Gladys Smith who sat on a throne the People of the World had erected for her.

We do it today, the favored few of us who enter that shimmering silver-and-pastel room with the great bay window that faces out onto the gardens. We make that little bow, that courtesy, that will indicate to the small figure, propped up amid so many satin and lace pillows, that we accept and acknowledge her sovereignty though the royal insignia is now only a small smooth hand, almost a child's hand.

Still a Throne Room, the famed golden curls are piled as a

crown on top of her head, they shine against the pillows and I seem to see them again at the head of the royal table at Pickfair. Believe me where *Mary* sat was always the head of any table. When she sat at the table with David Wark Griffith and Charlie Chaplin and Douglas Fairbanks to form United Artists, even though her feet didn't touch the floor (they never did) *that* was the head of the table, and Women's Lib should have seen the small dainty gestures with which she controlled all negotiations. To *her* advantage.

Not too long ago when I went to Pickfair to see Mary I took with me a young writer friend of mine who had a real *thing* about Mary Pickford. A movie buff, Robert Thom regards her with awe and affection. He waited downstairs with Mary's husband. I told Mary of his interest in perhaps writing a book about The History of the Motion Picture and its effects on the sociology of the known world and when I told her of his devotion, of how he would travel miles to see one of her films, she said I might bring him in and present him to her.

She looked up at him and was suddenly that character for which she was once given the Academy Award—*Coquette*. "It's too bad I'm not pretty any more," she said, and the playwright came up with a line of first-class dialogue. "But Mary," he said, "you never were pretty. You were always beautiful and you still are."

It was *true*.

Beauty belongs to her now in her eighties as much as it ever did and this, remember, while it was not the face that launched a thousand ships it *was* the one of which the world's leading cameramen have said to me, "It is impossible to get a bad photographic shot of Mary Pickford. She has the only totally cameraproof face that has ever been known."

I had telephoned that most remarkable and blessed lady, Esther Helms, who has been Mary's Secretary of the Household for many years. She has been my friend partly, I suppose, because Mary still includes me among hers, but also we have together done a number of jobs to raise money for the Motion Picture Country House, which Mary Pickford helped found years ago and to which she always gives large contributions. This day I had called just to ask how Mary was and to send her my love—but Esther said, "She would like to see you."

So I drove out Sunset Boulevard, turned up beyond the Beverly Hills Hotel, circling the small hill where on Summit Drive Pickfair looks down upon Mary's domains, for she still owns a great deal of that real estate. "Mama," Jack Pickford used to say, with a smile that enchanted, "Mama always bought corners," reminding me that so much of Mary's enormous wealth came to her from the acute business sense and advice she got from their mother.

I thought of this as I passed the guard at the gate, and was met at the door now used, which opens on the circular driveway, and then found Mary's husband Buddy at the head of the stairs to the main floor.

He has always been one of the handsomest of men. He still is. Older now, and with silver in the heavy black hair, he has gained a distinction that somehow makes you forget he was an actor and a bandleader, not but what it is okay indeed to be either or both of those, however usually they have a sort of theatrical flare, which suggests the lights of Broadway, lights over theater marquees, the magic spell of all that is the theater—or was. Buddy Rogers, to me, suggests an ambassador, the kind I used to see at White House dinners or receptions wearing red ribbons across their shirtfronts, or decorations of a kind as exclusive as the Victoria Cross or the ribbon of the Legion of Honor.

When I came down from my visit with Mary—that day it had been rather a long one—Buddy said, "What did you talk about today—Douglas?" I suppose I looked guilty for actually we very often did. "I've been married to her now for almost forty years," Buddy said gently, "and she still thinks, half the time, she'll always be married to Douglas Fairbanks. So do lots of other people, I guess."

"Mostly," I said, "we talked about Charlotte."

Truth to tell Hollywood in those early days was a matriarchy. The *mothers* dominated the scene partially because if there was a *father* around no young girl would have needed or been allowed a career as an actress, being as it was a potential primrose path leading to sin. Nor was there any doubt as to precisely what was meant by sin. So the mothers also hovered near to protect the fledglings they had launched and, since most of these lovelies were not of legal age, to sign their contracts and run their business affairs.

Some of them were powerhouses with organizational brains far beyond those of their photogenic offspring. A few of them were bloody nuisances who overestimated the talent of their poisonous little offspring because about 92 per cent of the child actors who arrived at the early studios propelled by their ambitious female parents should, as my writer friend Mark Kelly once said to Darryl Zanuck, have been exterminated with a good strong pesticide.

On the other hand there was Mrs. Gish, pretty Mary McConnell as they had called her in Urbana, Ohio. Mrs. Gish spent much of her later life in a wheelchair. A delicate, silvery-haired, exquisite *lady*, just the mother you would expect Lillian Gish to have, and a potent factor in the lives of young Lillian and Dorothy. Humorous, shrewd, forthright Peg Talmadge's advice was followed not only by her beautiful daughters—Norma and Constance as they became big stars, and little Natalie who chose instead to become full-time wife to the incomparable Buster Keaton—but by the Schenck brothers, Nick and son-in-law Joe, among the builders of the industry. There was, too, Phyllis Daniels, truly a daughter of early California aristocracy, whose own mother was a member of the Spanish nobility and still wore her exquisite shabby gown, her carefully darned lace mantilla, her air of elegance after thoroughly and happily depleting the family fortunes, Phyllis Daniels who passed on her faith and her hope and her courage to her lone chick, Bebe.

But the first of the great founding mothers was Charlotte Pickford. As she launched little Mary, then Lottie, then Jack on the stage after her husband died when Mary was only five, as she herself became a wardrobe mistress, as they took to the road sleeping on the worn not-too-clean plush of coaches on trains between towns when they looked for work, as they separated to go out with road companies and knew loneliness, Charlotte and her children also knew what it was like to be hungry. Charlie Chaplin had said to me, "Either you know what it is to be hungry, or you don't. If you do, you never forget it." The Smith-cum-Pickford family of Toronto, Canada, didn't forget. But because of Charlotte, because of her great faith, her loving heart, her Irish humor and good cheer, the Pickford family—and Charlotte *kept* it a family—was never embittered by those early struggles as was Chaplin.

I am still sure that Charlotte was at least half of Mary Pickford. Without Charlotte, there would have been no Mary. Charlotte it was who encouraged Mary at fifteen to take a chance on the "flickers" when they were in even greater disrepute than the stage. When Mary left Griffith to sign with Adolph Zukor at Famous Players, even when her stardom and her fortune were assured, Charlotte was omnipresent on the set and in the business offices, and she went right on putting up Mary's hair in rags to produce the most famous curls ever known.

Mary adored her mother, she knew I did too. So of course we talk of Charlotte. And I remember one of my favorite stories of all time, one I love to tell even though I've probably told it before.

Beloved stories, like loved tunes, stay close in the heart and can be sung over and over again.

When, at long last, Mary Pickford and Douglas Fairbanks were free to marry each other and become the world's favorite lovers, it meant that Mary must give up her church, for both she and Douglas were divorced and the Catholic Church in which Mary had been born and reared, as we used to say, did not recognize the marriage of divorced persons. And so Mary, who was at heart then and always and now a truly religious woman, must find for herself another church in which to worship. She chose the Christian Science Church, whose founder, a saintly lady, had herself been divorced, and Mary persuaded herself that her mother had come along with her. At the time when Charlotte knew she was dying of cancer I went to see her as often as I was allowed and one day when I arrived Mary was there and looking down at her mother with great love and exasperation she said, "Adela, you've studied Christian Science. You believe in the healing power of the Presence of Christ, don't you?" Without waiting for my reply she said with a rush, trying, I thought, not to cry, "Mama isn't giving us any help at all. She doesn't read her Christian Science lessons as she should and she doesn't do anything really to help the practitioner. You tell her she should," but Charlotte looked up at Mary and then at me and said with all the strength she had, "Don't you believe her, Adela. You know there isn't anything I wouldn't do to be able to get up and go to Mass again."

And I have always been glad that Bebe Daniels' mother Phyllis and I managed to conspire so that Charlotte was able to have the last rites of her beloved church. For years Mary never knew. Then when she and I were working on an article under Mary's name that appeared as a best-selling book called *Why Not Try God?* she looked up one day at Charlotte's portrait and began to cry. "I have no right to be talking about God when my mother didn't have her last sacraments," she said. So I told her how Phyllis and I had brought a priest over one afternoon when she was away— and it was a glorious moment to see those guilty tears tremble into an April smile.

Yes, we talk about Charlotte sometimes, Mary and I, and we talk about the Motion Picture and Television Country House and Hospital because it is very dear to Mary and I'm going to stop right here to tell you about it for it is very dear to me too. Also because it most truly shows the heart of Hollywood as we two know it, and because no one else does, tell about it I mean.

This I do not understand. In none of the tomes on the history of the movies do I find mention of this unique achievement by the industry.

The Academy Awards, which millions view on television each year, are supposed to show the film industry at its best. Don't you believe it. I remember so well the night we founded the Academy, we wanted to Reward and Award the artistic pictures, the pictures that were experimenting with acting, with camera work, with lighting, with scripts and direction. To give encouragement and applause without considering box office receipts, to trial flights and test hops aimed at bettering the art and techniques of the movies. And I can tell you now that, no matter how they shine up the production, this aim gets dimmer and dimmer by the year.

No no, to find the best today you would have to go to twenty green and gardened acres in Woodland Hills at the western tip of the San Fernando Valley. But it started a long time ago. And it started with Mary Pickford.

It came about in this wise.

When America at last entered World War I, Mary Pickford came out of the ivory tower where, we remember, she led her secluded private life and, often with Doug Fairbanks and Charlie Chaplin or sometimes Marie Dressler, began her war work, her Liberty Bonds drives, her hospitality tours. Now every day great crowds were seeing her in person, the Little Queen on platforms in factories, on stands in public squares, in ballrooms and ball parks, crying, "I am only five feet tall and I weigh 100 pounds, but every inch of me and every ounce of me is fighting American" —and the crowds bought bonds, millions of dollars' worth at a meeting, in answer to her plea.

This for her country. But there was also, for the Little Queen, the Motion Picture Industry, *her* industry. "If you've been hungry . . ." Most of these stars had, they didn't forget. Even Chaplin, so thrifty with his wives and children, kept his studio crew on payroll the year round whether they worked or not, put many of the funnymen from his Keystone days under contract, paid Edna Purviance, his leading lady in his early films, her full salary until the day she died.

Now when Mary Pickford saw *her* men, the men of her industry, march off to war leaving behind wives and children, some of them *hungry*, she became every inch a fighting Film Star. She enlisted Griffith, Fairbanks, everyone she could command; they appealed from the stage of Clune's Auditorium to two thousand of their fellow workers ranging from stars and studio heads to grips and extras and again the dollars rolled in, with, I might add, Mary's right up front. They raised $50,000 that night.

"We take care of our own," cried the heartbeat of Hollywood.

This was the beginning.

In time this cry took form as the Motion Picture Relief Fund.

Among the early presidents were such stars as Mary herself, Marion Davies, Conrad Nagel who arrived amongst us via Broadway to become a pillar in our community and head usher at the Fifth Church of Christ, Scientist at the corner of Hollywood

Boulevard and LaBrea; such studio heads as Joe Schenck, Jesse Lasky, Jack L. Warner, Carl Laemmle. On the first Board of Directors were Harold Lloyd, Douglas Fairbanks, Mae Murray—former Ziegfeld Follies star who raised herself to a coronet by marrying Prince David Mdivani—William S. Hart—contender with Tom Mix for the Cowboy Crown—Donald Crisp—favorite character actor—Cecil B. DeMille, Charles Christie, Hal Roach, and the Young Turk, Irving Thalberg, who was beginning to make waves out in the San Fernando Valley at Carl Laemmle's Universal Studios which he would eventually ride to the top as the Boy Genius with Louis B. Mayer at MGM.

I don't know why it comes over me again with such amazement that this august body was so *young*, mostly in their twenties and thirties, Thalberg, I think, was about twenty-three. Perhaps because the current youth crop, poor things, trained as they are to expect to be taken care *of*, would never have dared such a dream. "We take care of our own!" A formidable undertaking in those pre-welfare days, requiring vision plus faith. Well, we had both, and we all shared the fun of making the dream a reality. And we thoroughly enjoyed it.

I daresay that anyone who has been misled by the current fantasies of the Golden Years in Hollywood thinks we were wont to go from orgy-to-carousal-to-brawl constantly when at play. Here and there—now and then—perhaps. But I can only submit courteously, as one who was *there*, that money-raising for the Motion Picture Relief Fund, a hit-or-miss affair in those early days, was one of the real rallying points in our social life. When what was in the kitty had been given away there'd be a benefit premiere or show—I recall one featuring Mary Pickford in a comedy skit, Chaplin with a pantomime, Will Rogers doing the rope-twirling act he'd perfected in the Follies, where the pièce de résistance proved to be a large stationary suit of armor stage left throughout which suddenly came to life and turned into Doug Fairbanks—or as the need or mood demanded we had a charity ball, a fashion show, a card party or even a polo match.

You-all come! And since we were small-town neighborly and dearly loved parties of any description, we would don our pink coats and ride to the rescue of the Fund.

The dispensing of the money was unique and also neighborly—

without red tape and practically instantaneous—the thinking being that when you needed a funeral it wouldn't wait, or, alas and alack, if the need was drying out after what I believe is now called alcoholic abuse to get back on the job, or an ambulance to take you to the hospital, or the money for your mortgage payment or that tux without which no actor can travel was in hock, you needed the help at once . . . *now* . . . not at the farther end of a long line, four forms and two or three interviews. This instant help was made possible in a large measure by the remarkable ability of Anne Lehr, the voluntary director, whose husband was an executive at Goldwyn Studios, and her staff of volunteer interviewers. I remember particularly Mrs. Samuel Goldwyn herself, Charlotte Greenwood and Mrs. Conrad Nagel, a trio of gals who knew their Hollywood, knew why it was necessary for an actor to have a good toupee, a promising young actress to have dental assistance with crisscrossed teeth or, Came the Talkies, to be sure that the ones that weren't their own *fitted*.

Even when, during and after the Depression and Came the Talkies which put a tremendous strain on the Fund, it had to be more organized, the same policies continued. While our haphazard Happy Times were no longer sufficient for funding and the industry as a whole rallied to its own support, began and continues to this day voluntary payroll deductions of a half of one per cent from the mightiest to the lowliest, and our volunteers had to be augmented with more and more paid personnel as the industry grew, had its ups and downs, and more and more assistance was needed, all assistance offered was still direct, personal, prompt. Which leads me to believe that such is at all times *possible* if the heart is in it. If in the beginning and at the core "We Care." No loans or notes or fine print required here. No intimidating bureaucracy. No human indignity.

Thus eighteen years after the Fund was founded, Mary Pickford, now President Emeritus, could still say, "We don't ask a lot of questions. We see the need and we fill it. Pride means a lot to people in our business."

Indeed! "It's not so much the cold and the hunger. It's the shame that gets you."

This was, and has continued to be, one of the differences between our Fund and other aid plans I have observed springing up, particularly within government—this recognition that individual dignity is as important as individual help. "Everybody," as my minister grandfather was wont to say, "wants loving." *First*. Upon this premise and with the aid of this Fund in time was built to the everlasting glory of the Industry—and a possible beacon to others?—the Motion Picture Country House and Hospital.

I have called it unique. It is. So far as I know there is nothing like it elsewhere in the world.

I went out there the other day as I have done often during the years, sometimes to make a fund-raising speech, sometimes to give an informal talk or visit old friends, and stopped as I usually do for a cup of coffee with executive director Jack Staggs and May Hoffman, the administrative assistant. A cheery old man sitting in the sun outside May's office hailed me. He had, he said, met me when I visited the set where Vic Fleming was directing Judy Garland in *The Wizard of Oz*. For a moment I couldn't quite—then it flashed. The *"green" man*. I must confess that after the advent into our simple do-it-yourself-movie-making of sound, color, unions and efficiency experts much of the jargon baffled me. Particularly the "green" man. Here before me was the one who had explained that this was no extraterrestrial being but the prop man exclusively empowered by the union to handle "green" things—growing plants, flowers, trees, and any part or reasonable facsimile thereof.

"Yup," he said, "I *was* a 'green' man. Here they treat me like a *star*."

I thought of that as I walked along the manicured path of the Country House, between neat white cottages all bright with flowers, toward the Hospital on the other edge of the estate whither I was going to visit Dorothy Reid, the widow of Wallace Reid, whose story I see next on my tapestry. Twenty tree-shaded grassy acres with another twenty to grow on. Fifty-four double and single cottages plus the Lodge, a separate self-contained building with its own dining room and kitchen. The best medical facilities in the 180-bed Hospital. And all the guests getting *star* treatment.

Yes. The latest movies provided twice weekly by the studios shown in a private theater as luxurious as the projection rooms on the studio lots where the Bosses do their viewing. Trams designed by Walt Disney that cover the grounds and make scheduled runs to the nearby shopping center. Forty "Blue Angels," women volunteers who run errands, plan parties, drive the station wagons when guests need to go into Hollywood, or Beverly Hills, to the airport, or wish to attend their own church. A glass of wine served with meals at the small tables in the elegant dining room where the cottage dwellers forgather. A darkroom for photographers, art classes, trips to Disneyland, the Ice Follies. A full-time beauty salon and barbershop furnished by the Cinema Hairstylists where your volunteer operator may yesterday have been shampooing Faye Dunaway or currying Peter Ustinov.

Myself I'll skip going into Hollywood, the Ice Follies and the shopping center if I can have my beauty salon right across the lawn. The only time *I* feel like a star is when my own hairdresser insists on coming with me to the TV studios. "She says," I told Dorothy Reid—we always talk about our hair even though hers is no longer auburn red and mine is no longer blonde because we were the first two women in Hollywood to cut ours *off*—"My hairdresser says my hair is always a *mess*." "That," said Dotty, "is because you cannot keep your hands out of it. You never could." Too true. I daresay I've never gotten over the relief of ridding myself of those thick *braids* and steel *pins*.

We were sitting in the garden outside her room but through the sliding glass door I could see the small picture of Wally on her bedside table. Wally, *so* handsome, *so* talented, dead now for over fifty years. And here we sat, Dotty and I, who had raised our children together, fought together for Wally's life, lost, shared our grief, a couple of great-grandmothers, talking about him as he—and we—were in that long ago. Suddenly time telescoped and we were with him in his youth and were ourselves young, and his youth was with us in the here and now—as close as close. I could feel a joy in him, I could, I *could*, a joy that the lovely young wife he had oh-so-reluctantly left behind was being cherished like a *star*.

Growing older is a rich experience—the accumulated memories, the bird's-eye view of the sweep of years, the accelerated curiosity about what's to come—but I am frank to confess it isn't always

easy. There's a falling away of much that has been our life. I
remember the time I realized that I didn't come *first* with anybody in this world any more. My children had children who had
children who must take top spot. They had husbands and wives of
their own. I had no husband to come first *to*. Then I realized I
had a lot of seconds and thirds and these add up. Above all I, like
my blessed Marie Dressler, had my work. But for many it can
mean empty retirement, the end of an active career. For others it
is struggling to make ends meet *alone* as families scatter, friends
go on before us, a husband or wife is left behind. Or there is trying to live in someone else's house, quite possibly with a large,
noisy family; dearly as I love my children and grandchildren and
great-grandchildren as of today their ways are not my ways. Now
there is a need for a bit of peace and quiet, a space, so to speak, in
which to "make my soul" as my own grandmother would say.
Surely a sense of independence, of dignity, a measure of security
both physical and financial, a feeling of being *cared for* are the
pearls to be strung on these later years. It is precisely these which
the Country House and Hospital offer, "without money and without price," to those who have given their years of service to the
motion picture and television industry.

And it is done without discrimination *even in reverse*, which is
the way it seems to me to operate most often these days. The
white is as welcome as the black or brown, and without a quota.
The needy rich or the overburdened middle class are as welcome
as the needy poor although the latter do get priority. The welcome is as beneficent for a star or director as for a studio janitor
or fireman. It's all a question of need—"We see the need and we
fill it," as Mary Pickford said. That need may be financial,
physical, psychological, spiritual—which about covers the field.
And no one knows what particular need brought his neighbor to a
cottage on the grounds or whether her dinner partner in the dining room is on social security or a millionaire—as was the case
with that member of the first Board, Donald Crisp, who spent the
last years of his life at the Country House. As did Mae Murray,
the erstwhile Princess Mdivani. And Mack Sennett himself.

When Reece Halsey, a young friend of Mack's and his literary
agent, found Mack in bed alone at the Garden Court apartments
with a miserable cold, no one to fetch his aspirin, dependent for

his meals on the Hollywood Roosevelt Hotel across the street, Reece gave him a choice. "I'll take you to the Hollywood Presbyterian Hospital where they can take care of you for a few days," said Reece, "or I'll take you to the Motion Picture Country House where they'll take care of you for the rest of your life."

"I can't go to the Country House," said the King of Clowns. "That's charity. They wouldn't take me anyway."

Reece assured him that it wasn't and they would. He told Mack pretty much what May Hoffman, who has had her fingers on the pulse of the Country House for years, told me. "Those with financial needs come first, of course," May said, "the rest pay for the service as determined by the committee. They come here because they'd rather be here and if we have empty rooms we don't turn them away."

Whether Mae Murray was broke, as rumor had it, what Mack Sennett who definitely wasn't or the very wealthy Donald Crisp paid or contributed is not a matter of public record. Which is also true of the Hospital. "Circumstances, cases," says the Fund. But anonymously. Always. Nor is there exploitation for publicity or any other purpose of their guests. They are as anonymous as they choose to be.

Two weeks after Mack Sennett had settled himself in his single cottage he called Reece Halsey. "The food here," he said, "is better than Romanoff's," this establishment being then the *in* restaurant of Beverly Hills. Mack, who had no taste for anonymity, made occasional appearances at Romanoff's and elsewhere, loudly singing the praises of the Country House where he had found good food, good care, good people, *his kind of people.*

Two years later he died there. As did Chester Conklin and Minta Durfee Arbuckle, early members of his Keystone team. As did Hattie McDaniel who won an Oscar for her supporting role in *Gone with the Wind.* And Brian Donlevy, for years our Mayor at Malibu Beach. And Mme. Maria Ouspenskaya whose dramatic school was one of the finest in Hollywood. And Jack Benny's Rochester. And my beloved friend, Edmund Lowe, a star I had known since I was a kid at Notre Dame Convent in San Jose and he was a dashing pre-law student at Santa Clara over the way. Eddie lived at the Country House for years after the death of his wife, Lilyan Tashman, an ex-Follies girl who was known as the

Best Dressed Woman on the Screen—but that is another story, the story of Lil and Eddie, which I told in full when I selected Lilyan as one of my gallant women in a book I wrote called *Some Are Born Great*.

"Do you remember," said Mary Pickford to me one day at Pickfair, "when film people were dying all alone in rooming houses?" I remember. So, too, did Jean Hersholt, the fine Danish actor who arrived in Hollywood shortly before World War I and became President of the Motion Picture Relief Fund and a beloved and valued citizen of our town.

Shortly before his death at a banquet honoring him when he had been President of the Fund for eighteen years Jean Hersholt said, "When I came to this country forty-four years ago, I had twenty dollars in my pocket. The good heart of the picture industry was immediately opened to a virtual stranger when I hadn't the money to pay for hospitalization. That was my basis for my interest in people who needed help."

It was Fund President Jean Hersholt and President Emeritus Mary Pickford who, in 1941 just before America's entry into World War II, turned the first shovelfuls of earth for the Country House they had dreamed into being, and five years later for the Hospital. But what gave bite to their shovels was that "good heart" of Hollywood.

It beat in the Screen Guild Theater, a concept in the fertile and kindly mind of Jules Stein, then head of MCA, wherein the Screen Actors Guild was joined by the Directors Guild and Writers Guild to produce what was for thirteen years one of the most popular shows on radio. All salaries, in the end totaling over five million dollars, going to the Fund. The first show, as I recall, starred Jack Benny, Joan Crawford and Judy Garland, but over the years I can't remember a single major star who didn't make an appearance.

It beat in donations and bequests—the John Ford Chapel, Samuel Goldwyn Plaza which includes sixteen double cottages and a recreational area, the Louis B. Mayer Memorial Theater, the Y. Frank Freeman library, the Warner and Laemmle wings at the Hospital. Cash gifts running into hundreds of thousands of dollars have come from so many of the famous faithful that it hardly seems fair to single out a few, but I am personally pleased to report $220,000 willed in memory of the Vampire, Theda Bara —and somehow tickled that the donation made by Elvis Presley in person was received in person by Chester Conklin and Frank Sinatra, although why I should be I'm not quite sure.

Nor has the social scene been neglected. You-all come! To a Friars Club benefit in the Forties which raised $300,000 in a single night—what else?—with Gene Kelly leading the ensemble and a skit featuring Humphrey Bogart, Frank Sinatra, Alan Ladd, Van Johnson, Harpo Marx *plus* midgets. To golf tournaments. To a Celebrity Benefit Race at Ontario Motor Speedway with James Garner and Paul Newman among the drivers. To an extravaganza only a few years ago at the Los Angeles Music Center celebrating the Fund's half century and featuring the greatest entertainers in show business.

Somehow it is particularly warming to see that heart beat in the people who remember. Ingrid Bergman who never comes to Hollywood without going to the Country House to visit Joe Steele, for years her publicity man. Dan Dailey who was there one day when I was visiting producer Leo Taub. Greer Garson who keeps in constant touch with her old friend Ivy Wilson, once a Follies girl and then a highly successful syndicated columnist. Almost every week sees George Bagnall, for years vice-president and treasurer at Paramount Studios and President of the Fund since the death of Jean Hersholt, hosting at lunch someone who is about to tour the Country House looking up old friends; director George Cukor, Howard Strickling who drives all the way from his ranch at Chino, Gregory Peck, head of the Fund's Development and Building Campaign. The list goes on and on. Hollywood, it would seem, has not only a "good heart" but a long memory. Could be you can't have the one without the other?

"Do you remember . . . ?" says Mary Pickford when I go to visit her.

I remember when the Motion Picture Relief Fund became the Motion Picture and *Television* Relief Fund thus making the Woodland Hills estate the Motion Picture and Television Country House and Hospital. And when the word "Relief" was

dropped from the Fund title on the request of some guests returning from the shopping center who said this legend on the side of
the Disney trams made them feel like charity cases. "Which we
are not," they said. "Each of us has contributed *something*." It
took the committee about three minutes to agree. But when Mary
and I take our trip down memory lane our chief ports of call are
the Charlotte Pickford cottage on the Country House grounds,
one of Mary's many contributions, and of course the Douglas
Fairbanks lounge. This large and charming room complete with
billiard tables and piano was built and furnished with money left
by Douglas in his will. In it are a pair of bronze busts, the one of
Douglas Fairbanks, the other of Mary Pickford. When they were
young. When they were married to each other. When they were
King and Queen of the World.

"Adela, will Douglas ever forgive me?" Mary Pickford said to
me the other day at Pickfair, and the eyes that are still so beautiful were swamped with tears.

One reason I am received at Pickfair and have an opportunity
to talk with Mary often is, I am sure, because we can talk of
Douglas. Because I knew Douglas—Mary knows I am not all that
impressed by the great Fairbanks but she likes to explain to me
how mistaken I am.

Once when I was living in the Malibu Colony, as we then
called that stretch of beach and where at the time lived Gloria
Swanson, Constance Bennett, Jack Gilbert, Wheeler and Wool-
sey—Mary's brother Jack dropped in around midnight, our hours
were twenty-four around the clock at Malibu when it really was a
motion picture colony and hideaway for stars, and he'd had a
good deal too much to drink—so few Irishmen drink well—so I
got him to bed and didn't have any conversation with him until
he got up with the sun the next morning. I look back on that as a
significant moment in my Hollywood incarnation because he
came out wrapped in a patchwork quilt my grandmother had
made for me, his dark curly hair combed into a crest, and in what
we may well call a talking hangover. After a bit, he got himself a
pint of champagne from my small liquor closet, opened it with a

pop that delighted him, and began a round-the-world journey with his sister Mary Pickford and her husband Douglas Fairbanks.

I have known most of the wits of the times—Wilson Mizner used to spend every Sunday at my beach house, I even bought a special big upholstered chair to give comfort to his ample proportions, Dorothy Parker often visited me later in Beverly Hills, and I was lucky enough to be a member of that famed round table in the Twentieth Century-Fox Commissary when Harry Brand, Mark Kelly, Doc Martin (Louella Parson's husband), Jerry Wald, and Tyrone Power used to sit there and sometimes Darryl Zanuck —who when he forgot how important he was could be as sparkling as Chinese firecrackers. But for that effervescent wit that won't travel but is as joyful as Paul Lynde on today's television or Groucho Marx in his great theater days, Jack Pickford was number one. No, Jack's wit won't travel. I can give you the words but you'll have to fill in the music.

Within fifteen minutes after he began to talk it was plain that he adored Mary, not only with the usual Irish family love and loyalty but with his omnipresent sense of humor and his actor's passion for drama.

"Though how," Jack said, his Irish blue eyes bright with question, "*how* she can be so madly in love with that faker Douglas Fairbanks, I do not know."

This was, to tell the truth, more or less my own feeling. While I realize that Douglas left a much greater heritage to today's movies and TV with his swashbuckling image than Mary with her curls, at the time I was never able to see his personal magnetism for her or anybody else. I admitted it but never shared it.

"You're not fond of Doug?" I said. "Why?"

"If," said Jack Pickford, glancing out the big windows to where the sun was rising majestically over the vast blue Pacific, "if just once I could feel that he was—was *natural*. That he spoke a single sincere and simple word, that honesty was there without—what's the word?—dissimulation. He's always *on*, to use a theater expression. Listen, I went around the world with them—*around the world*. And it took us a hell of a lot longer than eighty days. Not once—*not once*—he was always acting! I was tempted to peek in some night and see if when he was actually making love to his adored wife he forgot himself. I never did—"

"Why?" I said. "You are obviously without scruples of any kind —why didn't you peek?"

Jack Pickford gave a whoop and fell off the window seat, for a moment he sat cross-legged and then he got up and said, "I was afraid he'd still be acting and I thought the sight of *that* would finish me and I'd have to go home and I really wanted to go around the world."

I recall now sitting one day with Douglas Fairbanks in the outer room of a bathhouse he had built for himself with hot and cold pools, showers and solariums, and a real gymnasium, fully equipped with every device for the physical fitness of man. Here also on call were gymnasts and gymnasium instructors and masseurs, ready to add the final touches.

While Douglas talked about climbing an alp or a trip he hoped to make soon into the wilderness, young Jack Pickford walked through on his way to the shower with only a towel around his middle. He gave us a friendly but disinterested wave, and Douglas watched him disappear into the pool area with an expression of total incredulity on his well-tanned face.

"If," he said, and his voice had the same quality, "you can explain to me why that little guy right there can *fascinate* more women—women like Marilyn Miller and Olive Thomas, women who really fascinate the whole known world—I mean these were the tops, Marilyn was the *star* of the Follies, and that New York artist called Olive 'the most beautiful woman in the world,' they married him, and Bebe Daniels, who—I just don't get it."

"It could indicate," I said, "that there are twenty-four hours in every day 365 days in the year."

He thought about that one, and finally nodded. "All right," he said, "you mean you can only make love a pretty small proportion of the time and—"

"Once," I said, "I talked to your young brother-in-law for about twenty-four hours—and I wish, oh I wish I had a *reel*—I wish there could have been a way to record it—" I thought then of some of the hilarious comments Jack Pickford had made about Douglas and was glad he'd never have to hear them, for I felt sure Douglas couldn't survive that kind of exposure. I wondered if Mary knew—but it wouldn't matter. If you are really in love its magic, black magic as it is sometimes, can withstand even the truth. I've seen women in love, I've been there myself, but I never saw a woman more utterly under the spell than Mary. Which makes it all the more inconceivable that when he wounded her pride—her vanity—her idolatry along with the rest of the world of MARY PICKFORD—she could never forgive him.

Unfaithful to *Mary Pickford? Off with his head*. And though I *know*—for they both told me—that he flew to get on the *Chief* at Albuquerque and pleaded on his knees all the rest of the way to New York, he couldn't get through that shield of hurt pride.

In the early days I had grave difficulty in selling *true stories* about Hollywood as truth. I had to put them together as *fiction*. This I did for *Cosmopolitan* magazine and *Good Housekeeping* and *Collier's*, in the days before TV when magazines were our great at-home entertainment.

Could be that Hollywood itself was *fiction*.

Today it is hard even for me to believe the story of Mary and Doug—and yet—I was *there*.

Upon a day in June about a year after the founding of United Artists Mr. and Mrs. Douglas Fairbanks sailed for Europe on their honeymoon.

Will my people ever forgive me?

Mary knew the answer when, as she once told me, she spent most of her honeymoon on a balcony waving and bowing to crowds. They not only forgave her but the people in five European countries plus the United States turned the trip into a Royal Progress unequaled in history.

At the Ritz Carlton in New York the crowds were so thick Mary and Doug couldn't walk outside their hotel. As their ship sailed into Southampton garlands of roses were dropped from planes flying overhead. Throngs waited all night and slept in the streets of London to get a glimpse of them. And in Paris. And Rome. In England, France, Holland, Switzerland, Italy, they were pressed with invitations from crowned heads, government officials, society leaders, just plain folk. They were deluged with gifts, besieged for autographs.

Frances Marion, Mary's closest friend and favorite screen
writer, and her husband, Fred Thompson, had gone along as traveling companions. "They were prisoners of the crowds," Frances
told me. "I don't think they ever had time to eat—or sleep." She
thought Mary was overwhelmed but a little homesick. And
Douglas? Douglas was in his element. He had a naïve taste for titles and there were titles galore. He had a taste for being *on*, as
his brother-in-law had noted, and he was now *on* the biggest stage
of his life. He could not resist scaling the side of an American
warship in the harbor of Venice in full view of the adoring fans
who were then seeing him on the screen laughing and swaggering
and *leaping* in *The Mark of Zorro*. He could not resist swinging
Mary up in his arms ignoring police cordons and striding through
the pressing throngs. "You could almost," said Frances, "see his
cape flowing on the wind. Fred and I rarely caught up. I felt like a
lady-very-much-in-waiting to the King and Queen of the World."

When the couple returned to their royal residence at Pickfair in
their capital city beyond Hollywood I was sure I could hear, and
not very faintly at that, the majestic strains of *Pomp and Circumstance*.

Along about this time my husband, Ike St. Johns, and I moved
with our two children into a large white frame house on the
corner of Franklin and Bronson *in* Hollywood, and there lived on
the hill behind us a kindly gentleman named L. Frank Baum who
had already written *The Wizard of Oz*. I used to meet him taking a little soul-and-back-stretching stroll down Bronson Avenue
to Hollywood Boulevard and certainly it didn't impinge upon either of us that his book was to become the second most famous
and successful of all movies. *Gone with the Wind* held first place
for many years. Now they tell me that some of those alleged
movies that are merely a record of physical catastrophe *or* pretty
dull pornography—for after age eleven most pornography *is* pretty
dull to any adult out of the idiot class—have piled up more customers. But these are in the decline of our country into a Permis-
sive Mess where the God in whom we trusted is supposed to be
dead and skittish middle-aged women are all too much alive and I
don't think myself it is a fair comparison.

I like to remember Mr. Baum, his extraordinary twinkle of *joie de vivre*, as he companioned no doubt with the Scarecrow and the Tin Woodman and the Cowardly Lion, and of course *Dorothy*, though he didn't know *then* that Dorothy was to make a movie star immortal and the movie star, Judy Garland, was to make Dorothy immortal.

Upon occasion when we met as we strolled beneath the pepper trees that lined the sidewalks I asked him if he found what was happening around us almost as amazing as what happened when Dorothy was whirled from the plains of Kansas into Oz. He said he did.

Hollywood at that point was the land of the Munchkins on the very edge of the new country but we were all on our way willynilly to the Emerald City—or something quite like it—and the yellow brick road led straight to Pickfair where all kinds of wizardry was going on.

First let us consider the disappearance, without a puff of smoke, of Owen Moore and Beth Sully Fairbanks.

It was unthinkable that America's Sweetheart, now Mary, Queen of the World, who looked like the Littlest Angel and could be seen on the screen in any hamlet as *Pollyanna*, The Glad Girl, had divorced with a suitable financial settlement a husband in Nevada; that King Douglas, that cavalier *sans peur et sans reproche*, or as we might say today Mr. Clean, had been divorced by the mother of his nine-year-old son, Douglas Fairbanks, Jr., citing as correspondent an Unnamed Woman—whose name anyone of us could have supplied anytime during the last three years. Presto. It was unthinkable, so of course nobody thought it.

Now let us look at the isolated hunting lodge in that nonplace to become Beverly Hills. Two very important artists have created a world-around illusion. And what have we here? A palace! Fourteen live-in servants, solid gold dinner service, a footman behind every chair. The Royal Couple of Hollywood entertaining the King and Queen of Siam, Crown Princess Frederica of Prussia, the Duke and Duchess of Alba, Babe Ruth, Amelia Earhart, Albert Einstein, Lindbergh, the Crown Prince of Japan, Alfonso XIII, the ex-King of Spain. The glamorous Lord and Lady Mountbatten honeymoon there. Within a few years mansions, like magic mushrooms, have sprung up all over the landscape, and when a titled pair arrive at Pickfair with an entourage of seventeen, Charlie Chaplin's is at hand an acre or so next door to take up the overflow.

One afternoon when Colleen Moore and I were having a dish of tea with Mary Pickford Rogers, Mary began, as she needs must do, to recall those days of grandeur. As she discoursed on the problems of entertaining royalty, the disruption of protocol at table since Douglas insisted on sitting at her left hand, she looked thoroughly English—which she was on her father's side. This, I may say, was the least endearing side of our Mary. But Mother Charlotte's maiden name was Hennessey, her people came from County Kerry, and in Mary the Hennessey would out. Suddenly she dismissed her worrisome crystal place-card holders with a wave of her hand and began to tell instead of a day when one of her royal ladies took a tumble on the tennis court and required a bath. "I took her to my own suite," said Mary looking thoroughly *Irish*, "shut her in and stood outside the door saying to myself, 'Imagine you, Gladys Smith, of Toronto, Canada, with the Queen of Siam in your bathtub.'"

Truth to tell, I think we all felt a little like that.

Picture if you will the city of Los Angeles—this included Hollywood which is not now nor ever has been more than a district within that city—as it was when Mary Pickford arrived there on location with D. W. Griffith barely ten years before she married Douglas Fairbanks. A sun-baked Spanish pueblo enlarged to a little over 300,000 souls by oilmen, cattlemen, citrus growers, riffraff from the Gold Rush, only recently rescued from a turbulent and bloody past and converted to righteousness by militant churchmen and *clubwomen*—of whom my own Aunty Blanche was one. Thus I may tell you that the signs on rooming houses which read "No Dogs or Actors Allowed" meant *movie* actors. They were considered a dangerous and immoral species and my Aunty Blanche would have questioned the sanity of any prophet willing to foretell that one of them, and a not very important one at that, would one day within my lifetime occupy the governor's mansion at Sacramento and make a good run at the White House itself.

As each year brought more and more of this ragtag and bobtail swarming like locusts to spend their winter in our sunlight, building ramshackle studios or converting the Eastside Zoo, a Chinese laundry, or the old car barn to their purposes, there was real indignation. Including a committee who called themselves the Conscientious Citizens who had over 10,000 signatures on a protest to force the invaders *out*. Before they succeeded the motion picture progressed from "flicker" to "film," few citizens objected to hosting this shiny new industry *if* the people therein kept themselves to themselves. Which they did. Actually they weren't interested then or later in anyone or anything not connected with the *movies*.

.It was the elfin spell of Mabel Normand that forged my first real link with the *movie* actors.

The second—the which expanded link by link into the tie that binds—was my abiding taste for excitement and drama. Newspapers and newspapermen were my first love (and still are) because they had it all, but there was something about these extraordinary young people, a tempo so swift it caught you up like the cadence of marching music—*You'd better move fast or you're left!* . . . *You're right!* . . . *You'd better move fast or you're left!* . . . *You're right!* . . . *Hurry up!* . . . *one, two* . . . *Hurry up!* . . . *three, four* . . .—they didn't know where they were going yet but they were determined to get there without pause.

Early on there were maybe a thousand in the entire industry (there were eight thousand at MGM alone when I worked there thirty-odd years later). Everybody knew everybody, they worked together, had breakfast, lunch and dinner together, ate out of each other's stewpots, slept on each other's couches, traded whatever money was around back and forth over the poker table. It was like one big, lively party. No one owned a car, or a house, they were poised like quicksilver ready on the instant to *move fast*—back to the stage—back to New York—or simply to vanish into the cyclone that had first dumped them in our backyard.

Until Mary Pickford arrived from New York around 1917 to take up permanent residence in a large square rented house with a veranda on Sunset Boulevard.

Then everybody unpacked.

They had, as it were, arrived in the land of the Munchkins. My husband and I along with them. For shortly there I was, a

fledgling Mother Confessor contributing to *Photoplay*. And Ike
was a *press agent* at Triangle Studios.

The Hollywood Press Agent. You will meet him from time to
time throughout these pages.

If it didn't happen that way, it should have!
This, according to my son Richard who had it duly inscribed
for my office, should be my motto.

Well, maybe. Upon the proper occasion (which is fiction) or
when the temptation with fact is irresistible. I do recall that once,
when I was writing of Margaret Sanger, in three separate drafts
my typewriter announced that her mother died in childbirth. Now
somewhere within those layers of the mind I knew the *facts*. But I
ask you—Margaret Sanger was the sixth of eleven children. Her
mother, to whom she was devoted, died at forty-eight, her father,
of whom she took a dim view at all times, died at eighty.
Medically her mother's death was attributed to tuberculosis, but
daughter Margaret didn't dedicate the rest of her life to fighting
tuberculosis, she spent it pioneering *birth control*. You see what I
mean?

Should such an error get by my conscious mind I am sure to
hear from my editor immediately, or if it gets by *him*, from my
readers immediately thereafter. For a writer to mix fact and
fiction is a no-no!

There was, however, in my Hollywood, a freewheeling, happy-
go-lucky group who could and did have it both ways. They could
adopt that motto and turn fact into fiction or vice versa as the situation indicated. They were called *press agents*. If sometimes
Hollywood itself was fiction you may be sure they had a hand in
it.

It is true that the press agent started with the advance man sent
out to ballyhoo the Barnum and Bailey Circus, but it was brought
to a fine art by the independent press agents of Hollywood and in
the publicity departments of the Hollywood studios. Within its
ranks were some of the wisest, wittiest, most loyal, innovative and
imaginative agents I've ever known. And I have to add that the
greatest of these were first *newspapermen*.

I give you now the late great Russell Birdwell; when I first knew him we were reporters covering a particularly nasty kidnaping in Tacoma, Washington, both for the Hearst Service. In due time Birdwell became the most outstanding as well as highest priced of the independent press agents.

Birdwell turned fiction into fact when David O. Selznick hired him to publicize *Gone with the Wind*. He took the Cinderella story, placed the glass slipper in the hands of David O., and sent him forth with great fanfare in search of the unknown beauty to play Scarlett O'Hara. The suspense built in the press for months with stories and pictures and not only every female star in and out of Hollywood but every extra girl, every beauty contest winner in every state, every star-struck fan dreamed that she might be the one the slipper fit.

Or Bird could turn fact into fiction, take an unknown girl from the San Fernando Valley who had given her life to Christ when she was six, helped her widowed mother raise four kid brothers and take care of a small ranch, gone steady with one guy since she was fifteen, and using only her physical endowments, the which were not all that uncommon around our town, plus a haystack, a jersey blouse, large billboards and a tape measure to thoroughly document what was visible to the naked eye, create Jane Russell, *the* Sex Symbol of the Forties. Birdwell made a Big Star of Jane *over a year before anyone saw her on the screen* in Howard Hughes' *The Outlaw*. So potent was this illusion that although Jane married her high school sweetheart, football hero Robert Waterfield, and stayed married to him for twenty-two years, spent her leisure hours helping her family build their own chapel in the Valley, adopted three children and founded WAIFS, an international organization to help other would-be parents and orphans get together, the public continued to ignore the facts and believe in the sexy sultry image created by Russell Birdwell.

Or let us take the very rich young lady who wished to become known, recognized, as it were, by the Hollywood aristocracy, not to crash the movies, mind, but to call her presence and identity to the attention of headwaiters, hostesses, columnists et al. For a sizable fee Birdwell agreed to undertake the assignment. First he had her photographed full length and beautifully accoutered and she went home to prepare for the long siege—not knowing Birdwell. Bird simply took the entire back page of both of Hollywood's rival trade papers which are read assiduously by the entire industry and its satellites, cut the photo in half and placed one half in each paper. On the top half, which appeared in the *Hollywood Reporter*, under the lady's name appeared a caption which read: *See Variety*. Upon the lower half in *Variety* it read: *See the Reporter*.

I am reminded that my son Mac, at one time editor of the *Hollywood Reporter* and currently business agent for the Publicists Guild of America, was for some years a reporter on the New York *Mirror*. In his days as an independent publicist it was the newspaper training that gave him the ability to know what *is* a story, and how to keep a story *alive* for more than one day.

When Mac was working on *Cold Turkey*, a picture in which Dick Van Dyke quit smoking, the company went on a forty-day location to Greenfield, Iowa, pop. 2,700. Greenfield, according to my son, is a town of great charm but not a focal point for the eyes of the world. The problem was how to draw the attention of the media to Greenfield. He and producer Norman Lear, one of the few creative producers around these days—and Norman, I now recall, was once a publicist—considered this. And went to the Mayor. The Mayor passed an ordinance and took it to the people. It caught the people's fancy and Mac spread the word. Over the next weeks the national press, TV cameras, *Time*, *Newsweek*, and a senator from Utah descended on this small Iowa town.

The people of Greenfield had quit smoking for thirty days.

If the Emerald City isn't *green*, my children, it *should* be. Just put on these spectacles with the green glass. . . .

Among the earliest of the early press agents were four good friends of Ike's and mine who set the pattern for all time for the studio publicity department—the studio publicity man. All of them came out of the sports department of the old Los Angeles *Tribune*, Arch Reeves—sports editor, Harry Brand—his assistant, Al Wilkie—sportswriter Howard Strickling—office boy. Al and Arch went to Paramount, Harry to Fox, Howard to Louis B. Mayer. Their primary purpose was ballyhoo and I daresay Howard was responsible for presenting that handsome homebody, Francis X. Bushman, as the EXALTED SUPERB SOULFUL STUPENDOUS STAR.

I know they banded together with other publicity pioneers to create the Wampas Baby Stars, youngsters they deemed likely to achieve stardom, and launched them yearly with great excitement and much to-do at a lavish banquet. My husband, Ike, and Danny Danker dreamed up the first advertising tie-ins putting male stars in the national magazines and on billboards jauntily waving from Stutz automobiles, the ladies displayed glamorously garbed in large DeMille type bathrooms holding a small bar of Lux soap.

They turned the dingy little red Santa Fe Station not far from the old Plaza in downtown Los Angeles into a newspaper *beat*, the train then being our only link with New York. And there were some of us always coming or going on the Santa Fe *Chief*.

Famous trains. There have been a few, although there are fewer and fewer every year, more's the pity. Their very names conjure up images.

> *The Orient Express*—Paris to Istanbul
> *The Flying Scot*—London to Edinburgh
> *The Blue Train*—Paris to Monte Carlo
> *The Golden Arrow*—London to Paris
> *The Santa Fe Chief*—Hollywood to New York

To those of us who lived and worked in Hollywood the *Chief* had a special magic, it provided a little oasis of peace in the headlong pace of our lives, a few short days in which we did nothing with a clear conscience, attended no story conferences, saw no cameras, world famous stars took their hair down and put their feet up. We visited each other's drawing rooms or stayed holed up in our own, were thoroughly pampered by protective porters who brought us Utah celery or Colorado trout, or a bucket of ice with a fan to blow over it when we crossed the desert.

And there, at the beginning or end of every trip, was the drab little Santa Fe depot but the press agents had it *en fête* for the arrival or departure of the stars, the red carpet treatment, armloads of flowers, dignitaries, flashbulbs, crowds of fans. Later the fashion shifted to the Pasadena station, the publicity departments simply moved the red carpet.

The press agents' first task was to create the appropriate illusion. When the snares and pitfalls and disasters began to catch up with us, as they had in the Arbuckle and Taylor scandals, as they would with Wally Reid—and when Mr. Hearst brought Louella Parsons out from New York as the first *gossip* columnist—came the second phase which was to *preserve the illusion*, to keep un-savory items *out* of the papers and their clients *out* of trouble. Thus they became troubleshooters, and *friends*, involved in the personal lives of the stars and moguls, expected to arrange mar-riages, divorces, parties, funerals, as well as interviews and public-ity campaigns.

As of today we have also the public relations counselor, invented when one Ivy Lee gave John D. Rockefeller a pocketful of dimes to pass around in the hope of changing his public image, although whatinhell *is* a public relations counselor I have yet to discover except that, like today's lawyer, his work is dark and mysterious, he never goes to *court*. My surmise is that the Hollywood public relations counselor sits in an air-conditioned office and says "yes" to his clients, something no good press agent would dream of doing. It was by saying "no" at the right time that the best of the early press agents rose to the top of the industry. And rise they did.

John McCormick, Colleen Moore's first husband, came from a San Francisco paper into the publicity department at First Na-tional and wound up head of the studio. Perry Lieber, for years head of publicity at RKO, was one of the handful of men Howard Hughes really *trusted*. Ike St. Johns was vice-president in charge of advertising and publicity at Universal Studios under Carl Laemmle, Jr. Howard Strickling retired as vice-president of Metro-Goldwyn-Mayer.

There was nothing these men couldn't do—and their loyalty was prodigious extending—well, let me tell you my favorite story about Howard Strickling. Howard had gone to a famous under-taking firm to complete the arrangements for the majestic services in the synagogue and out for the funeral of Louis B. Mayer—after all religious, floral, musical and other details were settled Howard asked automatically, "And what time do you want me to have Mr. Mayer there?"

John Gilbert
Rudolph Valentino
Irving Thalberg
Paul Bern
Carey Wilson.

I put them in separate paragraphs like that because I was to look at them that way myself. These young men lived close by our house in Hollywood. Jack and Rudy in moderate and separate establishments on the hillside amidst the poppies and lupines and Peter the Hermit used to amble down from his cave high above, looking like an Old Testament prophet with his beard, his staff, his flowing robes, and try to redeem them from the evil. So Jack Gilbert told me. I wish, how I wish, he had succeeded—while there was still time. Irving, Paul and Carey lived together within hailing distance in a California bungalow of dark brown shingles. We used to hobnob from time to time, shouting over the back fence in gay inconsequence. Sometimes they would stop to hold conversation with my small daughter Elaine or my even smaller son Billy, and once I remember young Thalberg, who seemed a well-mannered youth with a pleasant way about him, came over to take a closer look at a birthday party I was having for Elaine in our garage.

I am trying to paint for you a picture of the Neighborhood, as they have it on Sesame Street, for that is what Hollywood was for the few short years between the time Mary Pickford arrived to stay—with Douglas Fairbanks in what I can only call Hot Pursuit —and their marriage.

Over on Las Palmas, Wally and Dorothy Reid lived in a small gray bungalow, Colleen Moore and her Grandmother Kelly in another on Fountain. The house occupied by the Gish girls and their mother boasted a large sleeping porch. The only estate we could claim was a very modest one directly across the street from Ike and me on Franklin Avenue and belonged to another pioneer producer, one of the great ones, Thomas H. Ince. His was an estate by virtue of a large lawn upon which were both a fishpond and a marble bench.

When our young stars married they went no further than the nearby Wilshire or Los Feliz districts, there to establish themselves in big square stucco houses of what we might call California Italian design, all with four square bedrooms and two white-tiled baths, and usually decorated in a kind of Grand-Rapids-department-store style.

The ragtag and bobtail, the waifs, strays, and starveling pioneers of yesterday had *arrived*.

Life was good. Our town was beautiful. By day a beneficent sun filled crystal air with light for movie making. The palm trees etched against a dark blue sky spangled with stars, the scent of sage and eucalyptus and orange blossoms and hill earth and sea foam were part of every Hollywood night. Thus our merry bachelors and unattached ladies made light love, occasionally between darkness and dawn, most often between Friday and Monday.

The social life of the young married set was mild—I do not say in all cases as I shall tell, but in the main—and was also conducted between Friday and Monday. The rest of the time the entire industry labored like ditchdiggers. On Friday nights the men went to the fights, the ladies grouped in Hen Parties. Saturday night affairs were most often in the homes catered by the genteel Pig 'n' Whistle, as were the Sunday brunches, since Hollywood was not yet really geared to servants. Drinking was light—the *drunks* of course we had always with us, but where the alcoholic obsession had not taken hold, their careers came first—health, sleep, beauty, before pleasure. And yet—at every gathering the real *pleasure* was shoptalk. The *movies*. This was the common obsession.

So there we were.

What with homes, an automobile in every garage, money in the bank, and being able to make *movies* twelve to fourteen hours a day five days a week, who could ask for anything more?

Then came *Pickfair!*

In the space of a breath it seemed we were in a land of vintage wine and caviar in iced swan boats, glittering jewels and French chefs, aviaries and peacocks in formal gardens.

In sheer headlong flight we were all off to make of the Emerald City a reality.

The Stately Homes of Beverly Hills during the short, glorious Golden Age of the Twenties. True, they were scattered hither and yon, as were the studios of "Hollywood," but because of Mary and Doug, "Beverly Hills" became a word symbol that casts a spell unto this day.

If it seems that I am coming to our Royal Couple by a circuitous route it is because it seems necessary to show their capital city, the climate and conditions thereof, during the years of their ascendancy.

Much much later, when the Golden Age was tarnished beyond recall, Colleen Moore, by now Mrs. Homer Hargrave of Chicago, came west to sell her baronial Bel Air estate. She had rented it over the years—to Marlene Dietrich when she first came over from Germany, to Countess Dorothy di Frasso when the Countess was playing a leading role in the love life of Gary Cooper, eventually to Bruce Cabot and his playboy pals. When Mrs. Hargrave, at coffee in her Chicago apartment, read that Errol Flynn had been accused of *rape* in *her* house on St. Pierre Road, she decided to sell. It was a sentimental journey for the two of us, friends for so many years, strolling around the two acres of gardens and orchards, past the Olympic-size swimming pool, the guesthouse, the dark-shadowed private theater. In the house itself Colleen admitted it was so big she had never been in all the rooms, "but Adela," said Mrs. Hargrave, who besides being an expert on Modern Art and Thai temples, knows her architecture, "isn't this an outstanding example of Early Hollywood Movie Star?"

Few such examples, except for Pickfair, still stand, or if they do they have been so altered as to be barely recognizable. The original mansions came in all shapes and sizes—English manors, Spanish haciendas, Italian villas, to say nothing of Hollywood French Provincial. As the neighborhood dispersed to regroup in their Stately Homes, swimming pools and tennis courts were *de rigueur* with a little something extra thrown in. Thus Cecil B. De-Mille built for himself *two* houses on the ridge of a hill, one for his family, the other for his office and retreat. Tom and Vickey Mix had *two* enormous drawing rooms, one all gilt and crystal and Louis XVI for Vickey, the other early Wild West for Tom, and on the roof of their Italian villa Tom's beloved TM Bar brand blazed in electric lights. Studio executive Carl Laemmle maintained a private zoo; in Benedict Canyon Valentino blasted away half a mountain to keep his Arabian horses happy; near to Hollywood and straight out of the Arabian Nights rose the exotic Garden of Allah, home of Alla Nazimova. The unusual feature about Chaplin's mansion, which we called Breakaway House, was that it had been built by Charlie's studio carpenters when they were not otherwise employed. Unaccustomed to building foursquare they had created a fine confection from which bits and pieces were constantly detaching to roll into the canyon below.

What with press agentry on the rise, and me selling original stories and treatments to Tom Mix, Richard Barthelmess, Gloria Swanson, and my first novel, *Skyrocket*, as a film for Peggy Hopkins Joyce, a diamond-loving lady for whom the words Gold Digger had to be coined, Ike and I joined the merry madness with an English manse near the little Quaker community of Whittier. Complete with swimming pool and tennis court, we also had a stable full of hungry horses for Elaine and Billy, a spring-fed stream that regularly overflowed its banks and wiped out my rose garden, and sixteen acres of very expensive walnut trees. Director Frank Lloyd, much taken with our country life, built a Colonial mansion with great white pillars, a curved staircase, and an enormous crystal chandelier, across the dirt road from us.

On a day when I was sitting beside my pool gazing down on my rippling stream and eating my very own walnuts, Robert, our butler, announced Mr. Harold Lloyd on the phone. Harold was in what I must call a state. He had, so he said, just gotten the architect's plans for his *house*, he did not like them atall, atall. He admired my house very much, and would I please come right over to Beverly Hills and *help* him?

Now Harold Lloyd, that master of Gag Comedy, who started at three dollars a day on the extra bench, was a very sensible young man and when he and his wife, Mildred Davis, once his leading lady, embarked upon a stately home, Harold did it in a most sensible way. First he bought eighteen acres and spent the first million on gardens. By the time he was finished his Green Acres was probably the most extravagant of all Beverly Hills estates—a nine-hole golf course, a champion-size squash court, fountains patterned after those in Italy's famous Villa d'Este, a large waterfall that cascaded over a cliff to become a canoe course, a hothouse where Mildred could grow her own orchids, thirty-three servants including gardeners and a gatekeeper. *But* Harold wouldn't build his *house* and *move in* with Mildred and their two children until he had enough *income from his investments* to pay for the upkeep of the whole place. This came about before he reached the age of thirty and at that point, amidst the fountains and gardens and lush lawns, he and I laid out his house with wooden stakes and *string*. Later, when the thirty-odd rooms were completed, Mildred Lloyd, a little Quaker lass from Philadelphia, as she walked from empty room to empty room knowing full well that somehow all of them had to be furnished, said wistfully, "It looked so *cozy* in string."

Over and above all this was our Mme. Pompadour, born Miss Marion Davies to us, at whose disposal Mr. Hearst placed his Enchanted Castle at San Simeon, and when magnificent beach houses for weekend revelry began to extend along the Santa Monica sand, gave her that beach establishment of her very own with four tennis courts, a marble swimming pool, and a house so big it was later turned into a hotel.

Around us opulence rolled like lava from a volcano. Everywhere were foreign cars, gowns and furs from Paris, boots from Savile Row, rugs from Persia, art from Europe and the Orient. Pipe organs were more common than pianos. And our *bathrooms*.

When William C. DeMille wrote his "Hollywood Saga" he said of his brother Cecil, "He made of the bathroom a delightful resort which undoubtedly had its effect upon bathrooms of the whole nation." Now I am prepared to question whether anything Cecil B. did could be termed "delightful" but I will not deny his effect upon the bathrooms of Hollywood. They came in onyx, in marble, in mirrors, with murals, with fur rugs; tubs were sunken or elevated or shaped like swans or gondolas. Whether these were used as resorts deponent knoweth not, but I do know they were the source of much speculation. We could always tell when there was a variable wind in the love life of Jack Gilbert because he began at once to redecorate his guest bath. Black marble with solid gold fixtures was Greta Garbo, whom he hoped to marry. Pink marble mirrors were stage star Ina Claire, whom he did marry. White marble and silver were delicate little Virginia Bruce, his last wife.

In all this we were aided and abetted by the decorator, the architect, the landscape designer, the jeweler, the courtier, who delighted to show this *nouveau riche* society how to live—and spend.

Midst all this grandeur our social life altered. We played bridge instead of poker. We had a British colony wherein C. Aubrey Smith captained the cricket club. We rode English instead of Western saddles when we took our Sunday promenades on the bridle path that ran down the middle of Beverly Hills. Will Rogers introduced polo. In the place of the genteel caterer were highly trained major-domos and servants who unobtrusively taught very talented and decorative actors and actresses how to play the roles of ladies and gentlemen. Or Lords and Ladies. Or King and Queen, as the case might be.

Once when we were playing charades at the Hill, my home when I worked at nearby MGM in the later years—Wendell Corey, Van Johnson, Mickey Rooney, Colleen Gray, who had just made a sensational hit with Richard Widmark in *Kiss of Death*, Frances Marion and an assortment of my newspaper friends—we had been working our way through T. S. Eliot. Who started it I do not remember, but we had gone from *The Love Song of J. Alfred Poufrock*—

> I grow old . . . I grow old . . .
> I shall wear the bottoms of my trousers rolled.

To *Murder in the Cathedral*—

> The last temptation is the greatest treason:
> To do the right deed for the wrong reason.

Mickey Rooney, who hadn't uttered a word in some time, stood up, got center stage with some little effort, said "I know places where this game is played on a lower plane," and went home.

I do not wish to give the false impression that everything and everyone in Hollywood during the reign of Mary and Doug, including the Royal Pair themselves, achieved flawless elegance. Nor that all of us were paying our way out of the income from investments. Far otherwise. A lot of us had never heard of investments, let alone interest on same—which is why so many of these reckless, untrained young millionaires died broke.

Hollywood in the Twenties showered gold with one hand and took it back with the other. There has been no other place where fortune and debt could lie down together as odd but frequent bedfellows. There has been no other place where the disaster of sudden riches was accompanied by the flattery and adulation such as the world had not known since a Corsican corporal became Emperor of France.

In the Klondike, at Kimberley, in the California gold rush of '49, a man might find himself a millionaire even while he tightened his belt against the belly-hunger that rode him. But it would take him a long time to learn to spend the gold. A man can buy only so much liquor and so many women. The subtle lures of extravagance, the standards of tinsel grandeur, the methods of spending money which took the rich centuries to devise, were generally lacking.

Hollywood was different. It was like a fantastic fair, where the wheel on one side of the midway provided unexpected wealth, and the irresistible opportunities for squandering amid the baubles of the gaudy booths on the other side tempted it back again.

There was no place in the world where it was so easy to learn to spend money—where the spending of money was so necessary to keep up the illusions, where spending money was one of the few pastimes for a hard-working people.

Splurge. Front. Show. They were monstrous.

The elegant veneer of our society was paper thin, and just below the surface we had also to accommodate thoroughly unsettled, suddenly liberated young women, bootleggers, wild hot jazz music, this both inside our stately halls and further afield, the game was often played on a lower plane.

One of our first playgrounds, the Vernon Country Club, was a combination of the Barbary Coast, a cakewalk dance hall, a discotheque, and a superexclusive restaurant. There was the Sunset Inn where we could dance all night to the music of Abe Lyman. The Montmarte, a smart club, where Joan Crawford was snatched from the arms of meat-packing heir Mike Cudahy by his irate Mamma. Fatty Arbuckle's. After scandal drove him off the screen Fatty opened a place at the beach. We had the Biltmore Hotel ballroom, where were held our Mayfair subscription dances which we thought were *some* punkins, the Cocoanut Grove, the old Hollywood Hotel *and* joints and dives and gambling hells and a favorite drugstore where we went for ice cream sodas.

Yes yes, as I have said. A glory that was Greece, a grandeur that was Rome, a golden slum with tinsel trimmings, the Land of Oz with Hammerheads and Winged Monkeys and deadly poppy fields as well as the Emerald City. This was the background for the entire tapestry of the Golden Years.

And at the heart of it all stood Pickfair—the center of our aspirations. And Mary and Doug living the Perfect Marriage—the focus of our admiration.

I have called it the most important marriage in Hollywood because this young couple was the strongest stabilizing influence in our explosive milieu.

Mary and Doug during the years of their reign.

Together and separately they opened bazaars, reviewed parades, laid cornerstones, headed charity drives, set and condemned fashions in clothes, manners, society. All this Mary did with a kind of dedicated self-abnegation, Douglas with a robust goodwill.

It was as though Mary said, as had young Queen Victoria on coming to the throne, "I will be good," and meant, "I will live up to what is expected of me, and be *here* as long as my people need me." And I am sure Queen Mother Charlotte backed her to the hilt. If Douglas said, "I will be good," I'm certain he meant, "I'll go along with this as long as it amuses me," and for a good many years it did.

For despite shock waves of scandal and tragedy that rocked our community, Pickfair stood *firm*. *The rock*. Thus we viewed with alarm the first signs that there might be a crack in it. The loss of her mother came first; truly Mary was wild with grief. By the time she somewhat recovered Douglas had grown restless—Mary, for the first time in her life without Charlotte's wise counsel, fought for control. I can describe in a brief scene better than I can tell of the beginning of the end of the romance we did not believe could ever end.

There we were on the sand at Fairford, their beach house in Santa Monica, Doug, *young* Doug, and his wife, Joan Crawford, when Mary appeared. She wore a deliriously becoming outfit, at once making us all too conscious of the whole messy business of bathing suits, sunburn, oil, sand. Jumping up to kiss her hand Doug said, "Let's go see this dance marathon up on the pier. One couple has been dancing seventy hours . . ."

Mary said gently, "Douglas, love, you know we can't be seen in a place like that." She stood there tiny, tiptoe, enchanting, still Douglas said to her, "Tupper, love, your steel hand is showing through your velvet glove."

Trouble in Paradise. No other woman, no no. Douglas wished to consort with the whole wide world and take Mary with him. Mary was only happy in her protected ivory tower. Douglas wished to go to far places and *do* things. Except for rare state visits to foreign lands, the little Queen wished to stay in her Capital City and make movies. And so we have Douglas, no longer amused, rushing madly off to Europe after each picture—and Mary remaining silently alone at Pickfair. And then—well— maybe Edna St. Vincent Millay said it best:

> The fabric of my faithful love
> No power shall dim or ravel
> Whilst I stay here,—but oh, my dear,
> If I should ever travel!*

Poor Douglas, alone in England, encountered that other woman —and in his innocent snobbery failed to recognize just another come-hither chorus girl whose maiden name was Hawkes, because she had married a title and was called *Lady* Sylvia Ashley. Even when rumors reached Mary she maintained her silence. Douglas was still very much in love with her, and she knew it—a woman does. Also Mary had suffered much from Doug's excessive and, if I may say so, unfounded jealousy—of her mother, her family, any man who ever looked at her—and I'm sure Mary, the woman, could have overlooked My Lady, the wound she had sustained would have healed. But Douglas was still *on*. When a photograph of him clinging to the balcony outside Lady Sylvia's room

---

* From the poem "To the Not Impossible Him," from *A Few Figs from Thistles*, by Edna St. Vincent Millay (Harper & Brothers, Publishers, 1922). Used by permission of Norma Millay.

was published, he had offended against her Public Image, MARY
PICKFORD, and although Doug fought the divorce, begged and
pleaded and vowed undying love until the eleventh hour, Mary
could not forgive him.

Thus the Perfect Marriage ended. After fifteen years.

"Will Douglas ever forgive me?"

The last time I saw Douglas was at Claridge's in London, he
said wistfully, "Have you seen Mary lately? How is she?" I feel
sure now that he had already forgiven her. He knew his Mary.
"Pride means a lot to people in our business." A coin with two
sides, that one. It could build the Motion Picture Country House
—or topple a throne.

Two or three times when we met here and there in our newspaper days, George Jean Nathan would say to me, "You knew
Lillian Gish well, didn't you? Doesn't it restore your faith in
human nature to realize she was desired in marriage by more dis-
criminating men than any other woman who ever lived?" I agreed
that it did . . . I still agree.

It occurs to me, champions having been much on my mind this
last week what with Elizabeth II celebrating her Silver Jubilee
and Seattle Slew coming from nowhere and nothing to win the
Triple Crown, that Lillian Gish is a champion among the great
artists produced by Hollywood. I once asked Jack Dempsey what,
with all the talent around, it took to *make* a champion. He said,
"You have to be able to do it on Wednesday night in Madison
Square Garden—and keep on doing it."

The Big Four could live up to the first half—but what then?
Douglas Fairbanks—a cavalier is always young—died before he
had to face the test. But Griffith? Chaplin? Pickford? We have
seen the end of D. W. Griffith. Charlie Chaplin lived for twenty-
five years in self-imposed exile in Switzerland. Queen Mary in self-
imposed retirement at Pickfair. It is that Fifth One, Miss Lillian
Gish, who is still to be seen on TV, on the New York stage, who
has toured the country with a one-woman show, *The Art of the
Film.* It is Lillian who sixty-five years after her first appearance

with Griffith, is making another motion picture; and believe me, Miss Gish doesn't have to work for a *living*.

And this, too, says something to me about human nature. "A truly great artist willing to sacrifice all ego . . ."

A rose is a rose is a rose is a rose—or words to that effect.

Chapter Four

The Beautiful and the Damned

Valentino, the all-time sex symbol among stars for women, wasn't ever at any time attractive to *women*—as a man in person to women in person. I will always remember spending an entire afternoon sitting on a black velvet divan with *Valentino* at his home in the Hollywood Hills and wondering whether the Giants had taken two games from the Dodgers again in a doubleheader in Brooklyn!

One man—one man only—in all Hollywood history who was the Prince Charming, the Idol, the irresistible man to all women —*all* women.

His name was Wallace Reid.

I have seen a brilliant New York society lady, as they were then called, put a half-million-dollar emerald necklace in the hands of his valet just to let her *in* to his dressing room. I have seen famed beauties from all around the world follow him from room to room at a Hollywood party. I was there when his wife, Dorothy, to whom he was quite honestly devoted, used to drag them out from under the bed, from inside the music cabinets, from attic and cellar and car pits.

Wally was—yes, Prince Charming, Sir Launcelot, and by some quirk of the Fates that made of him first their odds-on favorite and at the last the object of their incredible mockery—Wally was a star in the days of the silent film, before music had come to be part of the appeal and charm of a Crosby or a Sinatra or a Nelson Eddy—Wally was a first class musician. A composer, a singer, a violinist—he could even play the not yet popular saxophone.

Remembering his looks, his prowess as an athlete, his irresistible personality, combined with his musical ability, I wonder what would have happened if he had toured the country as stars did later. Those first crushes that greeted Sinatra at the Paramount in New York at the beginning of his career, Frankie had a great voice—he sang with sex appeal and warmth—and he looked like Frank Sinatra. Imagine if he had looked like Wallace Reid, the handsomest man any of us ever saw.

As we came into our Golden Years, Wally was already established as the world's Matinee Idol and the most—I know it is difficult to use the word *beautiful* about a man and not make him seem less than *man*ly especially in these our Decadent Days—but Wally Reid was as beautiful as a Greek god, or the statues of Greek gods whom we are allowed to call beautiful—Apollo, the ancient deity of light, healing, music, poetry, prophecy, youthful *manly* beauty. He was as far as I know the only amateur, as it were, allowed to drive in the Indianapolis Road Race, for if there was one thing the great professional race drivers like Ralph De Palma and Barney Oldfield and David Bruce Brown could do without on the dangerous course it was some movie star amateur. That way indeed lay death and destruction. Yet they welcomed Wally, who didn't finish in the money but didn't do any damage either and who had the most wonderful glorious time of his life and thereafter kept on making automobile race movies for as long as his studio would let him. He had a stable of racing cars himself and used to drive to the Lasky Studios on Vine Street in a different one every day. My house was between Wally and the studio and he stopped by most mornings, sometimes to talk to me in my role as Mother Confessor, sometimes just to say Hello and play with Elaine and Billy.

Oh yes—he was a tormented soul.

Oh yes again. I have a few hates. Much as I try to rid myself of them, I do not believe that hate is the opposite of love—the opposite of love is indifference, apathy—*I know that thou art neither cold nor hot: I would thou wert cold or hot.*

Concerning Cecil B. DeMille I am cold and hot all right.

For I think he destroyed Wally Reid, who died and wanted to

die before he was thirty-five. Wally was young—supersensitive, not only a gifted musician but a passing-fair poet. Life swept him with emotions of violence—but he loved it, he loved life and music and driving automobiles as fast as they could be made to go.

Clark Gable was a very strong man. Born on a farm, growing up in a small town with a strong stepmother, poetry and music were all very well in their place—but their place was not central in Clark's life. He married early a very wise, rich, older woman who helped to safeguard and build his career. And men admired and sought Gable just as much as did women. He had as his closest friend one of the all-time great men and directors of Hollywood, Victor Fleming, and of course, Howard Strickling, and Clark had his part in a tough war on equal terms with other men.

Wallace Reid was born into the theater—his father was the well-known author of some appalling, dreadful but very successful melodramas and his mother, Bertha, who kept in close touch with him always, was an actress-singer. He began an acting career in New York when he was a kid, and before he was twenty-two came to Hollywood not perhaps with D. W. Griffith, but to work for him in *The Birth of a Nation.* It was a small part, the blacksmith who rescued Mae Marsh from a villain, but Wally Reid was so outstanding in it that it made a star of him before the picture was twenty-four hours old. He was a guy who really started at the top and maybe that was too bad.

Cecil B. DeMille spotted him at once—

I am carried back to a luncheon in Cecil B. DeMille's elegant suite of offices at the Famous Players-Lasky Studios, which along about now became known as Paramount. I was working then for both the Hearst Service and *Photoplay* and Cecil B., who was already making such smashes as *Why Change Your Wife* and *Don't Change Your Husband,* was part of my beat. I was supposed to know what he was up to at all times because he was always up to something and usually it was news.

When I said earlier that D. W. Griffith's name had stellar drawing power unequaled by anyone on the dark side of the camera until Walt Disney came along, I could hear the movie buffs breathing heavily—or wrathfully—because I omitted Cecil B.

DeMille. Let me say that this was a purposeful omission and I stand by it.

You see, I *knew* Cecil B. DeMille.

He was, for sure, one of the most successful directors of that era and he called attention to himself at all times, sported shiny puttees, yelled through his megaphone at *extras*. But there was nothing *stellar*, I do assure you, about his drawing power. He got it straight from the nether world. While Griffith was lifting audiences into living history and poetry, while Fairbanks was shining as our Cavalier and Pickford as our Sweetheart, while Chaplin was binding us together with the golden chains of laughter, DeMille pandered to every base instinct that lies hidden in man.

Making his own the new postwar morality—or immorality—he flouted conventions, encouraged the hedonistic pursuit of pleasure, emphasized sophisticated sex. I daresay his ladies of the bathtub would be mild by present standards since, like Queen Marie Antoinette, they always wore a garment when they entered the waters, but they were then both daring and risqué, and it was DeMille who introduced the thin edge of the wedge that has widened to the ugliness and vulgarity of these, our Topless days. Only—C.B. didn't show it as ugliness and vulgarity. No no, he made it *haut couture*, glittering, shining, more-to-be-desired-than-rubies.

I do not say that the morality of Hollywood, or of individual you or me, should be governed by the Three Monkeys—*See no evil, Hear no evil, Speak no evil*. BUT evil must be shown *as* evil. DeMille dressed it up and called evil *good*, and that is the sin against the Holy Ghost.

Even after Wally Reid's death, when he saw what he had done to this young man whom I believe he really loved almost as a son, even after the advent of the Hays office and censorship, when the great man appeared to have reformed and gave us *The Ten Commandments*, it was the same old DeMille bowing to expediency. He gave us Moses on the Mount, receiving the Commandments all right; then he gave us the Golden Calf and all manner of bacchanalian revelry on the plain below. D. W. Griffith, that gentleman of the Old South, was appalled. "I'll never use the Bible as a chance to undress a woman," he said.

No. I will not admit greatness for Cecil B. DeMille—his pictures have not stood the test of time—and if he has left us a legacy it can only be found in the tawdry X-rated films of today wherein once again materialism, the almighty buck, has swept away all integrity.

This then was the man who was Wally Reid's mentor.

Oh yes, I am cold and hot, and perhaps if I *show* you, take you with me to that luncheon in DeMille's suite at Paramount—

At the table that day were Wally Reid and Geraldine Farrar, the prima donna from the Metropolitan who was in Hollywood to make a movie, Jeannie McPherson, Mr. DeMille's scriptwriter, a girl named Julie Faye, myself and my buddy, a brilliant press agent and fellow fan magazine writer, Herbert Riley Howe, one of the joys and delights of my life. Herb not only wrote of this budding art and industry with wit and vision, he talked of it that way as well. So he was an inspiration and a light at all times.

We were served by a deft and careful Chinese boy in a white coat who joined in the conversation at his pleasure, and once when Wally Reid called attention to the fact that he had missed Jeannie McPherson in the handing of a dish he said loudly, "But Mr. DeMille does not sleep with Jeannie any more—he is tired of her—now he sleeps with Julie—" We were not as free and easy in our conversation then as we are now and actually it was the first time I'd ever heard the words "sleep with" pronounced in mixed company and apparently I changed color for Cecil B. said to Wally, "We have shocked our young reporter here but that will be very good for her. To debauch any kind of innocence is one of the last and greatest pleasures of the sophisticate. When you become jaded, my boy, with the overripe charms and activities of the experienced, always find innocence to violate or corrupt. There is nothing like a good orgy to cleanse the palate or the—" he used a word which also began with *p* to describe the male sexual organ, and I got up and left the table, Herb Howe right behind me, but the words followed us out. Wally was under contract, he stayed.

This is the kind of thing that dragged Wallace Reid to drugs and degradation and death. I do not say that DeMille encouraged his star to take drugs because obviously he did not. He didn't have to. What he did was constantly flaunt his philosophy of hedonism, of virtue begging pardon of vice, of wickedness as the *most fun* of anything. DeMille made Wally feel that his natural lovingkindness and tenderness, his desire for true love, was ridiculous and immature and, again that horrid word that can somehow tempt and mortify people—unsophisticated.

Sophisticate: To change from being natural, simple, artless, etc., to being artificial, worldly wise, urbane, etc. This according to Mr. Webster.

Truth to tell Wally was about as *un*sophisticated as it is possible to be or he would have possessed some immunity against what happened—*for the children of this world are in their generation wiser than the children of light.*

He was natural in his affections, loved his wife Dotty and two children, Bill and Betty; when he built his unpretentious mansion just below what is today the Sunset Strip and had one of the first swimming pools it was his delight, when he could find time, to teach not only his kids but my kids and all the neighbor kids to swim. Sunday brunches were mostly family, we all helped ourselves at the buffet, the children sat at second table right beside the big one where Wally presided.

He had to be artless—that squat little Italian who went by the name of Kelly and was Wally's dresser and make-up man, finally got very rich taking cash bribes from women on the agreement that he would get them into Wally's dressing room or hide them in Wally's car—which of course he never did. But Wally didn't even know it was going on, and Dotty and I made a point of not enlightening him. We liked him the way he was.

And then—just after the Arbuckle verdict and the William Desmond Taylor murder a national publication stated: "The unfortunate breakdown from narcotics of another film favorite now so complicates the case for Arbuckle as to revive the criticism of Hollywood as the graveyard of virtue."

The tragedy of Wally Reid is still one of my deep personal sorrows, and when I meet with his wife, Dorothy, I know we are both wondering, somewhere down below the verbal level, if we'd been a little older or wiser, we might have prevented the waste of Wally's ruin and death.

The causes of Wally's drug addiction were deep.

One was a severe head injury suffered when a giant redwood fell near him during the filming of *Valley of the Giants*. A doctor first introduced him to narcotics as a release from those blinding, unbearable headaches.

Another was that the pace of work and play kept him from sleep. His popularity was so great, the public demand for more Reid pictures so constant, that he never had even a day off between, and many of his pictures, such as the automobile racing ones, were dangerous and nerve-racking.

If he played, it had to be at night. His idea of heaven was to get the gang at his *home* and play the violin, the piano, the sax and banjo, all of which he did brilliantly, till dawn. He always overdid athletics, fencing, swimming, boxing, fast driving.

I have to think this was all a part of it. But the truth is, I am sure, that if this so *un*sophisticated young star had had for his friend and mentor someone, *anyone*, other than Cecil B. DeMille, he could not have been trapped in the deadly poppy field.

The Deadly Poppy Field as we read of it in the Land of Oz— where Dorothy fell asleep. Opium—the juice of the poppy and its most important narcotic principal morphine. Today's illusion of drugs as a pastime, *très chic* and socially acceptable, we did not have, and if we had we would have been *dis*illusioned at once. Wally Reid's decline was swift and terrible to behold.

A drug ring was exposed, Wally's name on its records. Dotty and I went together to the newspaper that had the story. Four hours in the hot, noisy city room, Dorothy Davenport Reid, tears streaming down her face, told newsmen the truth, and convinced them that she was thinking, too, of all the kids whose idol Wally was. In the end, they did a magnificent thing. They told only of the fight Wally was making to be cured, leaving out the ugly details, and let his wife ask in their columns for the prayers of all who loved him.

If Hollywood was sometimes the graveyard of virtue, it was also sometimes the graveyard of high hopes, great talent, and the fault was not always with those who erred, but sometimes with those who built them up beyond what youth and human nature could stand in the way of temptation. I think Wallace Reid must be remembered as a sinner who died to prove his repentance.

Through such hell as you can never realize unless you'd seen it, Wally's courage held. He was cured, but the body itself had been damaged beyond repair. Only return to the drug, under medical supervision, could save his life.

In that bare hospital room, clinging to his wife's hand, white and thin and haggard, a boy still, Wally said quietly:

"Then I will die. I am free at last; I will stay clean. Only promise me, my darling, that somehow you will use this to save others from this horror if you can."

On an even lower note he said, "*Can* you?"

Today, *today now*, I saw two teen-age boys walking in front of me in a Southern California town. They were high school age, I thought, and one of them had the kind of tow hair that comes from spending a lot of time in the California sun, possibly surfing in the California waves.

One of them was in that kind of condition, but the other had a couple too many layers of fat on him. I don't know why I instantly found it repulsive. Sure, most of my sons, grandsons, and kid brothers have been in shape to play at least a quarter or so of football. So are a good many of the teen-agers I see around now, this one wasn't—and it disturbed me. More profoundly in my stomach than the situation warranted. A psychic warning of some kind, and just then the boy swayed, staggered, and fell into the gutter, his arms flung out in frantic supplication.

I ran and knelt by his side and said to the other boy, "Find a telephone and ask them to send an ambulance. I don't like the way he looks—" The second boy didn't run, he didn't even walk. He stared down at his prostrate companion, then nudged him aside with his toe. "I told him not to take another of those shills," he said disdainfully. "He takes too many of them, the schnook."

"What are they?" I said, and knew that my voice shook. That break startled the boy, he pulled back and away, with a scamper he was gone leaving his fallen friend. Since the days of my friend, Wally Reid, I have known something of drug addiction, we used to take drugs very seriously indeed. I don't think we do today. The woman of today shrugs her shoulders, raises her carefully made-up eyebrows, puts down her cocktail glass and says, "These dreadful young people. They use drugs, you know."

Someday soon I am going to lynch one of those women. I say that in deadly earnest. I hope I can get some other vigilante women to help me, but if I can't a wrathful God will give me strength to do it by myself. To string up some of these modern women who have permitted the drug use among our youngsters to grow into a national menace.

Women can do anything!

They always could, of course.

Dorothy Reid and I *know*. We couldn't save Wally individually, but we could and did make a picture, *Human Wreckage*, in which we fictionized to some extent his tragic story. We showed evil as *evil*. And we took that picture out personally, barnstorming around the United States, to inform, to arouse, the women of our nation. And the *women* banded together to halt that drug wave.

Yet now they are too busy working, or playing, to take time out to prevent the growing horror of easy drug sale to our young people. If they'd unite and give out with a warning they could stop it in a couple of days. The drug ring has poised astounded not to have had orders from the mothers and teachers that would stop the traffic at once, for that terror which the underworld used to have of the American woman is still there. She *could* come out with a warning and stop the whole thing, but the American woman of today is too busy with her own work, her own life, with something she calls her identity crisis, whatever that may be, to bother about drug addiction in the young.

Wally had said, "*Can* you?" and a week later his short life ended. Now I am the Old Woman of the Sea and have not the time nor the patience for Friendly Persuasion, but if young Wallace Reid, with his beauty, his irresistible charm and kindness, could come back to us and if Wally reached out and said to these self-centered females, "*Will* you?" I wonder—but no, neither will they be persuaded, though one rose from the dead.

BARBARA LA MARR

There was a girl in Hollywood a long time ago named Barbara La Marr.

She was the most beautiful girl I or anybody else had ever seen.

I am often asked these days to list the truly memorable beauties I have known or observed over the years and I am always happy to oblige. There aren't all that many.

Madeleine Carroll
Elizabeth Taylor when she was young
Lady Diana Manners
Vivien Leigh
Gloria Morgan Vanderbilt
Barbara La Marr

And the *most* memorable of these, and the least prepared to handle the burden—for that is a burden any beautiful woman will tell you—was Barbara La Marr.

Barbara belongs at the end of the pioneer days, the beginning of the Golden Era. Like Wally Reid she has been dead now over half a century. Her dazzling day in the sun was so brief—three or four years at the most—yet she is more real, more vivid than the faces I see around me today. Believe me, Barbara La Marr has been forgotten by no one who ever saw her on or off the screen.

I am aware that *Esquire* magazine has hailed Catherine Deneuve as "one of the most remarkably beautiful actresses of our time" and I agree that Ms. Deneuve is pleasant to look upon, but in the time of which I speak, and side by side with our most beautiful actress, she would have gotten no more than a passing glance.

Real beauty is rare through the centuries, so because she was the most beautiful of all women who have ever appeared before the camera Barbara La Marr has a place in Hollywood's history and because beauty is so often a magnet for tragedy that place is here.

I am going to tell it as it happened to me, I was part of it and nobody knew Barbara so long nor so well.

One day, 1920 or '21 this was, Douglas Fairbanks' press agent,

Mark Larkin, called to say that at long last they had found the girl to play Milady in *The Three Musketeers*. In its time the search for Milady as evolved by Mark Larkin had almost, not quite but almost, as much suspense as the great Russell Birdwell managed to generate in the search for Scarlett O'Hara.

A dancer, Mark said, Barbara La Marr. I rushed to the studio immediately and Doug and Mary, but recently returned from their honeymoon, told me with great solemnity that they had found the most beautiful woman in the world.

Doug took me to her dressing bungalow and introduced me to a tall girl with satin-black hair and violet-blue eyes. We stared at each other without a word until Doug left and then the great unknown discovery and I fell into each other's arms consumed with laughter. Finally, we wiped our eyes and the most beautiful woman in the world said simply, "What now?"

This was not my first meeting with the beauty, though it was with "Barbara La Marr." I had known her as Reatha Watson and seen her first in juvenile court when she was fourteen and I was a very young cub reporter on the *Herald*.

The manner of it was thus: On orders of J.B.T. Campbell, the toughest city editor who ever beat a cub into shape, I covered courts looking for feature stories and front page pictures. Naturally, I always dropped into the juvenile department and there one morning I entered just as Judge Monroe from the bench was saying sternly:

"You are too beautiful to be allowed alone in a big city. You are too beautiful to be without constant protection from your parents at your age. You go back to them in Imperial Valley and stay there under orders as a ward of this court."

The old judge was not a man easily fooled. If he said this girl—I could only see her back—was too beautiful, then she would stop traffic. She did. As she turned, I lost my breath. But I got it back in time to persuade her to come down to our office so we could take some pictures. When I took her into the city room everything stopped and I remember Jack Campbell staring at her and then saying to me, "Helen of Troy, I presume?"

We carried three pages of pictures and a story about her, quoting the judge. Reatha Watson was the Too Beautiful Girl.

She didn't stay with her folks in the valley long. If I wrote *this* as fiction nobody would believe it, but it's on the court record. A wealthy young rancher eloped with her and they were married, but she ran away for, as she told me, good and sufficient reasons, the chief being that she did not wish to be eloped *with*, and got an annulment.

A year or so later, she asked me to her wedding. Naturally, I took a photographer and we printed the pictures of a well-known judge performing the ceremony for the Too Beautiful Bride, in wedding dress and veil, the bridegroom was said to be one of Los Angeles' most promising young lawyers. I was very glad for Barbara. She looked so happy and he looked almost demented with love and joy.

The next morning he was arrested for bigamy. He had a wife and three children when he took out the license to marry Reatha Watson. In his cell he said Barbara's beauty had driven him out of his head.

Barbara—Reatha she was then—hadn't known about a wife. Barbara was terribly in love with him and stunned by his explanation of what had happened. She said to me, "It looks like it would be better if I was a lot uglier, doesn't it?" But she went to work studying dancing. "I like it," she said, "and I might as well get a living out of all this beauty."

In 1915, she was a sensation at the World's Fair in San Francisco, where she and her partner danced divinely. He was a handsome blond lad, a college graduate of good family, and they were married that year. He showered her with jewels, furs, laces, cars. His allowance from his wealthy family back East paid for some of that. But not all of it we discovered when he was sent to San Quentin for forging huge checks. Barbara did her best to save him.

"It's my fault," she said, "I didn't know, but I should have. He did it to get things for me. I didn't want them but nobody would believe that."

After he got out and Barbara was dead, he told me he used to see her as a vision—Cleopatra with peacock fans and pearls, on a barge with perfumed sails and decks of burnished gold. It was a spell, he had to get the money somehow to surround that beauty of hers with beauty worthy of it.

They say if Cleopatra's nose had been an inch longer the history of the world would have been different. "I wish," Barbara said to me bitterly after her husband went to jail, "mine was as long as the Elephant Child's."

I knew that day Doug took me to her new dressing room she was glad to see me. But I also knew that her "What now?" asked whether it had to come out that Barbara La Marr, the unknown cast as Milady, was Reatha Watson, the Too Beautiful Girl of the juvenile court, teen-age heroine of situations involving abduction, bigamy and forgery.

I said, "You'll be a sensation as Milady, a star in a year. You're well remembered around here. I'll keep quiet if you ask me to, but it won't do any good. If I were you, I'd tell it myself, right now, the way you want it told. That's the best advice I can give you." A few months later she took it.

Of course *The Three Musketeers* made her a star. You could hear the audiences gasp when the close-ups were shown. They were looking again at the face that launched a thousand ships, and its road was to be no smoother than it had been in Helen's day.

At first she thought it was going to be, she was happy in her work, she tried writing poetry, sold a few original screen plays.

Paul Bern's attempted suicide—he would have succeeded if Jack Gilbert and Carey Wilson hadn't come in the nick of time—killed her last hope. A spell of death and disaster seemed to be on her beauty as it had been on Trojan Helen's.

Barbara thought Paul her best, her only, man friend. She never defended herself publicly against his wild charge that her marriage to an Irish actor had driven him to try to end his life. But privately, to me, she said, "No, I wouldn't marry Paul. He knew that always and he knew why. Adela, we've been friends so long, I have to make you understand—" which she did. Then she said, "Paul has no right to marry any woman." Later he did marry Jean Harlow. When he set his mind on suicide the second time he used a gun and nobody could save his life.

Barbara and I were alone one night at her house playing records. Relaxed with her huge shepherd dog at her feet, Barbara was telling me of her trip to Rome, where she'd gone to make *The Eternal City*. A young actor broke in on us. He began raving about his love for Barbara, shouting that he'd kill himself, she'd driven him mad—at that, I saw Barbara's face go bleak with rage. Those words had been said too often. In a flash she gave the great dog a word of command. He leaped and the young man ran for his life. Barbara sat with her hands over her face, weeping bitterly. I saw that scene—yet later I heard gossip that Barbara, a married woman, let herself become romantically involved with that young actor who was engaged to a very nice girl.

Things piled up. Her third husband developed an unreasonable jealousy, too. Another man tried blackmail. Blackmail in our Hollywood was a terrible thing. Innocent people often paid it for years in torment rather than face the damage to careers. Barbara La Marr said, "I won't pay blackmail. It's a lie, if it ruins me I can't help it." She went into court and sent the man to prison. That took courage—and the whispers grew around her.

Suddenly, Barbara went to pieces. Drank too much, threw money away, told idiotic lies, let herself go, went with horrible men, neglected her work, as though she didn't care what happened. I guess she didn't.

I saw her last in the garden of a sanitarium—dying. She seemed so young to die that I couldn't keep back the tears. "No, no," she said. "It's better this way."

Barbara pointed to where a host of butterflies danced above a flower bed. "Their little moment is almost over," she said. "Butterflies aren't meant to live long."

When the end came the doctors called it galloping consumption, but in a way I think the truth is that Barbara La Marr died of being Too Beautiful.

Chapter Five

One of a Kind

GLORIA SWANSON

It always seems to me that Gloria Swanson sprang full-formed from the foam of the sea, like Venus.

People thought Gloria was mysterious about her past. I don't think it was that. She never denied being born in Chicago, her father an Army officer, that as an Army brat she spent her childhood in Army camps from Puerto Rico to the Philippines. But I think her life before she became a movie star was always as unrelated to her as some previous incarnation.

Nor could anybody else think of Swanson as anything but a movie star. Temperamental, extravagant, dramatic, exciting, sensational—no other screen actress has ever topped her as all that star means.

Certainly the movie star of today is Elizabeth Taylor with her jewels, her Rolls-Royces, her husbands and lovers, her million-dollar film deals. But as we compare the two, diamond for diamond, husband for husband, pictures, fans, staying power, love affairs and all, Liz gives off a dim light.

Gloria Swanson remains *today* the all-time prototype image of a movie star.

Swanson was not a beauty, as were Barbara La Marr and young Elizabeth Taylor—although she created the illusion.

She had not the pristine single-minded dedication to her art of a Lillian Gish, indeed she found ample time for some spectacular love affairs, which I will mention at their proper—or improper?—time and place, five husbands and three children. Her first hus-

At the premiere of *Boom Town*, I (right) seem to be listening intently to Hedy Lamarr and Spencer Tracy. (San Francisco *Examiner* photo)

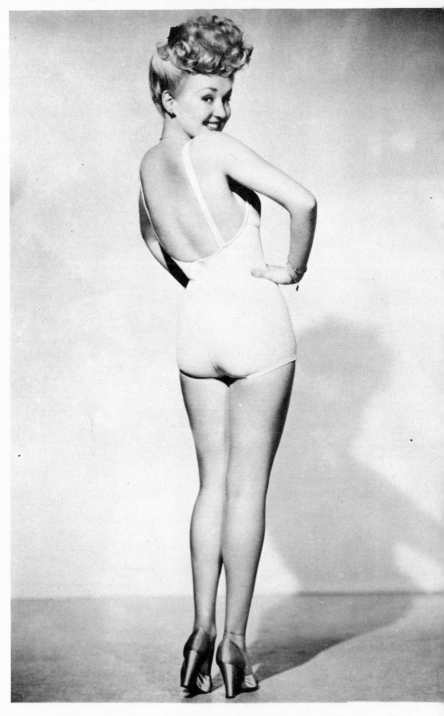

This is the photo that made Betty Grable the GI's pinup during
World War II.

A rare photo of Howard Hughes during the more sociable years of his life. Hughes (center, in dark suit) is flanked (left to right) by motion picture stars Charles Farrell, Billie Dove (to whom Hughes was once engaged), the Baron de Rothschild (in whose honor the party was being held at Mary Pickford's Pickfair home), Mary herself, Andrew Lawlor and (unknown) a friend of the Baron's. (Collection of Colleen Moore)

One of the most secretive yet most torrid romances in the history of Hollywood was the odd coupling of Charlie Chaplin and the Mexican actress Lupe Velez. The ill-fated Lupe, years later, killed herself over another love affair. Here they are, in the late 1920s, arriving at the Hollywood premiere of Colleen Moore's *Lilac Time*.

Bebe Daniels in her most famous role in *Rio Rita*.

Ben Lyon, Bebe Daniels and English actresses Margaret Lockwood and Margaret Leighton (left to right) being presented to England's King, George VI (out of picture), and his wife, Queen Elizabeth (mother of the present Queen of England), at Buckingham Palace at the end of World War II.

Lieutenant General Ira Eaker, in 1943 commanding officer of the U.S. Eighth Air Force in England during World War II, pins the Legion of Merit on actor Ben Lyon, after honoring Lyon's wife, Bebe Daniels, with the highest nonmilitary medal in the United States, the Medal of Freedom, during ceremonies at March Air Force Base in California in 1946.

Colleen Moore in the role that made her a star in the First National picture *Flaming Youth*.

Colleen Moore, New York's Mayor Jimmy Walker (center), and
Colleen's husband, John McCormick, at the Hollywood première
of her most famous motion picture, *Lilac Time*. Mayor Walker went
to Hollywood as the guest of honor for the premiere, a unique recognition for those days and times of the power of the motion picture
industry by one of the country's best known and most powerful
politicians. (Collection of Colleen Moore)

Mabel Normand (left) and her husband, Lew Cody, at the premiere
in Hollywood of Colleen Moore's *Lilac Time*.

In the Hollywood of the Twenties and Thirties, costume parties were as common as Thursday's Maid's Night Out. This one was held at Harold Lloyd's estate in Beverly Hills. (Left to right) Mrs. Harold Lloyd, Lloyd, Gertrude Olmstead, Colleen Moore, director Bob Leonard, Camelita Geraghty, and Patsy Ruth Miller, the famed stage actress.

Having a soft drink with the lovely Fay Wray, star of the first *King Kong*. (San Francisco *Examiner* photo)

band was also a movie star, our beloved Wally Beery; next came a businessman, Herb Somborn, elegant as only a young New Yorker can be, who with some help from Wilson Mizner founded Hollywood's famous Brown Derby restaurants. Then she made Hollywood's first international marriage, with the Marquis de la Falaise de la Coudray, followed by her marriage to Michael Farmer, a British playboy, then businessman-industrialist William Davey.

Yet, despite husbands and lovers, Swanson was never a sex symbol as were Clara Bow, Jean Harlow, Jane Rusell, and tragic little Marilyn Monroe. Nor did she have the endearing quality that made Pickford our Sweetheart. Another Pickford quality she didn't have was executive ability, Gloria made millions, but money know-how she had not got and never was more than two bucks ahead in her palmiest days.

What *did* she have?

Glamour!

She was the first of the glamour girls.

In my dictionary it says Glamour: Charm or enchantment; witchcraft; a magic spell; radiant illusion; any interest or association by which an object is made to appear to the mental vision magnified, glorified, exalted.

Wonderful words. I can still do it in two. *Gloria Swanson.* As Theda Bara brought the word Vamp into common usage so Gloria gave us the word Glamour when she first hit stardom and we started to reach for something new which might describe her and the unique element she'd brought to the screen and to femininity. After sixty years I find no other.

Gloria rose to the top in the mad lush years of the Twenties. Her first DeMille hit, *Male and Female,* was released one week after the Armistice ended World War I. Her first big talkie hit a few weeks after the market crash of '29 ended an era.

Always she attracted drama, aroused violent emotions, stimulated wit and comedy, everything seemed to magnify in her presence. Through it all Gloria went her own way—at all times—with complete aplomb which is to say with self-possession, assurance, poise and perfect confidence. Thus it was that Swanson, unlike Wally Reid, could go through her DeMille years, and emerge from his bathtubs unscathed.

I well remember Gloria's first battle with her studio. It came about not because of Bathtubs, Billing or *Money*, no no, but because she was *pregnant*. In her very early twenties Gloria, divorced from Wally Beery and now Mrs. Somborn, was delighted to find she was to become a mother. Paramount, already referring to her as the Swanson Gold Mine, shrieked in pain and protest. Said the moguls, "You can't do that now."

"Nobody but God," said Glorious Gloria firmly, "can dictate whether I'm going to have a baby." Nor could they. Furthermore she, who could have commanded all the luxuries of modern medicine, sent the studio into fits by having her first daughter in her own home by natural methods and breast feeding her.

No other star could have gotten away with it—but with Swanson the months off the screen, the madonna image, did nothing to impair her glamour.

No other star ever turned down a contract which agreed to pay $26,000 every week, fifty-two weeks every year for five years. That would have amounted to $6,760,000 in the days before big income tax. La Belle Swanson, at twenty-seven, then the best dressed woman in the world, a public idol, brushed it aside and two years later she was broke—and I mean flat broke.

She was broke because she had cast aside Cecil B. DeMille *and* Paramount, with its vast production organization, its theater chain, its sales and publicity forces, to make her own pictures. This has unfortunately often been catastrophe for actresses, but never did the pendulum of success and failure swing to such violent extremes as it did with Swanson.

From *The Loves of Sunya*, a little dilly that should never have been made at all and was one of the biggest flops on record, to the smash hit *Sadie Thompson*, the first screen version of "Rain"; from *Queen Kelly*, one of the biggest financial disasters in movie history, which swallowed Gloria's fortune, to that box office gold mine, *The Trespasser*, which proved Swanson even better in the talkies than she'd been in the silent films.

She took the chances and the consequences—and never squawked once.

Whatever the state of her finances she didn't let down her glamour, she still hit New York with a full court of maids, secretaries, chauffeurs and cars, still wore the magnificent furs and elegant jewels. At one time she ran four establishments, a Beverly Hills mansion, a country place at Croton-on-Hudson, a New York apartment and a palace in Paris. Sensible? If you ever saw Gloria Swanson, then off the screen for years, stop a big New York stage show as she walked down the aisle, which I've seen, you'd know they come like Swanson only once a century and they are seldom sensible.

Wild speculations, true and false, buzzed around Gloria like bees around a honeypot. People were always talking about Swanson—discussing the Eastern millionaire Joseph P. Kennedy by name, who at one point helped finance her pictures, or that she had sable and chinchilla automobile robes. I remember once when every newspaper in America was besieged by wild calls to ask if it was true that Gloria Swanson was dead, having either died on the set as the result of a fatal but long-concealed illness or been shot by a jealous wife or suitor. It took her personal appearance, stunningly gowned, very much alive and scintillating, at a mass press meeting in New York's Astor Hotel ballroom to settle that rumor.

Nothing trivial ever happened to Swanson. How could it? By instinct she dramatized everything for all the traffic would bear and got away with it.

Why, there never *was* a night like the one on which her picture *Madame Sans Gene* opened at Grauman's Million Dollar Theatre in downtown Los Angeles.

She was at the very peak of her fame then. She'd gone to France to make this spectacle of the washerwoman who became Napoleon's favorite and whom he forced the French aristocracy to accept as a social leader.

And in France, Gloria Swanson, hailed by the Parisians as their favorite, married the handsome, blue-blooded French war hero, Henri Marquis de la Falaise de la Coudray, and came back triumphant. Her landing, her progress across the United States had been a royal pageant of cheering mobs and now this night of nights she had Come Home to Hollywood.

Outside the huge theater mounted policemen held back the crowds that jammed the street for ten blocks in every direction. Inside, there was such a Hollywood audience as I had never seen.

Cheers resounded in the distance and swelled down upon us like the roar of a football crowd.

Lights dimmed, the orchestra struck up the *Marseillaise,* heads turned, you could hear drawn breaths as a spotlight hit the top of the aisle.

Gloria Swanson stood there wrapped in cloth of silver, glittering with diamonds. Behind her, in white tie and tails, red ribbon across his shirtfront, color flashing from decorations and medals, the Marquis, Hollywood's first titled bridegroom.

Then that audience of hard-boiled critics, every rival star, founding fathers, presidents and vice-presidents of vast film companies, social leaders and workers in every branch of picture making, began to yell like Indians, until cheers still going on outside faded before those inside.

I saw men standing on their seats waving their arms, other women stars tearing off their orchids and flinging them into the aisle for Gloria Swanson to walk on—and I saw Mack Sennett frankly wiping the tears from his proud face. One of his girls had certainly made good. Hollywood paid her a tribute that night it has never equaled for anyone else before or since.

She didn't fool around belittling her title at any time. Soon after the opening of *Madame Sans Gene,* a lady-in-waiting voice called me on the phone: "Madame la Marquise wishes me to ask you to come in for tea Friday at five."

Wonderful part of that was when you got there you found Gloria, who was above both triumph and disaster. I've heard it said that she denies she was a Mack Sennett girl. That's not true. No one has been more loyal, more openly appreciative of all Mack Sennett taught than Gloria Swanson. She couldn't possibly deny it, anyway, because there are always bits of her slapstick comedy showing, either on a Night in Grand Central Station, or those all too brief sequences in *Sunset Boulevard,* or, for that matter, in a real-life love affair.

To Gloria each romance seemed the first and only one. If you mentioned a former matrimonial or heart venture, she would give you a wounded look and say, "This is the first time I've ever been in love," and as far as she was concerned it was.

This nearly got me drowned once in my *own* bathtub. Gloria

had come across the street in Beverly Hills for a visit and found me scrubbing and sat on the throne to tell me about Michael Farmer. As I saw the exquisite face, starry-eyed and glowing, heard the husky, mesmeric voice saying, "At last, at last," I had to remember the number of times she'd said—anyhow she shoved my head under the water because *I* said the *one man* she really loved wasn't any one of her husbands.

"Wonderful One"—
One of the all-time great standard hit songs—
Written by Marshall Neilan for Gloria Swanson when, after her divorce from Herb Somborn and before her marriage to the Marquis, he was the head man in her life.

The mad devotion of Mickey Neilan, the curly-haired Irishman whose name must go down with the first five directors who built the motion picture industry and who was pursued at all times by a bevy of stellar beauties, has got to be the star turn in Swanson's exotic love life.

Later, much later, after she and Michael Farmer broke up, there was Herbert Marshall, a fine actor and a suave, urbane member of our British colony; together Gloria and Bart always reminded me of a Noel Coward play, dialogue and all. I'm sure it ended with a "Don't think it hasn't been charming."

The romance of Gloria and Mickey Neilan was quite otherwise. I am sure they had more laughs, more fights, more *fun* than any other two people who ever lived.

Once Mickey told me of a lovers' quarrel in London when Gloria bounced a magnum of champagne off his head. With a chuckle Mickey said, "Any woman might, if you annoyed her enough, hit you over the head. Only with Swanson could you be sure it would be champagne and a magnum at that."

When they weren't fighting—well, I remember one birthday when Mickey Neilan had given La Swanson a theater and projection room complete in her home, he also had bought every American Beauty rose in Los Angeles, Santa Barbara and all points in between and had them arranged on her front lawn.

Such high voltage romances are, of course, too hot not to cool down. When theirs did Swanson cabled Mickey Neilan from

Paris, "Forget me. Gloria." To which he cheerfully cabled back,
"Forgotten. Mickey." Funny, but it wasn't true. Nobody ever forgot Swanson.

Yes, I think Gloria was more in love with Mickey Neilan than
any other man in her life, but in a way the one she liked best was
Henri de la Falaise. "He was the finest, kindest, nicest man I ever
knew," she said once.

Then why did she divorce him?

The public believed Constance Bennett had stolen the Marquis
from Gloria. The true story is different—the woman was never
born who could take a man away from Swanson, in this case Constance Bennett almost brought them together again.

As early as 1928 shortly after Gloria started to make her own
pictures, the Falaises went to Paris and when Gloria came back
without Henri rumors of trouble hit Hollywood. In 1929 when
she ran over to France and returned for the premiere of her first
talkie, *The Trespasser*, and it became known that Henri had a job
with Pathé in Paris, there were more rumors.

Fond as they were of each other, Henri and Gloria had begun
to drift apart. Gloria had been married to Henri for three years,
almost four by that time. Love for Henri had become domestic.
Gloria was ever devoutly maternal, but domestic she was not. To
put it bluntly, witty and gay as Henri was, charming, cultured, distinguished and handsome as Henri was, Henri was an old shoe.

Henri came from Paris to talk things over with Gloria, and he
was seen about a good deal with Constance Bennett, who had
known him well in Paris.

With a great flash and flair, the first and eldest of the three
Bennett sisters—Constance, Barbara and Joan—had become a
screen star, chiefly because she knew how to wear clothes. Daughter of the great stage actor Richard Bennett, Constance had been
a pet of society, lived much in Paris and in her teens married millionaire Phil Plant. At twenty-one she was a sophisticated divor-
cee. In my personal experience I found Connie Bennett a girl of
considerable integrity, but she had a reputation around Hollywood for attracting other girls' men, though whether on purpose
or not I don't know.

The rumors about Henri and Connie almost needled Gloria

into holding onto her husband and title. Soon, Henri was arriving more and more often at what had once been his own front door.

I met him leaving it one day as I came in. I found Gloria in a smock, a towel around her hair, sculpting her small daughter's lovely head. She also wore her most dramatic expression. I said, "What goes with you and Henri? I thought he was going to live in France; I thought you were going to get a divorce." Patting clay, Gloria said, "Henri is sweet, isn't he?"

Somebody, I think it was Lilyan Tashman, gave a party. Henri was there, so were Connie and Gloria. The other guests were therefore in a state bordering on hysteria. I know that before she went, Gloria had intended to stage a public reconciliation with Henri, thus retaining her championship and giving the younger challenger a black eye.

Her own sportsmanship would not let her. Gloria rarely kidded herself, and to herself she had to admit that only feminine cattiness, professional pride and personal vanity could lead her to show off her power, to give Henri false hopes that could only be followed by worse heartbreak. Gloria knew that if she had wanted to continue as a wife to Henri, he would never have looked at any other woman. So, if Henri was finding solace in Connie Bennett, Gloria would have to take her own medicine. And she did.

She went home, cried all night, and next day began divorce proceedings. In a beautiful wedding, attended by her sisters, Joan and Barbara, Constance Bennett became the second Marquise de la Falaise. But before that very social event in Hollywood, Gloria had met, fallen in love with and married Michael Farmer, who was rated a catch that season. I think Gloria had always been disappointed that she and Henri never had a baby. Gloria always wanted babies. She and Michael had one.

That brought her total to three—Gloria Somborn—little Gloria we always called her because she looked so like her mother—a son, Joseph, adopted in 1923, and Michelle Farmer.

I have never known as devoted and wise a mother as Gloria. She worshiped her children, she drove directors mad when she insisted on driving sixty miles home from location at night and sixty miles back in the morning just to see them. At Malibu I lived two houses from her for several summers and even the other stars waited breathlessly each day in anticipation of Gloria's ap-

pearance, surrounded by her handsome offspring, followed by a
maid with bags, robes and slippers, a houseman with surf mats
and paraphernalia. But it was Gloria herself who built sand castles
with her children and taught them to jump the waves.

I believe because she was so strongly maternal Gloria could, and
in one department always did, kid herself, make herself believe
over and over that she *was* domestic. Even after her marriage to
the handsome sportsman, Michael Farmer, broke up—"I find it
necessary to earn a living for my children, while Michael finds
nothing so important as hunting and fishing"—she eventually
married William Davey for about a minute and a half. And when
I heard the other day that Glamorous Gloria, somewhere in her
late seventies, had married again it didn't surprise me.

Once just after her enormous success in *The Trespasser* Swanson said to me, "I hit the peak at thirty and have nowhere to go
for the rest of my life but down." Then, musing, she gave me a
fey look with those hypnotic, slanting, gray-blue eyes and said,
"Or—can it be a series of peaks? With valleys in between. Maybe
you have to climb each peak all over again."

Peaks—and valleys. A good description of the life of Gloria
Swanson. And Gloria walked it with courage at all times. She had
no fear of the future.

The moment her film career actually appeared to be waning
Gloria didn't linger in the fading light. She promptly disappeared
from Hollywood and reappeared scintillating in Paris, New Orleans, Dallas, New York as head of a huge dress-manufacturing
company featuring her own designs.

When she climbed out of the valley on the other side of that,
there were touring companies, a bit of this, a bit of that and then,
twenty years after *The Trespasser* came *Sunset Boulevard*, a Hollywood classic and a personal triumph.

After a studio showing of *Sunset Boulevard* I heard Groucho
Marx say to Fred Allen, "Here is the real place for that immortal
line, 'What Happened? I feel like I'd been hit by an earthquake.'" Gloria's tour of the country ahead of the picture's
release was as triumphant as when she returned from Paris with
Henri, they spread red carpets and cheering throngs showered her
with flowers.

But despite fabulous offers, when she didn't find another story she felt had substance Swanson disappeared again to emerge on television, on the stages of two continents, finally in a big Broadway hit. And whenever or wherever she appeared she was enveloped in that aura of glamour.

Attending the Academy Awards in her late sixties she swept down the aisle midst the miniskirted modern maidens of the movies in a long, flowing gown. The audience of her peers rose spontaneously to applaud her.

Age cannot wither her, nor custom stale her infinitive variety; and in honesty I have to say that Swanson, now eight times a grandmother, is perfectly aware of this—when she was given a standing ovation on the opening night of a play in Hollywood she said, laughing, "I don't know whether you're applauding my acting or my age, I'll be seventy my next birthday"—and perfectly willing to use it to convince one and all that we can go and do likewise. How? Gloria is a leading advocate of the sound mind in the sound body—positive thinking plus the elimination of pollution from the atmosphere and the consumption of organically grown foods.

As she approaches eighty, divides her vitality between her family, her work, her friends, her philosophic studies, flies from her apartment in New York to her apartment in Paris, from her home in Palm Springs to her villa in Portugal, she still finds ample time to put her glamour and her aplomb at the disposal of this cause. And it takes both. No other star, repeat, *no* other star but Swanson, could show up at New York's elegant "21" draped in sables carrying her own organically grown lunch in a brown paper bag—and get away with it.

Once when I was covering a Presidential Convention, Gracie Allen, bless her, and I chanced to meet at the Pump Room in Chicago. We fell to discussing the upcoming youths of Hollywood and I said one of them, I forget just who, seemed to me to have talent, and Gracie said, "Oh sure, everybody's got talent nowadays. But can he wrap it up?"

In this our day, what with cosmetics and rinses and Exercycles and *dentists,* the means to glamour are everywhere available. Certainly in Hollywood the commodity has been demonstrated by many of the stars. Connie Bennett had it—and Ava Gardner. Joan Crawford achieved it, after considerable effort as we shall see. The Gabor sisters, Zsa Zsa and Eva, were trained to it. We have Lena Horne, Lauren Bacall, Sophia Loren—oh yes, I will admit to glamour all over the place. But I have to say that, from first to last, from beginning to end without letup or letdown; Gloria Swanson was the only one who could really wrap it up.

RUDOLPH VALENTINO

With Rudolph Valentino the motion picture camera for the first time really showed what it could do in the way of creating a personality. How it could transform an ordinary mortal, a simple Italian youth named Rudolpho Guglielmi, into a god, *Valentino*, who could enter humdrum lives, create friends and foes, worshipers and bitter scoffers, bring disaster and delight, touch hearts to flames of both passionate adoration and furious hate, become a real part of daily lives and social circles which knew that personality only on the screen.

So that Rudolph Valentino could live the strangest double life that ever man knew.

Of all the stars with whom we have to deal in this tapestry of Hollywood's people, the camera did more to, for, by, with and about Valentino than anyone else who ever walked before it. And don't fool yourself, the camera can lie.

When a distinguished novelist once came to our town I took him to meet Rudy. Later he wrote: "I could not reconcile what I had read of him with the lad himself. He was splendid."

Our novelist had read of the Sheik, and the distance between the Sheik of the screen and "the lad himself" was so great that in the end it utterly destroyed him. Nor was the Sheik acting. Though he worked and studied to improve, Valentino was never much of an actor. No, it was a photogenic accident.

Let us take the hypnotic Valentino stare, that steady dark peering look that pierced feminine hearts. Quite simple. Rudy couldn't *see*, and he refused to wear glasses. *Myopia*—not passion. He didn't want to sweep you into a mad embrace, he just wanted to see where you *were*. The camera recorded it as romance, mystery, menace. A grim jest.

On the screen, *Valentino* was every woman's ideal, secret lover. Men hated him because of that, because he was the foreign type on whom the word gigolo could be hung. In real life, had they but known, *Rudy* was more henpecked, woman-dominated than any of them.

Missing in the millions of words written about Valentino is how young he was. Not on the screen. There he was the Male in his virile prime. But Rudy himself was always so young. Why, he was only twenty-five when he made *The Four Horsemen* and literally overnight became the idol of women of all ages.

It was barely twelve years from the day an eighteen-year-old immigrant arrived steerage in New York from his native Castellaneta to seek his fortune to the day the female worshipers of the Sheik were prostrated by his sudden death. In his entire career Valentino made only a dozen pictures and was off the screen more than he was on it. His career, his private life, his love stories were so different in fact from what fancy painted them, so much more heartbreaking.

I have written briefly of Rudy's strange story elsewhere, now I must in more detail do so again. For no picture of my Hollywood would be complete without it.

He was, still is, the most completely misunderstood of all our town's great figures.

It is natural to think of women in connection with Valentino. Women went mad over him on the screen, determined his destiny, gave him his fame. The popular conception of Rudolph Valentino at the height of his success *was* the Sheik, flaming from one Grand Amour to another.

The truth is stranger.

Only two women were ever important to Rudy. The bizarre Natacha Rambova was one. June Mathis was the other.

Fabulous as he had become Rudy had real humility, a desire to *learn*; he welcomed the chance to play Armand to Madame Alla Nazimova starring in *Camille*, Nazimova being then a most widely acclaimed actress of both stage and screen, as they say. On the set, he met Madame's designer, whose real name was Win-

ifred Hudnut but who called herself Natacha Rambova to match
the turbans with which she bound her black hair, the clanking
jewelry, the slinky gowns, the Oriental make-up she wore.

Nazimova, who tried to break it up, said, "Natacha is the most
ambitious woman I've ever known. She will sink herself in no
man's career, she will swallow him like a boa constrictor to feed her
own ego."

It was too late. For the first time, at first sight, the Great Lover
was madly in love.

But before that he had met June Mathis.

No more extraordinary friendship between a man and woman
exists in all Hollywood history than that between the youthful
idol and that brilliant eerie genius, June Mathis, ten or fifteen
years his senior.

Misunderstood, ridiculed, this affinity cost June the man she really loved. It instilled into Rudy, over whom her influence was
unshakable, her own fanaticism to keep the movies an *art*, and
this led to the contract fight that kept him off the screen two
years out of his brief span.

In those days of his frantic, feuding popularity, Rudy's idea of a
good time if he couldn't get you to come to his house and let him
cook spaghetti, was to sit in a Turkish cafe hidden in a side street,
eat meals especially prepared for him, and talk.

On one such night, he and Herb Howe and I talked our way
through horses, painting, religion, philosophy and travel to *friendship*. I quoted Emerson, rather sententiously I admit, but we were
much given to quotations in those dear dead days beyond recall—
Omar Khayyám, Millay, Shakespeare—and it seems to me now
forgivable, even commendable. We were in truth interested in im-
proving our minds, and sharing the gems we gleaned was a popular pastime, which to me is more plausible than trying to blow
your mind at a pot party. At any rate when the subject of friendship came up I *did* quote Emerson. "There are two elements that
go to the composition of friendship . . . One is Truth . . . The
other tenderness . . . The laws of friendship are austere and eternal . . ."

Rudy leaned forward to peer at us through the smoke of a
Turkish water pipe. His strange sloe-black eyes had a glow of emo-

tion that showed ruby-red. "These words I could never say my-self," Rudy said. "Yet this is what I have wished to say to my sweet friend June."

In the first months of their friendship, June and Rudy saw each other every day, every night. It is ridiculous to dismiss her merely as the woman who discovered Valentino, for she molded his thought, taste, and work.

First woman executive in the industry, there has been no one like her since. When June Mathis swept through the studio, onto sets, into offices and dressing rooms, appearing as by magic wher-ever there was a crisis, her fierce authority lit in others some of her own divine fire.

Short, stocky, with blazing brown eyes, brown curly hair forever untidy, Paris clothes that on her looked dowdy, she had an in-domitable will and a dangerous temper.

After World War I there had come to Hollywood a young lieu-tenant of the Royal Flying Corps named Rex Ingram. Rex Ingram and June Mathis became one of the writer-director teams that were part of the foundation of the industry. June had done a magnificent script on the Ibáñez classic, *The Four Horsemen of the Apocalypse*. Ingram was to direct, they were testing for an actor to play the lonely Argentine soldier who danced the tango.

Then June, on the Metro lot, spotted Rudolph Valentino.

At that point he had been seven years in the United States, working as a busboy in New York restaurants, dancing when he could, as he had done on the Riviera to earn his passage money, until Lady Luck found him. Someone saw him dance and men-tioned him to Bonnie Glass, whose dancing partner did not want to go on the road. Rudy got $50 a week with Bonnie on the Orpheum Circuit.

After that, Lady Luck forgot him again. He made a bare living dancing in hotels, in occasional stage shows, finally made his way to Hollywood, lured by the movies. But—Hollywood did not con-sider Rudolph Valentino romantic. Even the great D. W. Griffith saw nothing at all in Valentino, who played a bit for him in a Dorothy Gish picture, and when Dorothy suggested Rudy might make a romantic leading man, D.W. thought he was too "foreign-looking," that women wouldn't accept him.

So, for four years, sometimes with a year between small parts in

pictures, Rudy went on dancing in taverns, cafes, hotels, pro-
logues, so he could eat. Until at last one woman, June Mathis,
saw in the young Italian what millions of other women were to
see. June didn't fall in love with him. She had already given her
heart as well as her brains and talent to Rex Ingram. But she did
see Rudy as Julio and insisted, over Ingram's violent objections,
that he play the part.

For Valentino to build Rex Ingram's *Four Horsemen* at the
box office might have been palatable. But audiences didn't even
see the beauty of the Ingram sets, nor the skill he'd used with
lighting. They were watching Valentino dance. Forever after *The
Four Horsemen* was to be known as the picture that made Valentino.

Oh, it was a famous victory for June, the triumph of Valentino.
But Rex Ingram's resentment went deep and soon, finding beautiful Alice Terry, an extra girl he'd promoted to dance with Valentino, asleep on the set, Rex Ingram woke her up, took her to dinner and married her.

The marriage rocked Hollywood. What would June do? In public June showed the magnificent condescension of a duchess. If
her heart broke in private, nobody except her friend Rudy knew
it.

Nothing could shake the friendship between June and Rudy,
but Ingram could and did break up what might have been the
greatest three-way combination in all picture history. Valentino
went to Paramount and when a little later he needed his beloved
June, she was in his native Italy with *Ben Hur*.

To others, Natacha Rambova was a very tall, very thin woman,
with a dark Egyptian type of face, but from first to last she was
enshrined for Rudy in Oriental mystery, beautiful beyond all
other women.

While all the women in the world, it seemed, now courted him
by mail, in person, singly and in droves, Valentino followed only
his tall, remote goddess. Between hope and despair, he asked Jean
Acker to get a divorce. Even his rise to fame hadn't made people
remember his wife; she was a small ghost waiting to make a brief
appearance when she got her divorce decree.

They had found each other, Rudy and Jean, during the lonely

years. And Jean Acker wasn't any more in love with Rudolph Valentino than he was with her. She was a nice girl, a pretty girl so like dozens of other thin blonde girls in Hollywood that nobody could pick her out of a crowd, except she had gentler manners and a sweet smile. They met at a party and, knowing nobody, talked to each other in a corner.

After that they saw each other often, and one day had a forlorn little wedding. When they arrived at the door of Jean's room in the old Hollywood Hotel, Rudy said good-night and went back to his hole-in-the-wall and had a fight with his landlady, who had discovered the electric iron with which he kept his trousers so sharply creased.

When I once asked Rudy why he and Jean married, Rudy's answer was—well, actually typical of Rudy. "We were the two lowliest and loneliest people in Hollywood," he said. "It was like starting to climb a mountain, if you saw someone beside you look as alone and lost as you felt, you'd offer your arm, it would be easier if you held onto each other."

Always Jean and Rudy remained friends. She was at his bedside just before he died. Yet theirs had been a marriage-in-name-only, and they didn't even hold onto each other for long.

Nothing was important about that sad little marriage except its end.

For—came a day when Rudy persuaded the icy Natacha to join a house party at Palm Springs. Perhaps in that desert setting Valentino was the Sheik, as the camera created him in a performance which exerted more influence, had more impact, than any other part ever played by any screen star. Whatever it was, one night he carried her away across the sands. In Mexico, they were married.

They put him in jail for getting married before receiving his final divorce decree. Only one thing concerned Rudy. Shaking the bars of his cell, his face wet with tears, he shouted: "She is my wife. I will rot here forever before I will deny our sacred marriage. She is my wife."

When Valentino stood trail for bigamy, all he said in that packed courtroom was: "I did not understand it was against the law. But I expect I would have done it anyway; I would do it again to make her my wife." Acquittal time—two minutes.

It was in the months that followed that, after the extraordinary smash of *The Sheik* and *Blood and Sand*, Rudy walked out and refused to fulfill his Paramount contract. The studio retaliated with an injunction forbidding him to work elsewhere and once again he was out of a job.

The motive behind Rudy's stand was supplied by June Mathis' idealism—her insistence on *quality* motion pictures. The fuel was furnished by Natacha Rambova's ambition—her hope that his break with the studio would eventually help her fulfill her long-cherished dream of producing Valentino's pictures herself. But the fight, the first of its kind, Rudy fought alone.

In an open letter, published by Jimmy Quirk, a historic document in Hollywood annals, Valentino set forth his case and I set it down here on the forlorn hope that it may inspire someone else to go and do likewise. Rudy, overwhelmed with letters asking why he left the screen, wrote:

The contract producers offered me after *The Four Horsemen* was my first. When they told me not to bother my head about details, everything would be as I wished, I signed without hesitancy. I am not a good business man. Besides, $1,250 a week seemed enormous. I do not know that after I pay for clothes worn in my pictures, answer hundreds of thousands of fan letters, send my pictures to all who request, have a valet for the set which I must, it does not leave a fortune!

But I was not temperamental. I do not consider myself a great actor yet. But in me I have a deep feeling for the art of the motion picture. Of my gratitude to the public, my responsibility.

When I am offered $7,500 a week by the same producers if I would go back to work on the same cut-and-dried program basis, I refused. Is that grasping? I am not selfish of money. I have done without it long enough, it means little to me, but I don't want to be a cog in a machine that grinds pictures out. Cuts them to put in cans like sardines. I am selfish to make good pictures. It is not good enough for you, the public to measure art by celluloid inches. I say here in print if this company will permit the writer and director in whom I have all the confidence, people recognized as capable great artists, to have the last word on pictures in which I appear, if they agree not to destroy my pictures with cutting, if they give me the contract I thought I was getting in the first place without those little clauses that make all the difference, I will go back to work today. I will never go unless they let me make good pictures.

My salary of $1,250 a week is less than any prominent star gets today. Mary Miles Minter gets $8,000 a week. William Farnum the same. It is a provable fact at the box office that my pictures make much more money than theirs. I don't care. The point is if I go back to making any kind of pictures any way, as the producer says, I would not be true to myself nor to you. I ask you to believe I fight that you may have the best pictures.

June Mathis had done her work well. Now it was Natacha Rambova's turn.

In March 1923, the studio's injunction against Rudy was modified by the court to allow him to make a living as long as he did not act. He and Natacha were remarried at Crown Point, Indiana, and began a dancing tour which filled Midwest theaters with hysterical, fighting, screaming mobs.

Valentino—who knew all there was to know about dancing, most especially romantic dancing. Ballroom dancing we called it, and we found it most beautiful in those days when it still took two to tango. Comes now a picture of the first time I met him.

One day, when Ike St. Johns and I hadn't been married too long, who should drive up to the little shack where we were living on the beach at Santa Monica but our good friend, Norman Kerry, an Annapolis graduate who preferred not to go to sea and became instead a favorite leading man to such stars as Mary Pickford and Marion Davies. With Norman was a dark, foreign-looking young man in a sweater and the first beret I'd ever encountered. Kerry had seen the young man dancing in a Jolson show in San Francisco and befriended him when he came to Hollywood.

Ike was out of town on an assignment and Norman decided he wouldn't want me to mope but to come with them that evening to Nat Goodwin's cafe on the pier. So after a swim they went off to change. Came the appointed hour. To this moment I don't know what sidetracked Norman, but the dark young man, whose name I had discovered was Valentino, drove up alone.

His blue coat was elegant, he wore a natty straw hat with a ribbon, but as he got out over the door of his old car, which wouldn't open, he caught the pocket of his white trousers on the handle and I heard a healthy rip.

"Don't bother, I really don't care whether we go or not," I said. "Run along and we'll go some other time." At this he became voluble in three languages. His friend, his mentor, his benefactor, Mr. Kerry, had told him to take me dancing. "That demon!" I said. "All right, I'll wait while you go and change."

He couldn't. Valentino didn't have another pair of pants.

My well-known maternal instinct aroused, I shooed him inside, gave him a blanket and mended his trousers while he sat with his nether extremities wrapped, looking pretty silly and most discomfited. I was worried about letting him finance this expedition but, when I saw that the boy was really going to be chagrined, wounded and scared to face Norman if I didn't go, I said I would, though by that time I felt as though he were my small brother. So young, always, to the women who knew Rudy without benefit of the camera.

"He was never anything but a boy," Natacha told Herb Howe years later, and she treated the Sheik as a boy always.

That night on the pier it was immediately plain that broke or not, this Italian youth would spend his last dime on food. He liked everything done in rich, heavy, spiced sauces. It seemed harmless enough then. But it wasn't. Combined with other things, it was to be fatal.

At last he asked me to dance. I didn't want to hurt his feelings so I said I would, reluctantly, knowing that I was a bad dancer. Only—that once—I was not. I was terrific—joyous, light, graceful! I like to remember it now. Oh, I do I do. It was sheer happiness to dance with Valentino, to flow with ease, like flowers blowing in the wind, moonlight sparkling on water, never touching the earth.

In that ridiculous two years when he was off the screen, at his peak of popularity, when he and Natacha went on that dancing tour of the United States and I heard that people who saw them dance together used to weep with joy, I could believe it.

"I held Natacha in my arms and that was life itself," Rudy said to me. "Only one woman makes a man whole. No other woman ever made me touch ecstasy, all the rest were stuffed with saw-dust. Why? If you know why—how—"

This explains the mystery of Valentino, of Natacha's domina-tion. He loved her like that and she didn't love back. From the day his contract fight was finally settled out of court, and he re-turned to finish out his Paramount contract, Natacha played an ever-growing role in his work.

It is not given us to like everybody. I didn't like Natacha. It was mutual.

The Valentinos, having returned from a tour of Europe where they had been the toast of Paris and Natacha had bought $10,000 worth of Spanish shawls, $10,000 worth of Italian ivories, and $40,000 worth of Moorish costumes and jewels for a picture, *The Hooded Falcon*, which she had made up her mind all by herself Valentino must make, gave a dinner party.

The rooms at the Ambassador Hotel were exotic with orchids, a Paris showing couldn't have topped the gowns; everyone was there, even Mary Pickford and Douglas Fairbanks, a triumph in-deed for the Valentinos' social position. Charlie Chaplin, Bebe Daniels, the Tom Mixes, Vickey wearing all her diamonds, the new Flapper sensation Colleen Moore, the so-beautiful Tal-madges, young Richard Barthelmess, Irving Thalberg, Jack Bar-rymore who had just deserted the theater for movies, Jack Gilbert, Mae Murray, Dorothy Gish, Harold Lloyd, Gloria Swanson, the beauteous Barbara La Marr, Marion Davies, everybody, in fact.

Mrs. Rudolph Valentino, in a jeweled turban and clanking bracelets, reduced that dazzling company of great stars to a court as she made her royal progress through the rooms. Here and there she paused to bestow a word, sometimes she swept by with a faint, fixed smile, or a slight inclination of her head. Poor Rudy trailed behind, trying to be friendly and natural.

Despite this splendor I was hungry. Having been brought up to punctuality, I had arrived at eight. When there was no food by ten-thirty, I left.

Next morning Rudy's voice on the phone said, "Natacha is very angry. When it was time to sit down, where were you?"

"Tucked in my little bed," I said. "I'm a peasant. Did you want me to stay there and starve to death?"

"I am the one on the pan," Rudy said. "I asked you be put at

my table, so there is an empty chair, my good wife says fine kind
of friends you have, no manners . . ."

"You want me to write and apologize?" I said.

Rudy whispered, "Please." So I did. I never got an answer and
she never spoke to me again.

In the man who worshiped her and who happened to be the
greatest movie star in the world Natacha found clay for her hands.
Her ambition was to make him her masterpiece. Just here, Madame really began to meddle a leettle too much.

There it is again, the double life. Poor Rudy. His wife was married to Valentino.

Natacha started telling the cameraman how to photograph him.
You can monkey with a lot of things in motion pictures, but if
you have any sense you let the cameraman alone.

Nobody would make Natacha's *The Hooded Falcon*. While he
shot *The Eagle*, Rudy agreed to let Natacha make a picture of her
own called *What Price Beauty?* Its cost of $100,000 was consid-
erably more than it took in at the box office. Rudy didn't have
that kind of dough and he began to have real money worries.

She was never home. Rudy thought perhaps the simple stucco
house where he'd lived was not splendid enough, so he bought
Falcon's Lair, a sprawling seventeen-room Spanish hacienda on
eight acres.

Natacha never spent a night at Falcon's Lair.

A kinder man than Joe Schenck never lived. Nor one more im-
movable. He made up his mind when Rudy went from Paramount to United Artists where Joe was now head man on a
magnificent deal, that Madame must keep out of the Valentino
pictures Mr. Schenck proposed to produce. In the contract clause
barring her from the set, in a manner of speaking the ambitious
Rambova was divorced from Valentino, the star. After that, without warning, Natacha got a boat for Europe where she divorced
Rudy, the man.

That separation from the only woman he ever loved broke the
mainspring for Rudolph Valentino. Eight months after Natacha's
Paris divorce, he was dead.

"He hadn't," said the doctor, "taken care of himself . . . chronic
stomach disorder . . . holes in the lining of his stomach big as
your finger."

Taken care of himself? Years of struggle, poverty, the most sudden and sensational smash ever made by anyone in picture history, the idolatry of women, the jealousy of men which tore him limb from limb, the long fight with Paramount, the money worries, his desperate, unhappy love—and then between the time Natacha left him and that 1926 August day that was his last, came the Pink Powder Puff editorial.

He saw it in a Chicago paper on his way to New York for the premiere of *The Son of the Sheik*. It told of a pink powder puff vending machine that had been installed in the men's washroom of a North Side public ballroom and said, in part:

A powder-vending machine! In the men's washroom! Homo Americanus! Why didn't someone quietly drown Rodolpho Guglielmo, alias Valentino, years ago? . . . Masculine cosmetics, sheiks robes, floppy pants and slave bracelets . . . London has its dancing men and Paris its gigolos . . . Rudy, the beautiful gardener's boy, tries to become the prototype of the American male. Hell's bells! Oh, sugar!

Shaking with rage, Valentino wrote with his own hand and sent to all papers this letter:

To the man (?) who wrote the editorial headed Pink Powder Puff: You slur my Italian ancestry, you cast ridicule upon my Italian name, cast doubt upon my manhood, I call you, in return, contemptible coward . . . I challenge you to a personal test . . . I, therefore, defy you to meet me in boxing or wrestling arena to prove, in typically American fashion (I am an American citizen), which of us is more a man . . . Hoping I will have opportunity to demonstrate to you that the wrist under a slave bracelet may snap a real fist to your sagging jaw . . . I remain, with utter contempt, Rudolph Valentino.

In spite of his Continental manners and lovemaking, no one who knew Rudy ever questioned his manhood, his utter masculinity. But—it was the insult to the slave bracelet that sent him berserk. Always Natacha! In those days men didn't even wear identification bracelets, but Natacha had given him the slave bracelet and put it on. You'd have had to take Rudy's arm to get it off, he wore that symbol of his enslavement into his grave.

No answer came from the Pink Powder Puff editorial's author. Although all of us, Herb Howe, Jimmy Quirk, me, begged him to, Valentino couldn't let it alone. "I have not the hide of a rhinoceros," Rudy shrieked. He wrote the papers more letters, his anger remained red hot. In nervous hunger he ate huge, highly seasoned meals, until the sweat broke on his forehead. It was a last straw, somehow.

Also there was Pola.

There was a terrific thunderstorm going on outside. The building shook with the rumbling roars of it and the lightning opened the heavens with flashes of blue light. Valentino didn't seem to notice it.

We were both staying at the same New York hotel, he had appeared unexpectedly at my door and finding me in the hands of a hairdresser, who nearly swooned at the sight of him, began just the same to pour out his troubles. The girl who was doing my hair was shaking so with excitement—this was before permanents—that every once in a while the hot curling iron landed on my scalp or my ear. The which I bore in silence because Rudy's need to unburden himself seemed so urgent that no Mother Confessor worth her salt would interrupt him with yelps.

The problem was *Pola* who, the press said, would marry Rudolph Valentino.

"To be engaged to Pola," Rudy said, the wild gestures, flaming black eyes I could see only in the dressing-table mirror as he paced the floor behind me, "is like when I am a little boy and live near Mount Vesuvius. She erupts." Pola had telephoned, Rudy said, that she could not live separated from him by 3,000 miles, she was coming from Hollywood to New York to join him.

"What's wrong with that?" I said.

"I do not wish her to come," Rudy said. "This engagement—it is all a drama, what a great romance it makes for Rudolph Valentino and Pola Negri, thus Pola sells to herself the Grand Amour. But me, I do not. Myself I am not dramatic. In the home, I love quiet. Pola in the home is like the falls of Niagara. That is all wrong for me, Rudy. Poor Rudy. But what can I do?"

As he talked, my thoughts went back, I remember, to the first meeting of these two spectacular foreign stars. I saw again the stately, flower-filled ballroom of Marion Davies' home in Beverly Hills, filled with a grand company of Hollywood stars, in costume for another of Marion's famous masquerades. Marion in elegant blue and rose hoops, Pola robed and jeweled as the Empress of All the Russias, and I were talking together when Pola saw Valentino across the dance floor, in scarlet and gold braid and a sword, and her eyes narrowed.

"Ah, Valentino," Pola said, in her purring, throaty voice, with its strange accent. "I must meet him. Present him to me, please, Marion."

Marion, a little reluctantly I thought, made a gesture with her fan, Valentino crossed the room with his famous grace and bowed over her hand and the introduction was made. The music began, Pola looked up at Valentino with melting eyes, they took the floor together and so gorgeous and striking were they that for minutes no one joined them.

"They hardly seem real," Marion commented absently.

"It's the costumes," I said.

But here was Rudy telling me Marion had been right, it wasn't real, it had always been "in costume."

"Tell Pola not to come," I said to Rudy.

"Pola?" Rudy gave a shrug. "You know Pola. She will only say on the phone in that voice, 'Rudy, someone is trying to come between us. When your Pola is with you once more, you forget everything except Pola.'"

"You'll have to take a firm stand," I said. "If she comes, tell her you want to end it."

"But you know Pola," Rudy said. "With those eyes she will look at me like she looked at the King in *Dubarry*, even when I say to myself, Rudy, this is merely the supreme of acting, remain cool, be brave, I believe her—she will say Kiss me, Rudy and—no, I am too tired. I am a quiet fellow—it is too much—"

In the middle panel of the triple mirrors, he was framed for me, Rudolph Valentino, the great lover, then he moved, he was just Rudy, my friend, a simple young Italian whom lady luck had, for a while, befriended.

He disappeared into the bathroom and shouted, "The bicarbonate of soda, I cannot find heem."

"There isn't any," I shouted back.

He returned looking unhappy. "I ate too much snails with my lunch," he said, "I need the soda." He grinned unexpectedly. "Pola always drives me to the bicarbonate of soda."

It came to me to say, "You are still in love with Natacha, in spite of the divorce."

"She is my love," he said. "In the courts, she divorces me. Can you divorce in the heart?"

Poor soul, if he'd been able to look ahead one short week, Rudy might have spared himself all that anguish. He was never going to need advice about another crisis in his life.

Pola did come, but it no longer mattered to Rudy, who was beyond the sound of her voice, the glance of her beautiful eyes. A few hours after he said good-bye to me there in that hotel room he was stricken and Pola put on widow's weeds instead of a bridal veil.

When he collapsed they took him to the Polyclinic Hospital. All day, all night, during the week of his fight for life, thousands upon thousands of people stood outside the tall, grim building. Police reserves and mounted officers were there to keep order, but it was a quiet—a waiting crowd.

In the corridors, Joe Schenck, face drawn with pity, and his beautiful wife, Norma Talmadge, kept vigil. Rudy's first wife, Jean Acker, slipped in and out, a ghost of the past.

Not once did Rudy admit death was near. He consoled everybody. "Don't pull the curtain," he said. "I want to see the first sunlight."

He wasn't to see sunlight again.

Public demands Sheik's body lie in state, read headlines.

I wondered if Rudy could see the weeping wailing thousands that walked by the ornamental gold casket in which, Jimmy Quirk told me, lay not the body of Valentino but only a waxen effigy.

Jimmy, in charge until Rudy's brother should arrive in New York, had done a wise and sane thing. A sculptor was called and from the camera's 1,000 images a figure was molded, of the Sheik while the tired body of a young Italian lay peacefully elsewhere. With the wild, disgraceful riots and hysterical women and cursing

Spencer Tracy and Jimmy Stewart don't see eye to eye in their starring roles in Metro-Goldwyn-Mayer's *Malaya*. Always fighting, they're still buddies as they conspire to smuggle rubber out of Jap-occupied Malaya early in the war.

Colleen Moore starring in *Flaming Youth*, the movie that made her one of the all-time biggest attractions in the history of the motion picture industry.

Marvelous promotion shot: Bill Powell, Myrna Loy, Jean Harlow and Spencer Tracy in Metro-Goldwyn-Mayer's comedy-drama *Libeled Lady*.

This photograph, taken by Colleen Moore, shows that the legendary Garbo could relax just like the rest of us when she was among friends. Colleen took this picture at John Gilbert's home during an afternoon swimming and tennis party. (Left to right) Seated in front are Ralph Black, actress Eileen Percy, writer Barney Glazer and Garbo, resting against Gilbert's arm. In the second row (right to left) are Gilbert, Alice Glazer, producer Carey Wilson and Lothar Mendes. (Collection of Colleen Moore)

Gary Cooper in one of his most famous motion pictures, *The Hang-ing Tree*.

A now rare still picture of three of Hollywood's most famous stars, Wallace Beery, Jean Harlow and Clark Gable, as they appeared together in the highly successful motion picture *China Seas*. (Photo by Clarence Sinclair Bull)

Ingrid Bergman is visited on the set of her film *Cactus Flower* by Joel McCrea, a longtime friend. (Photo by Mac St. Johns)

Director Victor Fleming, Adela Rogers St. Johns and child star Judy Garland on a sound stage at Metro-Goldwyn-Mayer. (San Francisco *Examiner* photo)

Hattie McDaniel, as Mammy, and Clark Gable as Rhett Butler, in
Gone with the Wind.

The Motion Picture Country House and Hospital is in one of the
most beautiful and semirural sections of the San Fernando Valley,
which lies north and west of Hollywood. Pools, covered walkways,
trees, shrubs and the surrounding hills make the facility one of the
most beautiful in this country. (Photo: The Motion Picture and
Television Fund)

Attending the dedication ceremonies of the new hospital section of the Motion Picture Country House and Hospital in 1947 were (left to right) Y. Frank Freeman, executive vice-president of Paramount Pictures, Jean Hersholt, Shirley Temple, Robert Young, Dinah Shore, and Ronald Reagan. Man at far right is unidentified. (Photo: The Motion Picture and Television Fund)

Elvis Presley donated very generous amounts to the Motion Picture Relief Fund. This photo, showing Chester Conklin, famed silent screen comedian; Frank Sinatra, an active Fund supporter; Presley and George L. Bagnall, MPRF president, was taken the day Presley gave the Fund $50,000. (Photo: The Motion Picture and Television Fund)

men outside, I, for one, was glad it was Valentino who lay there in state and not Rudy. I'm sure Rudy was too.

At heart he remained always a very simple unpretentious peasant lad who had wanted a very few things from life; peace and quiet—Natacha—and to save enough money to buy a vineyard where he could retire with his love and grow grapes.

Alberto and Maria, his brother and sister, said, "Our brother belonged to America. He shall go to California, he so loved it."

As the *Chief* bearing Rudy's body made its way west, according to Jimmy Quirk who was aboard, Pola bore up well except when the train stopped and she saw the thousands who waited moaning on the platforms to say goodbye to their lost idol.

VALENTINO COMES HOME.

In war-size type, the papers hailed Rudy's last return.

They laid him in the place his beloved June Mathis had prepared for him. Standing with his brother and sister alone beside the quiet grave, it was his "sweet friend" who said the last farewell to Rudy. To the end, there was always Rudy and Valentino, and the woman who discovered Valentino was the only one of them all who really loved Rudy, in the truth and tenderness of Friendship, great, austere, eternal.

BEBE DANIELS

The true story of Bebe Daniels, the first *girl* singing star after Came the Talkies, the girl with the golden voice and the golden personality, has to start for me when I decided to let her live. Not figuratively, actually and literally. Because for a flashing moment of unutterably strong temptation, I was about to bury her so deep in a haystack nobody'd find her until next spring, or kick her nervous bronco off the side of a steep cliff high in the Sierra Madre mountains.

I was around eleven at the time and she must have been five or six.

This began in the riding ring of one of the big California ranchos up back of Glendale—a Spanish land grant still in operation in those days when the Spanish, whom our Bebe was a direct descendent *of*, were still our aristocracy. But even then Miss Bebe Virginia Daniels, whose grandmother had been Señorita Eve Guadeloupe de Garcia de la Plaza, was the center of all masculine eyes. Oh sure, the Little Princess of the empire—and I was stuck with her. I had seen it coming, and I was so mad I could feel the freckles standing out a foot.

The Vaqueros had gathered, mounted their gleaming horses already bearing silver-trimmed saddles and bridles, and lined up as the dawn light began to grow brighter over the Sierras. Ropes coiled, hats at the dashing angle of the early California Spanish, soon they'd take off for the long day's ride on the trails. A barbecue would be waiting somewhere at noontime. My father was among them, I'd come out with him and had of course expected deliriously to go on the ride. I had my own hat at a fairly dashing angle and a pair of regulation cowboy boots, my first. They didn't actually make cowboy boots that size but somehow Papa had managed it. I remember that Señor Leo Carrillo was there and Francisco Dominguez and Alfredo Shorb and nothing—*nothing*—was lacking to a moment of supreme satisfaction and anticipation. There were no other women and children in this *caballada*, which suited me profoundly.

Of course there was Bebe.

In *her* little britches with a small riding hat pushed back on her masses of gleaming blue-black curls. But she was too little.

"*We* are going to have to wait till *you* grow up," I said darkly, but she just began singing and smiling up at me and pretty soon, well, the moment passed. Bebe had a way with her even then.

Have you ever read a citation for the Medal of Freedom, one of the highest awards that can be bestowed upon an American civilian?

If not, here's one.

Bebe Daniels Lyon, American civilian, for exceptionally meritorious achievement which aided the United States in the prosecution of the war against the enemy in continental Europe from 16 December 1931 to 26 May 1945.

During this period she distinguished herself for initiative and unselfish interest in the welfare of the American soldier. With outstanding ability she organized, produced and acted in theatrical productions presented to troops and civilians and was the first woman civilian to follow the troops into Normandy in order to make recordings with wounded American soldiers six hundred yards behind the front line. Her unselfish services and willing sacrifice under the most dangerous conditions contributed immeasurably to the maintenance of a high state of morale among the troops, thus materially contributing to the success of the war effort.

To *Bebe Daniels Lyon*— is what it said.

Bebe was Mrs. Ben Lyon.

And a long and happy marriage it was and lasted until she died not too long ago in England where she had become an idol next only to the Queen—if not equal to.

But I do not see Bebe as one-of-a-kind because she was a real life heroine; other Hollywood stars have made outstanding contributions to causes in both war and peace. Nor because of her highly successful marriage and motherhood; we've had those too. Nor because her talent ran the gamut from comedy in the silent days to drama to magnificent musicals like *Rio Rita*, from motion pictures to variety tours and theaters and radio during World War II, all topped off with twelve years as the television star of Britain's favorite family show, "Life with the Lyons," in which she was joined by her husband Ben, her daughter Barbara and her adopted son, Richard, and much of which, I might add, she wrote herself, another thing she did brilliantly.

No, it is because looking back through the years I'd have to say that Bebe Daniels was the best-loved and most all-around popular girl who has *ever* been in Hollywood at any time.

Also because I think, in time, she came to represent to us all that is finest in an American girl—and woman—though early on she got herself into more trouble than most! And that for a number of reasons. Among them the fact that so many men fell in love with her.

The quality of Lillian Gish, how did Shelley put it?—*The desire of the moth for the star . . . The devotion to something afar*—was totally reversed with Bebe Daniels. She was George Herbert's *quick coal of mortal fire*, and both men and women drew close to her warmth.

Come to think on it there was even something special in the relationship between Bebe and her fans.

Fans—short for *fanatics*. Yes indeed. We had them in all sizes, shapes, varieties and stages of frenzy. When I see Valentino's fans I see the wild-eyed women at his funeral being forcibly restrained from desecrating the casket in which, unbeknownst to them, lay a wax dummy. Mary and Doug, with police protection fighting their way through the wild throngs of London and Paris. Colleen Moore, after the opening of *Flaming Youth* in Dublin, when the ten thousand madly partisan Irishmen broke through police cordons and affectionately tore her gown and feathered cape to shreds.

With Bebe I see the time she went to jail in Orange County for breaking its rigid speed laws, and Abe Lyman, who didn't impress easily, took his entire orchestra from the Cocoanut Grove all the way to Santa Ana to serenade her with her favorite number, "Rose Room Tango."

I see two daring young men in their flying machines and a rendezvous arranged when it was announced that Bebe would go to New York by air for a holiday. There were no regular passenger flights; we flew, if we flew at all, and Bebe and I were among the first who did, in an open twin-cockpit mail plane, complete with helmet, goggles and parachute. Halfway Bebe, eastbound, suddenly found herself in a hayfield, where the westbound mail pilot had persuaded his buddy to land so he could get her autograph.

I see a famous underworld boss reading in the papers that Bebe Daniels' jewelry had been stolen in a Midwest hotel while she was on a personal appearance tour. The following day her jewels were returned intact on orders from her secret admirer, Al Capone.

Or I see six little boys who lived across the square from her in London ringing her doorbell to ask wistfully, "Can Bebe come out to play?"

Then, too, there was that Boeing B-17 bomber named "Bebe's Boys," American boys very far from home who kept in touch with her thoughout the war.

Yes, I'd have to say there was something special between Bebe and her fans. And the first man in her life, Harold Lloyd, was something special too.

"We will have to wait until you grow up," I heard myself saying again to my little friend, Bebe, who by now was thirteen and, having done small parts on stage and screen, wanted me to help her get a job as a leading lady.

Of course Bebe wouldn't wait. There was no wait in Bebe Daniels.

Three days later, she came by my house very early in the morning.

I have no words to put down what she looked like. Her hair was done in a knot at the nape of her neck, and only a few curls strayed, and she wore one of her aunt's dresses! Her aunts were all Spanish, and they wore dresses even more *respectable* than other aunts.

"Where did you get that *dress?*" I said in horror.

"It's my Aunt Alma's," Bebe said, her eyes burning with excitement. "Isn't it stupendous?"

"It's a fright," I said, "all you need now is the coffin."

I don't think she heard me, if she did she paid no attention.

"I don't look thirteen in it, do I?" she said.

"No," I said, "I . . . you look like what you are, a kid with her mother's dress on."

"I don't and it's not my mother's, Phyllis keeps hers locked up," Bebe said and looked at herself in a full length mirror. "I think I look at least eighteen and I'm going out and get me a job as Harold Lloyd's leading lady, I heard 'em talking about his needing one, and it's going to be me."

Whereupon she tucked up her stray curls, went out to Hal Roach Studio in Culver City where Harold was making one- and two-reelers and not only became his leading lady *but* he fell in love with her and spent a lot of time and energy trying to get her to marry him. For some years the romance of Bebe and Harold was Hollywood's favorite boy-girl love story. There was at all times something so refreshing, not to say naïve, about the two of them that even Phyllis Daniels, whose elected role was more that of the loving and protective duenna than the Queen Mother as portrayed by Charlotte Pickford, even Phyllis smiled on Harold and allowed Bebe to go with him to Venice or Ocean Park on the streetcar to eat popcorn and ride the roller coaster, and later to the Sunset Inn to dance.

Harold Lloyd, then forging ahead as a comedy star, eventually as I have said was to become, and as far as I can add it all up, to

remain, the greatest of all gag men. A gag is any contrived piece
of wordplay or horseplay and at this Harold Lloyd, young as he
was, was a *genius*.

He knew—he aways knew, he had known from the beginning
of his work in the movies—that he was *not* a comedian. He was
never funny, as Charlie Chaplin and Buster Keaton were funny.
As Mabel Normand was funny just by being herself—no no,
Harold was at all times and in all ways a gag man. And a gag, as
he had been early taught by Mack Sennett, must have continuity
and substance.

With his *glasses* as an identification mark first seen in one of
the smash hits of those days called A *Sailor-Made Man*, Harold
not only became a true star by election at the box office, where
more and more people cast their nickels and dimes to see his pictures, but an innovator. In *Safety Last*, in which for the first time
he used the camera to bring about comedy effects, he invented
the danger comedy, as it were. He made it funny that he might at
any moment be precipitated to his death from the hands of a large
clock. In the trade one of the first top three laugh gags of all time
was considered to be the one in *The Freshman* where the leg of
the tackling dummy came off and Harold thought it was his own.

Harold, who deeply respected the art of the motion picture and
of comedy therein, worked on these gags with the care and preci-
sion of a great sculptor. His mind was clever, quick, dramatic—
and he was also and in every way quite the nicest young man in
town.

From him Bebe learned a great deal about comedy and to him
she gave her very young heart.

But she wouldn't marry him.

When her contract with Harold was up she went on to Paramount where DeMille had long been beckoning and where Jesse
Lasky, after six months, set her up in her own company producing
comedies in which she starred. Harold finally married his pretty
new leading lady, Mildred Davis, because he was a marrying man
and wanted a home and family, but he said to me once, many
years later, when we were sitting in Toots Shor's in New York, "A
man has different kinds of loves in his life, and after you stopped
being *in* love with Bebe, you went right on *loving* her. She had
something *special* . . ."

Yes, always, *always* when we met Harold found a moment to talk to me about Bebe. Some little tale of the dance trophies they won, they regularly got *all* the applause at those dance contests at the Vernon Country Club or the Sunset Inn. About the funny old car, a Ford runabout with no hood and a crank, that Harold drove before he'd begun to make big money, how they huddled under her umbrella if it rained, or how he used to put newspapers down so Bebe wouldn't get dust or dirt on her pretty little frocks.

Why wouldn't she marry him—or for that matter anyone else for years and years when she was the most popular girl in town?

Once young Bebe showed me her Rules for Success, very fashionable in those days, some running to pages. Bebe's were short and to the point:

1) Don't get married.
2) Don't get into scandal.
3) Work hard.
4) Always pay cash.

Come to think of it she kept the last three all her life—but the first? No no, that wasn't the reason.

Partially it was that Bebe, unlike Harold, had no desire at that time to *settle down*. None at all. Quite the contrary. Bebe, in those early years, was right out front among the Hollywood hellions, Constance Talmadge, Dorothy Gish, Lottie Pickford, Bebe Daniels—all high-spirited, mischievous teen-agers, fond of deviltry, and young enough, funny enough, pretty enough to make it very engaging. I remember Connie Talmadge and Dorothy Gish playing hooky from the Griffith set to go to baseball games. Bebe "borrowing" the bicycle used by the delivery boy from in front of the Western Union office and calling up later to tell him where to retrieve it. With perfect good humor Connie Talmadge, runner-up for our most popular gal, sassed the great Griffith, drove the chariot and four which were her "prop" as the Mountain Girl of *Intolerance* over his sets, and sometimes all over town with Bebe or Dorothy Gish or Lottie Pickford or a combination of same, hanging on behind. Healthy, happy, hilarious as their pranks were, they caused much commotion, and Harold Lloyd was ever and aye a most *serious* young man.

Also, and most important, for all those years Bebe wasn't *sure*. And Bebe, cradle-born Catholic, convent bred, had to be *sure* because when she married it would be forever.

And because whatever she did, she must do with all her heart.

When Bebe danced, she *danced*, and not only with Harold. With Valentino to "Rose Room Tango" at the Grove. With Wally Reid when in a DeMille picture they danced together— they even did a series demonstrating jazz dancing for an illus- trated magazine—and right there and then Wally, who also did everything totally, *loved* her.

Like Wally, when she drove she drove *fast* and, oh, I almost forgot, a man who was in love with her—*Jack Dempsey*. The time Bebe went to jail in Orange County—she was driving Dempsey and Phyllis to San Diego in a big open roadster—the Champ rented a hotel suite nearby in Santa Ana and stayed there through her entire sentence. Serving it along with her, he said, he wanted to be sure she was quite safe in jail, that they didn't treat her badly. Not likely, with the press and the press agents coming and going, her mother Phyllis actually insisting on being locked in with her, the judge welcoming her with a bouquet of flowers, furniture companies bidding to furnish her cell, restaurants to provide food and services, friends lavishing gifts and flowers, and so many fans and *suitors* that her jailer kept a guest book and brought in their visiting cards until, upon occasion, Bebe said Tell him I'm out and the jailer said I can hardly do that, and let Phyllis take over. No, Dempsey wasn't there as her protector; he just thought he had her immobilized for nine days (one off for good behavior), could press his suit intensely, shower her with her favorite red roses, and bring her a tamale for lunch. Much good it did him!

And when Bebe *gambled*—Bebe was the Number One gambler, it turned out, we ever had in Hollywood, not perhaps for as big sums as David Selznick, but Bebe would bet you on *anything*— and give you odds.

To gamble—to take risks.

One way or another early Hollywood, like early California itself, was the territory of gamblers. If you wanted security, if you were afraid to take risks, you didn't go West in the first place.

Indeed if Bebe Daniels' grandfather, the wealthy and distin- guished Colonel George Butler de Forest Griffin, after he finished his stint as Consul in Bogotá, Colombia, where he had married the Governor's daughter, had been seeking security he would have returned by boat to New York and New Haven whence he came. Instead, with his aristocratic little wife and their children including Bebe's mother Phyllis, he undertook the perilous trip over the Andes by muleback to start for his destination—California.

In her early starring comedies granddaughter Bebe personified the girl of the Roaring Twenties suddenly freed for *action*—driving fast cars, jumping off ten-foot walls, capsizing boats, piloting racing aquaplanes—doing it all herself and risking her neck with right good cheer. She took another kind of risk, when, after the Talkies, one B. P. Schulberg, risen to control at Paramount, refused her a voice test and let her contract lapse. Bill Le Baron, head of RKO, then called the "quickie" studio, was proposing to film a Ziegfeld spectacular. Now that I consider it the whole affair was one big gamble. Le Baron, with *sound* and *color* so new and all, was preparing to make the picture half in color, half in black and white with *much* very ambitious sound, including the sound of music.

When word got around that Bill was considering a silent-comedy star and not a trained New York stage voice to play opposite singer John Boles, Hollywood didn't call it gambling, they called it suicide. But Bebe's test, after she worked for three months to make sure she could hit high B-flat, was sensational; and then she placed *her* bet—a very small salary against a percentage of the profits. The result—*Rio Rita!* Perhaps the first great musical. Hailed by the critics as "staggeringly beautiful." A comedy queen had become a great singing star. And Bebe Daniels had won herself a beeg pot.

It occurs to me that Bebe was a gambler beyond anyone I've ever known *except* my husband Ike St. Johns, who once said I divorced him because he stayed in with a busted straight and caught my fourth nine. It didn't help his straight and cost me the biggest pot of the night. Bebe never stayed out of a pot and she would bet you any sum which side of the slip a ferryboat was going to hit first, something even the pilot couldn't tell.

Bebe was one of the ranking bridge players in those early days when bridge swept the country—she had played at the famed

Knickerbocker Club in New York, also I remember Ely Culbert-
son selecting her for his partner when he came to the West Coast
—and she was very much a part of Hollywood's Big League. This
included Joe Schenck, his brother Nick, Harpo and Zeppo Marx,
Sam Goldwyn, Irving Thalberg, and I've seen Bebe play with them
for anything from one to five dollars a point with a side bet.

It is impossible for me to see Bebe at a bridge table without seeing also Jack Pickford, the second love in her life.

His sister Mary said an interesting thing to me about Bebe one
day. "I can remember her better than anybody," Mary Pickford
said slowly. "No matter how . . . how casually or for how short a
time . . . anyone who even so much as met Bebe Daniels, remembered her always afterwards with . . . with *vividness*. Some people,
maybe most people, you have to stop and bring them back so you
can see them and sometimes you never quite do. But Bebe is always there just as she was. She and Jack were . . . so wonderful,
so happy together."

I was recalling some of the Kilkenny rows I'd heard Bebe and
Jack have, most often at the bridge table. I can see one scene now.
Bebe playing with the great experts for a dollar a point, and so
much in love with Jack that she accepted him as a partner though
his reckless overbidding—Pickford was a player who wanted to play
every hand himself—cost her a fortune. And she wouldn't let him
have anything but *beer* to drink and I have heard first-class rows
between men and women in my time but never anything to equal
the one when she found he was spiking it with scotch from a bottle in his pocket.

Oh yes, they were in love. For quite a time Bebe and Jack were
a stellar turn among the young couples of our town; two of our
most irresistible, witty, attractive, vibrant personalities, their marriage seemed inevitable. But—talented as Jack Pickford was, and
he was talented, he was dedicated to as much play and as little
work as possible. Charming as he was, and he was charming, he
was a good deal less than after his first bottle of scotch. Bebe
wasn't *sure*, this was one risk she couldn't take, and so there was
no wedding.

In fact Bebe wasn't *sure* until, just before she made *Rio Rita*, she got herself engaged to Ben Lyon, and then she insisted on a year's engagement.

Ben Lyon was, at that point in time, a very romantic figure in a town that thought it had invented the word. A successful, handsome and popular actor who was selected by Colleen Moore as her leading man in *Flaming Youth* and had gone on to play with Swanson, Pola Negri, Barbara La Marr, Norma Shearer, he was also one of those daring young men who *flew*.

Flying. I know I know. Overcrowded air space, increasing decibels of sound, airport traffic, terminals like subterranean cities in which if you don't get lost your luggage will, the sonic boom, overflights, SAC—that is flying as we know it today. Yet I beg you to believe that only fifty years ago, in its Age of Innocence, flying was *the* great dream made real, a dream that man had cherished since first he watched the eagle soar.

The man who climbed into those early machines and rose above the earth to soar with the eagle and beyond, to touch the clouds and flirt with the stars, was somehow touched with glory. Whether he was an air mail pilot named Lindbergh who made it from Long Island, New York, to Paris, France, or the barnstormer going from one farmer's field to another to tempt paying passengers which Richard Bach makes live for us again in his new classic book, *Illusions,* or an actor named Lyon devoting most Sundays to giving free hops around an L.A. airport where public timidity dissolved before the temptation to fly with a *movie star,* whichever, that man—or woman—we viewed with a certain awe. Which meant that we had to find Ben Lyon, one of our own, who held civil transport license Number 373 and was a member of the U. S. Army Air Force Reserve, very romantic indeed.

Ben taught Bebe to fly. Bebe taught Ben to play bridge. And there they were at the altar.

I like to live again their wedding in 1930 for it was one of the last big social occasions the Golden Years ever put on. Constance Talmadge and I were among the bridesmaids, and our gowns with wide hoopskirts and trains of different colored gauze-net had to be made on us because we weren't allowed to sit down in them. Mine was the deeper shade of blue and Connie's was the palest of yellow. Young Howard Hughes, who at twenty-four after three years' shooting was about to launch his air epic *Hell's Angels* starring Ben Lyon and James Hall and introducing Jean Harlow, was one of Ben's ushers. I remember that he was taller than anybody so in the bridal procession we put him with Betty Compson who was the tallest of the bridesmaids. I don't recall that Howard was any different from George Fitzmaurice or Henry Hobart or Doc Martin, whose wife Louella Parsons was matron of honor. How we got around the Emily Post dictum of brides*maids* I don't know, for among us we had or had had a good many husbands. I daresay by never having heard of it.

I daresay, too, that when a couple of years later a daughter, Barbara Bebe, was born to the Lyons and toted around by her mother in a traveling basket to be lodged on the couch at Connie Bennett's, or Virginia Zanuck's, or at Pickfair when we ladies forgathered for bridge, when both their careers flourished mightily, and a devoted Bebe and Ben, now settled in Bebe's beautiful Santa Monica beach house, were Hollywood's most popular couple, we figured this was the End to that story.

Only it wasn't.

Three incredible things happened and five years after the glowing wedding Bebe, who we thought belonged so especially to us, left Hollywood not to return except briefly for the rest of her life.

First came the kidnaping of the firstborn son of our national hero, Colonel Charles A. Lindbergh, and the discovery of the baby's body in a shallow grave near the Lindbergh home in far-off Hopewell, New Jersey.

Second a series of kidnap threats hit Hollywood, always a target for that lunatic fringe which a major crime sets off. The children of the Harold Lloyds, the Darryl Zanucks, of Irving Thalberg and his star wife, Norma Shearer, were under constant guard.

Then an actual attempt was made to kidnap Barbara Bebe Lyon. District Attorney Buron Fitts advised her parents to leave the country until the insanity died down. So it was that Bebe and Ben found themselves having to build new careers in England, and so it was that they were there four years later when war came.

They could have left. They didn't.

From Blackpool where Bebe and Ben were doing a variety tour when war was declared Bebe said simply, "We're staying. The

British have been so wonderful to us, we couldn't run out on them when they're in trouble." I could hear Harold Lloyd saying to me, "One of Bebe's great virtues is loyalty."

As war clouds gathered after Munich eight-year-old Barbara Bebe and her four-year-old adopted brother Richard had returned to live in the Santa Monica house with Phyllis. Now Bebe and Ben began to repay their debt of gratitude to the British people. Together they played in war factories, camps, hospitals. While the Battle of Britain raged overhead, through the heaviest Luftwaffe bombardments with the danger of invasion only a thin channel width away, at a time when the people of the little island so desperately needed something to take their minds off their tragedies and deprivations, this American couple helped give it to them. With Vic Oliver, for two and a half years, they starred in BBC's top radio program, "Hi Gang," a fast-paced high comedy show, featuring such guests as Sarah Churchill, Noel Coward, John Gielgud. Broadcast from "somewhere in England," when the sirens sounded everything ground to a halt, when, during the daylight bombings their studio was hit, they moved on. Their effort was so effective that Bebe and Ben found themselves on Herr Hitler's preferential list for extermination. At the same time for forty-seven weeks they starred at the Palladium, providing a box each night for servicemen and an invitation to come backstage for "a drink and a smoke and a chat about home."

Until the Americans "came in" and Ben volunteered for active service with the Eighth Air Force, it was Bebe *and* Ben, side by side, but always the top billing went to *Bebe*, and Ben, bless him, was the first to give it to her.

"We in Britain thought Bebe was the best part of Lend-Lease," so said one London paper at the time.

The best part . . .

18 Southwick Street.
Purple Heart Corner.
I tell myself now, today, that they were separate things. The one a tall thin house with a blue door in the Paddington area of London as described to me in one of his last letters by my son Bill. The other a radio program beamed into thousands of Ameri-

can homes during the searing months when so many of our sons
and daughters and husbands were fighting and dying "over there."

But here on my tapestry they are, in some other dimension, *one*
because they are both Bebe Daniels.

"I saw Bebe the other day," Bill wrote. "Anytime you call they
say Come on over but this is the first time I've been able to make
it. All you have to do when you get to London is tell the taxi
driver Take me to Bebe and Ben's. Their Hyde Park house is a
pull-in for both British and Americans. Bebe is just like I
remember her. She's a peach, and can she *cook*. Somehow she
managed a tamale pie like you used to make. We talked about
you, and Elaine, and it was almost like being back home . . ."

Hacienda hospitality, warm generous American hospitality—for
Bebe was at all times consciously and deeply American—home
fires kept burning right in the middle of the Blitz by Bebe
Eschevero Daniels Lyon. No less an authority than American Am-
bassador John Hay Whitney said, "That home was a haven for
Americans from General Ira Eaker right down the line." And for
her friends from Hollywood. Clark Gable and Jimmy Stewart,
U. S. Air Force. Doug Fairbanks, Jr., U. S. Navy. David Niven,
Commando, British Army. Pilot Officer William Ivan St. Johns,
RCAF.

When the telegram came—*His Majesty's Government regrets
to inform you*—in time I remembered Bebe, the bit of home my
Bill had found at 18 Southwick Street, London, in his last days in
a strange land . . . and the tamale pie. There didn't seem much
to be grateful for right then, but somewhere in my frozen heart
was a ray of warmth, I was grateful to my little friend Bebe. As
were more and more American parents when our involvement and
our casualties increased.

Bebe, now in her forties, and with Ben no longer at her side,
redoubled her activities. Week after week at the Piccadilly
Theatre she starred in *Panama Hattie*, providing now two boxes,
one for American and the other for British servicemen, always
with time to welcome them backstage. For the duration she did a
radio program for BBC, "Here's Wishing You Well Again,"
dedicated to the men and women in Allied hospitals. And a spot
on a mutual network show, "The American Eagle in Britain"

heard coast to coast in the United States, called Purple Heart Corner. American families each week listened eagerly as Bebe Daniels visited different hospitals and recorded interviews with wounded men and the doctors and nurses who were taking care of them.

Then—the main event. D-Day. The invasion for which we had waited when the Allies turned the tide and got a tiny beachhead on the German-occupied continent. But at what a price! We in America hugged our radios, the instant impact making the holocaust of ships and guns and planes and *casualties* more real to us than when we had awaited the screaming newspaper EXTRA and read a written report. We were torn between the hope of coming victory and the present horror. Which the Allied commanders knew. Which was why General Paul Hawley, Chief Surgeon of the U.S. forces in the E.T.O., asked Bebe Daniels if she would go to Normandy and continue her Purple Heart Corner interviews right up to the front line. But—there was *Panama Hattie* and it wasn't possible. Then there wasn't *Panama Hattie*. At two o'clock one afternoon a buzz bomb blew up the Piccadilly Theatre and on D-Day plus twenty Bebe packed her sleeping bag, her helmet and typewriter into a C-47 and, under sealed orders, followed the First Army into France and for five weeks recorded her interviews, within sight and sound of the front lines.

She kept a diary of sorts—broken sentences, bits and pieces—sometimes written while soaking her feet in her helmet. I saw it when I visited her in London after the war. Fragments stick in my mind—"eighty-eights cracking all around, death everywhere, the mud and blood, dirt noise and horror . . . a kid says 'I'm going to get a map and find out where I've been out here' . . . A sign outside, Broken English spoken here . . . Up the single track here go the wounded on stretchers . . . Down it comes a G.I. in a jeep with mail . . . One guy gets only a bill for a suit he bought two years ago."

Bebe was not only the first woman civilian in Normandy but the first civilian entertainer of either sex, and of course she entertained, not only in France but in Italy where 100,000 troops in front-line medical stations saw and heard Bebe and a British-American troupe she put together at the request of General Ira Eaker.

But it was her *interviews* as a "civilian" in wartime uniform under orders that were the grim but essential part of her offering. They meant reassurance to the thousands of families and friends back home—myself included, as my son Mac stormed his way across France with a storming General Patton—that an injury, even a major one, wasn't necessarily the end, and that the absolute elite of our medical corps was right at the front with our fighting men. That was morale at *home*. Then there was the morale of the *men*. Every quality that had made Bebe the most popular girl in Hollywood went into those interviews.

As I listened to her broadcasts I had to remember the time Harold Lloyd was nearly killed by a supposedly harmless comedy bomb, it did blow part of his hand off, and as he stood there dripping blood he said Do you know where Bebe is—as though the sight of her might ease the pain and shock. That nameless quality, that warmth, would be there when she talked to the men, plus the aura of her mature, tested faith. Bebe once put that faith into words for me. "Faith in God—the power of prayer," she said. "I believe that these are the greatest part of a *fulfilled* life."

I am looking now at two pictures—another most beautiful screen star, Madeleine Carroll, also a gallant woman of deep faith, riding the hospital trains through France, and Bebe Daniels awaiting the wounded as they came up from the beach on stretchers. I can well believe the men thought the Angels of Mons had returned and were fighting again at their side.

To take risks . . .

When the Surgeon General, Mediterranean Command, requested that Bebe continue her recordings with the Fifth Army in Italy, General Mark Clark vetoed the idea. Too dangerous, he said, more so than Normandy. But the vital question of morale persuaded him. "Bebe," he said, "we've lost some good men in this war, and before it's over we'll probably lose some good women. Go ahead."

For two months she lived at the front with the wounded and the medical men and women who were taking care of them, and then, after one day of rest and one hot bath, moved over to the British Eighth Army for a month to record from their front-line medical stations.

"In all my life I've never seen such unselfishness and such real love of one's fellowman." That is what Bebe said of her British friends and her own beloved countrymen.

Her unselfish services and willing sacrifice under the most dangerous conditions contributed immeasurably . . . That is what her countrymen said of Bebe Daniels when she came home.

For she did come home to us after the war, but for only a little while. Ben, who had a keen eye for talent, having discovered among others Jean Harlow and Marilyn Monroe, was appointed executive director of casting for Twentieth Century-Fox in London and, with Phyllis and the two children, the Lyons returned to England. Hollywood would miss them but I, for one, was glad that Bebe had gone.

With the peace the famous British cartoonist Strube, who had created a rumpled, bespectacled little fellow who plodded through the Blitz patiently meeting one crisis after another, drew another picture. It showed his little man standing outside a London theater holding a giant bouquet of flowers labeled BEBE. The stage-door keeper is saying, "I told you she's gorn to America," and the little man says, "Then I'll wait til she comes back." That was the message the British sent to Bebe.

The lights of London shone again, true, but they shone on such ruins and rubble, such devastation as shocked those of us from America who had loved the great city. The British were faced with the heartrending task of rebuilding not just this city, but a shattered country. I'm glad Bebe didn't make them wait too long, and that we had her to lend to them once more, this time for the rest of her life.

Not long before her death Bebe and Ben were given the royal box at the Palladium on the night after Her Majesty the Queen and His Royal Highness Prince Philip had occupied it for a Royal Command Performance. As the curtain fell Ken Dodd came out front and pointing to the box said, "Last night we were honored with the presence of Her Majesty, the Queen, she sat in that box. Tonight we are honored to have another queen with us, someone

we all love, a queen of the theater and films, radio and television
—Bebe Daniels and her husband Ben Lyon." A close friend, Jill
Allgood, who wrote a warm biography of them for a British publisher, was there that night and reports, "the vast London theater
audience rose to its feet—applause and cheers grew to a great cre-
scendo engulfing the floodlit box like a wave. Bebe and Ben stood
side by side . . ."

The most popular girl in Hollywood had become one of the
best-loved women in the world.

When she died there was sorrow on both sides of the Atlantic
—but no regret. Regret such as we knew at the death of Wally
Reid and Rudolph Valentino, of Mabel Normand and Jean
Harlow, all gone on with what seemed to us so much unlived life
and unused talent. As we were to regret the death of Clark Gable
such a short time before the birth of his longed-for son. No no,
the quick coal of mortal fire which was the life of Bebe Daniels
here on earth had been lived with such a clear, steady intensity,
lived so completely, that it left no ash. A *fulfilled* life.

LON CHANEY

They billed him as LON CHANEY, The Man with a Thousand Faces.

At the height of his fame, the greatest character star of all time
was rated one of the seven best-known people in the world.

Yet in Hollywood nobody except people who worked with him
in a picture knew Lon Chaney personally.

None of his fellow stars or top executives had ever crossed the
threshold of his small, quiet home nor met his tiny wife, Hazel.

There were two reasons for this. First, Lon liked it that way.
Second, his studio biography, written by himself, listed Hazel
Hastings as his first and only wife and the mother of his son,
Creighton. Neither of which was true.

Newspaper and magazine writers could sometimes get into his
dressing room to discover the simpler secrets of his world-famous
make-ups, but of Lon's personal secrets and mysteries we could
learn nothing.

Until, after his death when I was working on his biography for

Liberty, I came upon a line in his will leaving One Dollar to Cleva Creighton Chaney—and unearthed first a birth certificate, then a divorce decree, and finally the mystery lady herself.

From the beginning Lon Chaney was a foster child of silence. Silent pictures were to be his golden opportunity.

All that Lon Chaney became—the first great character star—all his fame and fortune began in the quiet room where his mother, born Clara Hennessey, waited and watched for him. When she saw "her baby," Lon, her smile always broke instantly into sunshine. Lon never forgot that smile. It was the only way she could express her love, for she was a deaf-mute. Lon, last born of her four sons, was her chief contact with the world.

In time, the greatest critics were to rank him with Chaplin in the art of pantomime.

Pantomime was no new art to Lon Chaney.

When Lon stopped at the barbershop where his father worked—well known around Denver was Chaney, the deaf-mute barber—his eyes were alert for scenes, to "tell" his mother about when he got home. He had to show the frail little invalid everything, all without words. To fill those long silent hours without radio, TV, he became a one-man show, collecting events, characters, creating dances to bring that *smile* to his mother's eyes. He was a streetcar conductor, an entire baseball team, the clown from the circus. He designed costumes from old curtains, dish towels, discarded hats. He brought the whole world as he saw it into the invalid's room and *silently* acted it out for her. Lon's brother John once told me, "You'd hardly believe your own eyes, how real he'd make it for her. When she worried about not being well enough to mend, Lon learned to sew, and he'd sit beside her bed pretending he was an old lady." Vast audiences were to cheer him later as the Old Lady in *The Unholy Three*.

At twelve, to help out, he went to work. Ran errands, was guide up Pikes Peak, a handyman in a furniture store who laid carpets and put up window shades.

When brother John got his first job in the theater Lon Chaney was eighteen—at eighteen from the wings he saw Richard Mansfield's classic hunchback, *Richard III*. From that performance he got the pattern and feel for his own great hunchback, which was to startle a new art and establish that character actors can be great movie stars.

Scene shifter, property man, head property man, assistant stage director, at last manager—Lon worked his way up in the theater and on his twenty-first birthday he took the Columbia Musical Comedy Repertoire Company "on the road."

In each town, Lon picked up a few girls for the chorus. It was good box office and saved traveling expenses. Until they hit Oklahoma City, Lon left those gals where he found them. In Oklahoma City, Cleva Creighton came into the Opera House in answer to Lon's ad for chorus girls. She was a tall, gently budding child of fifteen.

By the time I found her and heard her story, Cleva Creighton Chaney was middle-aged, work worn, cooking for "the hands" on a sugar beet ranch near Oxnard, California. I could see, though, what she must have been at fifteen.

When Lon Chaney first saw her, the shell he had built around his heart on the theory that he travels fastest who travels alone, cracked wide open. At first he gave no sign—not, say, for the first hour. Had she ever worked in a theater? The tall girl shook her head shyly. No, Mamma didn't approve of the theater. She didn't know Cleva was answering the ad. But Cleva sang in the choir, she said.

Dance? Cleva shook her head. Mamma didn't approve of dancing, either. "I can teach you," Lon said. "I can teach anybody. Lookit, sister." Alone on the dusty, deserted stage, he whistled his own music and danced for her.

"My heart took wings," Cleva said to me so many years later, "and flew right to him."

He could never teach her to dance—never. But when her pure sweet voice soared into "Kathleen Mavourneen," he knew that this time he wasn't going to leave a girl behind him when the show moved on.

Nor did he. There was trouble with Mamma, but Lon won her consent and three days after they met, Lon Chaney and Cleva Creighton were married. About two years later their son was born in Dallas, Texas, and at seventeen and twenty-three the young Chaney's were troupers on the road with a baby.

Later, Cleva had to crouch in the bushes by night to peer

through lighted windows for a glimpse of her boy who was with Hazel Hastings Chaney, the woman he believed to be his mother.

But in those magic nomad days, Cleva stood shy and gentle behind the footlights and sang Irish ballads and then rushed back to where the boy was literally cradled in the top of her trunk and sang them for him.

No home but a hotel bedroom. Eating in restaurants, doing the boy's washing in the bathroom if there was one, under the pump if there wasn't.

Finally, they got to the Coast. One of their longest engagements was at Pop Fisher's famous Princess Theater in San Francisco. In the chorus of the Princess was a girl named Hazel Hastings. Lon Chaney didn't pay any attention to the kid, though he did notice that the legless man who ran the cigar store next door waited for her after every show.

Then Lon was out of work for seven months and Cleva Creighton was "the furor of the cabaret shows," singing "Curse of an Aching Heart"—which by then might well have been her theme song.

In the dusty files of the Los Angeles *Herald* where I began digging after I'd found her, I ran across two clippings. One said that "Cleva Creighton has come back to Los Angeles because her husband, Lon Chaney, comedian, is here for a brief engagement."

So Lon Chaney was merely Cleva Creighton's husband. That didn't last long. Cleva booted chance after chance.

Their happiness had begun to fade. Their love degenerated into a series of violent quarrels.

Theaters were always full of girls who made a fuss over the good-looking manager and Cleva was insanely jealous. Lon had become suspicious because in the cabarets men customers expected the beautiful Irish singer to "crack a bottle" with them.

"Don't be too hard on Cleva," his brother John said to Lon.

But Lon Chaney was a hard man always. When Cleva drank too much, when she wasn't herself, Lon worked, took care of the child, grew grim and bitter while Cleva went from storms of defiance to fits of deep melancholy.

I'll never forget what Cleva said when I found her cooking in that tent under a broiling sun: "I guess I was just a woman who shouldn't ever have taken a drink. Well, I quit that. You can't drink when you're lugging heavy trays or cooking over a hot stove —but I learned too late for my boy."

I suppose Lon, that rugged, cantankerous young man with his rugged background, found it impossible to forgive her after he discovered that silly letter to a bartender.

"My dearest boy," the letter read, "Creighton is in the bathtub. I am going to play at Clune's, Fifth and Main. Gee, you don't know how sick I am of work, work, work, work. The doctor says I have lost control of my nerves. I take medicine all the time. I wish I could be quiet for a while. Well, I must go wash the baby. Yours with love. Cleva."

The doctor was right. She had lost control of her nerves.

One night not long after that, Lon came off the stage in his clown make-up. Whoops and shrieks followed him. But the clown didn't come back to take his curtain call.

In the wings, a woman fell at his feet. They thought she was dead, but there was a wild rush and scramble for an ambulance. When it came the clown, still in his funny face, rode to the emergency hospital with his unconscious wife.

All night long while the doctors and nurses fought for Cleva's life, the clown stood there, never speaking. At dawn, when the doctor said, "She'll live, but she'll be a sick girl for a long time," Lon Chaney stared at him a moment and then without a word he walked away.

He never went back.

So we come to the second clipping. "Cabaret singer takes poison in suicide attempt. Doctor at County Hospital says Cleva Creighton calls continuously for her little boy."

She never saw her little boy again except through the window, until he was a grown man.

When Lon Chaney became a great movie star nobody remembered the little tragedy and by that time Cleva had vanished as though she'd never existed.

"What could I do?" she said to me years later. "I didn't have a penny. I didn't know where Lon and the boy were. The stuff I'd taken did something to my vocal cords. When I tried to get a job I opened my mouth and couldn't sing a note. Lon didn't know about that.

"I never envied him his success. I never felt bitter. You see, he thought I'd been unfaithful to him. I used to sit in movie theaters and watch him on the screen. I was proud of him. I figured the boy was better off with him. Only I thought Lon might have let me see him but he never answered my letters and then I heard he was married again."

It was in the early years of World War I that Chaney and Cleva were divorced in a Los Angeles court. He did not mention her to a living soul until in his will he left one dollar out of his millions to "Cleva Creighton Chaney to fulfill any and all claims."

By the time he met Hazel Hastings again, Lon was making forty-five dollars a week as a stock player at Universal, an embittered loner with a small son, and Hazel had been married to the legless man who ran the cigar store next to the Princess Theater.

It was his second wife who forced Lon out of his rut and drove him on to greatness, of this there is no doubt—but it was the hardships and suffering he had endured as much as his talent that gave him the capacity for it.

Lon Chaney, cap in hand, stood in Irving Thalberg's office—a small room, furnished by a desk, two broken-down leather chairs and a lumpy sofa.

Another battle was on. Young Thalberg, head man of MGM, identified in the Twenties as "The Home of the Stars," was able to handle any of this fabulous stable which included Chaney, Greta Garbo, John Gilbert, Norma Shearer, Ramon Novarro, Lillian Gish, Marion Davies, Buster Keaton and Joan Crawford. But when it came to Chaney, it wasn't Lon alone he had to handle, but that unseen, mysterious figure behind Chaney, his shrewd, farseeing wife, Hazel.

At that moment Irving Thalberg was the most powerful man in the motion picture industry. There was a Hollywood legend as to how Irving Thalberg got his chance when at twenty-one he was secretary to the grand old man, Carl Laemmle, who built Universal City, and since, *if it didn't happen this way, it should have*, I've never inquired too closely into it.

One day, so goes the legend, following a series of disastrous blunders, Laemmle lost his well-known temper and informed his staff that they were noodles and numskulls. His eyes fell on his young secretary, busy in a corner out of the storm's path, he *hoped*.

"You know less about making pictures than this boy that writes my letters," Laemmle stormed.

Goaded beyond discretion, somebody shouted, "If he's so smart, why don't you let him make your pictures then?"

"I will," Laemmle shouted back. "Irving, as of now you are head of my studio and if you don't make better pictures than these dummkopfs I will hang you."

Irving made better pictures. Carl Laemmle had called a bluff and discovered a genius. After a few years Irving went to Louis B. Mayer and when the great merger of Metro and Sam Goldwyn and the Mayer company took place, L.B. put Irving in the driver's seat.

Thalberg was then twenty-four years old and looked twenty. He was five-foot-six and weighed less than 120 pounds.

Lon Chaney, always the rebel, loved him and would have no truck with anyone else on the lot. Nevertheless he faced the little boss belligerently across the piled and cluttered desk.

"We've got 2,000 extras on your set, Lon," Irving said gently. "If you work fifteen minutes more we'll get through with them; we won't need to call them for a whole day to do ten minutes shooting. That would cost us $20,000. You could work until 5:15 couldn't you?"

"No," said Lon Chaney, "I couldn't. I quit at five. What do I care if Metro-Goldwyn-Mayer gets stuck for 20,000 bucks? What's that to you? But five or ten dollars for another day's extra work can be bread and butter or new shoes for the kid. I'm glad I can make you pay it."

Never will I forget the day when news broke that Chaney was dangerously ill and must have a blood transfusion. By afternoon, the switchboard at MGM had to close down. They could not handle the calls coming in from all over the nation, offering blood to the stricken Chaney. Outside Metro's grilled gates stood long lines of workingmen, many of them still in their overalls, stagehands in whose union Lon Chaney still carried his card, carpenters, grips, electricians, grim and silent, came to offer their blood to their idol and avowed leader.

It was, as you see, the result of Chaney's defiant, "I'm glad to give the extras another day's work," to the mighty Thalberg.

But that was only part of Chaney's refusal.

"Besides," he said, "I have dinner at 6:30. My wife cooks it for me herself. She wants me home on time. When she finally agreed to marry me I promised her I'd never be later for dinner. If that costs you $20,000, that's too bad.

Lon Chaney put on his cap and walked out.

Hazel Hastings had taken the reins the day they were married and she never dropped them.

They had the same aims—peace, security and quiet.

When Lon Chaney's salary was in five figures a week, Hazel Chaney did her own housework, ironed Lon's shirts, mended his clothes—Lon never did have but one suit of clothes at a time, his ever-present cap, usually of tweed and worn jauntily, was his concept of sartorial splendor. This great box office star and his second wife lived in their small house like a couple making as much per year as Lon actually made a week.

"It is enough," Hazel Hastings had said of the $45 paycheck Lon was getting, when he proposed they join their battered lives. Hazel not only made it enough every week for the two of them and little Creighton, but also saved something.

I always got the impression that the boy never quite forgave his father when after Lon was dead, young Creighton—known professionally as Lon Chaney, Jr.—found out about his own mother and went to see her. How he felt about his stepmother, who was always kind to him, when Lon Chaney left her outright his entire fortune to do with as she pleased, I do not know.

Perhaps Hazel Chaney had some rights to the fortune for—Lon was getting $45, then $60, then $75 a week, and then, though he was an actor, handyman, assistant director and about everything else at Universal, in an economy wave they cut him off the payroll.

Now Hazel Chaney made her first definite move.

"You will ask for $150 a week from now on," she said. "There are not many in movies with your stage experience. The motion picture will go much farther than most people realize. They are building more and more theaters. You are in on the ground floor. Now is the time to make your place."

"We're doing all right," Lon said. "I'll get another job for $75. I'll settle for that for the rest of my life."

"A man must never settle for less than he is worth," said Hazel. "We have saved money enough to last a year. Now is the time to make your stand for more salary and for parts worthy of your talent."

That was the turning point in Lon Chaney's career.

Weeks of idleness dragged by. Lon was nervous, hollow-eyed. The savings dwindled alarmingly. Lon begged for compromise. Hazel wouldn't give in.

In 1919 came the break for which she waited. Lon Chaney made motion picture history as the Frog, the fake cripple, in *The Miracle Man.* He got $150 a week for it, too. From the day *The Miracle Man* was released Chaney became a major factor in the development of the motion picture. He was to write the original chapter in the Encyclopaedia Britannica on the art of Make-Up and Disguise, the inventions that made it possible for him to be legless, hunchbacked, dwarfed.

On my memory reel I see most of the stars as they were in "private life," rarely do I see them *at* work *in* a studio *on* a set. I never saw Lon Chaney anywhere else except once after his death—and that is a picture I can never forget. But when I see Lon Chaney alive, now, today, his background is a motion picture studio as they were *then.* In 1924, when I wrote the novel *Skyrocket* about a movie star, I described this background—which has to be part of the tapestry for all the stars *at work* if you are to envision our Hollywood—and I do not think I can better it today. I was, I wrote of this composite over fifty years ago, describing "the most important studio lot in Hollywood."

The doors of the casting office and the publicity department, the main entrance with its swinging gates, the rickety steps to the wardrobe building and the dozen gray doors of the executive offices, all face upon a gravel walk. On the right, the huge dressing room buildings look exactly like stone warehouses and behind them the stages, canvas-walled and glass-roofed, tower gray and dirty and mysterious.

Walking through those stages, unbelievably crowded and noisy, you would have seen a dozen companies, with a dozen stars, at the daily grind of making pictures, in a dozen different sets ranging, in their two-sided illusion for the camera's eye, from gorgeous ballrooms to east-side tenements. Here and there a set incased with black cloth, where a temperamental star who cannot stand the public eye was working. You would have heard the continual hammering of carpenters, the hum of music, the occasional shout of an excited director, the yell of the head electrician ordering his crew on the lights to "Kill 'em," or "Hit her with that baby spot." Seemingly hopeless confusion.

And a single set—

A whistle blew shrilly. The kleig lights banked solid on both sides, flamed an instant in their tropical purple and green, and went out, leaving only a trail of carbon smoke. (Follow these lights, if you will, and you will see that the dark glasses made popular by the stars were not originally an affectation or disguise, but all too often the result of eye strain or injury from these new inventions that made year round indoor shooting possible.) The baby spots, glaring down like a dozen miniature suns from the tops of the walls of the room, winked once, and grew dark. The giant sun arc sputtered and hissed a moment in fiery splendor, so brilliant that the eye of man dared not gaze upon it, then followed suit.

The electricians took off their gloves, and waited at their posts, while rehearsals in the dim daylight that came in through the glass roof began again.

The four cameras, shooting into the open face of the room, their tripod legs sprawled in every direction, ceased grinding, and the head cameraman got out a piece of blue glass and began gazing through it at different corners of the set.

Across the open end of the set was a row of canvas chairs, each with a famous name painted in black across the back.

In the dusty corner, a portable organ and a cello and a violin dropped from the heights of Rachmaninof's Prelude to the latest lingering ballad.

The quiet small home with Hazel and his son was his refuge, but this, the studio, and his studio dressing-room bungalow, was the world of Lon Chaney, his only world.

And when throat cancer took him from it, it was his own little group of musicians from the studio, with their portable hand organ, their violin, their cello, who played him Home. At the simple funeral they played, not for us, but for Lon—the music he had liked best on his set. From where Polly Moran and Marie Dressler and I sat we could see Lon in his casket with his cap in his hands.

I am wondering now why we went to that funeral—and we all did—the funeral of the most private man who *ever* lived in Hollywood. And why we felt so deeply the loss of a man it was impossible to know well.

It comes to me that, by keeping his own personality so definitely out of it, Lon was able, through his superb characterizations, to transmit to us all a deep and sometimes disturbing emotion—and we knew that he put everything he had into those creations.

Try this one yourself some sunny day.

Get on your knees, bend your lower legs out and up until they parallel your thighs. Have someone bind them, first with bandages, then leather straps. Put your bent knees into stump shoes, made to fit kneecaps. Try talking, working, speaking, acting in this position for hours on end.

Lon Chaney did just that while playing the legless man in *The Penalty*.

We have called him the master of the art of make-up and, as far as the movies were concerned, he created that art. He wrote the preface to Cecil Holland's book on motion picture make-up and this he would always discuss.

Other actors, writers, interviewers, cameramen, directors, costumers were admitted to watch him choose shades and textures of greasepaint, put in wrinkles and lines, change the whole contour of his face with putty, create eyebrows—Chaney considered eyebrows an actor's greatest asset—and to view his wigs. All this he would demonstrate so the movies might benefit.

But there were secrets within secrets. These he guarded as jealously as Houdini did his. When he began to perform those profound secrets guards were posted outside his dressing bungalow. No one but John Jeske, his dresser, was allowed inside.

Some of those secrets I know.

When Chaney was doing the sensational *Hunchback of Notre*

Dame, he got to the studio at 4:30 in the morning. First he modeled on the hideous putty face, inserted the snagged false teeth, celluloid tubes in the nose, hair-by-hair shaggy eyebrows. Over this the greasepaint, applied as an artist paints canvas. Then the wig.

This much anyone could know—or do, maybe. From there on the ritual was behind locked doors, drawn curtains.

Inside his eyelids he inserted a piece of fishskin, held in place by collodion, to give him one poor sightless eye.

With Jeske's help he donned the harness he had designed.

Leather shoulder pads, like those of a football player, went tightly around his neck and upper shoulders. A heavy breastplate of steel was fastened behind, across his back. The neck and shoulder pads attached to this in front. From front to back, between his legs, a broad leather strap hooked to the shoulder pads behind and laced to the breastplate in front with leather thongs. Then he and John Jeske pulled the thongs until his own spine bent in the terrible curve of the Hunchback. These were tied in strong knots, so that Lon could not straighten himself a fraction of an inch.

Over this they pulled a suit of heavy rubber that clung to the distorted body and concealed the harness.

Twenty minutes at a time was all the doctors said he could work.

Lon, when he got into a scene, got the emotional quality flaming, would keep on for forty-five minutes, an hour.

I once asked Lon the question many fans wrote him: Why? "No audience on earth," I said, "demands such torture. I don't believe it's necessary to great acting."

"Acting?" he barked, black eyes snapping. "This isn't acting. This is truth. I'm not faking a bundle of straw on my back. I *am* a hunchback. I know how it feels. Let them know, too, in the audience. It may teach them compassion for such poor bewildered souls."

Why did characters with handicaps have such an irresistible fascination for Chaney? Where did he develop his understanding of them and his own deep compassion?

His wife, Hazel, had been married to a man with no legs; whether Lon entered that world through her we cannot know for sure. What we do know is that he had entered fully, through love, into that totally silent, isolated world of his adored deaf-and-dumb invalid mother. And he never forgot what he learned there.

When Lon Chaney could no longer make a sound through his tortured throat he spoke for the last time in his life to his brother John as he had spoken for the first time to his mother—on his hands. His final gesture was the two lifted touching fingers, the deaf-mute's appeal for help.

COLLEEN MOORE

Once upon a time a skinny fifteen-year-old girl named Kathleen Morrison, of Tampa, Florida, with one blue eye and one brown, pleaded with her parents to let her go to Hollywood on a six-month contract offered by D. W. Griffith.

"No," said Mr. Morrison, "your mother can't leave your brother and me. And I can't leave my business. Who'd go with you?"

Then up spoke Mrs. Mary Moylan Kelly, of Kilkenny. "Let me go with my granddaughter and no harm will come to her."

Kathleen and Grandma Kelly set out to conquer Hollywood.

And doggoned if they didn't!

Thus began the amazing incarnations of Kathleen Morrison.

It was to be many years before Kathleen came back and by that time she was known around the world as Colleen Moore, the Flapper.

When, after many more years, she came back again it was as the chatelaine of the world's most renowned Lilliputian treasure trove, a fairy castle designed by movieland's great experts, furnished with tiny art objects and a great movie star's fabulous jewels.

Later still, when Colleen returned to Florida, she was on tour with her best-selling book, *How Women Can Make Money in the Stock Market*, written, I might add, not because of her famous name, but because she actually *knew* how.

But the amazement of Colleen Moore started with little Kathleen Morrison. For Kathleen Morrison had a normal, happy childhood!

I do not believe I can make that claim for any other figure on my tapestry. Kathleen had a full complement of two devoted parents, a father in the machinery business who was neither rich nor poor, a full-time loving mother, plus a little brother, Cleeve, who, since no one in the family had ever heard of sibling rivalry, was her best friend, *and* Grandmother Kelly who was considered an adornment by the Morrison clan. There was even a bonus of childless aunts who had married well and showered their niece with gifts from Paris and London and New York, exquisite miniatures which were known as Kathleen's Collection.

It is good, from time to time, to take a look at a normal, happy childhood, to prove to ourselves that such a thing is not only possible but productive. It is good, too, to remember that Kathleen-Colleen, brave girl, never denied it, thus all her life, when she made mistakes, she had to carry the blame herself. No doubt a case could be made that this idyllic childhood left her singularly vulnerable to the major tragedy of her life—but if so it also provided her with a faith with which to meet it.

Very early her mother had offered Kathleen an old-fashioned maxim—*God opens many doors in our lives*—and this her daughter accepted. When the dissolution of her marriage to John McCormick came, when he seemed to have destroyed Colleen Moore, movie star, and actually attempted to kill Colleen herself, instead of shattering like a dandelion in a whirlwind she believed implicitly that somehow another door would open on her next incarnation. And it did. It always did.

The first of these opened for Kathleen Morrison when she was five and went with her mother to a matinee of Maude Adams in *Peter Pan*. In the darkened theater the imaginative, elfin child glimpsed the Neverland, companioned with Peter, Tinker Bell, Tiger Lily, Captain Hook; it took her ten years to walk through it, but from that afternoon Kathleen knew—not hoped, but knew—that she would become an actress. She studied piano, went to convent school, gave theatricals with her brother in the Morrison backyard, and practiced weeping when she rode the streetcar. By the time she was thirteen and a devotee of the Saturday movies she didn't just hope to go to Hollywood, she *intended* to go. Her entire family was sympathetic, including all the aunts and one important uncle, Aunt Lib's husband, Walter Howey, who was editor of the Chicago *Examiner*. But Uncle Walter and Aunt Lib, as well as the rest of the family, as well as Kathleen herself, knew that a miracle was required. So young Kathleen prayed earnestly for a miracle. Then it happened. We could call it the Miracle of the Press.

I present now Walter Howey—that paragon in the tradition of terrible men so terrible that two of his star reporters, Ben Hecht and Charlie MacArthur (who married Helen Hayes), immortalized him as the city editor in their smash hit play *The Front Page*.

Later, when we had both moved on to New York, I myself worked for Howey, considered him the greatest, would have covered a cannibal convention if he had sent me, and believed firmly that he had a heart of stone. He was an explosive fellow with a highly colored vocabulary who could, and did upon occasion, recite *King Lear* in its entirety. Howey it was who billed me as a Girl Reporter on twenty-four sheets all over New York when I was a grandmother, when I complained that as usual he was leading with *my* chin, I quailed before his cold, cold eyes—or eye, for one of them was glass. We always figured he had acquired this in a back alley circulation war in the early days in Chicago and were hard put to distinguish which was which, although Ben Hecht swore the glass eye was the *warmer* one.

Now, I ask you—Howey as a miracle worker? Howey as a doting uncle rechristening Kathleen—"we need an Irish star, Colleen . . . Colleen Moore"—*Walter Howey* as the author of one of Hollywood's most dubious fantasies foisted upon the poor child when he put her aboard the westbound Santa Fe *Chief* with a box of chocolates, a copy of the Chicago *Examiner*, and a *kindly* note? No. And again no!

Yet I have seen the note and we all read the story. The note said:

Dear baby. Hollywood, where you will be living, is inhabited by a race of people called Press Agents. The studios pay them a lot of money to think up stories about the players under contract and to persuade editors like me to print their stories. So the moral of this letter is, never believe one damn thing you read about yourself.

The story that Colleen read in the *Examiner* written by Uncle Walter had also been sent by him around the country via the wire services. It told of the night Mr. and Mrs. Walter Howey entertained at dinner the great D. W. Griffith. Mrs. Howey's niece, visiting with them, substituted for the maid. By the time the meal wound down to dessert Griffith, who couldn't keep his eyes off her, said, "Mrs. Howey, you've lost a maid and I've gained a new movie star." Thus was Colleen Moore discovered.

An impossible tale? Ah, but we were practiced in believing six impossible things before breakfast, and this one became part of the legends of Hollywood. Nothing Colleen could say ever canceled out Uncle Walter's illusory dinner party. In the end Howey believed it himself, for he told it to me several times in the city room in New York.

"He was child-proud," Colleen once said to me. "He couldn't bear to admit that I hadn't gotten that contract on my talent and charm, that I was a 'payoff.' "

A "payoff" however she was. Griffith's *Birth of a Nation* not only moved audiences and critics to cheers but, dealing as it did with blacks, the Ku Klux Klan, rape, and the Southern side of the Civil War, incited a number of riots, much controversy and was continually threatened with censorship in big cities including Chicago. Mr. Howey had used his considerable influence to overcome the censorship problem there, Mr. Griffith was grateful, how could Mr. Griffith show his gratitude? And Mr. Howey said We have a niece . . .

I'm sure D.W. signed the contract for a youngster he'd never seen stoically enough. The cherished myth of the "casting couch" as a sure way to stardom, or even promotion and pay, was early discounted. This route was extremely chancy, whereas forthright nepotism and the "payoff" were certain to move mountains. Already on the Griffith lot were Winifred Westover, whose father was another newspaperman who had done Griffith favors; Mildred Harris, she who married Charlie Chaplin, was the daughter of the brilliant costume designer who headed his wardrobe departments; Carmel Myers' rabbi father had served as his consultant on *Intolerance* and instead of payment had said to Mr. Griffith—I have a daughter.

To this galaxy, via Chicago and a screen test to see if her eyes matched on film, was now added Miss Colleen Moore.

From the very beginning Colleen was as enchanted with Hollywood as she would have been with the Neverland itself, and Hollywood was equally enchanted with this pert young Peter Pan, so eager to explore every adventure her new profession could offer. Which she did. From the ground up.

The Fates were kind to Colleen but she gave them a lot of help.

Our Hollywood by now had developed a pecking order that was simple and direct: extra, bit player, leading lady (or man), featured player (where three or four performers shared equal billing), and *Star*. And few there were who started at the bottom and went all the way. The "old-timers," Pickford, Gish, Chaplin, had, of course, grown up with the movies. There were the "instant" stars as well—Wally Reid, Valentino, Barbara La Marr, who skipped straight to the top. But for most aspirants there was the pecking order. Because of Uncle Walter our Colleen skipped extra, but she didn't skip anything else.

Perhaps it is because of this that I see Colleen's life, unique among the figures on my tapestry, as "a reel unwinding in a straight line with scenes presenting themselves one after the other." Or perhaps it is because of the continuity of our close friendship which has been one of my great blessings, and has gone on without interruption, wherever we have been, whatever we have been doing, for sixty years.

First I see Colleen climbing that ladder. As a fifteen-year-old contract player at Griffith's she did one bit part for the great man himself—and it wound up on the cutting-room floor. She learned to curl her hair, stuff her bodice, walk without a wobble on high heels, and play the "sweet young thing" as leading lady to Bobby Harron. From Griffith she went to Selig to make *Little Orphan Annie*, an adaptation of James Whitcomb Riley's much loved poem, thence to Ince to play opposite Charles Ray. She learned to shoot straight and ride hard in Westerns as leading lady to Tom Mix, our greatest Western star. And then—and then I took her a copy of *Photoplay* and Grandma Kelly darn near took her back to Tampa, for in it Colleen read Cecil B. DeMille's pronouncement

that no girl could be a top dramatic actress without comedy training. There were two great comedy studios—Mack Sennett and the
Christie Brothers. And the greater of these was Sennett.

It was in the small bungalow on Fountain Avenue that
Grandma Kelly found Colleen and me in Colleen's bedroom, her
granddaughter in her decorous bathing suit practicing before a full
length mirror, me on the sidelines coaching. Said Mrs. Mary
Moylan Kelly, "You'll not be a bathing beauty so long as I am
with you. If you have to parade around with only half your
clothes on to be an actress I'll be taking you home tomorrow."

Colleen went to Christie Brothers.

On that day when Colleen and I took our sentimental farewell
journey around the Bel Air estate she was about to sell, at every
turn we were met by ghosts of those other days.

Jack Gilbert had once confided to me in the library that he'd
run away from Garbo that night. "She won't go anywhere!" he
said furiously. Bebe Daniels and Ben Lyon used to play bridge in
the card room with Tommy and Frances Meighan and the stately
staircase brought a memory of Jean Harlow coming down, looking
like a silver statue brought to life.

Here too was another ghost, not young, not glamorous, a ghost
holding herself ramrod straight because she was first and foremost
a *lady*, who had for Colleen and me her own kind of beauty and
her own kind of wisdom.

"Remember Grandma Kelly peeking over the stairs to see
Gloria Swanson?" Colleen said. "Gloria was her favorite."

"Not Colleen Moore?" I said.

"Grandma Kelly," Colleen said, "didn't rate you an actress unless you had fine feathers. She'd say, 'It's a shame you won't give
the child a decent dress to her back. What's the good of Colleen
being a movie star if she has nothing but rags to wear.'

"When we made *Irene*," Colleen said, "the Sweet Little Alice
Blue Gown was designed for me and cost $850. Grandma was on
the set as I came down the stairs in it and the director said, 'Isn't
that a superb dress, Grandma, and isn't your Colleen beautiful?'
To which Grandma replied, 'Well, now, as to that, Colleen's a
good girl.'"

And that of course was the key, known to Grandma Kelly,

which, when Colleen came to realize it herself, she used to open the next door.

For—

Colleen went straight from the Christie Brothers to the Neilan Studio to make her first bid for stardom. Mickey featured her in *Dinty* and so powerful was the deathbed scene that Marshall Neilan, that connoisseur, believed he had discovered another Sarah Bernhardt and signed her to a year's contract. When he cast her opposite John Barrymore in *The Lotus Eaters*, Barrymore agreed and tried to lure her to Broadway. From then on she made bid after bid for stardom and—nothing happened.

Her salary climbed to $1,000 a week. She was in constant demand. The press agents and publicists voted her a Wampas Baby Star. Rupert Hughes, then one of our biggest writers, best known today, I fear, simply as Howard Hughes' uncle, did three vastly successful pictures with her at Goldwyn. But there she was, still only a featured player, one rung below the top of the pecking order, the one that made *all* the difference. And there she appeared to stick.

Once upon a time—

Peter Pan arrived in the Neverland—

And now, when the Princess couldn't find the door to the treasure a handsome knight rode over the hill—

Do not tell me I have got my fairy tales crossed for I well know it. This has frequently happened to me and a lot of other people who have had to do with Miss Colleen Moore, one of those magic folk who can weave a double thread of fantasy and fact, fairy-tale-magic and down-to-earthness, who can create a fairy castle with one hand and make money in the stock market with the other.

The Fates themselves wove a double thread when they brought together Colleen Moore and John McCormick, a double thread of talents that worked professional magic, a double thread in private life of high romance and genuine heartbreak.

The romance came first and John, tall, handsome, talented, Irish witty with a double dash of poetry mixed in, was the perfect knight.

He arrived, as a true knight should, right on cue.

For if Colleen's professional life appeared to be in deep freeze, her romantic life was as bare as Mother Hubbard's cupboard.

Colleen was persuaded that she was a perennial wallflower.

Although glamorous romances have been at all times the publicists' meat, the deep dark secret is that this condition, or some variation thereof, has not been all that uncommon in our town. Well do I remember when Lana Turner believed, by some odd twist of logic since she had been divorced at a very early age, that she was destined to be an old maid. "You'd be surprised," she said to me bitterly one day in her dressing room, "how many men don't want to *marry* Lana Turner." This story had a happy ending for, at last count, Lana had escaped being an old maid seven different times. On the other hand when Ava Gardner, who was what we were wont to call a "regular gal" with a deceptive veneer of glamour and sophistication, at the height of her screen popularity remarked to my son Mac, "Nice men don't want to go out with me," I'd have to say she was prophetic. Judy Garland grew up convinced that, because she was chubby as a kid, and thought she had a funny face, she would never have a beau, and a sort of gratitude to any male who noticed her accounted for some of her later romantic eccentricities. Jane Powell, when she was a big singing star at Metro, was at the same time a student at Beverly Hills High School, and on the night of the senior prom cried herself to sleep because no one had asked her to the ball.

So you see, it is quite possible to believe that Colleen Moore, that enormously popular actress, at eighteen considered herself a wallflower. She had had a grand total of two dates; one, a friend of her piano teacher, had taken her to a movie and treated her afterward to a soda, the other, a lad whose parents were known to the aunts, escorted her to a Pasadena society affair which, since she was secretly yearning to go dancing at the Sunset Inn, she said to me later was "about as exciting as going out with Grandma."

Of course there was also the Indian who rode his horse straight up to her buckboard when she was on location with a Tom Mix Western and tried to carry her off, kicking and screaming, to his tepee. But that didn't count since she was rescued immediately. There was, too, Mr. Al, the elder of the Christie Brothers, a dear balding widower of thirty-five, who once put his arm around her at the studio, lifted her chin tenderly and said, "Colleen, you're a very nice girl and . . ." That didn't count either because our terrified heroine, certain she was about to be kissed by the boss, said, "Mr. Al, if you were my own father I couldn't like you more," which, you may be sure, was the end of that.

It could not be said that her life was empty. Or lonely. Far otherwise. Besides making movies one right after the other, there were lessons—piano, ballet, riding. Her father had changed his business so the whole happy family—and it still was—could be reunited in Hollywood. Colleen was a popular member of Our Club, a club with Mary Pickford as honorary president formed by successful young actresses, ostensibly to help newcomers, but in reality just a group of girls doing what most girls did then, get together in each other's houses to sit on the floor, eat cookies, drink hot chocolate, and talk endlessly, in this case about the movies. One by one the girls became engaged—Carmelita Geraghty to Carey Wilson, Virginia Fox to Darryl Zanuck, Mildred Davis to Harold Lloyd—and Colleen, that very normal young girl from that very loving family, went on wistfully longing for a beau of her own.

Thus matters stood on the eve of her nineteenth birthday.

Mickey Neilan it was who now called and asked her mother to let Colleen join him and Blanche Sweet and a young man, John McCormick, for dinner. She was going to the Sunset Inn—at last.

John had taken Colleen twice around the dance floor before he said, "I'm in love with you. When will you marry me?"

Unsophisticated she may have been, but she'd seen and acted in a lot of movies, so Colleen said, "Call me up in the cold gray dawn and tell me that."

At five o'clock the next morning her telephone rang. John's voice said, "It's the cold gray dawn and I love you. When are you going to marry me?"

At nine a messenger delivered an enormous bouquet of balloons with a Happy Birthday card. At nine-thirty there was a telegram, the first of nineteen delivered that day which, put together, told a fairy-tale ending of course, "And they lived happily ever after." In between telegrams came candy, American Beauty roses, an organ grinder with a monkey, a carton of chewing gum (to which Colleen was addicted) with a funny jingle on every stick.

All this I heard the following day from my entranced young friend. A fairy-tale romance!

One year later to the day she and John became officially engaged.

A year after that, the day before her twenty-first birthday, Ike and I along with both families, attended their wedding. It was a simple, quiet affair and there was no honeymoon because Colleen was in the middle of a picture.

The picture that was finally to make her a star.

I have said that I do not usually permit myself IFs, but there are times when the game is irresistible.

If Cleopatra's nose *had* been an inch longer . . .

If Louis B. Mayer had *not* paid to have Clark Gable's teeth capped . . .

If Mabel Normand and Mack Sennett *had* married . . .

If Colleen Moore and John McCormick had *not* married . . .

But Colleen and John did, and out of that marriage came one of Hollywood's greatest stars, and one of its great producers.

A professional husband and wife team working together successfully *as* a team is a phenomenon rarely observed in the entertainment business. When it appears it has a particular magic. The two become more than partners, more even than one flesh, they seem to become one talent. The Lunts, the French favorites Sacha Guitry and Yvonne Printemps, our own Burns and Allen, Bebe and Ben, impossible to imagine one without the other. The producer-star relationship in Hollywood has been even more rare, and the separation of talents equally impossible—Norma Talmadge and Joe Schenck, Norma Shearer and Irving Thalberg, Jennifer Jones and David Selznick, Colleen Moore and John McCormick.

The Moore-McCormick team started with John before ever he met his Colleen. When he handled publicity for First National on *The Lotus Eaters* he sent out more on the leading lady than he did on Mr. Barrymore. He nominated Colleen as a Wampas Baby Star. It was John, infatuated by her pictures, who had persuaded Mickey Neilan to arrange that first blind date.

From the time they met, John's campaign to help Colleen achieve stardom was persistent and brilliant.

The first break came when First National, until then exclusively a releasing organization formed by the twenty-six owners of the most powerful theater chains in the United States to distribute films made by others, decided to go into the production end of the business. The board of directors proposed to sign eight young people with star possibilities and John went into action. With the aid of a bell captain a new picture of Colleen bearing a pithy caption appeared daily on the mirror of each of the twenty-six directors.

Colleen was signed for four pictures, John was made assistant to the West Coast head of production, the team of Moore-McCormick was launched. It struck a reef when Colleen's first starring picture was a box office flop. The twenty-six bosses decided she couldn't carry a picture by herself and she was bounced back to featured player.

Right there Colleen's down-to-earthness asserted itself. "It has to be me," she said, took a good look in the mirror and broke the mold for all girls for all times to come. For Grandma Kelly had been right. Colleen wasn't beautiful. She wasn't glamorous. Up until then all the great female stars had been one or the other or both.

Because she wasn't, Colleen created the Flapper—a new style of beauty—and the day when a girl had to be pretty-pretty to be popular ended. The era of the Personality Kid began with the Flapper. Every girl in America to this day has reason to be grateful to Colleen Moore. A girl born with a saucy turned-up nose, straight red hair, a thin figure had no chance to be the heroine until little Miss Moore changed all that.

The Flapper dispensed with those time-consuming Mary Pickford curls and wore a short Dutch bob—John McCormick and I sat mute and trembling while her mother personally wrought this daring transformation. The Flapper dispensed with fine feathers, with ruffles and laces—her clothes were so casual as to be almost slapdash, she got her name from her odd habit of wearing unbuckled galoshes. From "sweet young thing" she moved into the free spirit of the Jazz Age.

Colleen's Flapper was something new under the sun. No girl had ever appeared on the screen with straight hair, bangs, and boyish figure.

The Modern Girl as we know her was born into the twentieth century the night *Flaming Youth,* starring Colleen Moore, opened in 1923 to madly cheering audiences. John Held, Jr., drew the Flapper to replace the Harrison Fisher girl. Literary heroines began to conform, hairdressing was revolutionized, fashions followed.

College girls everywhere cut their hair in Dutch bobs. They copied her clothes. She gave every girl a new dream. Any plain Jane could be a Flapper. No wonder they grabbed her to their hearts and made her their idol.

How did Colleen feel when *Flaming Youth* won the surefire publicity boost of being banned in Boston? "After six years of treacle," she said, "it's heaven to be given a little spice."

Colleen's salary shot to $10,000 a week. John, even after he became production head of the entire studio, continued to handle all her contracts, selected her stories, supervised her publicity, personally produced her pictures. They moved into a big square house in the Wilshire district. After *The Perfect Flapper* and *We Moderns* the twenty-six bosses, more and more pleased with their new darling, built Colleen a four-room Spanish bungalow on the lot. Designed around a patio with a live oak tree, it had high beamed ceilings, a huge fireplace, an oversized bedroom, a sunken bath. Three years after *Flaming Youth,* Colleen Moore was voted number-one box office attraction in the all-powerful Exhibitor's poll, topping Mary Pickford, Gloria Swanson, Charlie Chaplin, Tom Mix. The following a year she was again top box office and the McCormicks bought a half-finished Bel Air estate which Colleen began to turn into her dream house.

Up and up went the Moore-McCormick team; John, no longer acting head of the studio, was receiving $100,000 a year for producing Colleen Moore pictures only. And in 1928, in that hiatus between silent and sound movies, when the industry couldn't make up its mind any more than a hippogriff, John produced Colleen's most famous film, *Lilac Time.*

I adapted the part in this World War I saga played by Jane Cowl on the stage to fit Colleen, Carey Wilson did the script, Colleen herself selected her leading man, Gary Cooper—it was Coop's first really big part. John McCormick spent a knee-shaking million dollars on the production which included blowing up a real village, aerial dogfights using real planes, and, while the picture itself was silent, he incorporated a theme song and an orchestral sound track featuring a one-hundred-piece orchestra. It paid off.

After a gala opening at Carthay Circle in Hollywood, *Lilac Time* went on to New York for an unheard-of six consecutive months reserved seat showing at the Astor Theater. This was not only top money, but top prestige.

The Moore-McCormick team was on top of the world.

The Bel Air mansion was completed. Colleen moved in—alone.

John had disappeared.

The Private Life of . . .

Came a time when I was doing those first pieces on Hollywood stars for the national magazines that my typewriter seemed to write those words automatically. It was what the public wanted. The Private Life of Rudolph Valentino . . . Gloria Swanson . . . Marie Dressler. As Mother Confessor of Hollywood I wrote them all except—

I never wrote the Private Life of Colleen Moore. I knew it. From the beginning. Little by little everybody·in Hollywood *and* New York knew it. It is a tribute to Colleen, to the affection we felt for her, the desire not to betray the faith and loyalty we saw her offer John, that *nobody* told that story until she chose to reveal it herself.

> This time he didn't disappear. He got drunk and stayed drunk and sat around all day in his dressing gown staring into space and not making much sense when he talked . . .
>
> Finally I said to him, "You make it tough on me having to go to work every day and be funny."
>
> He weaved over to me, a wild look in his eyes, and said in a menacing tone of voice, "You're nothing without me. I made you a star, and I can break you just as easily."
>
> Except for the time in New York when he had tried to throw me out the hotel window, I had never been afraid of him when he was drunk. But I was afraid of him now.
>
> I went over to my side of the house, took off my make-up, and sank down on the bed. Not to cry. I was past that.

This scene in John's bedroom at the Bel Air house is from Colleen's own autobiography, *Silent Star*, along with Lillian Gish's *Mr. Griffith and Me* the finest to come out of the Golden Era.

Brilliant as he was, the disintegration of John McCormick, who suffered from a classic case of that progressive disease alcoholism, had been in inverse ratio to the rise of his star-wife. As Colleen went up, John went down. The periodic binges came closer together, were longer and more destructive. Colleen, in advance of her time, recognized that the man she loved was ill, stood by him through the drying-out periods, the hospitalization, the gold cure, covered for him at the studio.

I was in her dressing bungalow when she got the rumor that John was about to be fired as production head of the studio. That was the year she had been voted top box office, she was bringing in millions. Colleen picked up her telephone, got the head man in New York, Richard Rowland, and said very sweetly, "This is *Mrs. John McCormick*, I just called to say 'hello.'" Mr. Rowland got the message, and later I adapted the scene in *A Star Is Born*.

When finally they had to fire him, John negotiated the new contract which paid him that fabulous salary as Colleen Moore's producer. He still controlled Colleen's career, but there was no one any longer who could control John—including John. Colleen had finally to face the hopelessness that, before the miracle of Alcoholics Anonymous—and a true modern miracle AA is—confronted the family of the suffering alcoholic. It came on a night when John, whose alcoholic cunning always managed to circumvent the constant vigilance of male nurses, had passed out cold.

There was a full moon outside, and I walked downstairs and out onto the patio and sat in a swing looking at the blue pool shimmering in the moonlight.

I looked at my garden and looked at my life. My great ambition to be a movie star had been realized. I had built the house of my dreams. I had a million dollars in the bank that I had earned myself. I had everything a woman could ask for, except the one most important thing in a woman's life.

It had always been easy for me to pretend. Whenever I played a movie role I identified with the character so much that for the time being I would lose my own identity—and get scared sometimes that

I wouldn't be able to find it again. In the same way I had pretended about John—made him fit my image of him, believed that one day he could wake up and say, "I'm never going to take another drink," and mean it.

I couldn't pretend any more.

I went upstairs, packed my clothes, and moved to my parents' house.

Yet she went every day to the Bel Air house to check on John, to try, if somehow she might, reawaken him to sanity by interest in their joint careers. When, shortly after the release of *Lilac Time*, First National merged with Warner Brothers, Jack Warner had offered $15,000 a week for Colleen Moore without John McCormick. John, as her manager, had turned it down because John, her producer, wasn't included. This Colleen didn't know until many years later; what she did know was that when her current picture was completed neither of their contracts was renewed. In an occasional lucid moment John mumbled about Joe Schenck and United Artists but—

The day that was to be the turning point of my life came a couple of weeks later on a Thursday afternoon. I went to the Bel Air house as usual. The servants were off, as well as John's day nurse. The night nurse was due at six. Why I took my chauffeur inside the house I will never know. But I did, asking him to wait in the hall for me while I went upstairs to John's room.

John was sitting in his large, gold brocade overstuffed chair, his face red and bloated, his mouth hanging loose, his eyes blank and staring straight ahead. He bore no resemblance to the man I had married six years before.

Sitting on the edge of the bed taking in this picture, I said, "John, I want a divorce."

As the words sank in, he turned to look at me. Getting up from his chair, he came over to me and grabbed me by the throat, pushing me back on the bed shouting, "You'll never divorce me!"

Before I could make a sound, his hands closed tight around my neck. The room began to spin. In the hall below, the chauffeur heard John's shout. He rushed upstairs and pulled him away from me. Gasping for breath, I tore down the stairs, the chauffeur following. When we got in the car I was trembling so I couldn't speak.

I was still shaking when we arrived home. My mother made me drink some brandy, saying, "You must never go back again." Then she went to the phone and called our lawyer, telling him to file for divorce.

Colleen charged "noncompatibility of temper," John moved to the Beverly Wilshire Hotel, and all that was left of her fairy-tale romance was the great Bel Air estate where she now lived alone.

It is not true that either the break with John or the Talkies were the end of Colleen Moore, movie star. She made six Talkies, four of them after the divorce. The last, *The Power and the Glory*, with Spencer Tracy, was the finest film she ever made, silent or sound—a dramatic role in which she went from a young girl to a woman of sixty. But the public wanted Colleen Moore, the Flapper, and Colleen, now in her early thirties, felt she was too old for that—and too tired. She bowed out.

The little girl who had fallen in love with Peter Pan had grown up—or had she?

A dream is a gift given us at birth by our Fairy Godmother. A lovely gossamer thought that floats in the secret part of our imaginations most of our lives. I was one of the lucky ones, for my dream came true.

This is what Colleen wrote in her delightful book with its exquisite photographs about her miniature castle. Begun at her father's suggestion during the darkest years of her marriage to John, this shimmering dream of fairyland, which eventually housed not only Kathleen's Collection but all of Colleen's jewels, was to become world famous as Colleen Moore's Doll House, more famous even than the doll house of Queen Mary of England displayed at Windsor Castle.

Horace Jackson, who designed the sets at First National, as the architect of enchantment insisted that the castle must be unreal, a fantasy, as if it came from the pages of a storybook. Harold Grieve, the distinguished decorator who had done the Bel Air house, as castle consultant decreed that the period should be Early Fairie, furnished by a princess who doted on antiques and from the shops in fairyland would unearth such rare pieces as King

Arthur's Round Table and Sleeping Beauty's bed. And Colleen's father, who engineered and supervised everything, decided that the over-all criteria should be, "What wouldn't *people* have?"

The answer was rose quartz and jade and mother-of-pearl floors, a golden chandelier hung with real emeralds and Oriental pearls and diamonds with a six-carat pearl-shaped diamond drop at the bottom. *People* wouldn't have a weeping willow tree in the garden that wept real tears into a bronze pool, or amber vases that belonged to the Dowager Empress of China five hundred years ago in the drawing room, or the smallest Bible ever printed in their private chapel; they wouldn't have miniature stained-glass windows and wall murals depicting fairy-tale characters done by celebrated artists or tapestries so fine the stitches could be seen only with a magnifying glass.

Nowhere outside of a fantasy land bookshop could anyone find tiny volumes one inch square containing manuscripts hand written by noted authors for a fairy library, or an album of the same size containing autographs of celebrities from De Gaulle to Nehru to Picasso to Toscanini and Henry Ford (who once spent two hours inspecting the castle's minute waterworks and electrical system) and Einstein and Queen Elizabeth II.

Yet after seven years a-building all this and more was a part of Colleen's dream-come-true. The scale of the building was one inch to a foot; the completed castle was nine feet square, the tallest tower twelve feet high; the whole weighed one ton.

It was this extravagant toy, built for her own amusement and amazement, that launched Colleen into her next incarnation, the incarnation in which she discovered America.

I have to say here that, in my opinion, one of the reasons God seems to have opened so many doors in the life of Colleen Moore was that she never sat around beating on a door that was closed. This would appear to be an occupational hazard for many one-time stars who have tasted the nectar of that supreme ego inflation. Furthermore Colleen had enough faith to follow any new light, however dim. In this case it was the recollection of a promise she had once made to herself when she broke her neck on a movie location, spent six weeks in the hospital, and became in-

terested in crippled children. Someday . . . someday she would do
something to help them.

Ten years later she decided the time had come. She called Children's Hospital and asked the ladies' voluntary association if they
would like to have a castle-viewing tea at her house to raise funds.

The next thing Colleen knew she and her Doll House were on
a nationwide tour of department stores, starting with Macy's in
New York, where crowds in droves came to view—their 10¢ a ticket
going to local children's charities—and stayed to shop. In Chicago
20,000 were clocked going by the castle in a single day. For two
years, traveling in a private car with an armed guard furnished by
Railway Express because of the castle's enormous value, Colleen
crisscrossed the United States. By the time it was placed on permanent display in the Museum of Science and Industry in
Chicago, where it is seen by more than a million people each year,
Colleen Moore's Doll House had raised over $650,000 Depression
dollars for the children of America.

It did something to—and for—Colleen as well. Emerging from
eighteen years in that most parochial village called Hollywood
where the focus was totally singular and "Rotarian" a term of
derision, Colleen discovered not only America, but *Americans*.
She fell in love with the world of Rotarians, Shriners, Elks, Lions,
and the wide generosity of their life-style. She was awed by the
women she first met in Chicago who served on the boards of the
various charity organizations sponsoring the Doll House, women
who gave not only of their money, but of their time, of themselves; they served in settlement houses, as nurses' aides, in or-
phanages, at the Art Institute.

"They don't have time to think of themselves," she said in wonder, "they're too busy with people who need their help. *They're*
what makes America great."

From city to city, as an onlooker, a visiting celebrity, her life a
continuous chain of trains and hotels and department-store receptions, Colleen found herself looking longingly into the world of
"private" women who seemed to have found that "most important thing in a woman's life" and everything else had been added
unto them.

It was in Chicago, the city from whence she set forth to conquer Hollywood, the city where she first met and admired these

women and where the Doll House found its permanent home,
that the next door opened for Colleen. She met Homer Hargrave,
a broker, an attractive widower with two young children; they fell
in love, were married, and Colleen stepped over the threshold into
"private" life. She never looked back. Hollywood beckoned off and
on for some years but Colleen continued to say No. She had
found real happiness by becoming one of those women who "give
themselves away."

I was visiting Colleen in Chicago, we had gone to lunch at the
exclusive Casino Club, and we were giggling over her latest incarnation. I must have put a foot wrong because she said firmly, "I
am not now nor have I ever been a social leader."

Well, as to that, she was as close as never mind. I must admit
that in Chicago, as in St. Louis and all those lusty Midwestern
cities, Society=Service. It has little to do with great fortunes and
even less with "blue blood," the great ladies of society are those
who contribute most to the community. Let us say then that, as
the wife of one of the original partners in Merrill Lynch, Pierce,
Fenner & Beane (now Smith), Mr. Homer Hargrave became a
great civic leader. The irrepressibly spirited little Irish girl who
had created the Flapper buckled up her galoshes and served with
éclat on the board of the Chicago Art Institute, the women's
board of the University of Chicago, the citizen's board of the University of Illinois, the board of the Chicago Boy's Clubs, the board
of Northwestern Hospital—and was four years president of same.
She conceived and was the guiding light of the Debutante Co-
tillion, so that the vast sums that would have been spent on individual debuts for the twenty-eight invited debutantes would be
put together and contributed over $100,000 a year to the hospital's
free bed fund.

In her spare time she became a devout needlewoman (the rug
that today graces her dining room took her seven years to complete) and member of the Needlepoint Guild of Chicago; as a
good wife should, she studied her husband's business interests and
became conversant with the stock market; she also became an outstanding hostess.

"How many parties have you given?" I said to her the other

day. "Seven thousand three hundred and fourteen," she said. Whether that is fact or fancy I don't know, probably she doesn't either. But she does know the secret for successful parties, whether for four or four hundred, whether catered or hostess-cooked. I heard her passing it along to another generation, her granddaughter Alice. "Give it for yourself," she said, "even if you have an important guest of honor, because if you have a good time at your party everyone else does too. So do your homework ahead of time . . . everything done the day before. Better a simple, unambitious menu and a happy hostess than a harassed 'good cook.' *The hostess is the heart—sets the pace.*"

Or, for hostess, we could read "woman." For twenty-seven years, first and foremost, Colleen was the heart of a family, a wife, a mother, a grandmother—but *wife* came first. Upon this most important cornerstone she built her whole life. Which is why her next incarnation is to me the most amazing of all.

"The final lesson of learning to be independent—widowhood . . . it is the hardest lesson of all."

These words of Anne Morrow Lindbergh were reported by my talented young friend, Julie Nixon Eisenhower, in her timely book, *Special People.**

In a letter I once received from Colleen dated April 20, 1967, she wrote in part:

> . . . Clare, who we all think of as being so self-sufficient, is having a *bad time* . . . She and Harry were great friends, and he was her greatest admirer. It was like Homer and me . . . Her life has been cut in two—and I think more than ever she realizes how much she depended on the partnership they had . . . The truth is she doesn't know what to do without him . . . She feels poor and forlorn . . .

Colleen Moore Hargrave had been a widow for three years when she wrote those words to me about her good friend, Clare Boothe Luce, after the death of Henry Luce, but they also revealed a great deal about Colleen. There are those of us—more and more I suspect as the tribe of the so-called modern woman increases—who will never know the poignancy of this particular

* *Special People,* by Julie Nixon Eisenhower—Simon & Schuster, 1977, p. 144.

grief, never having had the gift of such a partnership to lose. Nor, I further suspect, can we win through to that final independence.

Colleen, after a period of deep suffering and the ensuing growth, did.

In this incarnation called "widowhood" she wrote three very good books, built another dream house on a ranch up in the hills behind Paso Robles, California, where she "farms" a hundred acres, worries about crops and the weather, chases deer from her rose garden and rescues her poodle from rattlesnakes, gives wonderful parties for family and friends. But she has done more than that—with irrepressible spirit Colleen Moore Hargrave has discovered the *world* and all the wonderful people therein. Not just the Paris-London-Rome axis of the smart set, but Egypt, India, Russia, Tibet—shopping in Hong Kong, the Taj Mahal by moonlight, the sacred Book of Kells at Trinity College in Dublin. In fact she has now been *around* the world so many times that granddaughter Kathleen, who once accompanied her, said, "Next time Grandma will have to go the other way, up and down over the Poles."

"On my eightieth birthday," said Colleen.

And at seventy-five? She called yesterday to say So-long-for-a-while. Whither bound? "Up the Amazon," Colleen said. "I've never met a headhunter."

Not to worry. I assure you no headhunter has ever met up with Kathleen-Colleen Morrison-Moore McCormick Hargrave.

Or anyone *like* her.

For that matter, no more have I.

CLARA BOW

Which came first, Clara Bow or the Jazz Age, is as unanswerable as the one about the chicken or the egg. She was carnival, the first hot blues. She was syncopation and when they billed her as the Spirit of the mad whoopee that followed World War I they were right on the nose.

The It Girl.

This title was hung on Clara by Elinor Glyn, famous author of *Three Weeks.* Today, that novel would read like Goldilocks and the Three Bears. In its time it was a shocker and made the beautiful Englishwoman an international authority on matters of L'Amour. Soon after her arrival in Hollywood, Mrs. Glyn supplied the movies with a two-letter word for allure—"it." She also said Clara Bow had more "it" than anybody in the world. IT went up in electric lights to describe Bow.

At the time Clara Bow was nineteen. Having more It than anybody in the world is quite a load to carry in your teens.

Nobody in Hollywood was surprised at Mrs. Glyn's choice of Clara except the kid from Brooklyn herself, the kid whose proudest feat was still that she had once hooked a ride on a fire engine.

Colleen Moore's Flapper, while she moved in the free and easy spirit of the Jazz Age, was about as sexy as a Shirley Temple doll. Clara Bow, on and off the screen, was somebody else. She smashed through any lingering conventions.

Clara was the kind of girl you'd always known only you'd never known she was that kind of girl.

During the time of her most sensational success, the It Girl was engaged to director Victor Fleming. After their romance was ashes and Clara Bow had escaped Hollywood forever, Fleming said of her: "A temperament that responded like a great violin, touch her and she answered with genius. Her acting could have been developed to a power, a reality that would have led screen drama to new heights. What happened to Clara Bow is one of Hollywood's blackest marks."

What did happen?

In 1925 Clara made fourteen films. More than one a month. Today Liv Ullmann, and Barbra Streisand make one a year—maybe. In 1926, when Clara Bow was the hottest thing on the Paramount lot, in 1927, when she was getting forty thousand fan letters a week, an all-time high, she continued to work like a dray horse. Picture after picture after picture without pause, all capitalizing on her sex appeal. She made millions for her studio, but their young star was treated as a chattel, given, as she herself once said, "nothing but a salary, untrained leading men and any old story they fished out of the wastebasket."

At one of those crossroads so frequent in movie history where one signpost said Art and the other Industry, Hollywood was more interested in the huge profits of the It Girl than in a long-range view of a future great actress.

In her autobiography Elinor Glyn, commenting on this black mark, wrote that Clara "would have become one of the greatest artists on the screen, particularly in tragic parts, for which she had a far greater aptitude than for the comic scenes which I had to make her act in my films."

Mary Pickford—America's Sweetheart.
Clara Bow—the It Girl.

A turbulent decade of fantastic hothouse growth lay between Mary's long golden curls and Clara's aureole of flaming red bobbed hair.

In a way, Mary Pickord brought the new idol to Hollywood. The fierce little girl from Brooklyn was another in that new generation to whom the movies had opened doors into unknown worlds. When Clara Bow could stand reality no longer, she begged or borrowed a nickel and escaped into the movies.

There she saw open country, mountains, streams, fields of wheat. Stories you could understand better than any on a printed page you couldn't read very well anyhow. Miracles of beauty, fine homes, ladies in lovely clothes—above all, there was Mary Pickford.

With reason, Clara Bow hated and despised girls. They made fun of her rags, her tomboy games and fights. In return, Clara stuck out her tongue and called them sissies.

But every little girl needs friends. Clara found hers in *Tess of the Storm Country, Rebecca of Sunnybrook Farm, Amarilly of Clothes-Line Alley, Pollyanna*—the girls Mary Pickford made so real.

With her vivid imagination Clara saw Hollywood inhabited by all those wonderful people.

A small, secret dream began to grow into a resolution. Anybody in his right mind would have told her she was silly. No normal, happy childhood, no aunts, uncles, grandmother to back this little one's dream. Far otherwise. A sick mother, a timid overworked father. Clara Bow didn't have a dime, a decent dress, nor a whole pair of shoes. At school she had never been in a play. So far she'd never even crossed the Brooklyn Bridge to Manhattan—and Hollywood was three thousand miles away.

A few months later, she was walking into a room full of ninety-nine beautiful girls. Her first mile in the long journey.

Jimmy Quirk, whose magazine was running a contest to find a new star for the movies, said the hundred selected to appear that day were chosen from thousands of photographs.

The ninety and nine were blondes and brunettes, perfumed, groomed, manicured, wore silk stockings and luxurious furs. The last was carrot-topped Clara Bow of Brooklyn, who had gotten lost. She, too, was dressed in her best. Plaid dress she'd begun to outgrow, baggy sweater and cotton stockings.

Among the ninety-nine a snicker grew into a giggle. If they hadn't laughed, Clara might have run. Getting there had drained her courage.

From the moment she read the announcement she'd told herself the idea of entering a beauty contest was crazy.

Clara said, "Papa, I've got to have a dollar."

"A dollar?" Papa Bow said. "Well, now, honey . . ."

A dollar at one time didn't happen often to the Bows, but somehow Papa Bow got the dollar that paid for two pictures.

Certainly neither fourteen-year-old Clara nor the photographer would have believed that within three years twenty thousand photos of that same face would be sent out every week to eager fans.

The laughter of the ninety-nine girls didn't make Clara love women any better—she learned never to expect anything but betrayal and insult from women and in Hollywood that made her defiant and reckless—but it sent her forward into the crowded, perfumed room, head up, chin out.

"Who's the one with the gorgeous black eyes?" a man's voice said. That was Clara Bow's first compliment.

The committee of eminent artists, Howard Chandler Christy, Harrison Fisher and Neysa McMein, chose twenty girls for the first screen test, Clara among them.

Nobody, including Clara, realized what preparation she'd had. The movies themselves had trained her, the little neighborhood theater had been her university. Lillian Gish—Mary Pickford—Norma Talmadge—Charlie Chaplin—Mabel Normand—those supreme natural early geniuses of the movies had been her professors.

The sense of timing, that vital part of every screen performance, had soaked into her and she knew the other girls were wrong.

Her test was one of five to survive. It narrowed down to a willowy blonde in Paris clothes and Clara Bow in her same old plaid. And Clara won.

An unbelievable triumph!

She won a silver trophy, an evening gown, and a contract for a part in *one* motion picture—Billie Dove's *Beyond the Rainbow*. Clara's part was left on the cutting-room floor.

Then a long wait when in spite of being a beauty contest winner, Clara couldn't get a part. Her chance came when she played a hoyden in Elmer Clifton's first version of *Down to the Sea in Ships*, made in New England. Ben Schulberg saw her in that picture, he sent her a ticket, he promised to pay her $50 a week, if she came to Paramount and they'd see what she could do.

She was on the way to Hollywood.

If I could have said to that little figure alone on the train, whom I can see so plainly down the corridors of time—*You*, Clara Bow, sitting there with a heart cold with terror, hot with dreams, an ignorant seventeen-year-old from a Brooklyn tenement, in less than two years your name will be known to millions, you will be one of the biggest box office draws in the world, your lightest word quoted. From pulpits they will cry you have more influence upon Youth than the most famous bishop. Your love affairs will make headlines. Before you are old enough so that your country thinks you have the sense to vote, you will make more money than its President.

For your art? Your wisdom? Your work? Your character? Your beauty? Your vision or invention or service?

No. The public itself will make you all those things for the sex appeal you don't yet even know you've got.

Would the red-haired child have believed me? Turned back if she had? Guessed what the end must be?

You know better. She was on her way to Hollywood, a bombshell they weren't expecting. Her only worry was the competition

—the only thing she thought about was the odds against her which were about ten thousand to one.

Coals to Newcastle—another girl to Hollywood.

Between 1913 when Mary Pickford became the first movie star in the term as we now understand it and 1923 when Colleen Moore made *Flaming Youth* and Clara Bow made *Down to the Sea in Ships*, competition for movie stardom had become heartbreaking. Girls from every walk of life, every section of the country, wanted to get in pictures.

Girls? We had them in all sizes, blondes and brunettes, and redheads. What would you have given for the chance of penniless, friendless, little Miss Bow of Brooklyn? History shows that within eighteen months she was one of the top feminine box office draws and the henna market had tripled.

Ben Schulberg put her in two or three small parts, bits, all at once. Then she played the wild, impudent, reckless, super-flapper debutante in *Black Oxen*, which starred Corinne Griffith with Conway Tearle. Nowhere on the billing could you have found the name Clara Bow. But as one reviewer said, "When Clara Bow is on the screen, nothing else matters. When she isn't, nothing else matters either."

Here was an instant star.

I met her first when I was doing her life story for *Photoplay*. Later, when I had come to know her very well indeed, I still used that first interview in a piece I did for *Liberty* magazine which we called Clara Bow, The Playgirl of Hollywood—and I use it here because there is no way to give you a better picture of this audacious young star who appears splashed on my tapestry with all the Bohemian vigor and boldness of a Toulouse-Lautrec poster.

An appointment had been made for me through the publicity department, I arrived at the Paramount Studio on time, and a publicist, who annoyed me by becoming incoherent about her, conducted me to Miss Bow's dressing room.

Miss Bow wasn't there, which was an omen. Miss Bow was never, at least in my experience, where she was expected to be. Trying to locate her at any given time was a week's work, partly because she changed her mind with every new impulse and partly because she was always surrounded by thoroughly incompetent people whom she either happened to like or was sorry for.

After considerable excitement they found her in a projection room where she was looking at the day's rushes. We walked up several flights of stairs to said projection room and knocked. Explanations, and then Miss Bow tumbled out the door.

I saw a very young girl, with amazing red hair obviously but beautifully and effectively dyed, and the most restless, brilliant, and arresting black eyes I had ever encountered. Under an exquisite kimono, her figure looked a trifle plump but—if you will forgive me—luscious. The two hands that reached out for mine were hot and electric, but soft as a baby's.

"Darling," she said, in a throaty, vibrant voice, "I'm so glad you've come. I forgot all about you. Do come in and see the rushes. You'll like them."

We saw the rushes—studio name for the day's work—and Clara talked all the time in the darkness, telling me the story of this picture, explaining to the director what was wrong with her work and everyone's else's, and giggling throatily over the bad takes.

When we came out she looked at me with startled eyes and exclaimed, "Oh, you were to come to dinner!"

Back in her dressing room, which was gorgeous and disordered as a night club at 3 A.M., she said, "I'm so sorry. I don't think there is any dinner. I'll phone and see."

But unfortunately they had just changed her telephone number again because too many people knew the old one, and she couldn't remember what the new one was. No amount of cajoling Central could extract it, and no one else around the studio knew it.

Clara gave up calling wrong telephone numbers and said, "Darling, do you mind coming tomorrow night? I'm sorry, but I forgot. I'd take you to the Ambassador, but we couldn't talk there, and besides I have a date with a gorgeous man. At least, I think he's gorgeous. He'll probably turn out to be a dud."

She told me that I was to come straight to her house the next evening and she'd be home as soon as she got through at the studio. She wrote down an address, which turned out to be two blocks wrong, and I went home, debating in my own mind as to whether or not I would go back.

The next morning my phone rang. It was Clara. "Don't forget about tonight," she said.

I finally located the house, and after much parley with a suspicious maid—Clara had forgotten to tell her I was expected—was admitted.

It was a small house in Beverly Hills, down near Santa Monica Boulevard instead of up in the fashionable hillside district. A big living room with a sun porch behind, opening into a little garden. A dining room and kitchen. Two small bedrooms. A maid's room. Clara's Chinese room, which was originally a den. Just an ordinary stucco bungalow. But inside it was exactly like Clara.

The beautiful and the bizarre, the exquisite and the commonplace—mingled in hopeless confusion.

A gaudy doll in frowzy skirts and wig leaned against a wonderful Ming lamp. A huge fuzzy Teddy bear with a pink bow around his neck occupied a corner of the luxurious brocaded davenport. The center table was a really fine thing of carved oak and the rugs were awful imitation Chinese. Most of the lamps looked as if they had come from the five-and-ten-cent store, but the shawl on the piano might have been worn by a Spanish Infanta.

The Chinese room—which was Clara's lounging room—was one of those things you read about in novels of flaming youth and never saw. The walls were gleaming gold. An entire side was taken up by a huge soft couch of black velvet heaped with pillows of lacquer red and gold embroidery and jade silk. A Chinese god looked down from a carved pedestal. The lights were so dim it was five minutes before you could really see, and the place smelled of some strange incense rising in clouds from a brass burner. The curtains were full length black satin and they were always closed.

Yet next door was Clara's bedroom—as simple and unpretentious a room as you would find belonging to any high school girl in Cleveland or St. Louis or Atlanta.

I waited in the living room, unable to read because I couldn't find any books. Papa Bow came in finally. Our first and only Hollywood *father*, an unobtrusive little man to whom his daughter was devoted, was chiefly noted for his self-effacement. My presence apparently failed to register. He got up and went out without discovering me at all.

Pretty soon Clara arrived. She looked horribly tired. Her eyes were pitiful.

We had one highball, which Clara informed me was all she ever allowed herself while she was working. Then we went in to dinner, Papa Bow having popped up again like a jack-in-the-box. The fat and friendly cook served it, with appropriate comments. The food was marvelous. Real French vintage champagne was served in glasses of Venetian crystal. Clara didn't touch it. Instead she drank three large cups of strong tea. She hardly spoke throughout the meal. She just ate.

Papa Bow vanished, and Clara and I settled down on the davenport to talk. I was worried. Clara slumped in a corner. It seemed to me that she would give me nothing. She looked tired and almost stupid, in spite of the feverish glitter in her eyes.

Then, as we started to talk, she came alive.

There followed a night—for we talked until dawn filled the room with cold sunlight—which I shall never forget.

My business has taken me to talk with many great and strange and famous people. But I think I shall always remember that night with Clara Bow—who had come from nothing to be the greatest drawing card in her own game—as the peak of my experiences.

Clara turned on the radio at its loudest and the jazz beat against the walls of the room until I felt quite deaf. I asked her to turn it off and she did, with the sweetest apology, and ten minutes later forgot and turned it on again. It wasn't only on the screen that Clara was jazz-mad. Like the kids today who are turned on to hard rock, jazz was her national anthem.

I cannot describe the tension in that room as we talked. The clash of its furnishings, the dynamic colorings, the throbbing jazz from the radio, and *Clara*, who gave you the feeling that the world might come to an end before you could finish what you were doing unless you *hurried*—so that you found yourself talking breathlessly and more loudly than was your habit.

Her own tension was catching; in all the time I knew her I

never saw Clara relaxed. Even when she was dropping with fatigue, there was no peace in her.

During that first night's talk it was possible to gain a complete view of Clara's mind. I do not know why she talked as she did. It was as though a dam had broken and the words poured out without volition; as though she had not for years talked to anyone who might sympathize and understand.

Once started, she could not stop. I had the feeling that never before had she reviewed her life as a whole, even to herself.

She talked about her birth, a birth which the doctor had predicted would surely cause her mother's death. She talked about her childhood in a Brooklyn tenement, marked by indelible tragedies—her grandfather dropping dead at her feet as he pushed her in a little swing; Johnny, the dear little boy downstairs who was burned to death before her eyes; the poverty brought on by her father's bad luck and failures. She talked about the delicate mother whom she worshiped, and her own agony when she saw that mother's mind gradually give way beneath illness caused by bringing into the world children who did not live.

"As I grew up," she said slowly, "Mother began to be afraid for me. When I first wanted to go into pictures, she was so distressed that I gave it up. One night she came into my room while I was sleeping. She had long hair, and the first thing I knew the great braids of it struck against my face. As my eyes opened, I saw that she held a long knife against my throat. She told me she was going to kill me because I would be better off dead. She said life was brutal and terrible and death was better.

"Her eyes blazed. I grew cold with fear. I didn't want to die. And my heart was breaking for her—her suffering. I gathered myself and sprang past her and out the door. I locked her in and lay sobbing against the door outside until my father came home at dawn."

When her mother died Clara tried to jump into the open grave beside her—a child half mad with grief at losing the thing dearest to her in the whole world.

As she talked, I realized somewhere in my subconscious mind that I was listening to one of the greatest tragic actresses in the world. My face was wet with tears, though I was too fascinated to know I wept.

I realized, too, the thing that alone could give anyone even a partial understanding of Clara Bow. No success, no adulation, no amount of fame or gold, could ever wipe out the terrible scars of her childhood and adolescent years. There was hammered into her soul a fear of life—she had nothing with which to meet it—and she sought forgetfulness in mad gaiety as the pitiful youngsters of today seek it in drugs.

Before me that night unrolled a mind entirely untrained, raw and strong as the mind of a primitive woman, grappling its own way with the problems of a sophisticated and civilized world. The things which the average person has accepted as truths were not truths to her. She accepted nothing. Life was as new to her as it was to Eve.

Never before had I been conscious of how much of our thinking we have taken from books, from other minds, from traditional laws and culture. Clara took nothing from anybody. The effect was astounding. To watch a fresh, violent young mind tackling principles, life, God, laws of society, sex, as though they had never been touched before, and discarding axioms as so much dead wood, was like being at sea in a hurricane.

"Why can't we know?" she cried. "Why is life so difficult? Why are we born with such mixed-up desires? Why are we so ignorant of where we came from and where we are going? I don't understand."

A reckless, lawless, honest, rebellious young pagan, with a primitive mind and a beautiful body, both of them capable of every fundamental emotion at its peak, her one law was to cheat her enemy, life, out of every moment of fun and feeling that she could get.

Going home that first morning through the clear California dawn, I was eaten up with pity for this girl who was on top of the world, who occupied a position almost every girl in America envied.

That feeling of pity has never passed away.

It is with me today perhaps more than ever as I see another young generation half a century later seeking their answers, as Clara did, in "doing their own thing," without pattern, without faith, without God.

I didn't have those answers then myself so I had nothing really with which to help Clara, although I tried. A lot of us tried.

I am seeing Clara now upon a day when she arrived to spend a weekend at our Whittier ranch. As she walked in the front door, my Mary Poppins governess of whom I was much in awe, walked out the back, taking my children to Grandma's rather than allow them to spend the night under the same roof with Clara Bow.

I tried to explain to her about Clara. "I'm as careful of my kids as you are," I said. "With the childhood she had, no girl alive would be more careful around children than Miss Bow."

My governess didn't believe me. She had seen Clara on the screen and she'd read tales of Clara's romances. So, when Clara and I got upstairs and Clara said, "I'm crazy to see your kids. That little Billy is a darb, he reminds me of Johnny," I had to explain lamely a promise to let them visit their grandmother.

Clara was changing into country clothes. The scarlet satin which she held tightly around her with one hand, the feathered mules, her really amazing red hair blazing, made her quite as incongruous in my patchwork quilt four-poster guest room as a tigress in a rose bed.

Her eyes met mine and I winced. They began to smolder, her face hardened. "Oh well," Clara Bow said, "what'd I expect?"

I felt like a heel. Knowing about Johnny, I should have been the last one—

I have always wished I'd let Billy stay home that weekend. Yet the governess was right.

Just the same, what happened wasn't Clara's fault. She didn't do a thing except eat too many chocolates. A well-known leading man and his pretty wife came out for tennis. In one set both the wife and I were playing, so Clara and the handsome husband sat on a canvas swing beside the court, in broad daylight, four feet apart, watching the match. That's all.

When the set was finished, the pretty wife walked over and busted her tennis racket right over her husband's ears. They left amid tears and recriminations.

I made it worse, to be honest. My husband and Clara went out to the kitchen to scramble eggs for a late supper. So I got in a fury and my husband and I had a row. All Clara had done was put too much salt in the eggs. I trusted my husband.

Moreover I knew Clara's strict code about married men. When she gave a dinner party she put all the husbands next to their own wives, books of etiquette to the contrary notwithstanding. "I don't want to start any trouble," she said. She was fanatic when the husband was a friend's, and I was her friend. "Why do they always think I want their husbands?" Clara used to say wearily. "Most of them are no bargains that I can see."

No, the weekend at our ranch was not a success but—I went on trying. A fine scenario writer, Hope Loring, who had done a number of pictures with Clara, said, "It won't do any good. Clara is the complete nonconformist. She has a big heart, a remarkable brain, and the most utter contempt for the world in general. You'll fail just as I did."

I did fail as she had, as Elinor Glyn had. But I think now it was because we were offering stones, or maybe oyster forks, to a wounded creature who needed the true Bread of Life. Clara was sweet with us all, grateful, willing as a good child. She agreed with us, admired our platitudes—and went right on being Clara Bow. And we went right on loving her and hoping she wouldn't get into any real trouble.

Which, of course, was hope beyond hope.

As her fame mounted, everything she did exploded.

Her love affairs, which were legion, including such stalwarts as Gilbert Roland, Gary Cooper, Vic Fleming, Harry Richman, were wildly public. Scandal and rumor of scandal with a dash of blackmail attended her tempestuous passage across the Hollywood scene. At least two men who loved her tried to kill her, and one attempted suicide, which annoyed Clara; she thought him a fool and a coward and said so.

Her penchant for gambling led to the rumor that she had lost $13,000 at Cal-Neva which she would *not* pay, while a newspaper told tales of the wife of a Texas physician and an alienation-of-affections suit for $30,000 which she *did* pay. Nobody who knew Clara believed the one or the other.

Her health, which in spite of her vitality and zest was never good, sent her to the hospital in several serious illnesses. Mad, short, whirling years of fame, of overwork and overplay, ill-health, and after the Talkies came, one nervous breakdown after another. The Talkies didn't hurt her. She made a lot of successful ones, but they drove her crazy. She sometimes trembled so with fear and nerves the cameras showed it plainly. Often before a big scene she would weep for hours.

But it was the case of Daisy De Voe that finally put her under a psychiatrist's care for the first time in 1931.

Partly because of her fear of women, partly because of their suspicion of her, Clara never had but one *intimate* girl friend in Hollywood, which made the betrayal shattering.

On the witness stand in her theft suit against her secretary, Daisy De Voe, at the end of two days' examination before a jammed courtroom, Clara's quiet control cracked and she began to howl like a child.

Turning her wet face to the judge, she said, "My best friend, Daisy was. Why did she have to do me like that?"

It had all come out. The checks Daisy had signed, the fur coat and house Daisy had bought, the $16,000 cash missing from Clara's hard-earned money. When the verdict came in Judge William Doran said from the bench, "Miss De Voe, this jury has been generous in finding you guilty on only one count," and headlines told millions of eager readers who had suffered along with Clara as all the old scandals were aired at the trial, "Jury Vindicates Clara Bow"—but it was too late to repair the damage to Clara's heart.

Heartbroken, nerves shattered, Clara now sought forgetfulness in marriage. She had met Rex Bell the year before the De Voe trial. Rex was a big, quiet, honest, good-looking cowboy who'd done well enough in pictures to buy himself a big ranch near Searchlight, Nevada. After their wedding in Las Vegas, Mr. and Mrs. Bell went to live on his ranch. A year later Clara returned to Hollywood briefly to make *Call Her Savage* and the following year to make *Hoopla*. Then, at twenty-six, she retired permanently.

"I was glad to go," Clara said. She loved acting but the truth is that for ten long years she hated Hollywood. The dream world she'd created in the neighborhood movie house in Brooklyn never came true. "I'd had enough," she said. "It wasn't ever like I thought it was going to be. It was always a disappointment to me."

The Bells had two sons whom Clara idolized and for twenty years it looked like Clara had found her peace. No scandal touched the marriage, Rex opened an expensive shop in Las Vegas selling Western style clothes, got into politics and was twice elected Lieutenant Governor of the State of Nevada.

But the damage done Clara had gone too deep. Rex protected her from rumors, showed a deep affection for her at all times, but she continued to suffer from insomnia, to lapse into deeper and deeper depressions, and eventually moved with a nurse-companion into a small house in West Los Angeles where she could be near the neuropsychiatrist in whom she had confidence. The boys and Rex visited her, she made occasional trips to the ranch and the family home in Las Vegas, but Clara's ability to deal head-on with life had worn out long since. This was a black mark Hollywood could not erase.

Trying to explain what had happened to his wife Rex Bell once said, "If she had been Minnie Zilch instead of Clara Bow perhaps this never would have happened to her. But the emotional strain of her early years was just too much for her nervous system. It's like training horses. Sometimes when you're starting thoroughbreds, you break 'em in too early, while you take a saddle horse and bring him along easy."

Vic Fleming had said, "A temperament that responded like a great violin . . ."

Alla Nazimova once defined temperament for me.

She said, "There are people who are like big brass gongs. To get a sound out of them you must hit them hard with a sledgehammer." Others, she said, were like wind chimes, lovely little panels of glass—a summer breeze, the ripple of bird song, the cry of a child and they made music, rang sweetly, gaily, sadly . . .

"The brass gong," said Nazimova, "is what most people have. The wind chimes—so sensitive—that is the artistic temperament."

Sensitive, often to feel things others do not feel, see things others do not see. This can be good, it can lead to great art—and sometimes to strange experiences with which we were quite familiar in our Holywood long before ESP was a recognized phenomenon.

I remember well when Bebe Daniels stopped speeding—and why. It wasn't her trip to jail that did it, it was a dream. In her dream, Bebe told me, she was passing a big white house and some people we had both known who had died came out on the veranda and beckoned her in. A few days later she was racing along in her open roadster when the wind whipped the floating chiffon scarf she was wearing across her face as she approached a curve. She pulled it away, braking, and stopped the car just short of a crash. There, a few yards off the road, was the exact white house *with* veranda of her dream.

I remember, too, the strange tale told me by Mrs. Robert Morris Phillips, Social Registrite of Park Avenue, about a tour of the Austrian Alps she made with Marie Dressler. They arrived in a small Austrian village where the innkeeper suggested a visit to the local castle. "No more castles," said Marie firmly. "But, madame, *our* castle . . ." Eventually Marie yielded.

As they followed the guide Mrs. Phillips noted a strange expression on Marie's face—as if she was trying to remember something. "We've been here before," she said finally, "I'll slay that innkeeper. Who needs to see the same castle twice?" Mrs. Phillips assured her that, while all Austrian castles had points of similarity, this was not a repeat performance. "I've been here before," Marie said again. In one of the picture galleries Marie stopped abruptly before the portrait of a long-dead Austrian nobleman. "Hallie," she said in bewilderment, "that might be a picture of my father."

It was, they discovered, the portrait of a member of the family which had once owned the castle—a General von Koerber.

Marie Dressler's father's name was Alexander Koerber.

Irene Fenwick, the lovely actress who left her own career behind to marry Lionel Barrymore, once told me that the Barrymores communicated by telepathy without regard to distances.

And when her niece Gwynne called Chicago, Illinois, to tell Mary Pickford Rogers of the sudden death of Douglas Fairbanks in Santa Monica, California, Gwynne got as far as "Oh Auntie . . ." when Mary said, "Don't tell me—my darling is gone."

Sensitive? Oh yes. But what and if that sensitivity goes wrong?

Clara Bow had the true artistic temperament. Damaged already as a child those fragile wind chimes had been smashed by a sledgehammer at a studio where she was treated as an expendable commodity—or a brass gong. The music stopped and eventually plunged her into a silent world of fear and dreadful imaginings where those who loved her could not follow.

Once again, at the end of her life as at its beginning, the kid from Brooklyn, when she could no longer stand reality, escaped into that other world—this time through television. Night after night during the last years of her life in her little bungalow Clara Bow watched the Late Late Show.

She died, apparently of a heart attack, in front of her TV watching an old movie. She was fifty-six.

Chapter Six

Love Hollywood Style

Greta Garbo—the mysterious, unattainable she, the strangest girl Hollywood has ever known.

John Gilbert—the man who took the top spot after Valentino's death, the maddest, most lovable guy who ever lived.

Garbo and Gilbert meant millions at the box office.

Garbo and Gilbert in private life were a short chapter unequaled in Hollywood history.

To me the reason these two never married and this mad romance ended so abruptly is one of the stories that has to be marked Made in Hollywood—it could have happened nowhere else.

In the full flower of their romance Gilbert and Garbo were added by movie fans to the list of immortal lovers. Romeo and Juliet, Dante and Beatrice, Antony and Cleopatra.

They portrayed love between man and woman as Shakespeare wrote it into his sonnets to the Dark Lady. Nothing like it in acting has ever been on the screen at any time, this perhaps because from the very first they weren't *acting*.

Some enchanted evening, you may see a stranger . . . it does happen. It happened when these two met on a crowded movie set in the light of day. Their love scenes in *Flesh and the Devil* "caught fire," as we say, and when the director called "Cut" the stranger-lovers remained oblivious in each other's arms.

Seeing that enchanted love, which perhaps many of them had

missed, held audiences stunned, breathless, thrilled by Gilbert and Garbo.

And when the great screen lover actually carried his *svenska flicka* (little girl, as he affectionately called her) off to his eagle's nest, a Spanish house which dangled precariously on a hillside—and she *went*, for we already knew somewhat of Miss Garbo—all Hollywood was equally stunned.

When they parted, Greta told him, "You are a very very foolish boy, Yacky. You quarrel with me for nothing. I must do my way. But we need not part."

Maybe not. But it always seemed to me that the end was in the beginning.

Mix Greta Garbo and the camera and you came up with great gobs of gorgeousness—mythical, sphinx-like and Nile-scented. And a myth it was. Unmix them, you had a shy, awkward, stubborn young lady who didn't wish to be the Garbo the camera created, could not be, never was.

I didn't know Garbo well, and that is an understatement, but I knew Jack Gilbert very well. What I know of their romance is told here exactly as Jack told it to me.

"You are in love with *Garbo*," Greta once said gloomily to him.

"Damn right," the dashing Gilbert, then at the height of adulation and stardom, said to her. When he told me about it he said, "I told her yes, I am in love with *Garbo*. I want to marry *Garbo*. She wants to leave the screen and buy a wheat ranch and have seventeen children and don't think she can't. I love people and cities and *conversation*—so I say I will not marry her unless she goes on being Garbo. She says she will not marry me unless she can leave the screen forever. So there we are."

And there they stayed.

She was in love with him and when in sheer exasperation he threw her off the balcony and she rolled down the Beverly hillside, she climbed back up over rocks and through burrs and tumbleweed. But she would not move an inch from her determination.

I have called their romance high comedy—but as I look at it I'm not so sure. The incongruity of this pair made for laughter both between them and for the rest of us. Yet once again it shows how close to tears love and laughter are. I remember the night at my ranch when, sitting before the fire, Jack said, "There's never been a day since Flicka and I parted that I haven't been lonely for her. And I think she has always been lonely for me."

Incongruity! How far apart those two lives were when they began. Never were two people born at such opposite poles of temperament, background, experience, ways of life, aims and desires. John Gilbert was born in Utah, Garbo in Sweden. She was pure Scandinavian, Gilbert was an American with Irish, French and Spanish blood in his veins.

At one point only they were in complete agreement. Neither of them ever wanted, from beginning to end, to be screen stars in Hollywood.

Garbo meant and wanted to be an actress in *Europe*, where she understood the people, felt at home.

Jack Gilbert didn't want to be an actor of any kind anywhere.

His mother had been a popular stock company leading woman. He loathed the theater. His boyhood had been hideous in cheap schools and boardinghouses. Sometimes he was forgotten, his bills unpaid. That wound still bled.

At seventeen Jack was manager of a stock company in Spokane. From there on, his entire career was a violent struggle not to act.

While he played extra cowboys and Indians at Inceville, he did a little writing and was always in Tom Ince's hair to let him direct. He quit and starved until Maurice Tourneur signed him as assistant director, then begged him to "help out" playing leads.

In 1920 he cajoled Jules Brulatour into letting him direct Hope Hampton.

Another lean and hungry session followed and then he signed for three years with Fox, at the end of which he thought they were going to let him direct. They didn't. Nobody did. He went down fighting. Almost his last act was to sue Metro-Goldwyn-Mayer charging that they had not fulfilled their contracts to let him direct.

The reason was obvious. He was too valuable before the camera. No matter how he hated being an actor, he was an actor. Moreover, he was darkly, romantically handsome and photogenic.

Like Valentino, he was made the moment's great star by one of the greatest parts the movies ever offered. The boy in *The Big Parade*, circa 1925.

"That was worth doing," Gilbert said, "all the rest was balderdash."

Like Valentino, Jack insisted a man could have but one *great* love in his life. Garbo was his, but unlike Rudy, Jack had many others. While he was at Fox, before he met Garbo, he married Leatrice Joy, the New Orleans girl who had become DeMille's leading lady.

Leatrice was beautiful, intelligent, had a sense of humor, wanted beyond everything to make a success of her life with Jack Gilbert. The fact that she was so desperately in love with him made it harder to put up with his wildness, his neglect. Though he adored her, marriage to Leatrice didn't slow Jack down any. On a night a couple of weeks before their baby was to be born, Jack and a few of his cronies arrived at his house in the dawn to find the doors locked. Leatrice, through the window, explained in a few well-chosen words.

"It was all my fault," Jack said later. "I understood Leatrice's feeling, why she couldn't take it any more, but I was stunned when she filed an immediate divorce suit."

That added one more wound of what he felt was injustice and he carried it unhealed the rest of his life. It kept him expecting, looking for, injustice always—and getting it, of course.

Soon after that he met Garbo.

Louis B. Mayer wanted a Swedish director named Mauritz Stiller. He got him, but to his annoyance he had to take also a tall, gangling, gawky girl named Greta Garbo, who had been a barber's assistant, model and was Stiller's screen protégée.

Garbo didn't want to come any more than Mayer wanted her to. When Stiller, a flop in Hollywood, went back home she wanted to go with him although her first American pictures were a sensation. "I tank I go home now," became a gag line, but when Garbo's strange, husky voice pronounced it on the Metro-Goldwyn-Mayer lot, the studio fell apart.

Immediately after Stiller left, it was chiefly Garbo's love for Jack Gilbert that held her in Hollywood, which she continued to loathe.

I tank I go home now.

As far as I can figure out from what Jack told me and at this distance her famous bon mot was simply at all times Garbo's desire to *leave*.

Few people in Hollywood ever met her. Sometimes we saw her, in an old trench coat, walking alone by the ocean, bareheaded in the rain. She worked, she vanished. Her own studio didn't even know where she lived!

That other famous Garbo line, "I want to be a-lone," was on the level. She was afraid of people, shy to the point of panic. She hated parties.

On the other hand Jack Gilbert never wanted to be alone for five minutes. He loved people. He loved games, indoors and out, loved to sit up all night with a gang and drink and talk.

When Gilbert and Garbo first fell in love nothing mattered. Then for a while, Jack tried to persuade her to try his way of life, meet his friends. We would go to his house, Garbo would be there, white and speechless. They'd play two sets of tennis, which she played very well, or swim in the pool, which she preferred to do sans company and sans clothes, and then disappear. She came to a few big Hollywood parties, gorgeous in black velvet, clinging to Jack's arm. They never stayed long.

Then nobody would see Jack for weeks, until he'd appear unexpectedly, defiant, excited, quite mad with joy at being with his friends again.

"We must do my way," she said to him. "But we need not part."

Greta would *not* marry him unless she retired completely from the screen. She didn't want to be a star. She wanted to be his wife and have those seventeen children.

"But," Jack Gilbert told me, "the glorious woman I loved was the Garbo of the screen. I knew what would happen if we bought a wheat ranch. She'd wear flat-heeled shoes the rest of her life. No, no, it wouldn't work."

So part they did.

"A happy marriage must be a safe thing," Jack said to me wistfully about this time. "Why don't you and I get married?"

"Because," I said, "we're not in love with each other."

"Love!" said Jack Gilbert. "We're good friends. It would be peaceful."

"You're unhappy now," I said, "but you don't really want peace. You'll fall in love, more or less, with somebody. You once told me you'd rather spend an hour with Flicka than a lifetime with any other woman. I wouldn't care to be your wife on those terms."

Probably the two women who accepted his proposal didn't know about that. A fine, intelligent woman, a great stage actress, Ina Claire, tried to teach Jack how to read lines in the terrible adjustment to the Talkies. Having resented headlines which said Jack Gilbert Weds Actress—she thought it should have been Ina Claire Weds Movie Star—she took advantage of her great superiority in spoken drama to rub it in a little and Jack bucked.

Of Virginia Bruce, his last wife, he said: "She is an angel. If I'd met her sooner my life might have been different."

John Gilbert had just signed a new MGM contract calling for a million dollars. Came the Talkies and he was worth less at the box office than a bag of popcorn. No man ever hurtled from so high a pinnacle so fast. Three little words destroyed his fame, his fortune, his future.

He was the first man to say "I love you" in the Talkies.

The audience laughed.

That was the death knell of Jack Gilbert.

Partially I myself believe that laughter came from embarrassment—that disconcerted giggle women give when they have unexpectedly caught someone in an indiscretion. Here was their silent lover actually saying *out loud*, "I love you." The other part was that his voice didn't match the screen personality audiences worshiped. The latter was the official version, and on those grounds the studio tried to buy back his contract. Jack refused.

He begged to direct. But Gilbert had almost as many enemies as he had friends. Unfortunately, the enemies he'd made were in high places. He was difficult, a little mad, he drank too much. But he had creative genius, he had many virtues, he might have been turned into a great asset instead of tossed on the scrap heap like a worn-out rag doll. The movies can be brutal as my beloved Frances Marion attested when she titled her Hollywood memoirs *Off with Their Heads!*

When Jack Gilbert finished his contract his head was certainly scheduled to roll; only one person on the Metro lot had enough clout to stay the execution, Miss Greta Garbo.

It had been six years since these two made *Flesh and the Devil*, at least four since their final parting. Yet when Garbo, who slid into the Talkies as if they'd been invented especially for her, was scheduled to make *Queen Christina* and Laurence Olivier had been imported from England to play opposite her, of a sudden Miss Garbo did not feel Olivier was right for the part.

Who was?

"Jack Gilbert," said Greta Garbo. When the studio once again fell apart Miss Garbo simply continued to say, "Jack Gilbert."

The critics praised his performance in *Queen Christina* but— this time the love scenes did not "catch fire." The public it was who turned thumbs down. And that was the end of John Gilbert. It was he who left the screen forever.

"There's never been a day since Flicka and I parted that I haven't been lonely for her. I think that she has always been lonely for me."

Poor Jack. What Flicka really felt nobody ever knew. But she had made a supreme gesture to their lost love.

Garbo never married; she retired from pictures while she was still on top.

Jack Gilbert died, aged thirty-eight, a few years after they made *Queen Christina*. I think he was glad to go.

GARY COOPER'S LOVE STORY IN THREE ACTS

Gary and the Fiery Lupe

To this day, the only explanation I have of the fact that Gary Cooper's premarital romances fill me with laughter is that he himself was so grave in the midst of them.

Some of them had tears enough, nevertheless they also had a quality of magnificent comedy as far as I was concerned from the first night the big cowboy came to Sunday night supper at my Whittier ranch and I watched three Hollywood beauties maneuver to see which he'd take home.

Gary got away that time. On my desk the next morning I found a note explaining he didn't want to break up the party so he'd left without saying good-bye.

But the grave and silent young man from the great open spaces didn't get away from Clara Bow or Lupe Velez or the Countess Dorothy di Frasso, an international beauty who later went on the bizarre cruise of the "hell ship" *Metha Nelson*, along with gangster Bugsy Siegel.

When we think of Coop today (and we do, we *all* do, for he is one of the stars who live on in our hearts), we remember him as the husband of one woman who had a long, quiet and peaceful married life. And so he was. But in the Golden Days when he was Hollywood's most eligible bachelor his romantic life was far otherwise, the tempest that surrounded it evident in constant speculation as to whether he would or would not marry Clara, or the stunning Evelyn Brent, or Tallulah Bankhead, or the Countess.

But mostly Lupe!

When Gary finally found the one girl he wanted for his wife, it was swift and definite, but very formal and correct. Gary has always been the Cowboy to Hollywood, which makes you forget he spent two years at school in England, three at Grinnell College. His father left England to ranch in America, but he also became a justice of the Supreme Court of Montana. Gary did punch cows and break horses on a vast Montana cattle ranch and he always went along with the idea that the movies picked him off the range. Actually, he came to California looking for a job as a newspaper cartoonist or commercial artist and did movie extras to eat.

His courtship of debutante Veronica Balfe was chaperoned, their engagement announced at a formal dance given by the mother and stepfather of his fiancée, Mr. and Mrs. Paul Shields, of Park Avenue, East Hampton and the New York Stock Exchange, and the marriage was in the bride's Park Avenue home. That one marriage of Gary's lasted until his death twenty-eight years later.

It occurs to me that Gary Cooper walked the tightrope of a long, consistently magnificent career as a great Movie Star without ever making a false step. And as I write this today, not too long after our Bicentennial Year, I see him as the single star who most captured forever on film the way of life we long to remember.

In 1941, Gary Cooper was characterized as "the most popular man in the nation." With a beard, somebody once said, he would not look unlike Abraham Lincoln.

One by one, he put various states on film for an impressive and heartwarming record. *The Texan*, *A Man from Wyoming*, *Arizona Bound*, *The Virginian*, *The Plainsman*.

From the day in 1925 when Frances Marion spotted him on the Sam Goldwyn lot and persuaded Sam to give him the part of the young Westerner in *The Winning of Barbara Worth* which starred the English Ronald Colman and the Hungarian beauty Vilma Banky, Cooper was the *American*. We knew he had survived the Talkies when the mike picked up his first deep All-American "Yup!" Not only with his Academy Award performances as the World War I hero, Sergeant York, and the high-minded, tough sheriff in *High Noon*, but also as Lou Gehrig, Dr. Wassell, Mr. Deeds, the leader of the Confederate secret service in Marion Davies' unforgettable *Operator 13*, Gary Cooper put on the screen the real American with those qualities which made America, with courage, honor, decency, truth, old-fashioned virtue and morality and high ideals.

America owes Gary Cooper—and the movies—a great debt for that. It's been nice to remind ourselves and the rest of the world of those things.

I watched over the years as his acting grew in depth and stature but again I am overcome with laughter as I remember the trouble directors in the early days had with Cooper's *legs*. When he went directly from Goldwyn to a Paramount contract among his first pictures was a story I had written, and the ingenuity that Frank Lloyd, one of Hollywood's great directors, displayed in hiding the long Cooper legs remains a delight to me. For stage fright went to Gary's legs. They trembled like aspens in a high wind, and Frank shot him in scenes where only his head and shoulders showed, behind every conceivable piece of furniture, wearing long bathrobes and polo coats. No actor every played so many scenes sitting down as Coop did in *Children of Divorce*.

Lloyd had other difficulties with that picture. Its star, the redheaded It Girl Clara Bow, and her new leading man, the silent, sun-tanned twenty-six-year-old cowboy, Gary Cooper, fell in love.

However, like many young people in love they fought. And a black eye, even when bestowed by one's ladylove, is no help to the cameraman. Nor were the reconciliations, which took place all over the lot, much quieter, though Gary always forgave the redhead. Just the same that extra-celluloid romance must have cost the studio $100,000 in time lost, and the powers that be heaved a sigh of relief when this torrid romance cooled as suddenly as it began.

The three musketeers of those days were Gary, Buddy Rogers, and Richard Arlen. (Later there was Bing Crosby, who named his first son Gary.) Coop was low man on that totem pole until in *Wings* he stole the picture from Buddy and Dick in one little scene where his smile at his flying buddies as he walked out of the tent somehow said it was his last good-bye.

But they all trusted Coop and Coop only when it came to money, contracts, parts, promotion, publicity or trouble and, again like the Virginian, Cooper played a stiff hand of stud poker. At ease, relaxed, grave and courteous he would let the busy executives on the other side of the desk talk. Sometimes in that gentle voice, Coop would say a word. Mostly no. Usually, he was silent. A Big Shot said to me once in a burst of nervous exasperation, "Cooper is always polite but I feel he's got a gun stuck in his pants."

Maybe that was the time they offered him $600 a week and Gary stood pat for $1,750—and a raise for the other boys, too. Over the years, he handled his career with cool common sense, vision and judgment.

Only one person ever took Gary off his feet. The doctors called it "complete collapse." He grew so thin and haggard it shocked his friends and I wondered if he'd come back alive from the long rest his doctors finally ordered.

Strange, how up to a given moment it seemed so funny—tiny, tempestuous Lupe Velez and six-foot-three of slow-moving Cooper; her firecracker Mexican accent and her sparkling laughter against the slow drawl and slower smile of the big cowboy; Lupe's public demonstrations and declarations of love and Gary's embarrassment and adoration. Then, all of a sudden, it was a matter of life and death.

Part of what was called a nervous breakdown was overwork, but most of it was an emotional upheaval.

"Can I help what I am?" Lupe said to me once. "I am free to do as I please. I will never have a boss except Lupe. I earn my own money, why should I not live as I please?"

FUN WAS COCKFIGHTS,
DIRTY MOVIES, AND BOOZE.
MONEY CAME FROM SELLING
HERSELF AS A CALL GIRL.
HOLLYWOOD IN THE 30'S. (so it says)

I quote this from an ad for a picture Now Playing which says it is about a big-time Movie Star.

On all that I hold most sacred, I *promise* you that I never in Hollywood in the Thirties where I was *at,* where I lived and worked and had my being, a lot of it *covering* movies and movie stars, I never heard of a cockfight. *Never.* Dirty movies there were; they were made illicitly then as now by stinking little outfits in no wise connected with the Industry specially for and sold specifically to men's gatherings—lodges and clubs and alumni associations and such. As near as I can make out, this has been going on since Hannibal crossed the Alps and somewhat before. Seems to be very little question that when Nero fiddled while Rome burned he was watching—and fiddling for—some pretty suggestive dances and back in Egypt before Cleopatra decided she preferred the *asp* there was a rumor around that the tales would later be put together by an Italian writer named Boccaccio.

No movie star I ever knew, heard about or saw sold herself as a call girl. There were movie stars whose activities kept them pretty busy at the same occupation for which call girls allegedly got paid. But that any of them were movie stars and call girls at the same time I *know* is not true.

In those days there was a whorehouse run by a lady named Madame Frances. I say lady advisedly, because in manners, vocabulary, conversation and appearance she was more nearly what my grandmother considered a lady than most of today's Women's

Lib ringtail roarers. As Mother Confessor of Hollywood I was friends with Madame Frances and consulted her from time to time about the marital states and stages of various movie stars. Years before, I'd had a good friend named Pearl Morton who ran what we then called a House (many years later a *madam* named Polly Adler wrote a book called *A House Is Not a Home*) and it was their conviction that no man who had a happy home had ever entered their houses. Of course now that prostitution is a sideline and hobby with alleged respectable women and wives and an unmarried girl can keep her "virtue" and her clear conscience with the aid of the Pill and legalized abortion, it wouldn't be profitable to keep track of such things and in fact with so much sex for free and for nothing I can't quite see how a prostitute can make a living, and the gals who are movie actresses and whores at the same time wouldn't be doing very well at either, but I do know that in the Thirties—I mean this I *know*, they weren't doubling at that level *in the Thirties*.

Let us look on my tapestry at Lupe Velez. Never was a more effervescent, earthy female Latin personality on that scene. If Clara Bow stands there as a Toulouse-Lautrec poster, Lupe was pure Goya, all rich reds and strong colors, and as Clara fades as our Playgirl of the Twenties there in the Thirties is Lupe, the epitome of joyous, uninhibited lust-for-life. And yet poor little Lupe, who made everyone laugh, Lupe the breaker of Hollywood hearts, was to die by her own hand at thirty-three because she had *standards* and an ideal of virtue.

In the legends of Hollywood there has never been another like her, so stormy, so merry, so warmhearted. Our other Mexican star of those days, Dolores Del Rio, was of a far different type and temperament. A serene beauty, Dolores was born Lolita Dolores Asunsolo de Martinez Lopez Negrette on a great ranch in Durango, educated at a convent in Mexico City, presented at court in Spain at fourteen, married at sixteen to an Oxford graduate and playwright, Jaime Del Rio, who died. A genuine daughter of the Dons was Dolores, formally introduced to Hollywood by Edwin Carewe who saw her dance at a charity bazaar in Old Mexico. Not so our Lupe. What her background was we never knew but—what matter? There she was, as colorful and explosive as the

Fourth of July. Never for one instant had she the need of pornography or *booze* to put fire in her blood. Cockfights? No no. But to this minute we who saw her have no more vivid memory than of Lupe Velez at the Hollywood Legion prizefights. Visiting celebrities were always taken there but not to see the bouts, to see Lupe rooting, storming through the rope to assault the referee if she didn't like the decision, putting on a better show than the one in the ring. Things were never the same at the Legion after Lupe.

"Pooh," said Lupe, when United Artists announced they'd made her a star. "Pooh, I am always a star! When I come from Mexico I am not yet sixteen, I have not a peso, but even before Douglas Fairbanks puts me in *The Gaucho* I know I am a star already."

Two years after *The Gaucho* when they made *Wolf Song* together, she hit Gary Cooper like a Mexican thunderstorm.

I came back from swimming one day at Malibu Beach to find Gary sound asleep on my couch and Lupe kneeling beside him. Now I yield to no one in finding Cooper as attractive a man as has ever been in Hollywood, but Cooper asleep and snoring gently with his mouth open was a good deal like any other man asleep and snoring gently with his mouth open. Nevertheless, Lupe looked up at me and said in a voice throbbing with emotion, "Is he not beautiful? I have never seen anyone so beautiful as my Gary."

Just then, one of Cooper's eyes opened and I saw that he was utterly overcome with mirth. Lupe, turning swiftly, saw it too. "You laugh at your Lupe's love!" she cried, and it turned into one of those scenes that probably, in the end, caused Gary's nervous breakdown. Lupe adored scenes.

It seems incredible now when we think of the stature he attained as the wise, quiet, steadfast man, that in 1929 Cooper was at the center of a maelstrom of gossip: "What about Miss Velez and her Gary? Are they married? Most people in Hollywood think so."

In April, Lupe was quoted as saying, "Of course I love him. Marry him? Well, who will know what I do until I do it, eh? Maybe tomorrow, maybe next month, maybe never. But I think maybe."

In November she said capriciously, "I don't love Gary Cooper. I don't love anybody. I will never marry. I stay Lupe. I am sick of love."

She did love Gary Cooper. Just before her pitiful death, she told her loyal friend Estelle Taylor he was for her "the big love." She told me so, too.

On tour, she used to telephone Gary and talk $400 worth. "If I do not, I will die," she said. "I am so lonesome for him."

They never married. After three years of such fireworks as nobody but Lupe ever set off in Hollywood, Lupe said with her famous little shrug, "I have got tired of Gary, but he is one good man just the same."

Lupe had a real fear of marriage as the end of freedom. Once up at Jack Gilbert's house—she tried to tide Jack over the dark days—she said to us, "I must be free. I know men too well, they are all the same, no? If you love them, they want to be boss. I will never have a boss."

Nor did Gary Cooper want to marry Lupe Velez. He was wildly in love with her, but some inner self never gave in. Lupe wasn't the girl Gary wanted for a wife. She didn't belong in his picture of marriage as he'd seen it with his father and mother, who celebrated their golden wedding, and who had given him, I now realize, the same blessing enjoyed by Colleen Moore, a normal, happy childhood.

If either of them had wanted marriage, the other couldn't—wouldn't—have resisted. But I am sure neither of them did and without marriage such flaming romances always crash and burn up.

The paths of two people, who have been inseparable in love, laughter and tears, part.

They go different ways in the small town of Hollywood, meet only by chance, pass in the street, find themselves at the same party. Often you wonder whether, secretly, they've followed each other's careers and rejoiced or were sad as fortune was good or ill for the other.

Once when it was widely rumored that Gary Cooper was to wed the Countess Dorothy di Frasso, Lupe said to me with her most impish grin, "Ah, this time that Coop has got himself in a fix, no?"

After their romance ended there is record of only one meeting between Gary Cooper and Lupe Velez. They were by chance at the same place, and photographers asked them to pose together, Gary refused. The Mexican temper flared hotly, "He is no one's oil painting himself, that one," she cried.

How could Hollywood help but wonder what Gary felt the day he learned that his once-so-dear love had taken her own life? If there was one person in Hollywood of whom nobody would have predicted a sleeping pill exit, it was Lupe. To the last moment, she never gave a sign, never stopped laughing and making others laugh.

Don't misunderstand me. Lupe didn't carry a torch for Cooper, nor go around wearing a broken heart on her sleeve. But as she went her merry way, she was changed somehow, more reckless, more defiant, more the little savage.

I've never forgotten what she said to me at the time of her brief and hectic romance with Jack Gilbert.

Dark days, those, for the great Gilbert. After Talkies had crumbled his shining career to dust. He and Ina Claire had separated. And Jack was wild with hurt and defeat. As Lupe said, "He hide in that big gloomy house like the bear with a sore ear." And she added, "His wife has told him she is a better actor than he is, which is true, but no wife should tell a man such things. I will make him laugh, that cure him."

She could, you know, make anybody laugh.

"Big baby," I heard her say to Jack once in the now deserted house up on Tower Road, "you let Hollywood get you down. I say to Hollywood, look out, here comes Lupe. If my heart hurt me, I go to the fights and holler whoopee. Hollywood says, 'That Lupe, she is the wild one, nothing gets her down.'"

As for marriage to Gilbert, Lupe said, "I am not a one for marriage. Maybe—I don't know."

When I asked her, she said, "You know I don't love Jack except I am his friend. All this I say so to him it restores his vanity. It is good for a man's vanity which is beat up to have it said that Lupe, the heartbreaker, she loves Gilbert. No? But Gary is only man I have really love. There will not be him again."

But she did marry. It was the mistake she had always said furiously that marriage would be for her. She and Johnny "Tarzan" Weissmuller fought their way through several years, two divorce petitions filed and withdrawn. "I love to fight," Lupe said. And when it was over she said, "Now I do not wish ever to talk any more about my marriage."

"I love to fight." Yet just before the end, after her last quarrel with Harald Ramond, she cried to Estelle Taylor, "I am so tired of these fights I don't know what to do. People think I love to fight. Ever since I am little baby I must fight for everything I get. I have never had the man that I don't have to fight. They fall in love with Lupe, very much, the way Lupe is. Then quick they want I should be somebody else, the doormat, they wish to conquer the fiery one, to tame Lupe. I die first."

The only man who came close to taming her was Harald Ramond, a young actor. "I think I marry him," she said. But the last time I saw her, she said, "I am confused. Things happen like I do not expect. Say the prayer for me."

To Harald Ramond she wrote: "May God forgive you and forgive me, too. But I prefer to take my life away and our baby's before I bring him with shame . . . how could you, Harald, fake such great love for me and our baby when all the time you didn't want us? I see no other way out for me, so good-by and good luck to you. Love, Lupe."

It's possible that if he was right in the things he said in those first hours after they found her, Lupe might have lived out her life, her wildness and fears truly tamed by a baby, all the good in her having a chance.

Ramond was an Austrian who'd served two years in the French Army. He hadn't been in Hollywood long. His English was none too good. Lupe spoke a language all her own. The word "fake," Harald Ramond said, was what she'd misunderstood. The word fake which she in turn had used in her note, which from the first struck me as so unlike Lupe. He had loved her madly. Ramond said, "Who could help loving Lupe? I was proud she would consider to marry me"—he said that over and over. All he had meant was that they should fake a marriage—that is, pretend to have been married at an earlier date—so her friends would think the conventional interval of time had elapsed before the birth of their child.

Lupe had misunderstood. She'd flown at him in wild fury. She wouldn't listen to his explanation.

He only saw her once more. She was laughing then. She wouldn't let him speak, he said, she laughed loudly and said it was all a joke, she wasn't going to have a baby at all. She pushed him out and he heard her laughing loudly as she ran upstairs, even after she had closed the door.

There was a contract for $4,000 a week on her desk waiting for her to sign. She'd had enormous success on the New York stage, on personal appearances she was still as popular as any star in Hollywood.

She didn't sign the contract. She wrote: "I see no other way out for me." Then to her lifelong friend and secretary she wrote: "Don't think bad of me. Say good-by to my friends and to the American press that has been so nice to me. Lupe."

The room was all white. Thick white carpets, sweeping white satin drapes, mirror walls with carved white statues reflected in them, a crystal bar with hundreds of bottles of exotic perfumes. "It's the room of a movie star all right," Lupe said the first time she showed it to me. Against the satin whiteness Lupe's long black hair, her enormous black eyes, the dark olive skin made a startling contrast.

She must have seen it in the endless mirrors as she wrote, as she went in her gleaming white gown and lay down on the white bed where her love and laughter and tears were so swiftly to be stilled forever by her own hand.

Though she called herself a savage, Lupe tried to be true to the highest that she saw. In some terrible way she felt she had betrayed it. She had been conquered by something she could no longer cloak in wild gaiety and defiant adventure. What she called freedom had turned out to be a jungle outside the walls and Lupe could not live with herself any longer.

This, then, is a *true* life story of a big-time Movie Star of the Thirties—Played Then.

The Cowboy and the Countess

At the time that the romance of Lupe and Gary Cooper ended he seemed to be the one who was broken by their parting. It was

Gary whom the doctors sent on a long trip around the world to recuperate.

Gary landed in Rome in the spring of 1931 just one jump ahead of everything that could be wrong with a guy. Jaundice, flu, a nervous breakdown and at least a slightly broken heart. He was in a strange land, worried about his work. New faces, new stars were still flooding into Hollywood in the wake of the Talkies, and Cooper's place in our firmament was not then really secured. He'd been told he mustn't make a picture for at least a year and he knew a lot could happen even to the best career if a man stayed off the screen a whole year.

There and then he met the Countess Dorothy di Frasso, American-born daughter of multimillionaire Betrand L. Taylor. She had made an international marriage with an old and famous Roman title and was the first American woman to entertain royalty in the ancestral Villa Madama, a sixteenth-century treasure, which included a drawing-room ceiling done by Leonardo da Vinci, and which she had spent a million dollars to restore. There, before Gary Cooper showed up in Rome, she had received His Royal Highness, Prince Umberto, Crown Prince of Italy, at a nine-course dinner for two hundred. That put her in a position rarely achieved in those days by an American hostess.

When she heard the American star was ill, the American countess went to his hotel, took one look and said, "You young idiot, you ought to be taken care of." Gary was a very sick boy and she soon had him in bed in her historic villa surrounded by a battery of doctors and nurses.

With constant care she got Coop back on his feet. Then by way of recuperation she took him on a specially arranged safari to Africa to hunt lions and get fresh air, sunshine and exercise.

What might have happened to Coop if she hadn't rescued him we can only speculate. He didn't know a word of Italian. He was shy of strangers any time, any place. He was too miserable and ill to care. Could he have shivered and burned in that hotel until it was too late?

To the question of whether the Countess di Frasso had saved Gary's life the answer is that Gary thought so and was deeply grateful. A wonderful woman, he told me one night when I was having dinner with him at his house. He could never, he said, be grateful enough to her.

As soon as he was well, Gary got homesick. He wanted America; he wanted to get back to work. So he took a boat home and returned to Hollywood. A short time later Countess di Frasso arrived in Hollywood; her stated aim to visit her friend Mary Pickford. And practically before you could say Mazerowski, it was reported that the Countess di Frasso would soon divorce the Count to become Mrs. Gary Cooper. It was about that time that Lupe said to me with her impish grin, "This time that Coop has got himself in a fix."

The Countess Dorothy di Frasso, as a "nonprofessional" resident of Hollywood, handed that town more dramatic shocks than most of its stars, among them the unexpected ending of her romantic friendship with Gary Cooper, her cruise in the *Metha Nelson* with Bugsy Siegel as a member of the crew.

In spite of, or in some circles because of, her unconventional tastes and overgrown sense of humor, I would say that Dorothy di Frasso was the most popular of all Hollywood favorites who didn't actually belong in the movies.

She was the first outsider to become a social member and to give parties in the magnificent homes she rented that surpassed in lavishness and originality any that Hollywood had known before.

Along about this time, 1932, I was over at RKO studios working for David Selznick. We were short of offices so mine was on the back lot over the extra men's dressing room. There I first saw the Countess di Frasso. Behind her loomed the six-foot-three Gary Cooper.

I could not describe our meeting as quite *comme il faut* since in the office on one side, behind a thin wall, Bobby Clark, a great comic, was rehearsing a gag that sounded as if it involved barbells while on the other Gene Fowler and Jack Barrymore were developing an imaginary (I hoped!) scene in which Barrymore, slightly inebriated, was to drive a hearse.

The occasion for the Countess's visit was that I was to write a piece about her entry into Hollywood and Pickfair for a national magazine. Since at that point I was working around the clock for Selznick (David arrived at the studio at 5 P.M. and expected everybody to sit up with him until dawn) and trying to cover the Olympic Games in my spare time, I was desperate as to how I was to meet our distinguished visitor. Dorothy graciously agreed to look in on me.

Obviously older than Coop, she had a thoroughly American face, magnificent eyes with a twinkle, a wide humorous grin. The face was American but the attire was definitely Parisian. Probably this combination entranced Italian, French and British nobility, which prefers its Americans American. So that from the day of her international marriage Dorothy Taylor di Frasso had been really "in" the most exclusive circles of Paris, London and Rome, not merely on that fringe known as the Riviera's international set.

As Gary perched on my desk, I thought his eyes lacked their twinkle. Oh well, I thought, she has twinkle enough for two, if she's really going to divorce the Count and marry Coop. I wondered if the bachelor days of Hollywood's most-sought-after and eligible bachelor were now finally numbered. Hollywood had decided they were. Here, said Hollywood, is romance worthy to be in motion pictures. The Countess who had saved our Gary's life in her magnificent villa, the safari into Africa, the colorful and exciting episodes of Gary's rides with the famous Italian cavalry, the trips the Countess and the movie star made to European capitals, to Aintree to see the Grand National. The Cowboy and the Countess. Everybody in Hollywood loved it.

Everybody, I figured, except maybe Coop.

The Cowboy Meets THE Girl

That very day a girl walked under my windows on her way to the RKO commissary to lunch. A young beauty, her real name was Veronica Balfe—Rocky for short—though as a would-be movie actress, escaped from her boredom with New York society, she had taken the name Sandra Shaw. Though he hadn't seen her up to that moment, she was soon to be the determining factor in the life of Gary Cooper.

When some months later I went out to his big, comfortable ranch-style bachelor house to have dinner, he had seen Rocky. This was his girl and he knew it. But—if a lady had saved a man's life, if she wanted the rest of it, didn't a man of honor owe it to her? If she wanted it. To Hollywood it looked as though the Countess did.

Hollywood was in for a di Frasso shock. Whether Dorothy who, under that sophisticated, extrovert, woman-of-the-world exterior, was actually warmhearted and truly generous, also noticed the twinkle go out of Coop's eyes, that they truly lit up in another direction, or whether she was unwilling to give up her distinguished title and position in Europe to become plain Mrs. Cooper, we never knew.

Either way, one fine day the Countess packed her million-dollar Paris wardrobe and took off for Italy. As far as the Countess was concerned it had been charming; she adored Hollywood, Coop was her favorite friend.

The next thing Hollywood heard of her, she and her husband Count Carlo were introducing dog racing to Rome.

The next thing heard of Gary Cooper, he and Veronica Balfe were married on Park Avenue.

I cannot let Dorothy di Frasso simply vanish from these pages for Hollywood wasn't to lose the Countess with whom it had never a dull moment; she turned up again full of fun, frolic and good will, with still more interesting adventures up her sleeve, particularly the notorious cruise of the *Metha Nelson*.

Hollywood first heard of Bugsy Siegel during the cruise of the "hell ship," a cruise involving pirate gold, bloodied heads, marriage and charges of mutiny on the high seas, rum, romance, rescue and rebellion such as no producer has ever dared to put on the screen.

And again I have to wonder what Coop, who had once gone adventuring with the lady, made of it.

The old three-masted schooner *Metha Nelson*, chartered by Marino Bello, once Jean Harlow's stepfather, was in search of buried treasure on Cocos Island, off the Costa Rican coast.

According to Richard Gulley, a young cousin of Sir Anthony Eden, who was along, the treasure was $300,000,000 in diamonds, rubies and gold doubloons. They had a map.

Afterward at a Grand Jury investigation of mutiny charges, Captain Robert B. Hoffman, the schooner's master, said that before they sailed the FBI had shown him a picture of Louis "Lepke" Buchalter, notorious head of Murder Incorporated, who then was a fugitive from justice supposed to be hiding on a tropical island and who was later executed at Sing Sing. "They said this might be an attempt to pick him up," the Captain said, "and I was to notify them if he showed up."

The rest of the cast of characters was picturesque in the extreme.

There was Champ Segal, described as a prizefight promoter, Abe Kapellner and Bugsy Siegel, occupation gangster.

The Countess acted as maid of honor when the Captain married Bello to Evelyn Husby, a nurse. Later the jealous bridegroom almost fought a duel with a Costa Rican colonel who made eyes at the bride.

The *Metha Nelson* didn't pick up Lepke, though there is a strong suspicion that this may have been Bugsy's original plot. There was also a rumor that Dorothy, informed by the Captain, foiled the plot, and knowing Dorothy I'd have written the script that way.

The merry voyagers never found any buried treasure and a storm came up on the voyage back. The ship floated helpless for three days in the Gulf of Tehuantepec, in hourly danger of breaking up, but was rescued in the nick of time and towed to Acapulco where the Countess went ashore and flew off to Palm Springs. It was not long after this that Bugsy found his way into Hollywood's most exclusive society circles.

The handsome hoodlum never got over the way he was received by movie people. He was true to Beverly Hills until bullets mowed him down in that star-studded annex of Hollywood. So, too, was Dorothy di Frasso—who died quietly not at the Villa Madama outside Rome, but on a train traveling between New York and Hollywood.

Gary Cooper was thirty-two years old when he married Veronica Balfe, and now the career about which he had worried so much in Rome picked up new highs. Before his marriage he made *A Farewell to Arms* with Helen Hayes. Returning from his honeymoon with Rocky he played the lead opposite Marion Davies in *Operator 13*—this before Marion decided it was too much to be on the set all day and work with a Shakespearean coach all night to control her stutter.

Seven years after his marriage Cooper was the highest paid man

—not actor, *man*—in the United States. His $482,821 topped the salaries of the country's best paid business executives. The Cowboy, it seems, as happens in America, had made good.

It seems too that this grave, silent, modest guy with the aspen legs had known exactly what he was doing when he waited for *the* girl. A daughter, Maria, arrived and I have to say now that, over the years, the Cooper women, Rocky and Maria, displayed on all occasions an abundance of that magic quality, *class*, "excellence of style" in all departments which, truth to tell, has all but vanished from this bleak world. Gary himself grew in stature. He continued to sketch and paint as he'd done all his life. He continued to hunt, to search out the open spaces or high country whenever he could. The Coopers were part of Hollywood's best social scene. And more and more Coop was someone troubled folk sought out. A man *men* could count on. A guy who was tough *and* tender. A man of humor *and* faith. Later, as his faith matured, Gary without any fanfare was baptized into the Roman Catholic Church.

There was indeed a steadfastness about Gary Cooper.

The graph of his career and his work goes steadily upward. Principle, hard work, self-control, and great good humor went into it. He became, by his own efforts and study, a fine actor.

But—

The women a man has loved and who have loved him must contribute to his acting. Certainly his travels with the Countess showed results in his movies, especially *Lives of a Bengal Lancer*. I don't think he could have played Mr. Deeds so well if he'd never known Clara Bow. And I am sure the love scenes in *A Farewell to Arms*, among the most moving ever seen, and in *For Whom the Bell Tolls* had a fire, a warmth, he'd never have had but for little Lupe. *Sergeant York, The Pride of the Yankees, Meet John Doe* and *High Noon* owe more to his wife Rocky and the wonderful home and happy married life with which she backgrounded his career.

Class

Rocky Cooper. Maria Cooper.

The scene is a dinner at The Friars Club, oldest and most storied actors' club in Hollywood. On a winter night early in 1961 they were honoring Gary Cooper. It was a star-studded main event. At the close of his speech Gary Cooper said, "If you asked me if I am the happiest man in the world, I'd have to say 'Yup!' "

Only three people there that night knew that Gary was terminally ill. His wife, his daughter, and his close friend and lawyer, Dean Johnson. They had known for some months, yet not by word or gesture had they betrayed it to Coop. He had his night as "the happiest man in the world."

Courage

Gary Cooper.

Another scene. This in February in the offices of Dean Johnson, senior partner in the distinguished firm of O'Melveny and Myers. Gary brought Rocky there directly from the offices of his physician, Dr. Rex Kennamer, to discuss updating Gary's will.

"Dean," Rocky said. "You don't have to hide it any more. The doctors have just told Gary."

"And," Dean Johnson said later, "he kept trying to cheer me up. Twenty minutes earlier he'd been told he had a few months at best, and he's trying to cheer me up! Finally he said, 'Dean, don't feel so bad. Let me buy you a drink.' " So they went across to the Beverly Wilshire Hotel where Gary Cooper bought Dean Johnson a drink.

I know this is true because Dean himself told it to me. Thus I am equally willing to believe that Gary said to the doctor that same day, "It must be a terrible experience for you to tell a patient that he's dying." And that when he called his close friend, Ernest Hemingway, himself seriously ill, to break the news he said, "Well, Papa, I'm going to beat you to the corral."

Still Hollywood did not know.

Now it is April, the night of the Academy Awards; Gary Cooper was to be given a special statuette "for his many memorable performances and the international recognition he, as an individual, has gained for the motion picture industry." By now Gary had to ask another close friend, Jimmy Stewart, to accept for him and Hollywood and the whole world knew something was seriously wrong when Jimmy, after saying, "We love you, Coop," broke down on television and wept.

Two days later headlines screamed: "Gary Cooper Has Cancer"; it appeared the whole world loved Coop. Messages flooded the quiet house in Holmby Hills. President Kennedy called and talked for ten minutes with Cooper and his family. Queen Elizabeth's handwritten message was the first time a British monarch had made such a gesture to a Hollywood star.

In May, shortly after his sixtieth birthday Gary Cooper died with *the* girl and their daughter at his bedside. Another steadfast American, John Wayne, spoke his epitaph, "A part of our movie business died with Coop. No one will ever replace him."

JEAN HARLOW AND WILLIAM POWELL

Jean Harlow was known as a nation's Sex Symbol. In her own home town of Hollywood, her own home studio, we called her The Baby.

Somewhere, I wrote that of Jean.

How she hated being the nation's sex symbol. It destroyed her life. The only man she ever loved, William Powell, wouldn't marry her because, as he told her definitely, he did not wish to be married to a Sex Symbol nor a Blonde Bombshell. I have to tell you here that we were *not* totally preoccupied with *sex* at that time. In fact during Jean's short amazing career came a moment when the two top stars in the world were a woman past sixty and a little girl under six. Marie Dressler and Shirley Temple.

One time on a television show, a beautiful nun named Sister Margaret Marie, who was head of a girl's college on the Hudson, said in answer to this question, "Sister, don't you feel sometimes that you've given up all the *fun?*" "Oh—perhaps I've given up all the fun but I've kept all the *joy.*"

I think Jean Harlow lost the joy when she became the nation's sex symbol.

"I feel like a bitch in heat," she said to me once, at a superelegant party at Colleen Moore's estate in Bel Air. "With the way men behave, even my stepfather, even my best friends' husbands—that's what I feel like. And I'm not all that interested in *sex*. I mean it has its place—"

"My father always said," I remarked, as her voice ran out, "sex is like money. It's only of first importance in your life when you haven't got it."

"Maybe," Jean said faintly. "I'm so sick and disgusted with it. It spoils my friendships and—you see Paul married me but he never trusted me. Never. Why once when I stopped to sign an autograph for a young man and smiled at him—right in front of our house—when I came up Paul hit me. It was horrible."

"We love you, Baby . . . Your Gang." They did, too. The grips, carpenters, electricians, painters who wrote those words to go with the flowers they laid at Jean Harlow's feet after she was dead—loved her better than they've loved anybody in the picture business before or since. They'd worked with her through thick and thin and she was their Baby. Meanings of words do change. This one has become a low idiom. But her Gang, and the rest of us who awarded it to her, meant it as a title, a term of deep affection.

The girl had power to win devotion beyond any I've ever seen.

Yet the men who were in love with her never, never understood, never would believe in the Harlow we knew.

"Good night, my dearest darling." Bill Powell's words lay upon her heart, beneath the blanket of orchids he'd sent. It was some time before William Powell was on the screen again. Kneeling at her deathbed, he'd come at last to believe in his dearest darling, to know what her love for him was, what he was losing.

The men who were in love with Harlow were prodigal of endearments. Five years before, there was that other note beginning Dearest Dear.

Dearest Dear. Unfortunately this is the only way to make good the frightful wrong I have done you and to wipe out my abject humiliation. I love you. Paul. P.S. You understand last night was only a comedy.

Her husband, Paul Bern, wrote that and then killed himself with a gun in front of Jean's mirror. Nobody understood better

than Paul Bern that the public knew Harlow as the Blonde
Bombshell, that her *Red-Headed Woman* was in thousands of
theaters at that very moment. Yet he left that strange note, which
might be interpreted as an attempt to place the responsibility for
his suicide on her.

When Jean Harlow announced her engagement to Paul Bern,
by then Irving Thalberg's right hand at Metro, I was on a spot.
All of us who loved the Baby had our own assessment of Paul's
character. Frances Marion, who had worked closely with him, was
convinced this mild little man had a quirk that could make him
sadistic. Colleen Moore thought him kind, gentle, erudite, a natural teacher who would feed Jean's questing young intelligence on
good music and good books, as indeed he had done for many
Hollywood youngsters including Joan Crawford. I myself knew
Paul Bern well and believed he had a neurotic mind—brilliant
but neurotic. There were also rumors about Paul. Among them
that he had a common-law wife, recently discharged from a private sanitarium, who might well decide on either scandal or blackmail if he took to legal wife the latest and, as it turned out, all-
time greatest of the Sex Stars. My dilemma did not arise from any
temptation to reveal the rumors to Jean. It stemmed from the
fact that I knew the rumors couldn't be true in any normal sense
—and I knew why.

I had to remember Barbara La Marr trying to make me understand why she wouldn't marry Paul Bern. Barbara, who had the
direct, uninhibited honesty of a child, had been graphic, technical
and explicit. Then she had said, "Paul has no right to marry any
woman. This I *know*."

Barbara La Marr was dead. Jean Harlow was very much alive.
What was a Mother Confessor to do? I went to consult Jean's
greatest friend, Marie Dressler. "Why did a thing like this have to
happen to her?" Marie said.

Born of a fine Missouri family with tradition, position, gently
reared in a home where the library was lined with the classics and
there was a piano in the music room, the Baby had been the idol
of her grandfather, a highly respected gentleman of the old
school.

Her mother, to whom she was devoted, sent her to the best schools, including exclusive Ferry Hall at Lake Forest, where at a dance she met the son of a well-known Chicago family, young Charles F. McGrew. A few days later they eloped and were married.

Soon after they came to Beverly Hills to live the marriage broke up. They were too young—he was twenty, Jean was sixteen. They were socially too popular, had both been spoiled at home, but the real cause was a trouble which followed Jean to her death. Men who were in love with her not only were jealous of every other man who looked at her, they also always refused to credit her love and loyalty.

When I went to see her after her engagement was announced, I learned that Paul hadn't told her about himself. I told her.

"Then it's true," she said, and began to cry. "Paul loves me as he says he does, for my mind, my spirit, my companionship, for me. He's paid me the highest compliment I've ever had." She could, she said, get along without sex. In fact it would be a relief to sit at Paul's feet and let him *read* to her.

So the Sex Symbol of the century entered into a marriage that she knew would be a marriage in name only.

Would things have been different if Jean Harlow's first picture had been for someone other than Howard Hughes? After her divorce Jean stayed on in Hollywood where her mother joined her. She did some extra work, a bit part now and then, nothing serious *until* that day when Ben Lyon spotted her and took her along to young Howard Hughes who had decided to reshoot *Hell's Angels* as a Talkie.

Let us pause for a moment to consider one more baffling aspect in the character of this Texas billionaire. When, sometime later, Leo McCarey and I went to work for Howard who had by then acquired RKO studio, Leo and I had offices three doors down from our boss. We never once saw him. So far as we could discover he spent most of his time alone in a darkened projection room looking at rushes of Jane Russell in *The Outlaw*. But, so Jane told me, and knowing Jane I believe her, he never even asked her for a date. It is a matter of film history that Howard Hughes spotted and, with the help of Russell Birdwell, flamboyantly exploited Miss Russell's most obvious charms. Looking further back I can see now that a younger Howard, only twenty-four at the time remember, and considered by many of us, to my present confusion, as a little naïve, did exactly the same with Miss Harlow.

Harlow was eighteen, ignorant of pictures, excited by getting as her first part the lead in the most expensive picture ever made up to that time. She did what the producer and director told her to do, and what they told her to do was all pretty sensational for that day and age.

Within two months after the release of Hell's Angels, in a listing of the world's one hundred best-known people, Jean Harlow was placed seventeenth. Harlow lingerie, copied from what she wore in Hell's Angels, was in every store. Girls dyed their hair platinum blonde. Women stampeded to buy clinging satin gowns with plunging necklines to look as alluring as Harlow did on the screen. The pattern was set and no producer in his right mind would throw away the box office draw represented by Harlow to put her in another type of role. So when she went from Hughes to MGM those were the roles they handed her.

The public still preferred to believe what it saw on the screen; Harlow was to them a hard-boiled femme fatale. When she was only twenty, people in Hollywood who should have known better were telling exaggerated and untrue stories of Harlow's private life. Yet those who really knew Jean knew how different she was off the screen.

There was no actress in Hollywood who didn't envy Harlow when she won the coveted role in Red-Headed Woman. It turned out to be bad luck for Jean. People were seeing her right before their eyes as that ruthless siren who lured men to their destruction when the news broke that her husband of only two months had killed himself.

No, her marriage hadn't lasted long. A few weeks after the wedding we were all at a party where Paul made a scene. Coming home from work, Jean had left in a taxi a pair of the heavy white gauntlets she often wore. The driver called to return them. That night, in front of a dozen people, Paul accused Jean of making an appointment with the taxi driver and Jean went home weeping bitterly.

The tragedy followed on the heels of a dozen such scenes.

According to the story, Jean had spent that fatal night at her mother's because her stepfather, Marino Bello, was away fishing with Clark Gable. There was a great closeness between Jean and her mother, idolatry on her mother's part. Certainly Jean was in bed at her mother's home when the servants employed at her own residence, returning from their day out, discovered Paul's body the next morning.

Yes yes, that was the official story. But—she was there in that house that night. No reason not to tell it now. She'd heard the shot. She would hear it as long as she lived. After Jean's call for help we went, another close friend and I; we took her to her mother's. When the police and the press got to the house of tragedy they found only that hideous note that made her—a girl men killed themselves over.

Two days later, as I watched her walk down the stairs at her mother's like a sleepwalker, I knew Jean would never be the same again. As with Valentino the mainspring had broken. If she hated herself before, what must she have felt then? Trying to comfort her I said, "Look, Baby, it wasn't the first time Paul tried suicide. After Barbara La Marr married Jack Dougherty, Paul put his head in the *toilet* and got stuck. Jack Gilbert and Carey Wilson found him in time, got a plumber to unscrew the seat. He wound up wearing it like a wreath but—he didn't drown." I heard myself babbling as I looked at that still, white face, heard her mother weeping in wild distress. I said, "I wish they'd let him."

"So do I," she said in a thin, quiet, faraway voice.

It was the only bitter thing I ever heard her say about anyone.

I put my arms around Jean and said, "Baby, Baby don't look like that." But she did. All through the days ahead. She went on looking like a white statue until she fell in love with Bill Powell.

But she had courage. I'll never forget the day Marie Dressler brought her on the set to begin work again on half-finished *Red Dust*. It was the scene where she took a bath in the rain barrel. I remember Clark Gable standing there watching her, his eyes glinting with unshed tears. "There's the best gal that ever lived," he said over and over. Other men on the set were weeping openly.

Her marriage, a year or so later, to Hal Rosson stunned Holly-

wood. A great cameraman, Hal was a quiet, simple little guy, the
last man you could picture with Harlow. It was final proof that
Jean was looking for affection, for kindness, for peace and safety
from evil.

She didn't find it.

Then, for the first time and the only time in her life, she fell in
love. In the rosy glow of that adoration she knew William Powell
would understand.

Once when I went up to the Hearst Ranch, I was taking two
tennis champions, Fred Perry and Alice Marble, Mr. Hearst having decided he wanted a tennis tournament.

A night watchman was waiting our arrival on the terrace and I
was delighted to find I had one of my favorite apartments. As he
put my bags down the man said, "Miss Harlow's in the Doge's
suite and she asked me to let her know as soon as you came." I
protested that it was almost three o'clock in the morning and he
said, "No matter how late, she told me," and departed.

Ten minutes later Jean walked in, followed by Bill Powell.

Jean wore a pair of long soft, pearl-white pajamas of the kind
now fashionable again. Impossible not to wonder what Harlow
would have been like in Living Color. She glowed silver like the
moon, not golden like the sun, as Maugham says of Rosie in
Cakes and Ale. Her hair wasn't blonde, which suggests yellow. It
was platinum, silver with a glow, and it was real. Again as
Maugham has his famous painter say, "Your color is *the* miracle
of the ages, Rosie." So was Jean's. As Mary Pickford's face was
photogenically perfect, so was Harlow's body, so proportioned and
polished it wasn't obsessively "sexy" in the vulgar sense. That
night at the Hearst Ranch, she was a small statuette by a silver-
smith named Cellini.

As always, Powell with that *Thin Man* suavity and sophistication could—and often did—give the handsomest men in our
town a head start and beat them.

An extraordinary pair. Yet they looked as though they hadn't
slept within the memory of man. Neither of them said How are
you or Did you have a nice trip or anything trivial. Without smiling, Jean took Bill's hand and led him to a tall-backed king's chair
in which I do not doubt Caesar Borgia once sat and Powell, in a

robe of heavy blue brocade, could have played him without re-hearsal. In that room, with its tapestries and art treasures, its glittering chandeliers, the Renaissance colors, the stained-glass windows, you could believe you were anywhere at any period and whatever had moved under that ceiling in all the centuries since it was painted moved there still.

Nevertheless, what came startled me.

Jean knelt down beside him, held up her clasped hands, and said in a voice that had kept its Midwestern flatness, "Bill, will you marry me?"

He made a sound of pain and protest. The silence went on too long. I couldn't think of anything I could say, moreover I wasn't sure they remembered I was there. Bill broke it. He said, "Baby—don't. What's the use of this?"

Jean didn't alter her position kneeling beside Bill Powell's chair. She said, "I love you, Bill. I have never loved anybody else. Do you love me?"

Bill said, "More than I've ever loved anything. You know that."

"Then why won't you marry me?" Jean said.

As though an outside force jerked him, Powell was on his feet. He began to walk up and down, up and down. He picked up a red velvet cushion with heavy gold tassels and threw it at the wall—William Powell, so famed for his elegant equanimity.

Inside I was seeing, hearing, a life and death, love and passion, desperation and denial struggle played by two of the most dynamic and exciting screen stars who ever lived. A girl, who represented sex power, on her knees saying with all she had to give it, Bill will you marry me and a gifted highly trained actor shouting back, No I won't. On the screen, in theaters it would have moved vast audiences to tears, to pain. I was getting it for real, at firsthand, shut in one room. They knew how to play it, they had timing and gestures and voices, this made it more moving, but also it was as real, as sincere, as deep, and strong as though they'd been inarticulate and awkward and ineffectual outside. They were so sincere I could hardly stand to watch them. That scene made me know forever how much people *do* feel, can feel, how powerful emotions are. I have never from that day sold feelings short.

"Why won't you marry me?" Jean said.

"You know why," Bill Powell said. "I've told you why."

"I want Adela to hear you say it," Jean said, and got up for the first time.

"Children—" I said, though Powell was at least my age.

With icy distinctness, Bill Powell said, "She knows I was married to one beautiful blonde bombshell named Carole Lombard. I was younger then and Carole wasn't *Jean Harlow* by a long way. I couldn't take it then. Now I am a middle-aged gent, my hair is getting gray, no doubt I will soon have a pot. I wish to remove my shoes of an evening and live a quiet life. You're still so—so young, Baby, so terribly young—twenty years younger—"

Furiously Jean Harlow said, "I'm not a blonde bombshell. Oh Bill—I had a worse time than you did, it wasn't my fault that Paul—he had no reason to be jealous, did he, Adela?"

She looked at me and I said, "No, but Paul wasn't a normal man. He believed in Jean when he was sane, Bill."

"Even if he started sane," Bill Powell said, "no man can cope with being married to the world's sex symbol. There are biblical words—no no, but I have to say—I don't want in my declining years to be married to a girl men kill themselves over. Not if she's pure as a lily."

In the terrible silence, the Baby began to weep.

I felt as tired as I ever had in my life. This was hopeless and we knew it. The silver girl, weeping silently, was hearing that shot again.

I felt empty and useless—as I watched Bill Powell, up and down, up and down. The scene hung fire. I thought, Something is wrong here. He is in love with her, insanely in love with her. All he has said is probably true, it's not enough, something is missing. This marriage means everything to her, is there a way she can persuade him, something she hasn't said or done? With the speed of light my mind slipped a cog back to a night after a Hollywood party. I couldn't remember how long ago, it didn't matter.

Dick Barthelmess, young Griffith-made star, had taken me, and he said he was starving, and why didn't he and I and Bill Powell and Bill's girl friend (I can't remember her name, but she was a sensational redhead) go back to Barthelmess's house? He had some ham and I could scramble eggs and onions to go with it. I had broken said eggs into a bowl when Bill Powell made some witty jest which sounded innocent enough to me but did not amuse the redhead and I saw that she had picked up the LARGE carving knife with which I had been slicing the ham and I only got out, *What are you going to do with that?*—when I could see for myself she was going to cut Bill Powell's throat with it. Bill, who hadn't been out of a walk since before Christmas, broke into a trot around the kitchen table, holding up his hand and saying with a charming chuckle, Now Precious (or whatever the hell her name was) that isn't nearly as funny as when you played Lady Macbeth in Peoria—give it to me, Aspidistra darling—and *she* said, It'll be less funnier and funnier when I catch you, you wisecracking two-timing bastard, I'll show you how to slice *ham*. Barthelmess picked up the bowl of eggs but he was a slow thinker and by the time he threw it Powell had taken off into Beverly Hills' wide-open avenues with Medusa *right* behind him. The eggs missed their target and decorated the kitchen wall like a Picasso painting. I know Roger Bannister gets credit for the first four-minute mile but when Powell came around the block into Rodeo Drive the first time, he had to be close. His style was more that of a hurdler, a man in a car stopped and broke into a couple of U.S.C. cheers before the sight sobered him up and he abandoned the battlefield. I said to Barthelmess, Tackle her the next time around, and *he* said, Powell brought her let *him* tackle her, but she began to run out of gas, after she'd leaned up against a palm tree and said, God, how I hate men, Bill kept on sprinting for a couple of laps and then came cantering slowly back his eyes rolling like a bronco's and said, When I arrived here I was hungry and I'm a lot hungrier now—the wit of which hasn't traveled down the years but in that moment of exhausted relief—I mean girls have cut men's hearts out, especially redheads—it seemed the funniest thing we'd ever heard. We were still laughing heartily when I served the ham and eggs, and *that* dawn came up over the patio and the tennis court and the garden and Miss Eye-of-Newt-and-Toe-of-Frog was giving Powell the full I-only-did-it-because-I-love-you treatment and he was smiling at her with his eyebrows way up. But I thought, No no, sweetie, you will never eat scrambled eggs with us any more.

A couple of weeks after that I laughed when I should have luffed, and Barthelmess chased me and scrambled some phonograph records over my head and I decided that with *actors,* whether you were chasing them or they were chasing you, you could soon get into a rut, so I wasn't there any more either.

Now here was another dawn in a far far other place, and Bill Powell and I were in it but everything else was different. The birds in the garden were wakening and I knew Bill Powell would never marry Jean Harlow any more either and I knew why.

He hadn't even met the girl named Mousie whom he did marry, but I knew he wanted to marry the kind of a girl who could be nicknamed Mousie.

Some people want to follow Schweitzer to darkest Africa or play second base for the Cubs or dance like Ray Bolger—desire may be the first thing but it isn't *enough.* Jean had an awful lot of things going for her but the ability to make Bill Powell believe in her as Mousie she did not have.

As the dawn grew into bright California sunshine I said, "Look, my children, lunch is always late up here, let's get a couple hours sleep?"

Bill looked at the Baby, he held out his hand, and she smiled at him and said, "Run along, I'll have a nap here on the couch."

As she watched him go, still debonair after that night of emotional turmoil, I saw that Jean had accepted that final verdict, too. She curled up on the long velvet divan still smiling, and I kissed her and tucked a fur robe over her and went up the circular stairs to the balcony where my bed was. Tears are no less bitter under a fur robe and so at last I went down again and found her sitting up and I never saw a girl cry like that. Usually Jean's courage managed to mask the terror she had felt with Bugsy Siegel. And the horror when she knew her stepfather's cane had acid in the handle, and even the despair over Paul Bern's deadly suicide note. This time she wasn't trying any more. I think that last hour and Bill's debonair exit had wrenched her heart loose from her body and I don't think she ever got them back together again in the little span of life left to her.

She was twenty-six years old when she died.

It was Bill who bought the stately white marble tomb at Forest Lawn, and for years Jean Harlow's was the only sepulcher in that vast park which was never without flowers. Sometimes a spring basket from her old friend Lionel Barrymore, who'd been with her at Metro all the years of her short life. Sometimes white orchids from her boss, Louis B. Mayer, or chrysanthemums from Clark Gable, to whom she was "My kid sister." And every day white roses from Bill Powell.

Now they are all gone but Bill Powell and it's possible that even a wife called Mousie can hear too much of her husband's love for another woman, though that woman be dead as Juliet, and so there are no more white roses either.

THE DRAMA OF INGRID BERGMAN

The bar sinister may well have crossed the coat of arms of some of our Hollywood young. Certain it was that there was much speculation as to whether or not Mickey Neilan was the father of Gloria Swanson's son. I know for a fact that one of our most famous directors in the Twenties had a daughter by one of our most beautiful foreign stars; the resolution was that the director stayed married to his nice childless nonprofessional wife of whom he was really very fond, the petite brunette wife raised a large blonde Valkyrie daughter as her own, and the star went back to shine on Europe.

For that matter I am frequently asked if Clark Gable is the father of my youngest son to which I reply that no woman in her right mind would deny that possibility. So I won't.

But I will tell you right now that no woman in such straits in our Hollywood, before the dim and dreary days of Mia Farrow and Jane Fonda and Marlo Thomas, was striking a blow for women's lib or the so-called sexual revolution. "The past is a foreign country—they do things differently there." So said L. P. Hartley in *The Go-Between*. They do indeed, and it isn't only in the distant past but the recent past that we fail to consider this, and misread the lives lived *then. Then*, less than thirty years ago, the situation in which Ingrid Bergman found herself was unacceptable to her, and to us. *Now* a famous actress can write a book dedicated to her illegitimate daughter with nothing more than regret that her work keeps them so much apart. More than years —a total reversal in attitudes and mores—separates these two points of view. To understand the drama that took place *then* we must step back into that foreign country. Thus when it is claimed that Ingrid Bergman stands as flag bearer for those poor unfortunates who wish to step down and be equal with men, that she "did what she wanted, shook a defiant fist at those who scorned her, and came out on top," I have to remember the true story of Ingrid Bergman.

It is the story, above all, of a most *womanly* woman. A woman who came to a time when she cried out in pain, "They say an artist cannot have a private life. Then I will not be an artist. I will live as a woman at last."

She came out on top because she was eventually able to drive those two mules in tandem but her life as we watched her live it showed clearly where her priorities lay.

The announcement in December, 1949, that Ingrid Bergman was expecting a baby in three months rocked Hollywood like an atom bomb. Ingrid was still the wife of Dr. Peter Lindstrom. As the news circulated and the realization grew that unless there was a swift divorce, Ingrid could not marry Roberto Rossellini before their baby was born, the studios looked like New York after the stock market crashed. Crowds huddled on sets, on street corners, in cafes, the phone exchanges and cables were jammed.

This was a deep, a painful excitement and despair for Bergman and the art of the motion picture for which she'd stood. Emotions must always be the top hazard of an industry founded on an art. Art has artists and artists are superemotional people. But Ingrid Bergman? The most withdrawn, self-possessed star since Garbo? We couldn't believe it.

Though I didn't see it at the time, I suppose my first contact with this news that shocked the world was in Santa Barbara, where in a little theater venture conceived by David Selznick, who brought Bergman from Sweden to Hollywood in 1937, Bergman was playing Anna Christie. In the scene in a waterfront cafe, as Ingrid sat at the table, smoking a cigarette, from the select audience came an audible titter. The sight of Bergman as a "bad girl" had inspired a wealthy dowager to mirth.

Ingrid finished that scene, then put on a better one backstage.

She wanted the dowager ejected, but since the lady had backed the theater this wasn't practical.

"I'm an actress," Bergman stormed. "I can play a bad woman. Do I have to be a bad woman to act one? What is this Frankenstein they build around me? It is not fair. I can play anything. I'll show them. I'll show them."

The icy Bergman, regarded by people who worked with her as either shy or rude, as either proud or righteous, showed a fiery temperament that stunned the company and on the opening night in San Francisco she gave a performance that had them standing to cheer her.

Around Bergman, as around Garbo, grew the legend of the cold, silent personality, the Snow Maiden.

As a person she seemed to wear a cloak that made her invisible. No one ever knew what Bergman was doing. They took it for granted that the Snow Maiden, the artist, was above all human passions, all temptations, all emotional earthquakes. It seems ridiculous now. It was ridiculous then.

And always in that background of the "private life" she guarded so desperately, which we were to see with the quality of an Ibsen drama, was the silent figure of her husband, the neurosurgeon who dominated her.

When I think of Ingrid Bergman on the screen, I see her as the young nun buying the baseball bat in *The Bells of St. Mary's* and as the tortured wife in *Gaslight*, for which she won an Academy Award.

Two images off the screen are clear before my eyes this minute, as far apart as the nun and the tortured wife.

For three years, as a memorial to my son Bill who was killed over Germany, my son Mac and I had one night a week provided entertainment and visitors for the men in the incurable wards at the Long Beach Naval Hospital, who were too sick to go to movies or regular Red Cross shows.

In this, we had the magnificent help of the movie stars. You can have no vague idea of the calls upon Hollywood's stars, but my friends responded nobly. For over one hundred and fifty weeks, we never failed to find someone to go, holidays and all.

The men's favorite was Lloyd Nolan. Alan Ladd went; and

Celeste Holm, June Allyson and Dick Powell; José Iturbi, to play on a tinny piano; and Audrey Totter, Elizabeth Taylor, Mona Freeman, Gordon MacRae, Jane Powell, Betty Hutton and Wendell Corey. Teresa Wright sat all day beside a boy who said he'd die happy if he could see her. He died happy, I hope, for Teresa was holding his hand.

One day my phone rang and a deep, sweet voice said, "This is Ingrid Bergman." As I knew Miss Bergman but slightly and had a reverence for her as an actress, I merely gasped and the voice went on, "Leo McCarey tells me of your work in the hospital. Why is it you do not ask me to go? Nobody ever asks me to go anyplace, but I should like to help if you think they would care to see me. When could I go?"

"Whenever you want to, of course," I said.

"Then we go tomorrow," Miss Bergman said.

Thus my first image. A figure taller than most women, moving with long, easy strides through my garden, the late afternoon sun making her hair a golden helmet, something clean and strong and wholesome about her, a Viking's daughter in a simple, one-piece print dress.

My son drove down with us, thoroughly accustomed to movie stars, he was still shy and a little awed at the sight of the legendary Miss Bergman, and she was even shyer. But soon they were talking, shouting, laughing together like Army buddies.

Our routine at the hospital was to take the "serious wards" from 5:30 when the patients finished dinner to 8:30 when the hospital closed for the night. We went from bed to bed in the incurable ward. Ingrid stopped at every bed to talk.

Halfway through an orderly came to say that the rest of the hospital knew Miss Bergman was there, the Captain would set aside the closing hour rule if Miss Bergman would consent just to walk through.

How many miles of corridors, wards and beds there are in that hospital I cannot tell you. Blocks and blocks, Ingrid Bergman walked them all. The strain was terrific, but she never faltered.

In the eyes of the Captain, who had joined us, admiration turned to adoration. "I never saw a woman do that before," he said.

It was almost midnight instead of 8:30 when we left. She'd had no dinner, so we stopped at a roadside cafe, owned by Esther

Williams. Suddenly Ingrid looked at her watch. "I must phone my husband," she said nervously, "I have said I will be home by ten." When she came back her face was white, her hands shook.

"I must go home at once," she said, "at once, oh, please, I must."

"An emergency?" I said.

"No, no," she said. "But I *must* go . . ."

We went. Without anything to eat.

The true story of Ingrid Bergman is the stuff of which immortal novels are made. A story of human hearts struggling, suffering, sinning, loving and hating. Of those things which are done only in the grip of powerful love or hate.

In this drama we have the brain surgeon, an icy, silent, graying, sharp-featured man-in-white. Life and death lie daily in his hands that must be steady even on that day when he was told his wife, thousands of miles away, had borne another man's son. We have the fiery, witty Italian director, hailed by critics as a creative genius for his pictures *Open City* and *Paisan*, a man articulate in many languages or none, wise in the ways of women, a little world-weary but still filled with a Latin zest for life.

Between them is the eternal triangle, the actress, in her high moments the greatest of our day, as Duse was greatest, or Ethel Barrymore, a movie star adored and respected by millions, an international beauty who by her mere presence and performance could lift an ordinary melodrama like *Casablanca* to greatness.

Dr. Peter Lindstrom. Roberto Rossellini. Ingrid Bergman.

It was quite a cast. Hollywood has produced none to equal it, on or off the screen.

There are other characters. Minor indeed.

Pia Lindstrom, a schoolgirl of ten known to her playmates in Beverly Hills as the daughter of a famous movie star. A baby, her half-brother, named Roberto Rossellini for the man who said boldly, "I am the father."

This drama came to us as running news, unfolding day by day to the greatest audience any love story has ever known except that of the Duke and Duchess of Windsor, in a series of shocks, of contradictory viewpoints and battles coming one after the other.

Time has given it a measure of perspective; it can be told now exactly as it happened, allowing the facts to speak for themselves.

One thing must be made clear. I heard from the man who actually told him face to face, long before Louella Parsons' scoop told the world, that Dr. Peter Lindstrom knew what Ingrid's situation was.

Dr. Lindstrom was told the whole truth, with a plea for a divorce.

During those long months, Ingrid Bergman's heart hammered with pain, with hope, then with panic, finally with desperation to every tick of the clock that brought closer the inevitable day when her secret would be, could be, secret no longer.

During the heat and turmoil that ensued upon his refusal to free her, Dr. Peter Lindstrom, in the corridors of the General Hospital, cried out to photographers and reporters, "I am being persecuted. Why should I be persecuted?"

There is another point that I believe must always be considered. It is one which could happen only to Hollywood people. During the time that Ingrid was begging her husband to grant her a divorce, and later when the whole world knew that she was to have that baby, that world was watching her on the screen as St. Joan of Arc. So when Ingrid's millions of fans learned of her situation, many of them probably could not separate her from the role they saw her playing on the screen.

The forbidden thing she had done, therefore, must have seemed all the more appalling to them.

They must have thought of her fall from those heights not as that of the great actress, the artist who is perhaps all too often unconventional, but as that of a revered person—and the fall must have seemed farther.

The story line for our drama is a simple, fundamental one.

A woman, married when she was very young and inexperienced, after twelve years fell in love for the first time with another man.

We have a child who at four determined to be an actress; at eight amazed everybody with her talent before her father's amateur movie camera; at twelve entertained her five cousins for hours with plays in which she did all the roles; the girl who at sixteen won a scholarship to the Royal Dramatic Theatre School in Stockholm and before she was twenty-five rated leading stage and screen actress of Sweden.

It was while she was attending the Royal Dramatic Theatre at Stockholm that Ingrid Bergman first met Peter Lindstrom, a dentist. He was ten years older, he was a commanding, important figure to this teen-age devotee of art who, as far as I could discover, had never had a beau.

In person, then, she was a tall, lanky awkward young thing, who paid as much attention to her appearance offstage as a colt. All her emotion, thought, heart and soul poured into acting, which of course is one way to become a great actress. Boys had never bothered her, but this experienced man of almost thirty persisted, was waiting when she got out of school, took her to the theater, invited her to dinner. For the first time she met people other than her family and her fellow students.

In 1937, when they married, her success was assured, her genius had been recognized by those who counted. A year later their daughter Pia was born. Pia, who was her mother's great delight. In Hollywood the little family lived in almost total isolation. For years, Ingrid didn't care about all the other things. As long as she had her work—"I wish I could work twelve hours a day, 365 days a year," she said once—the actress in her allowed Peter Lindstrom to run everything else.

In the end it was the woman slumbering within the actress who rebelled.

The rebellion had been building for some time. The Bergman whose life was so private as to be a legend was seen here and there, talking in cafes with people from other countries, as though hungry for companionship. Once at least there is record that Dr. Lindstrom came and took her home. Little eddies of talk said Bergman was restless, unhappy, smoldering.

Certainly this was a different Bergman from the quiet, repressed young woman who had gone to Rochester, New York, to stay there away from her own work while Peter Lindstrom who had long pursued medical studies in neurosurgery got his degree.

Miss Bergman had been interested then in his career, but now it had swallowed him up completely. She still had her own career, but before she went to Italy, Ingrid's work began to suffer. Her screen Joan of Arc was far below her Joan on the New York stage; critics said so.

It was after this picture that she decided to go to Rome to make a picture with Rossellini, whose work in *Open City* had so fired her imagination. She couldn't have been in love with him then. She'd never seen him. But it is an interesting fact that she met this other man through a fan letter of admiration for his art, his work in motion pictures, which was also her art and her work.

To Rossellini she wrote: "If you should ever want a Swedish actress who speaks good English, who has forgotten most of her German, who never did know French, and who in Italian knows only 'I love you' I am ready to come and make a film with you."

In any civilization which can still be called civil it is considered wrong for a wife to fall in love with another man, but it has been happening since Bath-sheba, the wife of Uriah the Hittite, first caught the eye of King David.

Ingrid Bergman was called upon to pay a bitter price.

In the tidal wave of unrestrained emotion which she had never expected to know, on the lonely, barren island of Stromboli, where day after day and night after night they waited for the smoldering volcano to erupt so that they might make the scenes in their motion picture, she turned her back on the rest of the world. She was not held prisoner on that island in the sense suggested later by Walter Wanger, who as producer of *Joan of Arc* could not believe the woman who had played the Saint for him would or could stay there of her own volition. But she was held voluntary prisoner, in a sense, by that tidal wave of unrestrained emotion which she allowed to sweep over her and make her indifferent to all else. She did not want to hear the voices of the outside world. When she returned from Stromboli to Rome she seemed bewildered and confused like a woman coming out of a drug.

Let's follow her story step by step, beginning with the fact that on February 15th, 1949, Ingrid for the third year in succession won an annual award as the most popular actress in motion pictures, voted so by the public. About that same time, Roberto Rossellini arrived in Hollywood to consult her about the script of a picture called *Stromboli* in which he wanted her to star.

March 7th—Rossellini returned to Rome. Ingrid did not see him off. She was up in the snow with her husband, skiing.

March 12th—Ingrid left by plane for Europe to make *Stromboli*.

April 1st—Rossellini, Bergman and company left for the island to begin shooting the picture.

April 17th—First pictures of Roberto and Ingrid together, and rumors of their falling in love were in the papers in Rome.

April 21st—Dr. Peter Lindstrom left Hollywood for Italy.

May 2nd—Six-hour meeting between Ingrid Bergman and Dr. Lindstrom took place in hotel in Messina. Later Lindstrom saw Rossellini alone.

May 4th—Dr. Lindstrom issued a statement that his wife would return to Hollywood and neither of them would say anything further at this time.

August 4th—On her return to Rome, Ingrid Bergman announced, "I have instructed my lawyer to start divorce proceeding as soon as possible."

August 6th—Through a friend in Hollywood, Dr. Lindstrom said his wife's request for a divorce was a stunning, shocking surprise to him.

September 3rd—Dr. Lindstrom refused his wife's request for a divorce.

September 12th—Pia was told her mother would not return.

September 23rd—Dr. Lindstrom again refused to free his wife when she sent a lawyer from Rome to ask him.

October 17th—Dr. Lindstrom again refused a divorce request.

December 12th—Louella Parsons in headlines broke the story that Ingrid Bergman's baby would be born in three months.

January 29th—Dr. Lindstrom agreed to allow Ingrid to file for a mail order divorce in Mexico.

February 2nd—A son by Roberto Rossellini was born to Ingrid Bergman in Rome.

February 9th—Bergman got her mail order divorce.

May 24th—After clearing international difficulties, Ingrid and
    Rossellini were married by proxy in Mexico.

All the time this emotional drama was going on in her private
life, that guarded private life that now above all others had become public in headlines around the world, Ingrid Bergman's
work, her art, her cherished profession chosen when she was a
child, was on the auction block and she knew it. Yet not one word
did she say about her career.

Over the transatlantic telephone, Rome to Hollywood, her new
baby Robertino by her side, her ten-year-old daughter so far away,
Ingrid said, "I will never give up Pia. Whatever I have to do or
say or prove, I will do it. I will never give up my daughter." For
two years the custody battle raged, to be settled only when Pia
herself told a judge, "I like my mother. I love my father. I don't
want to go to Italy."

A bitter price.

It was five years before mother and daughter were reunited at
Orly airport near Paris. They were long years for Ingrid Bergman,
both the artist and the woman.

"Out of the ashes of Ingrid Bergman will arise a better Hollywood." This public inanity from United States Senator Ed Johnson, of Colorado.

If there were ashes after the romance that erupted on Stromboli
they were the ashes of the self-styled genius of Roberto Rossellini.

Once upon a time a brilliant scenarist in our town announced
to me that she was through with *love*. She said, "I am sick of
crawling on my hands and knees so I can look up to the men I
marry."

A world well lost for love is one thing. A world lost for Rossellini was another—as Ingrid Bergman was to discover.

We come now to the irony of the final act of our drama, the
story line no longer simple.

Despite the public castigation Ingrid Bergman received at home
and abroad, there was never a time when Hollywood, for better or
worse, would not have taken her back into its Art and Industry.

They tried. Producers offered. It was Signora Rossellini, more domesticated than ever when twin daughters, Ingrid and Isabel, were born in the second year of her mariage, who said no. And kept on saying no. Her husband didn't want her to work for any other producers, ergo she would work for no one but her husband. Their personal life was a far far thing from any Ingrid had ever known; Roberto's friends ranged from circus performers through the Italian cinema crowd and race car drivers into the nether world in and around Rome. She didn't complain, although later she said, "Roberto was not easy to live with. He thought flying dangerous but he drove his Ferrari at speeds of more than 150 miles an hour." Nor did she complain of his inordinate jealousy, but it must have shocked this very professional actress when her husband, whom she'd worshiped as an artist-director, refused in a film they made to let her kiss a youth with whom she was supposed to be in love. An even greater shock when after making four very bad films together in five years the lovers of Stromboli found themselves on the verge of bankruptcy in Rome.

It was now that Ingrid Bergman Rossellini wrote to a friend, "Perhaps a good movie will turn up—we can at least buy the children shoes." It did. For Ingrid Bergman. Fox offered her $250,000 to make *Anastasia* in Europe. Her husband objected violently.

The insoluble paradox for the career woman who honestly tries to give her marriage, her children, first places in her life comes all too often not because of her passion for her work, but because of her earning power.

This the dilemma of Ingrid Bergman.

If she did *Anastasia*—a deadly blow to her husband's brittle ego.

If she did *not* do *Anastasia*—no shoes for the children.

Bergman made *Anastasia*, for which Hollywood gave the actress another Academy Award. The Genius of Stromboli was volubly furious. Yet the *woman* pleaded for her husband, "Don't say he was jealous of me. He so wanted to have a big success. He was just hurt when I went out and did it on my own."

She went on to another critical and financial success on the Paris stage in *Tea and Sympathy*; Rossellini announced that he hated the play and hated her in it; she replied tartly that he never saw her in the complete play. Said the *actress*, "That I can't forgive. It was so small, so petty. When he returned from India his only comment was, 'Are you still playing in that piece of junk?' "

When he returned from India.

Rossellini, discredited, largely ignored, more angry with his wife after the play opened, had gone to the subcontinent to make documentary films. Rumors, news stories, tales told by friends came to Ingrid about her husband and one Sonali Das Gupta, wife of an Indian director. She flatly refused to believe them, proved her faith by going to London to plead personally and successfully with Prime Minister Nehru for an export license so Rossellini could bring his documentaries out of India. When the films and Rossellini arrived in Italy, with them came Madame Gupta. Madame Gupta was pregnant.

Signora Rossellini permitted her husband to file for an annulment of their seven-year-old marriage on the grounds that her Mexican divorce was illegal—and Ingrid Bergman left Rome for Paris to begin another humiliating public battle in an unsympathetic Italian court, for the custody of the three Rossellini children. This time she won. Two weeks later she quietly married Lars Schmidt, Swedish producer and heir to a shipping fortune, in London's Caxton Hall.

That was some twenty years ago and today Lars and Ingrid Schmidt live part of the time on their country estate twenty-five miles out of Paris, part on their private island off the coast of Sweden. Mrs. Schmidt visits her daughter and good friend, Pia, and her grandson, Justin, in New York where Justin's mother is a television newscaster; she visits Robertino and Ingrid and Isabel who are studying in Italy. Ingrid Bergman does films in Hollywood, another Oscar in 1974, for her supporting role in *Murder on the Orient Express*, and does plays in New York and London and Paris when she finds one she likes, "I want to hear people laugh in the theater. They have so many problems now and I don't want to add to their anguish."

Yes, Ingrid Bergman came out on top as a woman, a mother and an artist. But the final irony has to be what this woman, whose tumultuous love affair was the scandal of the decade, said when asked why she married again so soon after winning custody of her three children. "No one will know how many years I lived without any love at all."

Chapter Seven

The Miracle of Two Cowboys

TOM MIX

The miracle of the man who created for all time the art form
we call the Western, who wrote the code of the Good Guys and
the Bad Guys, and made the Cowboy our National Hero was that
he wasn't an *actor*.

Tom Mix was the genuine article.

A cowboy, a marshal, a Texas Ranger, a Pendleton Roundup
winner, he showed us a way of life he knew because he was part of
it. Not in song or story but in moving pictures he immortalized
the West he had helped to win.

It could have been otherwise.

For some time, under the tutelage of that brilliant showman
Tom Ince, one William S. Hart fought to mold a different, a
leaner meaner image of our cowboy heroes, but—Bill Hart was an
actor whose lean mean countenance Ince had spotted when Bill
played Messala in the original *Ben Hur* on the stage. Bill Hart
was a postman on the sidewalks of New York when Tom Mix at
fourteen was punching cattle in Texas. William S. Hart was on
the road playing Shakespeare in Schenectady and Jersey City
when Tom Mix was starring with Buffalo Bill in the 101 Ranch
Wild West Show. Tom never had a double in his entire career.
Bill Hart never had anything else—he was scared to death of
horses. He just never was the Real Thing—as Tom Mix was and
somehow the public knew it. If the first great Western star hadn't
been the real thing it would have all come out phony.

A lot of people liked Bill Hart. I wasn't one of them. But then
I was a friend of Winifred Westover's, an innocent, sweet little

creature of seventeen or eighteen when Bill, at forty-eight, married her. One of the first pieces of Hollywood fiction I ever wrote for *Cosmopolitan* was about Winifred, poor baby, and the brutal way Bill Hart let his sister drive her out of the house.

No, the code of William S. Hart would never have done. On the other hand—

As Tom Mix and I sat at dinner, I began to wonder. The great cowboy star came often to our Whittier ranch, but he had never before "dropped in."

He gave me no indication of why he was there. Instead, he entertained me with a tale about the time he and Will Rogers went calling. Blondes, Tom said they were.

"We were mighty young then," Tom Mix said, "and apt to travel double, hunting adventure we called it. This sister act lived a ways out of town, so we hired a rig.

"We drove up in style and the girls agreed they'd come for a spin. There was an awful pretty moon and I was too young to have any second thoughts, so I acted on my first one, which was that a little kiss was indicated.

"But the girl I was with let out a yell and hollered for Will to drive us home.

"I was for saying adieu on the doorstep. But Will, knowing my general harmlessness and respect for the weaker sex, wasn't going to admit I'd strayed off the reservation and he could get mulish.

"So he tied up the horses and we went in. After a half hour or so, I said we had a long ride back to town.

"Only it wasn't a ride. Will'd been so mad he didn't tie the horses proper, and they had better sense than me or Will. They knew when they weren't welcome and had taken off for home sometime previous.

"Will became so melancholy in the moonlight he gave off a seventeen-mile monologue about how plumb ridiculous a cowboy was without a horse and the tragedy of a young man who'd discovered he couldn't trust either women or horses."

Suddenly, Tom Mix doubled up with laughter.

"Look here," I said getting more and more puzzled, "have you and Victoria had a fight?"

Tom looked surprised. "Not recently," he said. After a moment

he said, "Vickey worries about my future. Vickey says I haven't
any more regard for a dollar than a cowboy."

Nor did he.

Later I was to know that a murderer that my work as a newspaper reporter helped to indict had declared that since he
couldn't hang but once he'd get *me* before the cops got *him*.
Somebody, knowing Tom was my friend, sent him a warning,
which was the reason he appeared that night without notice. And
stayed, talking, until dawn's early light. Now there is a Code I
buy.

After Tom Mix had won the Cheyenne roundup in 1909, for
the third time, he went to work for Colonel Selig, making motion
pictures out of Chicago.

They made one- and two-reelers in Oklahoma, then Madero
started a revolution in Mexico. Mix never could resist revolution.
He fought, was captured behind enemy lines, stood against a wall
to be shot, escaped, had a fine time helping Madero take Ciudad
Juárez and arrived in El Paso with a bullet in his leg.

A couple of years later he rode into Hollywood on his horse
Tony, carfare having run out in Arizona. The Colonel had set up
a cradle of the industry called the Selig Zoo and there Tom went
back to work in pictures. And there he met and married a cowgirl
actress named Victoria Forde.

Wyatt Earp—a Folk Hero—to be seen over the years on motion picture and TV screens as played by Randolph Scott and
Hugh O'Brian. The Marshal of Tombstone of whom that Western authority Lee Shippey wrote: "Already Wyatt Earp had become one of the greatest traditional figures of American history,
comparable to Kit Carson, Davy Crockett and Daniel Boone. He
is the outstanding Peace Officer, the only one to become a legendary hero."

Wyatt Earp, eighty when I knew him, made me understand all
that Mix was when he hit Hollywood, all he stood for in the eyes
of men of the Old West. For Wyatt Earp regarded Tom Mix as
his equal, looked up to him as one of the men who had fought
the desperadoes for control of the West.

We always pictured Wyatt Earp of Tombstone standing with

guns blazing to quell a mob bent on lynching, to capture cattle thieves, bandits, train robbers. Tom Mix, too, had been a Frontier Marshal, in Two Buttes County, Colorado, and Washington County, Oklahoma.

"It's a great thing for the movies they got Tom Mix," Wyatt Earp said to me. "He knows. He was there."

That is why Tom Mix, the man, and Tom Mix Westerns were a motion picture miracle.

And that is why, even when the studio begged him, ordered him, to use a double for dangerous stunts, he never would. He had five or six doubles for his horse, Tony, but Tom's own idea of a real good time was jumping a horse off the top of a freight car just before it went into a tunnel.

In every Art, certain gifted ones reach heights which establish what is called a School. Rembrandt, Raphael, Velásquez, Dickens, Jane Austen, Michelangelo—their art form persists for centuries and others follow them.

The motion picture is the people's Art; this same law holds true in its history. And since pictures for some unfathomable reason abandoned the classic comedy school originated by Mack Sennett, it is a fact that the school of Western melodrama founded and brought to its supreme height by Tom Mix shows itself the only permanent, important and satisfying form over the long range of motion picture art.

When you see Gary Cooper or John Wayne, you still see Hollywood's golden link with the Real West, Tom Mix.

Harry Carey, Buck Jones, Hoot Gibson, Art Accord, Ken Maynard and others helped nail down the pattern. From them to Joel McCrea, to Jim Arness, to any "legitimate" star like Alan Ladd or Yul Brynner, Gregory Peck, or Kirk Douglas who has made a Western to bolster the falling box office—Topper and Trigger, Chad and Fury and Thunder—all these follow an unbroken line from Tom Mix and Tony.

Gene Autry and Roy Rogers only diluted the Western with songs, the form remained the same.

From his first meeting with Selig in Chicago, Tom Mix went to greater profits, wider fame, more idolatry than any other Western star ever knew.

Then it ended as though cut by the shears of Fate.

Victoria and Tom separated. The separation stunned Hollywood.

The truth was stranger than all the wrong guesses Hollywood made at the time.

There was no other man. No other woman. So the next guess had to be—whiskey.

It was easily apparent that no all-white man ever moved with Tom Mix's grace, and further that no one-quarter Indian should ever uncork a whiskey bottle. Tom wasn't an alcoholic in the sense that John McCormick was. No, when Tom drank he was a cowboy with Indian blood on a spree. If he left the firewater in the bottle, which was most of the time, all was well. If he didn't, it wasn't, for in the end it killed him. He tried to mix alcohol with a bucking Cadillac which even the greatest cowboy cannot do. But Vickey, despite the fact that she now kept the fabulous diamonds with which Tom showered her spilling out of an Ali Baba casket when she wasn't wearing them to breakfast, had been a cowgirl, and was a pretty fair hand with a bottle herself. No, she didn't object to an occasional drinking spree.

Nor was their separation due, as some hazarded, to that usual scapegoat, "incompatibility," although in very truth, as we regard those twin living rooms in their Italian villa, the one distinctly Marie Antoinette with French china, Fragonards, gilt and crystal, the other decorated with priceless Indian blankets, Remingtons, Western saddles heavily ornamented with silver, a case for incompatibility could be made. Vickey by now wished to forget the Old West that spawned her and become somebody else—like maybe a French duchess before the Revolution. Tom never wanted to be anything but himself. Trouble was Tom was delighted with his would-be duchess and Vickey found her cowboy irresistible until—

William Fox, founder of that company to which Mix went when he rode out of the Selig Zoo and for which he worked most of his career, sounded the keynote when he said, "Vickey Mix is a great little businesswoman."

This Fox knew. Vickey had handled the contract by whose

terms Fox agreed to pay Tom Mix's enormous salary as she had every other Mix deal.

Under her flashing elegance, Tom Mix's wife was haunted by a specter. Tom was over thirty when he came to Hollywood, when they met, married. Ageless as the actor seemed, Tom Mix had been shot more times than he could remember. He had been hit by an artillery shell fragment during the Boxer Rebellion in China. For all his dynamic virility as he neared fifty his stunts and riding were harder to do. Even Tom Mix, his wife thought, couldn't go on forever.

Suppose they went broke, their money vanished via Tom's extravagance, his mad generosity, his gambling investments, just when he grew too old for his dangerous work and his enormous salary ceased?

The climax came when Tom went on one of his *spending* sprees, which had to be the supreme exaggeration of a cowboy on a spree. At a fabulous price in six figures, he had a famous diamond cut to insert in a watch for Vickey. Dozens of made-to-order white silk shirts with his monogram, a dozen new suits from Hollywood's most expensive tailor, a crate of handmade boots, two new imported cars (they already had five cars) arrived. Along with the news that Tom had lent a fortune to a slightly demented prospector he'd known somewhere in the good old days.

So they separated and were later divorced. Vickey had the millions he settled on her.

But she didn't have Tom.

He was out of Vickey's life, and he proceeded to walk out of the movies, and kept on walking. Pleas from Will Hays himself, staggering offers from every company, public demand didn't shake his determination to move on. Four thousand letters a day from "the kids" during a severe illness brought him back for a couple of Talkies. "They are no different," Tom said. "You're too busy in a Western to talk much."

The love that began when he and Will Rogers started a little Wild West Show drew him now. The circus. And the circus paid him $25,000 a week. But—Vickey was right. He didn't have any more regard for a dollar than a cowboy. In spite of the circus he died broke.

HOPALONG CASSIDY

In Tom Mix we had the story of a man, the Real Thing, who made the Cowboy.

This is the story of a cowboy who remade a man.

The man was an actor; his name was William Boyd.

The cowboy was Hopalong Cassidy, a purely fictional character who did not exist. Or did he?

That I am not prepared to answer. I can only tell the story as I saw it unfold. But this I do know. Only once in the history of the movies has a star become the character he played on the screen to the extent that he himself no longer existed separately.

Half the millions, young or old, who in the Thirties and Forties and Fifties worshiped at the shrine of Hopalong Cassidy cannot tell you now when they are in their thirties and forties and fifties the name of the actor who was Hoppy. They didn't want to know. Even more remarkable, since actors have enormous vanity, Bill Boyd didn't care whether they did or not. He was willing to sink himself out of sight to make Hoppy's legend more real.

For the actor himself had been so affected by this imaginary hero of another era that his whole life was changed.

Before this change, Hopalong Cassidy's first miracle, but by no means his last, Bill Boyd was a big roisterous guy who married a number of beautiful girls. One in Ohio, before he came to Hollywood, an older woman when he was still a kid extra, then two Hollywood lovelies.

Going back through those early years when he was only Bill Boyd, perhaps the handsomest leading man in Hollywood, I can't remember any open scandals. But he certainly lived a life of fun and frolic and a little thing like buying a yacht one morning before breakfast because the skipper thought he and his party were too wild and irresponsible to be safe guests at sea was all part of the picture. Great good nature, outstanding good looks, popular with the gang. Took what came and such things as the brotherhood of man, and the future of American youth didn't bother him.

Everybody liked Bill Boyd. He had plenty of pals, spent money freely, loved a big time—and nobody cared. Then Hopalong Cassidy got him. He was Hoppy's first convert.

Came the time when the nonexistent Hopalong Cassidy was part of American life and had more influence among 150,000,000 people than any political leader, sports champion, movie star or college president. His figure, tall in the saddle, his silver hair, his smile were Hoppy's, not Boyd's, and the youth of America was clothed, fed and led by an idol who was purely imaginary except that Boyd had made him live and breathe. And because these old-time Western films were finally brought right into the living rooms by the new medium of television, we saw *for the first time* the phenomenon of millions of kids wearing Hoppy clothes, carrying Hoppy guns, eating Hoppy bread and living by his code of honor, courage, honesty and service to your neighbor. Oh, yes. Hoppy had become intensely *real* to millions of people—children and their parents and their grandparents—for a check made in the early Fifties showed that 65 per cent of his fans were grownups.

Why and how did Hopalong Cassidy awaken a public love and idolatry which transcended anything known in the picture business since the Golden Days of Tom Mix, Mary Pickford or Valentino?

Actually, the Hopalong Cassidy movies weren't in point of background, action, stories so very different from other Westerns in the theaters or on TV. But the results were different.

I'm going to try to piece together Bill Boyd's own explanation as he once gave it to me, though he wasn't very clear about it himself. The miracle of Hoppy was to him, a sort of miracle of grace.

It happened, yet he didn't know why it happened to him.

Bill Boyd was born in a Midwestern state where he worked in a grocery store, a gas station, as a salesman and finally drifted west. A good many people, impressed by his looks, said he ought to be in pictures. So he went into pictures but nothing much happened. When Cecil B. DeMille said it, Bill was in pictures for sure and under DeMille's direction made a success of *The Volga Boatman*.

The next years are a Hollywood pattern. Bill Boyd thought it was swell, got a big salary and spent every penny, married a lovely leading lady named Elinor Fair. After they were divorced he married the stunning Dorothy Sebastian. He and Dorothy lived near me down at Malibu and had a big time all the time, fishing, swimming, sunbathing, all-night parties and no more thought of the morrow than grasshoppers. Young, beautiful, rich, popular and complete materialists. Bill went on playing leads opposite well-known women stars. For quite a while. Never got any higher than all-star billing.

Somewhere in there he and Dorothy got a divorce, and after a while the ole Hollywood grapevine began to whisper that Bill Boyd was hitting the bottle a leettle too hard. It wasn't doing his looks any good and his looks were all he had. According to the pattern, there wasn't much of anywhere for Bill Boyd to go but down—and eventually out.

Then one day Bill Boyd met Hopalong Cassidy.

After four lean years his day as a handsome young leading man done, Bill, in 1935, needed a job and though the Hopalong series was regarded pretty B stuff, Westerns written by Clarence Mulford, to be produced by Pop Sherman—he went to talk about another character in the stories—and ended up with Hoppy himself.

Bill Boyd wasn't a Westerner, he'd never been a cowboy, he couldn't ride much, he knew neither the lore nor the tradition nor the work as Tom Mix had known them. But Hopalong taught him. Quick. Hoppy got him. I can't explain it. Transmigration of souls, reincarnation, maybe some big words I don't understand too well. Anyhow, Bill Boyd knew it all, could do it all, became the character in about a week. Things he hadn't known he knew all at once—instinctively.

From the beginning, in the small theaters and neighborhood houses where the Hopalong Cassidy series played, the kids went for Hoppy and then something fantastic happened to Bill Boyd.

The only emotional parallel of which I know was described to me by my good friend, Paul Gallico. It happened at a baseball writers' banquet at a time in history when George Herman "Babe" Ruth was baseball's number-one idol and home run king, the King of Swat, *and* its ace bad boy. During that season Babe Ruth had managed to break training, quarrel with his manager, be suspended and fired. At this memorable banquet his friend Mayor Jimmy Walker took him to task for his delinquent behavior, made a personal, public appeal that Ruth heed his responsibilities to the youth of the nation, that he reform himself for "the dirty-faced kids in the street who worshipped him." And the Babe stood up, tears streaming down his big ugly face, and promised. And then kept his promise. He was never in trouble again.

Something like that happened to Bill Boyd. Something from outside himself moved in and created Hopalong Cassidy. Only it was Hoppy himself who made the plea to Bill Boyd, and Bill always had a soft heart.

The story of the newsboys who stood outside the ball park in Chicago at the time of the Black Sox scandal and cried to Shoeless Joe Jackson, "Tell us it ain't so, Joe, tell us it ain't so," is legend. Well, kids began to stand outside the studio gates to see —Boyd? No. Hopalong. Hoppy said to Boyd, "You see?"

One day Bill Boyd, because he was Hopalong Cassidy, was asked to go out to a reform school. Real tough boys. Bill Boyd looked at those bitter young faces and the miracle happened. Hoppy took over.

Bill Boyd couldn't put it into words, even into clear thoughts. But he began to think of Hopalong as somebody that had come to do something—be something—to those lonely kids whose folks were not much interested, unhappy kids, all the kids who needed a *hero*, somebody to look up to and love and admire. A man— well, Hoppy sort of explained it to Bill Boyd that truth always comes along to people in a form and a language they can understand then. God speaks through many instruments. He, Bill Boyd, a very ordinary guy, an actor who had made his own mistakes, he couldn't do anything for these kids. An almost pathetic and terrible humility about Bill Boyd possessed him, though like George Herman Ruth, he would try to live up to the Hero, he wouldn't let Hoppy down, not if Hopalong Cassidy wanted to use Bill Boyd—like the Babe, he'd have to behave for the dirty-faced kids who loved him.

That was the first miracle. There were to be more along the road.

One of the greatest was the fight Bill Boyd put up to have Hopalong for his own so no one else could ever let him down— ever touch him—and that took miracles.

The first of these was that in this fight he had the inspired support of his wife Grace, his great love.

The timing was extraordinary, as Bill's life marched in step with his creation of and possession by Hopalong.

In 1937, two years after he began making Hoppy movies, he met a beautiful young movie actress named Grace Bradley.

Later Grace's mother showed Bill the girl's schoolbooks, with "Bill Boyd" scrawled all over them. In the fashion of high school girls, Grace had written "Mrs. Bill Boyd" and "Grace Bradley and Bill Boyd" with the letters crossed in the immemorial custom. In fact, Grace's mother thought Grace came to Hollywood as much in a forlorn hope of meeting the man she'd fallen in love with on the screen as of getting in the movies.

If that's true, she was successful. Three weeks after they met they were married. Bill Boyd said to me seriously, "I had been looking for Grace all my life."

There had been previous Mrs. Bill Boyds.

There was to be only one Mrs. Hopalong Cassidy.

Came the day in 1944 after forty-four Hopalongs had been made, when Bill Boyd and Pop Sherman broke up. A strange phenomenon, never known in the movies before, had taken place. True, no one but Mickey Rooney could be Andy Hardy, but Mickey could and did play other roles. But not only could no one else play Hopalong, Hopalong was the only part Bill Boyd could play. They were one.

Bill Boyd was inspired with the idea of getting Hopalong Cassidy for his own. From the first, Grace told me, his deep motive in owning his alter ego was to protect Hoppy, to continue him as Bill felt him.

It cost them nearly $400,000, most of which they didn't have. They sold the ranch, Grace's car, mortgaged Hoppy's for $1,500, sold Grace's jewels and furs and rented a four-room cottage where Grace did her own cooking and Hoppy mowed the lawn. They borrowed every penny they could and even cut down on meals.

Common sense made the odds against this B Western hero, popular as he was, becoming the leading idol of the nation. Only Bill Boyd and Grace had supreme faith in Hopalong.

Even with faith Bill couldn't see into the future—but maybe Hoppy could?

For six years later, with the assist of television, Hopalong Cassidy had become a folk hero right along with Paul Bunyan and Wyatt Earp and Daniel Boone and Davy Crockett.

He was the power of good always trying to down the power of evil. The blazing guns of Hoppy, shooting down bad men, had been heard around the world.

Somewhere along the line Bill Boyd had picked up the talent for showmanship that's so essential. Too often, as today, we have left showmanship to the wrong side.

Add up the 70 million dollars' worth of Hopalong Cassidy merchandise that was sold in 1950; the TV showing of his movies; the radio; his daily column (except Bob Hope, a comedian, Hopalong was the first star to have a widely circulated, much-read daily newspaper column since Mary Pickford); the cartoons and comic books; the personal appearances; *The Trooper*, his own paper sent to his kid followers; and you had a man in direct and friendly touch with more folks than any other man in the world at that time.

Hollywood's Bill Boyd was an extravagant man who always had the biggest, flashiest cars, the best clothes and at one time five places in which to live, besides the yacht and an extensive wine cellar.

It was Hoppy's idea that as he encouraged kids to buy—and he insisted on values from the people who handled his merchandising program—he must also encourage them to save. This began a Hopalong Cassidy thrift program display to teach children to save—three thousand new accounts were opened in one Los Angeles bank the first week.

A lot of people who made possible Hopalong Cassidy activities had a percentage of the earnings, including the man who started the whole thing, author Clarence Mulford. Out of the million dollars more or less that Hoppy earned in one year, Bill Boyd himself kept only around $50,000. He turned over vast sums to an enterprise for child welfare work and stayed up nights to work out a scheme for free dude ranches for city boys.

But nobody but Bill owned one per cent control of what Hopalong did, said, or was. That belonged solely to the Hopalong Cassidy-Bill Boyd union.

"Doesn't it scare you sometimes?" I asked Bill one day along about then when we were lunching together. "Being the best-known and best-loved man of your times, because Hoppy is."

Hoppy—Bill—it was hard to know which to call him, had the bluest eyes ever seen. In his deeply tanned face, under the silver hair, which had been silver-white since he was a very young man, they were startling. Now he turned them on me.

"It would if it was me doing it," he said, with his appealing grin. Then, after a moment's thought, he added gravely, "No man who didn't believe in a higher power . . . I mean no man could try to do what I'm trying to do without help. But one with God is a majority, I learned that when I was a kid in Sunday school, back in Ohio. I thought I'd forgotten it, but it turned out I hadn't."

Or maybe Hoppy reminded him?

For Hoppy's creed had become Bill's only business in life.

The creed of love God, your country, your fellow man. Be decent, clean in speech, conduct and body, help your neighbor, be an unselfish member of your family, your community, never quit when you're right, tell the truth, fight evil.

The code of Tom Mix.

The creed of the Old West as updated by Hopalong Cassidy-Bill Boyd.

A trail blazed for those who would be pure of heart.

Corn? To be sure. And I say Hooray! If you don't give people a little corn they have nothing but husks—they perish—as happened to the youths of the post-Hoppy generation. What did they get? Beach boys. Surfers. *The Rolling Stones*. The Code totally reversed as in a Black Mass.

God is dead—or a member of the Establishment. What we need is Flower Power. *Drop out*—What did your country ever do for you? Or your family? What do you owe them? Or society for that matter? *Do your own thing at all costs*—in dress, conduct, morals. The scruffier the purer. Your neighbor must be someone your own age *or* a member of your cult or gang. All others are expendable. *Have a good day!*

And where did that creed lead them? Straight to Haight-Ashbury and drugs, isolation, insanity, death.

I saw *Star Wars* the other day in the company of some of my great-grandchildren who belong to the *post*-post-Hoppy generation and they were vastly taken with the movie and the tall gold humanoid robot, C-3PO, who speaks with a British accent and the little mechanized robot, R2-D2, who bubbles and squeaks. A few days later these two new stars were immortalized in cement in front of Grauman's Chinese Theatre not far from the prints of Tom Mix and his horse, Tony. I have to admit that C-3PO and R2-D2, as well as the bionic men and women of today, are a vast improvement over the Rolling Stones. I also have to admit that, whether I like it or not, and I don't, the Old West as a frontier is being replaced, in the imagination of the young at any rate, by the new frontier of Space. The glamour of the cowboy now rests with spacemen and robots while the trusty horse is, I suppose, the computer although I'm not too sure how far we should go with this.

I have had no faith in computers since one of them got us into all that confusion with the Russian scientists by translating "hydraulic ram" as "water goat" and no liking for them since they have been invited to take over the Internal Revenue Service, which didn't have much heart to begin with, and to interfere in every other branch of *human* affairs. Your friendly banker has become a mindless gadget which will not even admit its own mistakes. My granddaughter encountered one recently which took exception to the number 15 and upon encountering it, when ordered to either deposit *or* withdraw, perversely stuttered three times. The only suggestion the friendly teller had was that checks be made in the amount of $14.99. *We* have programmed them to pander to one of our lowest impulses, curiosity about each other's private business, and then gossip about these shamelessly at the flip of a switch.

I'm not even sure where a computer leaves off and a robot begins or what bionics have to do with either or both, *however*, since this is the wave of the future that may well engulf all those I hold most dear, some dark night I shall take to my trusty broomstick and set forth to improve the whole breed.

I shall program them with Heart—feed into them large doses of *corn*, as handed down to us by Tom Mix and Hopalong Cassidy. It may well blow their fuses but consider, today when it takes more guts to uphold or ever admit to the Hoppy creed than to break the law, it might well blow ours.

This I *know*. We, and all these extensions of ourselves, must come back to the Heart and *soon*—to a code of Brotherhood from which we can act—for the sake of this world and the worlds to come.

Chapter Eight

The Magnificent Gable

Television, or rather me on television, came as a late-blooming flower in my life.

I have enjoyed every minute of it. Even when it was nerve-racking and difficult. It's granted me those rare and wonderful moments when I could say what I wanted—*needed*—to say, and whether anybody paid any attention to me or not, it has been a real joy. Ma, as my children say, has an opinion about everything!

Hasn't everybody?

But more than that it has given me friends—friends to talk to —friends to argue with—friends to laugh with. And they are very much the same kinds of friends I was lucky enough to have in my newspaper life, the kind who were always at the center of whatever and wherever the action was.

My first television was—luckily for me—with that number-one guy, Jack Parr. A man as kind as a member of the human race can be. He took one look at me and realized that I was terrified and within a few seconds had made me comfortable, welcome and self-confident. Don't ask me how—just that if television was a world he lived in and was happy about, it had to be a place where there was nothing to fear.

And he gave me two definite *orders* that have controlled my TV life from then on. Never, said my Mr. Parr, see or hear yourself on television.

If you keep to that you won't take yourself too seriously. You'll have fun. Never either look at yourself or listen to yourself on TV.

Promise me!

I promised and I have kept that promise absolutely. And so I have had such friends as Johnny Carson, whose judgment and opinion I value the same way I did Damon Runyon's. I can't say better than that.

And my beloved Merv Griffin. I want you to know I loved him devotedly before ever he appeared in front of a television camera. Merv was a member of Dink Templeton's Stanford track team! Come right down to it I suppose I respected Dink Templeton as much as, maybe more than, almost any other man I ever knew. Most of us did.

My heart always goes out to Merv Griffin. He has parlayed what to him was a failure into one of the great TV successes. For Merv never wanted what is now a Talk Show, though it has given him fame and fortune.

All Merv ever wanted to do was *sing*.

Doing the Merv Griffin Show is one of the delights of my life. Think about it a minute. What is it but having a real fine visit with a man whose friendship I value highly, whose conversation always entertains me, and who brings together a variety of stimulating people I might otherwise miss?

This I could say, too, about Mike Douglas in Philadelphia, that blessed Kup in Chicago, and one of my favorite gals, Ruth Lyons, when she was in Cincinnati, and Bob Brown who took over when Ruth retired. In fact, with the great variety of hosts and hostesses I've encountered, I have to say all the television I've ever done has been fun.

I will admit to a few uncomfortable moments. The night I was on with an upstart author who had compiled a particularly vile tissue of lies about Jean Harlow—never having interviewed a living soul who knew her—if *he* wasn't uncomfortable it was not *my* fault. With the likes of Erica Jong and Truman Capote—let's just say we were not comfortable *together*. But the only time I ever wished I was someplace *else* was on a show where I was preceded by a lady who, as I recall, ran the San Diego Zoo.

She had with her a chimpanzee and smaller monkeys, a friendly coyote, and a witty parrot who left me with very little to say. Except that W. C. Fields told me never *never* NEVER try to follow children or animals. You could not top them. It couldn't be done.

Which brings me, circuitously I confess, to the magnificent Mr. Clark Gable. Who *could* do it.

Gable could follow chimps and children and all the stars in Hollywood—and still come out on top.

The life and the star career of Clark Gable can be divided into two parts, both complete, but strikingly different.

The first man was the most vital personal influence, the best-loved, most looked-up-to man who ever lived in Hollywood.

The second man, who came away from that mountain behind the broken body of his wife, Carole, killed in a plane crash, was a blind giant, maimed, wounded almost to death, trying afterward to find his way in darkness. A shell and a shadow, henceforth to give the world a gallant performance of the man he had once been.

Clark Gable's strength and sanity and integrity and character as a man and an actor helped lead the industry through the wilderness of reconstruction to sound. He proved to a confused art that a talking Movie Star could be bigger and more popular than ever.

The man himself took Hollywood by storm, but the Public saw him first. Proof again that the box office is the ballot box. The public, by a practically unanimous vote, elected Clark Gable what Tracy first called him—the King.

To men Gable was what they wanted to be, strong, resourceful, courageous, unafraid of life. To women he was what they wanted their men to be.

One thing about Gable puzzled me for years—his burning passion to be an actor in the first place.

The frame house in Cadiz, Ohio, where he was born; winters at school in a small Midwest town; summers, after his mother died, on the Pennsylvania farm of his grandparents; the simple loving woman who was the deciding influence of his youth, his adored stepmother, Jennie; his big, strong body and honest mind and utterly freakish sense of humor—these do not suggest a desire to act. His Pennsylvania Dutch relatives didn't know footlights existed. His father told him later "acting's no job for a fellow six feet tall, weighs 185." Movies hadn't yet gained much following in Clark's childhood neighborhood, he had never met an actor, talked with

any human being connected with the stage nor been inside a theater until he was seventeen—but the sight of his first play was
enough. He quit his job as timekeeper in a rubber factory and
started on the road to Broadway.

Mule skinner, lumberjack, tool dresser in Oklahoma oil fields,
telephone lineman, he worked at anything to keep from starving
"between engagements." He "rode the rods" like a hobo in a bliz-
zard from one town where his troupe had folded to another a
thousand miles away; eked out the winter there as a tie salesman.
But nothing took his eye off his goal which was to act.

He sat looking more like a cigar store Indian than a candidate
for the part of the smooth, sardonic ready-on-the-draw gambler,
Ace Wilfong, a leading character in *A Free Soul*, a novel I had
written, a best-seller soon to be made into a movie. He turned
down a drink I offered, perched on the edge of a rattan *chaise
longue* in a position of acute discomfort, and waited for me to
make the next move.

For a moment I couldn't imagine what had caused this with-
drawal, which it patently was. On the telephone when we had
made the appointment he had been warm, friendly, he had even
kidded me a bit about my time of service as a sports writer. Now
he was wary and worldly and faintly amused. What had brought
this about? And suddenly in the big window that gave on the
sand and the sea I saw the reflection of a figure—a figure decked
out in elegant and rather overpowering turquoise silk lounging pajamas, exactly designed for the leading lady to wear in the second
act of a society comedy-drama. These were, in fact, a gift Colleen
Moore had brought back from Gump's in San Francisco and I
had them on because they were, quite literally, the only thing I
could find to wear—the all too frequent state of my wardrobe
since my daughter, Elaine, and her girl-friend-in-residence, Jean,
Mark Kelly's daughter, had discovered my clothes fit. Thus it had
been on this morning in 1931 when Clarence Brown called to ask
if he might send down to Malibu a young New York stage actor
who he thought might be a replacement for Jack Gilbert as Ace.
Thalberg thinks there's a chance, he said, tentatively.

So there I was most inappropriately clad for a beach morning and there was the young actor whose name was Clark Gable, obviously cagey and on guard with ladies in silken pajamas who invited him into their parlor and plied him with liquor, but after I had explained that I had made it myself in the guest room from five gallons of very good alcohol—a Prohibition present from Little Augie who ran the bootleg art and industry from Brooklyn and for whose wife I had once done a favor—Clark drank his gin neat, with a wedge of lemon peel and salt on the back of his hand, a fashion the California Mexicans used with tequila.

Then he sat more comfortably, he relaxed and gave me my first version of the to-become-famous Gable grin of joy in living—and I had found not only my Ace Wilfong but a friend.

Our friendship was to last from that moment until his death almost thirty years later.

Why do I say that?

Has it ever ended?

In a book I wrote called *The Honeycomb* I find I say "The heart's dead are never buried." They live for us always, every minute of every day.

Friendship-love is the greatest.

It lasts.

Lovers come and go without making too much change in the scenery. Even husbands are around for a while—and then they aren't there any more, especially nowadays. The ups and downs of a love affair or a marriage are more or less like a ride on a roller coaster. You can see more from the top but there's always that downward plunge. Today I have trouble remembering the name of my second husband. What is there to remember? But with friendship-love you never want to try to forget—you sit on the terrace and watch a perfect sunset and the empty chair next to you can have sitting in it A Memory of a Friend, and both the memory and the friends still fill you with warm delight.

A lovely word. *Delight.* Music comes with it of course. With Clark, for instance, comes a tune he used to whistle absent-mindedly—a phrase from Tchaikovsky's Fifth Symphony, varied with the Halls of Montezuma and a note or two from the Maine Stein Song.

And fragrances—of good pipe tobacco, or pine woods, or a certain kind of shaving lotion, or in Gable's case a faint whiff of the best scotch.

I'm remembering now.

Our first days of horseback riding together.

He couldn't ride after the California fashion at all, nor for that matter the English one. An English saddle the size of a postage stamp completely disconcerted him.

I cannot recall under exactly what circumstances I offered to give him a few pointers and why I said to him, "But you *can* ride, can't you?"

And Mr. Gable, meeting my eyes with a cold glare, said, "Not what you-all call riding in these parts."

"But . . ." I said, "you were brought up on a *farm*. I thought all kids brought up on a farm could ride . . ."

"Did you?" said Clark Gable, and one eyebrow went up—his eyebrows were a kind of barometer of his state of mind, how far up or down and whether he was using one or both. "Let me explain to you one of the facts of farm life. Sure I rode. I rode a farm horse *bareback*. His back was just about as wide as a barn door. My legs stuck out at exactly right angles. That, my good wench, was all the riding I ever did—it was on a *farm*, not a *ranch*. You comprehend the difference?"

I did, so I said, "I've got a couple of horses out at the Bel Air stables . . . we could get on the trails early . . . nobody would notice us."

And the next thing you know there we were—me putting silver dollars between Clark Gable's knees and his horse, or attempting to.

"What in hell are you doing?" he said, and looking up I could see him silhouetted against the sky.

"When Papa taught me to ride," I said, "he used to put a silver dollar between my knee and the horse—one on each side. If I came home with them I got to keep them."

"How old were you?" Clark Gable said.

"Oh . . ." I said, "I guess I was eight or nine maybe . . ."

"I," said Mr. Gable, "am slightly older. And I am *not* going around at my age trying to imitate you when you were eight."

Both eyebrows made a straight black line. He was sore. For about five minutes. Then he said, "Do I get to keep the dollars?" and we both began to laugh.

Gable and I used to go out just as the sun came up behind us, and spend a couple of hours riding the trails. Often we walked our horses after a brisk gallop and then we talked. The basic purpose of these early morning canters was to improve Clark's horsemanship—but it turned out to be the ripening of that beautiful friendship.

They *don't*.

They don't go away! Never. If you have once had friendshiploves you can always bring them back, those friends-and-lovers. The groove of memory is deeper and stronger than anything else in life. I *know*. As time passes it tests and proves this—for I find William Randolph Hearst, who was my boss for over thirty-five years and my *friend* as well, and Mark Kelly, who made me a sports writer, which was the job I liked best in all the world. And Wally Reid, Jack Gilbert, Eddie Rickenbacker, John Aloysius Clements, Dink Templeton—and Clark Gable.

Oh, yes. I remember.

Clearer I guess than anything is a time he came down to Malibu, and we were sitting in the little outdoor pergola that overlooked the blue Pacific.

My son Bill, who was then in his early teens, but had grown to over six feet in the process, came out on his way to the water— none of the kids *knew* actually the difference between land and water, they went back and forth without ever seeming to notice and were as much at home in one as the other.

Bill found Mr. Gable sitting comfortably with me and his instant reaction of course was Does Mr. Gable want to go swimming? If he didn't bring trunks I expect we've something around he could wear. Gable, correctly garbed, went off with Bill and Joey Santley and Gloria Swanson's small son. The next thing I knew he came back just with Bill—and a more dilapidated and disreputable figure I have never seen. He had seaweed coming out of both nostrils, hair totally matted with sand, water still streaming all over him like Niagara Falls, and he was staggering just a little as he walked the hot sand.

"Ma," Bill said in what I am sure he thought was *sotto voce*, "you shoulda told me Mr. Gable couldn't swim . . ."

It wasn't *sotto voce* enough, for Gable heard him and let out a roar. "I can swim!" he shouted. "I'm a very fine swimmer. I been swimming in the ole swimming hole all my life. Nobody ever told me about a lot of water that keeps coming up all the time and banging around like it had eels on its bottom . . ."

He shook the water out of his ears and glared at Bill and said, "All right, Bud, let's go," and the next I saw a breaker had greeted his return, but he came up grinning and, as Bill said at the end of the afternoon, "Maybe he can't swim much but he's sure got guts."

After *A Free Soul* was released, Clark Gable's stardom was as instant and total as an explosion, as definite and complete as an Act of Nature—which actually I suppose it was.

And it brought with it an instant adulation, a loving idolatry and an outgoing admiration which Clark told me not once but many times dumfounded him in the beginning and actually never ceased to dumfound him all his life.

Even in Hollywood he was always a celebrity—which is very hard to do, nobody else ever did it except Garbo and she did it by being so elusive, seen in public so seldom, that it was the result rather of the rareness of her appearances than the size of her popularity.

Just now my daughter Elaine, remembering back forty or so years, reminds me with glee that in the days when he came often to our beach house, she was making herself quite a lot of money selling tickets at 50¢ apiece—and this to the children of the other movie stars who formed the Malibu Colony of that famous day. A blasé lot they were, as a matter of fact, but they were willing to pay that price to stand on an orange crate and peek through our living-room window at a movie star—*if* he was Clark Gable.

Never—never as far as my extensive Hollywood experience went did anyone in the movies or anywhere else take so dim a view of being lionized as Mr. Gable. Unlike Garbo he genuinely liked people, but those elaborate parties given by the elite of Hollywood, forgathering to show off in a Mutual Admiration Society, were anathema to this blazing new star.

Personally I will never forget a night when I stopped by the Gables' house to go along to a party with Clark and Rhea. She was the second Mrs. Gable and a nicer more charming woman never lived—and so thought Mr. Gable. She had been a Mrs. Langham of Texas, with a good many Texas millions tucked in her purse, when in New York she met a young actor named Clark Gable. Since their scene had shifted to Hollywood I had been, so to speak, shepherding my friend's wife through the social mazes thereof. On this particular night it appeared that I was off duty. Friend-husband was refusing to leave the fold.

The scene, the dialogue, could have been played in a million American homes. Mrs. Gable, lovely in a flowing gown, Mr. Gable, still in the pin-striped suit he had worn to the studio.

MRS. GABLE: But, darling, we've refused so many times . . .

MR. GABLE: (scotch in hand)

> I've worked hard at the studio all day . . . now you want me to get dressed up in my fancy suit and go *out* and talk to a lot of people . . .

Two or three scotches and a good deal of persuasive dialogue later, Mr. Gable agreed to go. As he was. Eventually a compromise was reached and we sallied forth, Clark triumphant, one eyebrow definitely raised, in an immaculately tailored dinner jacket— and striped gray pants.

He was, our Mr. Gable, about as Dutch stubborn as a man could get. His resistance to being lionized never changed—he was in most ways a very private person, you didn't barge into his home or his dressing room on the lot without phoning—and yet he was more friendly, more gracious, more hail-fellow-well-met with ordinary people, crowds or fans, than any other Hollywood star I ever knew. I was in his dressing room at the Capitol Theater in New York, this was during the heights of his fame and he was there at an enormous salary to make a few personal appearances, when the theater manager, all beaming smiles, came in.

"I've just arranged an exit for you through the building next door," he said, "then you won't have to fight your way through that crowd."

"Hell no," said Mr. Gable, "the time I'll begin to go through the building next door is when there isn't anybody out there! I'll be damn glad to say Hi to them."

. And he did. Day after day, he went out through the crowds and it was one of the astounding things about our Mr. Gable. *Nobody* laid a hand on him. It was the same thing at the opening of *Gone with the Wind* in Atlanta. A wild packed jam of fans, who'd attended the opening if they were lucky or gathered outside if they weren't, waited for him—and they opened a path as he came out and again nobody laid a hand on him. *Ever.* He had always some unmatched dignity of his own—he was a *man* before he was a Movie Star and people didn't paw him. There was, perhaps, a sort of dignity about him, and this may have added to the things that caused Spencer Tracy to nominate him the King.

Off the screen, it seems to me now, Gable did *naturally* all the things that were expected of him. And a few that weren't. Probably it was his pronounced talent for the unexpected that made him so believable in roles like the newspaperman in *It Happened One Night*—which next to *San Francisco* was the picture he had the most *fun* making. And that same unexpectedness gave an added spice to his friendships. Sure, you expected Clark Gable to go off into the woods to hunt and fish, which he did. You expected him to be virile in love and victorious in war, which he was. Off the screen as well as on. And I testify that he was. His work in the war as a gunner in our Air Force was honest and definite as that of any other man. He not only asked no favors, he turned them aside. You expected him to drink hard when he drank—which he did, preferably scotch whiskey.

But would you have expected the King of the Movies to be a Master at Jacks? Yes yes—*jacks*—with those little six-pronged metal pieces and a small bouncing rubber ball?

Probably not—but he was. And loved it! On my memory screen I can still see him, cross-legged on the floor in the living room of Howard and Gail Strickling's, their charming Encino house, which was the place Clark went oftenest to dinner or for an evening of gab—and *jacks*.

Last time I played with him he did in-the-barn-door, around-the-world, Flying Dutchman—and a few I'd never heard of!

Nobody, I guess, is without faults.

Gable wasn't.

But there are faults and faults!

There are faults that somehow make your flesh creep—and there are those you sort of shrug off or are amused by. Any kind of cruelty is the one fault I am still having trouble trying to forgive ever. It cost me the one man I truly wanted to marry and with whom I thought I could do a great newspaper job, but once I found out, he had done a minor cruelty on purpose—and it scared me out of my wits. Any form of unkindness seems to me of all things most dreadful.

Gable was *kind* to the point of tenderness. And that, by the way, is my favorite virtue. I want so much sometimes to point out to the generations now in control that the world is chill today from a lack of kindness—not sentimentality, not *luv* as it is currently misunderstood, but actual, warm, human kindness of the variety Clark knew about. After Carole's death there was a new dimension to it, his reaction to his personal grief was that he had something to share with others, that because of his own ordeal he could offer a special something that those who had not "been there" didn't have.

When a popular singer was killed in a plane crash Clark went straight to his widow, although he had never met her. He was my comfort and strength when I lost both my son, Bill, and my brother, Thornwell, in the Second World War. "Endlessly thoughtful and helpful . . . he checked up on me constantly to see if I was all right," so his friend David Niven wrote of Clark's unfailing kindness to him during the long months of despair after Niven's wife, Primmie, died in a tragic accident. Clark somehow kept track of all things going on, and showed up at what is now known as the psychological moment over and over again.

Perhaps his biggest *fault* was that he was right close with a buck. This I could understand. Clark had spent a lot of time being broke. He came to stardom and a big salary after the Income Tax as an insatiable monster had become a reality in all our lives. By now we have learned to live with it, I guess, but forty-odd years ago it seemed to us immoral if not illegal, and Clark's Dutch soul often writhed under the percentage of his earnings that went in taxes, agent's commissions, lawyer's fees, all the things that by then were required to keep the life of a Movie Star running smoothly in high gear. So that notwithstanding the care he took of what was left, he didn't have anywhere near as much money coming in as it sounded like he would have.

Gable countered this tendency to closeness with sudden bursts of generosity which he would take great trouble to arrange.

One time when I was at his Encino house I sincerely admired his front door. A few weeks later I emerged from the office in my home in Palms one afternoon to discover that my own front door was missing. This can discommode a person and I was considering my next move when a crew in overalls came around the corner of the house and across the terrace bearing a brand new front door, an exact copy of the one I'd admired in Encino. "Compliments of Mr. Gable," announced my butler with satisfaction.

His freakish sense of humor could also upon occasion spark these bursts of generosity.

Once when I was living in the East and came out at Easter time to do a picture I went to stay with a longtime dear friend of mine, Jessie Mestayer, in her big old-fashioned house with a plumbago vine over the front porch down on East Kensington Road in Los Angeles. Clark, having kindly decided I might be lonely for my family over the holidays, came to take me to dinner.

He was, as usual, drinking scotch. I drank martinis, of which Mr. Gable disapproved and which I could never drink in his company without his violent protests. He considered martinis the most dangerous drink he had ever encountered. Could be he was right because as Clark got pleasantly high my evening got dimmer and dimmer until it became a total blank. The next thing I knew I awakened to ribbons of daylight in Jessie's big front bedroom. I was laid out fully clothed on the great old-fashioned black walnut bed, my hands carefully folded on my bosom—and I was literally surrounded by banks and banks of Easter lilies.

I thought I was dead.

And with the logic of drunks decided to swear off martinis if they killed you.

Which was no doubt what Mr. Gable had in mind when he conspired with Jessie and his florist in the middle of the night to arrange my "funeral."

Gable "on the lot" could be a different guy.

The tenderness came through, as it did with Jean Harlow when she came back to the studio after Paul Bern's suicide. On his set, where he always arrived fully prepared and on time, he laughed and joked and generally enjoyed himself.

It was in the front office and at story conferences that Clark got tough. He was in no wise awed by the Brass and he was determined at all times to protect both Clark Gable and the Public.

From that first day at Malibu he had trusted my story judgment and when we both found ourselves at Metro one of my main jobs was as Clark's story consultant. So I sat in on a good many of those conferences. What I saw and heard convinced me that Gable had no illusions about himself as an actor. It has become fashionable to say that Clark Gable couldn't act; the truth is that he knew his limitations as an actor and was absolutely determined that the stories given him should be within his range; if not he was quite capable of walking right off the lot.

One talent Gable had as an actor has been too much overlooked—his ability to get the very best out of the women he acted *with*. With Jean Harlow in *Red Dust*, which assured Jean's stardom. With Claudette Colbert in *It Happened One Night* which won them both an Oscar. With Ava Gardner in *Mogambo*, the best thing Ava ever did. And, of course, with Joan Crawford in *Possessed*. He was even trying in the last picture he ever made, *The Misfits*, with poor little Marilyn Monroe. But there was one young lady who, without this particular talent of Clark's, would never have become a star at all.

We could call this "How Clark Gable saved Neptune's Granddaughter for The Movies."

Paul Gallico in his classic *Farewell to Sport* said: "The best-known group of girl athletes in the whole United States wasn't made up of tennis players, golfers, runners or jumpers, but swimmers. This is due to Miss Annette Kellermann and the art of the camera."

Today we'd probably have to concede the honors to the tennis players or the gymnasts, more's the pity, for while I admire Chris Evert and Kathy Rigby I can't quite compare them to the stars in the days of which Paul wrote—starting with Annette Kellermann and reaching its zenith with Esther Williams.

Annette Kellermann was one of the first movie stars as well as a diving champion. Hers was an inspiring career. As a child, she was paralyzed and swam her way out of it to national fame. I can still remember the beauteous Annette in that first one-piece bathing suit, the thrill when she dived from a high platform into a small tank on the stage of old-time vaudeville theaters. This was poetry of motion and chill-steel nerve. Movies gave her scope and in 1914 she made one of the first "spectacles" in motion pictures, a smash hit called *Neptune's Daughter*.

Movie companies kept on looking after that for another of Neptune's Daughters. It was over thirty years before they found her.

In the late Thirties a high school girl from Los Angeles, California, named Esther Williams showed up as a true contender for national honors, and in 1940 made the Olympic Swimming Team. She was received with cheers in press boxes from coast to coast, growing louder as sports writers, who are hard-boiled outside and sentimental as an Irish ballad within, found this new teen-age Water Queen, Bathing Beauty and Swimming Venus to be as nice a kid as the sports world had ever known.

Sports have always vitally interested the motion picture industry. It knows full well the hero-worship American fans have for sports idols and that the fans who pack stadiums are the same who will, they hope, keep movie theaters crowded.

Not only therefore has the industry made sports pictures, some as fine as *The Monte Stratton Story*, the life of Lou Gehrig with Gary Cooper, and more recently the deeply moving *Brian's Song*, but it has gambled fortunes to find out whether heroes and heroines of gridiron, prize ring, pool and diamond and court have what it takes to be movie stars as well.

Some didn't. After one or two appearances as "actors" Babe Ruth, Red Grange, Gene Tunney, Max Baer, Glenn Davis of the Army, Brooklyn's Jackie Robinson and even the most popular of all heavyweight champs, Dempsey, returned to their own fields of glory.

Leaving out the splendid and successful sport shorts made by Bobby Jones, winner of the grand slam in golf, four authentic champions became real movie stars.

Exquisite, doll-like Sonja Henie, in the opinion of experts the greatest all-time woman ice skater. Swimming champ Johnny

"Tarzan" Weissmuller, Johnny Mack Brown, star halfback of Ala-
bama's Crimson Tide in the Rose Bowl against Washington,
given a contract by producers before he could get out of the dressing room afterward to become a favorite Western star in movies
and on TV as well. Above all, Esther Williams, one of MGM's
top stars, who in 1951 was on the "first ten at the box office" list.

Yet if it hadn't been for Clark Gable, Esther Williams would
have quit before she ever made a movie.

The crucial drama that saved Esther Williams to become the
pride of Hollywood began in L. B. Mayer's office, consulting
room, safety zone and, I must admit, torture chamber for stars on
his Metro-Goldwyn-Mayer lot. It was Mr. Mayer, who had first
seen her in an Aquacade in San Francisco, who had put her under
contract, and then forgotten about her.

When the tall, slim young girl walked into Mayer's office one
day, she had been on the MGM lot over a year and never shot a
scene. What, the subproducers kept saying, could you do with a
swimmer? And Esther Williams sat down across the desk from
the head man and instantly burst into a flood of tears.

"What's the matter with you, young lady?" he said.

"Mr. Mayer," Esther said, "let me out of my contract. Please.
Nobody wants me. I'll never be any good in movies. I'm a
swimmer, not an actress."

Had that interview ended differently, Esther Williams' picture
career would have been over. But at that moment Clark Gable
walked in the door. Clark had to make a test for his next picture.
Lana Turner was to play opposite him, she was in the East, who
did L.B. want him to use instead?

"Esther Williams," Mayer said. "What's more, convince her
she can act."

Gable made her act. Esther Williams explained to me once
that Clark was patient with her, that he made her feel a warmth
about acting she'd never dreamed of before, made it fun and a
challenge. She said no more after that about quitting the movies
and, Clark Gable had rescued Neptune's Granddaughter.

Gable's own attitude toward his acting can best be described by
what Hollywood tried to build into a Gable-Tracy feud. Truth to
tell there wasn't any. They were Friendly Enemies *because* they
admired each other. Each had something the other didn't have—

each knew it. Clark would have given his right arm to be the actor Spencer Tracy was. And Tracy would have given his right arm to be the personality that Gable was. But feud? As in "a bitter, long continued and deadly quarrel?" Not so. Tracy was making *The Devil at Four O'Clock* when he got news of Clark's death. Spence closed down the set and didn't return to work for the rest of the week.

However, a feud there was, a regular Hollywood vendetta, between the clan Gable and the clan Selznick. On the Selznick side were ranged David O., who was about to produce *Gone with the Wind*, his brother, Myron, and his wife, Irene Mayer Selznick. On the Gable side were Clark, Carole Lombard Gable, Victor Fleming, Jock Whitney and the Public.

It really started when Louis B. Mayer didn't want his daughter to marry David O. Selznick, whom he considered an upstart. She did.

Then Myron Selznick, who was Carole Lombard's agent, didn't want Carole to marry Clark Gable. She did.

David O. didn't want Clark to play Rhett Butler. He'd have to go to his father-in-law, who held Gable's contract, for his loan and, said David, "He'll hold me up!"

Jock Whitney, the money man, speaking for the public, said, "Get Gable." After a good deal of infighting in the front office, it was agreed that Selznick would produce the picture at his own studio with Mr. Gable, but for a goodly share it would be released under the MGM banner. Then came the surprise—at least to those who had never sat in on a Gable story conference.

Clark Gable didn't want to play Rhett Butler. That is when he said to me, "They'll lynch me in Atlanta," and no matter what any of us said to him he remained convinced that he *couldn't* play it with George Cukor, Selznick's choice, as the director. "Sure," Clark said, "Cukor's great—as a woman's director. He directs women's pictures." He felt that, if he could do it at all, it would only be under the sturdy direction of Victor Fleming. Fleming not only understood Gable, he saw himself *as* Gable. However, shooting started on *Gone with the Wind* with George Cukor at the helm. When Selznick saw the rushes he persuaded himself that Gable wasn't giving his best performance, was holding out for Fleming. This was not true, but Clark, who *did* know his own

limitations, had been right; he couldn't give the strong performance needed under the gentle Cukor guidance. So Selznick had to
put Fleming on the picture.

Selznick never forgave Gable for what he thought was a touch
of professional "blackmail."

At the *preview* it was obvious to all that Fleming had done a
superb job for which he later received an Academy Award, but
Selznick took all the credit. This infuriated Clark and annoyed
hell out of Fleming. When it came time to fly to the *premiere* in
Atlanta, Vic wasn't having any. Carole and Vic's wife conspired
and cajoled, they bought Vic new luggage. But when the plane left
for Atlanta, Fleming wasn't on it.

Gable never forgave Selznick.

At the premiere the two barely spoke.

One of the persistent Hollywood legends is that this situation
led to an engagement in fisticuffs between them as the main event
in the garden at a large party; that blows and blood flew and
Gable was, of course, victorious.

I will admit that, from time to time, I have said—partially because no Mother Confessor would miss such an event and partially because *if it didn't happen this way*—that I was there. Well,
for the record, I wasn't. Nor have I been able to find anyone else
who actually witnessed the fight. This because I do not believe
this ever happened. I was talking to Howard Strickling about this
the other day, and Howard, who knew Gable as well as any man
alive, agreed it *couldn't* have happened.

For one reason, David O. Selznick, without his glasses, couldn't
have seen a standing let alone a moving target very well, and
Gable wasn't the man to hit someone who couldn't see him or to
take on an opponent with his glasses on. But the real reason was
that none of us who knew Gable well believed he could be made
to hit anybody.

Despite his terrible temper, or I should say because of it, not
one of us ever saw him fight that kind of a fight at any time under
any circumstances. Clark had his temper on an iron leash. He was,
as he once told Gail Strickling and me, afraid to let himself go,
afraid he'd *kill* somebody. We all figured that, in the distant past
before he came to Hollywood, he had probably come very close to
doing just that. No no, when Clark was really angry he didn't

turn hot, he turned *cold*, like he'd thrown up a cement wall. He'd slip off, refuse to see people, refuse to talk even to his friends, until he cooled off.

So I'm convinced the fighting between Gable and Selznick was a fantasy. The feuding, the fussing, however, was fact. As was *Gone with the Wind*, one of the all-time greats. And while he won his Oscar for another picture and none for this—although the picture itself and practically every other contributor thereto *did*—I am sure Clark would rather be remembered for the performance he gave his friend, Vic Fleming, as Rhett Butler than for any other. As, of course, he is. Clark was an actor for over forty years, a top motion picture star for thirty. He made over sixty pictures. But it was Rhett Butler who gave him the greatest scope for *acting*. And that was what Gable loved.

He didn't care much for "being an actor."

He didn't care all that much for "being a star."

Clark Gable loved to *act*.

Carole Lombard Gable once explained to me Clark's love of acting. "He's got so much more vitality and love of life, he wants to live more, faster, harder, crowd in more experiences. So—he's been boss of a rubber plantation full of man-eating tigers, and Jean Harlow; he's been a miner, con-man in a *Boom Town*, a test pilot, a gambler saving lives in a San Francisco earthquake, a minister, a killer, a prizefighter, a politician making speeches in Madison Square Garden, a doctor in *Men in White*, a hard-boiled reporter in *It Happened One Night*, a man with a dog in the Alaska gold rush. He led a *Mutiny on the Bounty*, sailed the China Seas, fought the Civil War—he's not an actor! That's just Gable having his idea of fun. Which puts into his performances that terrific quality of living to the full that makes people holler with joy."

I wish you could have known the Gables, Clark and Carole. They were wonderful folks.

Carole Lombard was a very big star in her own right, much loved by Hollywood. But everybody who went to the rambling white house overlooking the San Fernando Valley knew it was Clark's house. Carole had created and maintained it to suit him. It was the most joyous house I was ever in.

Theirs was an adult love. They were among the most attractive people in the world. They couldn't have avoided experience. Carole, as a kid, had been devoted to Russ Columbo, the radio idol who was killed in a gun accident; she had, of course been married to Bill Powell, and led him the merry chase which later made him afraid to take Jean Harlow as a second young blonde bride.

Clark's first two marriages were to older women. In his early twenties in New York he married Josephine Dillon, an intellectual, a fine dramatic coach. By the time he arrived in Hollywood the handsome widowed Rhea Langham was "Mrs. Gable." The quotation marks tell the story. When Clark suddenly became the biggest thing in pictures, the target for interviewers and gossip columns, "they" were all important for "Mr. and Mrs. Gable" had never been married to each other. Remember, we are back in that foreign country, the past, where we did things differently, and *living together* openly without legal sanction, as they had been doing for quite a spell, was one of the things our public idols did *not* do unless, of course, you were *living together* with William Randolph Hearst in exceptional circumstances. Disclosure could ruin even such a superstar as Mr. Gable promised to become. Howard Strickling and I agreed there could be beeg trouble, so Clark, who really didn't care much one way or another, and Rhea, who was very much a woman of the world, betook themselves to Santa Ana where Joe Sherman, of Howard's publicity department, had arranged a secret ceremony.

Now Mrs. Gable, very friendly, very chic, became a popular figure on the Hollywood scene. While she was not anybody you got to know well, Rhea was a charming, mature woman with tact and diplomacy, who handled herself very well—which was a good thing for, ironically, not too long after the wedding Clark made *Possessed* with Joan Crawford. And Joan was, from first to last, a girl to be reckoned with.

Joan Crawford was one girl Hollywood could never lick. Once or twice she lost a round, was down for a count of nine, had to outwait bad breaks. But overall Joan was never defeated by anything or anybody. She died last year a winner and still champion.

The evolution of Lucille Le Sueur from the day she was born in

San Antonio, Texas, to Joan Crawford, movie star and top flight business executive of the Pepsi-Cola Company, both of which she was on the day of her death, has to be Hollywood's best story of someone who rose from the ranks to command.

She was impelled by a life force within to improve her lot, a dogged determination to "make something of herself."

Joan Crawford came further, stayed longer, fought more challenges, had less help, was beholden to fewer and kept climbing more steadily, as woman and actress, than anyone in Hollywood history.

She had capacity for hard work, she had startling beauty, and, from the day of her arrival, Joan Crawford was as conspicuous as a circus in town. Of all people who've been in the movies, Joan had the highest voltage of personal impact. Like taking hold of a live wire.

The first time I saw it in operation was at the Montmarte, where my husband and I were dining with Tom and Victoria Mix and the town's then pet bride and bridegroom, Mildred and Harold Lloyd. This must have been in 1925 or '26. I don't remember who was there that night.

I found myself staring at an unknown girl dancing with a tall, dark youth I recognized as heir to the Cudahy meat-packing fortune. From her too-high-heeled shoes to her too-frizzy hair with an artificial flower, she was all wrong. Yet she stood out as though the light was too bright for everybody else.

Terribly young, showing off rather crudely, laughing too loudly, her fierce and wonderful vitality and grace made everyone else seem to move in slow motion.

Somebody told me her name was Lucille Le Sueur. She'd been in the chorus at Metro, was doing bit parts now, might be a comer.

Not many years later, I saw that same girl at Pickfair. A first appearance within those sacred portals was a top moment in any girl's life. By this time she was Mrs. Douglas Fairbanks, Jr., and being entertained by his father, Doug, Sr., and his stepmother, Mary Pickford. Every eye was on her to see how she got away with it. If, as she told me later, she was scared silly, she didn't show it. Slim gown of simple elegance. One fine jewel. Sleek burnished head held high, faint smile, perfect poise.

That night must have proved something to the girl who had been fighting and scrabbling her way *up* since she was ten.

Three months after Lucille was born, her mother got a divorce. Her first stepfather was important because he took them to Lawton, Oklahoma, where he owned a theater. "Billie"—her childhood nickname—smelled greasepaint, saw footlights and was sparked with the love of dancing that led her from behind a department store counter to winning a dance cup in a Kansas City ballroom. From there she went on to night clubs in Chicago and Detroit, into the chorus of a Broadway show, thence to Hollywood, where she achieved stardom in, appropriately enough, *Our Dancing Daughters*.

In her early Hollywood days, Joan had a reputation as the Hotcha Kid, a reputation for wild drinking and running around with men that haunted her for years.

"It was easy for a girl in pictures to meet a lot of men," Joan said once. "How could you tell what they'd be like? But you had to have men to dance with."

When she was seen, night after night making the rounds from the Cocoanut Grove to the beach clubs in the dawn with rich young playboys, people naturally thought it was the men she cared about. Not true. They were necessary partners for *dancing*. As for drinking, I saw her when I knew she hadn't had a drink. She'd start to dance and ten minutes later she was intoxicated with joy. Then you'd hear Crawford was seen tight somewhere.

In her teens, she was in love with young Mike Cudahy, who wanted desperately to marry her. But Mama Cudahy, sitting in a mansion at the top of Vine Street, controlled the purse strings and would have none of a little movie actress as a daughter-in-law. That's when Hollywood began to be in Joan's corner. Joan was a generous, kindhearted, hard-working kid with nobody to back her.

A few of us knew about Joan's childhood, too.

After Steppapa No. 1 went out for a walk one night in Oklahoma and never came back, her mother moved to Kansas City, opened a laundry and put Billie in a convent. The laundry failed, there wasn't any money to pay the convent, and her mother married again. Billie and Stepfather No. 2 didn't get along. Very soon, and very *young*, she was on her own. "My education ended in the sixth grade," Joan once told me.

Her self-education never ended. She became an omnivorous reader, and when she found out about them, a familiar figure at art galleries, museums, concerts, operas and lectures. In later years she was usually accompanied by one of her four adopted children.

Joan had made a few silents after Harry Rapf, a Metro producer, saw her in the chorus at the Winter Garden and gave her a contract. Her rich, husky voice, her incredibly quick ear, made her a natural when the Talkies came along.

About this time Paul Bern, who was advising her against so many spangles on her dresses and so many pink lamps in her living room, took her backstage to meet Douglas Fairbanks, Jr., starring in *Young Woodley*. Love at first sight, and an ardent romance exploded which, despite some Go Slow flags hoisted at Pickfair, culminated in their marriage at St. Malachy's Church in New York. The bride was twenty-one. The groom was nineteen.

Here again, though it was a love match, Joan was anxious to "better herself." Young Doug was a polished youth—precocious, with charming manners and an easy wit. This was all new to the girl who had been rechristened Joan Crawford. With her vital determination, her quick impressions and ability to learn and imitate, the bride picked up and put on all her husband had to offer. More rough edges smoothed away.

So it was a Joan Crawford at twenty-three, still with all the high voltage of Lucille Le Sueur, a live wire encased now in a thin veneer of simple elegance, who encountered Clark Gable, the most all-round attractive man Hollywood ever produced, on the set of *Possessed*.

Let it here be said that, with the exception of Carole Lombard, *all* Gable's romances, whether they led him to the altar or no, were made by the women. They decided they were going to have an affair with Gable and Clark couldn't run fast enough. It wasn't that Clark didn't love women—in fact in a way I think he was a little in love with every woman he ever met, at least they thought so, and I know that every woman who ever managed to have an affair always remained a little in love with Gable and always remained his friend—but the pursuit sometimes irritated him. His attitude was fairly simple, as he explained it to me one day when he confessed that the lady I had seen leaving was, indeed, an expensive import from Madam Frances' establishment.

"Why would you do a thing like that," I said, "when all you have to do is whistle? Or grin?"

"That's why," he said. "I can pay her to go away. The others stay around, want a big romance, *movie* lovemaking. I do not *want* to be the world's great lover and I don't like being put on that spot."

To be fair to Joan Crawford—in her case Clark didn't even try to run.

When these two came together in *Possessed* once again the love scenes "caught fire." They were both extremely fond of their respective spouses, they were both people of basic integrity, yet the chemistry as they made love before the camera day after day was volatile. How do such things happen? I dunno. They just *do*. Proximity—dynamics—sparks—*explosion!* Naturally folks around began to smell smoke. There were rumors, people speculated, talked. I, who really loved and admired them both, crossed my fingers, closed my ears, and hoped not.

The night I stumbled on them behind the bandstand at the Cocoanut Grove, with *his* wife and *her* husband sitting out at the tables, I literally felt stricken. Oh, no! I thought frantically. That torch'll maybe burn up two careers . . . neither of them has any *sense*.

I was wrong. The attack was short, sharp, and not fatal. As suddenly as they had come together, they moved apart. "It wouldn't have worked," Joan said me. "We'd have hurt too many people." And, being the people they were, this they could not do.

Their marriages held without a ripple to their previous course. They both denied then and later, and quite rightly, too, that they had ever been anything but friends. However—that these two were as mad about each other as any pair I ever saw, I *know*.

Why do I tell it now? Because I'd like to give credit to Joan Crawford—and to Clark—but mostly to Joan. For Clark this was a momentary madness, a temporary infatuation, which with his experience he has to have suspected. For Joan it was that potential great love.

She gave it up without a murmur, the Hotcha Kid with no

background, no "culture," because she put kindness before desire —loyalty and consideration before gratification. And that I have to admire.

Yes, a woman to be reckoned with was Joan Crawford.

As was Rhea Gable. If Rhea suspected anything, which I'm sure she did, she was too smart to let on.

I'm somehow sure young Douglas never did. That marriage lasted another couple of years, after which Doug, Jr., married socialite Mary Lee Hartford, had a family, and became a great favorite on both sides of the Atlantic, socially as well as professionally. Joan Crawford married Franchot Tone, then Philip Terry, and finally New York business executive Alfred Steele, who gave her an emotional stability she'd never had and to whom she remained devoted until his death.

Rhea Gable continued to run her husband's home smoothly, make sure the bills were paid and his clothes cleaned, and to try to build a social life of the kind to which she had been accustomed around Clark, who still wouldn't play. When she was convinced that their life together was over, Rhea distinguished herself by making the most graceful exit from Hollywood I've ever seen a lady make. She got a divorce and went back to Texas leaving many friends in Hollywood, including Clark Gable.

Women, I have to think, did not come at the top of Clark's list of the important things in life.

First, his men friends—and their masculine pursuits.

Second, his work.

Third, women and children.

Until he met Carole Lombard.

When you saw Clark and Carole Gable together, you could say this man and this woman are all-in-all to each other. This is a marriage. These two are one. And Carole Lombard Gable was a first class example of what a truly liberated female who is both feminine and funny can do when she makes up her mind to be a *wife*; Carole had made up her mind. After all those false starts they had found each other and she was going to make this marriage work.

To begin with, despite her own great popularity, she gave her career—and herself—second billing. Clark was the King.

This became clear when the protocol of announcing their marriage to the public was at issue. As an MGM star Clark was handled by Howard Strickling's publicity department. Carole Lombard, on the other hand, was handled by the great Russell Birdwell. So when Clark called Howard asking him to come out to the ranch, "Ma and I want some advice"—they called each other Ma and Pappy—Clark said, "We're gonna do it, we're gonna get married. Now, will you handle it, or Birdwell?" Howard thought a minute and said to Carole, "Well, if Clark is marrying you, we'll handle it. If you are marrying Clark, Birdwell will handle it." And Carole said without pause, "Look, you go ahead and handle it."

Mr. Gable, I may add, had no hesitation about marrying a blonde bombshell. He would take care of that. A woman would *try*, he said, but no woman was ever happy in marriage unless the man was head of the family. At the time he married Carole Lombard she had a reputation of swearing harder and talking dirtier than any other girl in Hollywood. A couple of days after the wedding she blued up the air some and Clark said to her, "Mrs. Gable. Around here *I* do all the swearing. If any language that isn't fit to print has to be used, *I* will use it. I don't ever again want to hear any of it from my wife." And he never did.

Carole, until she met Clark, was what we called a "negligee gal," her svelte, streamlined, subtle glamour more suggested the boudoir than the open spaces. After they married she became what he wanted her to be—she could and did drink drink-for-drink with him, don hip boots and woolen shirts to fish with him in icy streams, enthuse over shotguns and fishing rods and flies instead of jewels and furs at Christmas. She also became a farmer's wife, for Clark, who had never forgotten those summers in Pennsylvania, was a frustrated farmer.

By the time Clark and Carole came together Beverly Hills, that exclusive, quiet little hamlet which had blossomed around Mary and Doug, was all but unrecognizable. Douglas Fairbanks had wanted to build a wall around his sacred citadel to keep the mortals *out*, now only fifteen or so years later, Doug was *out* and the mortals were swarming *in*. The bridle path had disappeared beneath the asphalt and the commercial buildings were rolling out Wilshire Boulevard until you could scarcely tell where Beverly

Hills ended and Los Angeles began. It wasn't to the new King's taste and so before they were married Carole started looking for a place and finally found a ranch in the "country"—which the San Fernando Valley was then. It wasn't a ranch really, the Gable place in Encino. You might have called it a farm except *farm* isn't a word in California except maybe after *chicken,* which the Gables' certainly wasn't. But its thirty acres around the charming house were arranged so they gave it the aspect of a farm. They had their own eggs, fruit trees, vegetables, a tractor to drive . . . and here Carole created a home for her man. Except for Carole's own rooms, which were dainty as a spring dawn, everything in it was *big,* the *biggest* drinking glasses, the *biggest* dining-room table, the *biggest* chairs, with Clark's, of course, the biggest of all.

For all their fame abroad, at home they laid the warmth of a fine fire of coals. They were as comfortable as a pair of old shoes. She made him laugh as no one else ever could. They had a sort of slapdash kindly hospitality so united as husband and wife you thought, with a lump in your throat; this is happiness, they belong; you could not imagine them apart—

Nothing but death could have put them asunder.

Soon after the United States declared war in 1941 Carole Lombard Gable, at the request of the President, went on a bond-selling tour which started in Salt Lake City, covered the State of Texas, with a last stop in Carole's home town, Fort Wayne, Indiana.

Then she took a plane home to "Pappy"—and that plane hit a mountain outside of Las Vegas, Nevada.

Clark was getting ready to go to the airport to meet her when word came that there was something wrong with her flight. In a chartered plane Clark, with his friends Eddie Mannix, Howard Strickling, and Ralph Wheelwright, Howard's right-hand man, flew to Las Vegas. Carole's flight was still unreported, an explosion had been seen thirty miles away, and a fierce fire was sighted by another pilot burning on Table Rock Mountain.

It was at the foot of the mountain that they finally persuaded Clark to wait with Howard while Eddie and Ralph went up with the search party. Only the argument that if Carole was alive and in bad shape, she'd need him *there* ready to take care of her, turned him back.

Ralph Wheelwright told me later of the carnage, the charred and smoking debris flung across the snow—"Hell on a mountain," Ralph called it. "I was damn glad he hadn't come up . . . Carole wouldn't have wanted him to see it . . . you know, even on those camping trips she always kept herself so . . . so lovely . . ." Eddie Mannix identified her—chiefly by a pair of earrings he'd helped Clark buy.

I will tell you something I know. The heart of the great Gable died when the searchers, after weary hours of suspense, told him as gently as they could that they'd found his wife and she was dead. Clark never even looked the same again.

As in rage, so in grief, in those first hours Clark was icy cold, private, locked away. It was only when Gail Strickling arrived the next day with Jill Winkler that he gave any evidence that part of him was still in the land of the living—for Jill Winkler was the wife of Otto Winkler, and Otto had been on the plane with Carole.

Otto Winkler, a former police reporter who worked for Howard Strickling, had personally handled Clark, whom he adored, for years. Between the Gables and the Winklers was a great rapport, for Otto and Jill, like Clark and Carole, had been on the marital merry-go-round before they too found each other; the Winklers were married a week before the Gables.

Because Clark was in the middle of a picture and couldn't go with his wife, he'd asked Howard to send Otto. "I know Carole doesn't work for the studio," he said, "but I'd feel better if Otto was with her." Otto, real pleased, said to Jill, "He wants me to take care of his old lady," bought himself a gray pin-striped suit such as Gable always wore, kissed his wife good-bye at the airport.

Now these two, who had found their people and lost them, faced each other in that grief-laden room in Las Vegas; it is typical of Clark that he managed to set aside his own grief and let the warmth of his comfort flow over Jill.

For him there was no comfort. He made the arrangements for Carole's services himself down to the last hymn, then he went alone to the Rogue River up in Oregon and for three weeks let the studio fret. When he did show up on the set of *Somewhere I'll Find You* he knew his lines, he grinned and joked, he was *Gable*— and yet he wasn't, not ever again. He was a great guy giving that gallant performance of the man he had once been, a performance he was to give for the next nineteen years. During those years he did once again all the things you expected him to do; he hunted, fished, golfed, drank with his pals, he played jacks, he made movies—a lot of them—but he couldn't quite put it into any of it that "terrific quality of living to the full that makes people holler with joy" when the other half of him was missing.

As soon as the picture was finished Gable enlisted in the United States Army Air Corps and asked to be posted overseas. For months now he was flying, fighting—away from home.

His struggle, after he took off his uniform, to adjust to the old life, the studio, making motion pictures, trying to get up steam for his work, was terrible to see—and he let very few people see it.

At the ranch he faced *everyday* living, getting up in the morning, going to bed at night, in a house where you saw traces of Carole everywhere.

He wanted it that way. He didn't want to change the house— for a long time he kept Carole's rooms exactly as she had left them.

Clark did not want to *forget* his love. He wanted to *keep her alive through memory*.

In the difficult days before he enlisted, everyone who cared about Gable, a brilliant crew, rallied round to amuse, to distract, to entertain, but what he needed most was to *talk* about her. Most folks, as he said, are uncomfortable with grief, find it hard to mention the one who's gone on. "They mean well . . ." Clark said, but he wanted to keep Carole a part of his life. With Howard and Gail we used to look at Carole's pictures, not to be morbid, but to laugh—she was a great comedienne—to recall her, the funny things she did and said.

The same held true after the war. I was out at the house working with him—he had turned down a story I liked called "Haunch Paunch and Jowl" and we were trying to make sense of a thing later advertised as "Gable's Back and Garson's Got Him"—*a horror*—and right in the middle of a sentence he looked over at the fireplace, eyebrows slack, face lifeless, and said, "We used to sit

here evenings . . . we liked to be alone, just the two of us. She
was the best companion . . ."

And I said, "She was the one woman who always kept you
laughing. You are an unsentimental man. Whenever you were
afraid things would get sticky . . ."

He grinned then and said, "One day we were looking around
the ranch and it was beautiful—one of those California days. We
were just lazy—strolling around and gabbing and I said, 'Ma,
we're awfully lucky, you and I—all this and each other—anything
you want we haven't got?' You know what she said, standing
there looking as lovely as a dream? She said, 'Well, I could use another load of manure for the south forty.'"

He laughed then—and laughed again—but a few minutes later
he took me upstairs to her sitting room to show me her books and
said, "She'd like you to have any of these you want," and I saw
another side of Carole, for the books ranged from *The Prophet*
and Emerson's *Essays* to *The Cloud of Unknowing* and *Men
Who Have Walked with God*, and we talked about this other
side—a side that he *needed* to remember.

This need to remember did not change throughout his lifetime
—something no woman romantically involved with him could understand or, in some instances, could tolerate—except Kay
Spreckles. For, of course, there were romances. On the surface he
was still *Clark Gable*, and the girls lined up waiting for the whistle or the grin . . . mostly hoping to marry him. All his friends
wanted to see him married for we knew that Clark hated the *loneliness*. For a spell Anita Colby, a model and actress so beautiful
she was known as the Face, led the pack. Then the gentle, sweetly
pretty Virginia Grey, who looked like Carole by moonlight. One
day Gail Strickling, who could take certain liberties, actually said
to him, "Virginia would make a *good* wife," and Gable, instead of
turning his back and mixing a drink as he usually did if you got
personal, said, "Look, after all, I've got to face up to something. I
have a hole in me, it's never going to be filled up. It wouldn't be
fair to anybody. I haven't anything more to give."

Suddenly he was seen around the night clubs. Gable? At parties
he and Carole had avoided. There was a sensational swing
through Europe with a svelte, willowy blonde model. He mingled
with cafe society and his name was linked with Dolly O'Brien

Dorells, Millicent Huddleson Rogers. And then one day he turned up *married* to one Lady Sylvia Ashley Fairbanks, etc., yes, the very one who had befuddled our Douglas in his middle age. And we looked at each other and said, "What the hell is that all about?" And then, of course, since we knew perfectly well what it was all about, said no more and waited for the inevitable end—which wasn't long in coming.

Again Gable drifted until, at fifty-five, he ran into a small safe harbor with Kay Spreckles, an authentic if limited edition of Carole Lombard, and perfectly happy to accept the fact. Kay was carrying Clark's son when he died five years later of a heart attack. I'm sure it pleases Clark that Kay left the ranch which Carole had designed especially for him when he was no longer there to enjoy it, moved to Beverly Hills where she lives quietly today, and that his son, John, who goes to school there, is a nice normal teen-ager.

For myself, I am pleased to think of Clark and Carole Gable together again. It never made sense any other way.

Young Bill Hearst called to tell me Gable was dead, he wanted me to do some stories about him. As I told in *The Honeycomb*, I was at the time living in New York, halfway through a novel, and I started to say, No, I do not write about Hollywood *any more*. Then I thought, I cannot build my old friend a monument of marble, or carve his face on a mountain, but I can erect a small memorial of paper and ink. For a moment it may recall, for me, and perhaps others, some beautiful yesterdays, bid bygone times return.

So I went to my typewriter—I had trouble seeing the keys—I still do.

The King is dead. Long live the King.

There has been no successor, nor will be. The title died with him.

Is it strange that from the man who was an *exaggeration of life* I learned that death is a door life opens? As happens in wartime, we were confronted with death. His wife, my son, my brother.

The Army didn't want Clark Gable. An Air Corps officer followed by cheering mobs upset discipline. Once *in*, the studio fought to keep him out of active service. "He was a soldier," war correspondent Hank McLemore wrote in a dispatch from the front, "an airplane *gunner*, where the mortality rate is highest. He made it like any man had to. A tough guy up there where you know whether a man is really tough or only camera-tough. Facing death."

Most clearly I saw no thought of death nor fear of it would turn him aside from what *life* demanded, or rob him of joy as adventure. Nor would it occur to him to ask or allow anyone he loved to give up climbing the highest mountain, because death might be waiting around a turn.

Everyone has to learn how they feel about death. I learned from this simple sincere man of fiber faith, without spiritual pretense. He said to me that day in Carole's room, "They say in the midst of life we are in death, but I know now in the midst of death we are in life." It has served me well, that honest unpretending acceptance of a part of life called death.

I have to realize now how many of those who lived these legends, these beautiful yesterdays I've tried to recall for you, have gone through that door called death. Yet when I look at my tapestry it is teeming with life. Whether to our eyes they walked from this scene young and tragically, as did Mabel Normand, Wally Reid, Valentino, Carole Lombard Gable—or full of years and in triumph, as did Marie Dressler and Bebe Daniels—whether they were still at the top of the ladder, as were Clark and Gary Cooper and Joan Crawford—or fallen stars, as were D. W. Griffith and Clara Bow, one and all they had celebrated *life* in all its infinite form and variety. They were never afraid of it. They were willing to *love* deeply, to laugh *all* of their laughter, to weep *all* of their tears.

Yes, yes, death is a door life opens, and the more fully we live the more we carry through into the part of life called death.

So I look forward to seeing them again, these my old friends, in that Tavern at the End of the Road where we shall all meet someday.

Until then, I can say to them with my whole heart—and maybe now that you know them too you can say it with me—*Thanks for the memories.*